NO FEAR SHAKESPEARE

NO FEAR SHAKESPEARE

As You Like It

The Comedy of Errors

Hamlet

Henry IV, Parts One and Two

Henry V

Julius Caesar

King Lear

Macbeth

The Merchant of Venice

A Midsummer Night's Dream

Much Ado About Nothing

Othello

Richard III

Romeo and Juliet

Sonnets

The Taming of the Shrew

The Tempest

Twelfth Night

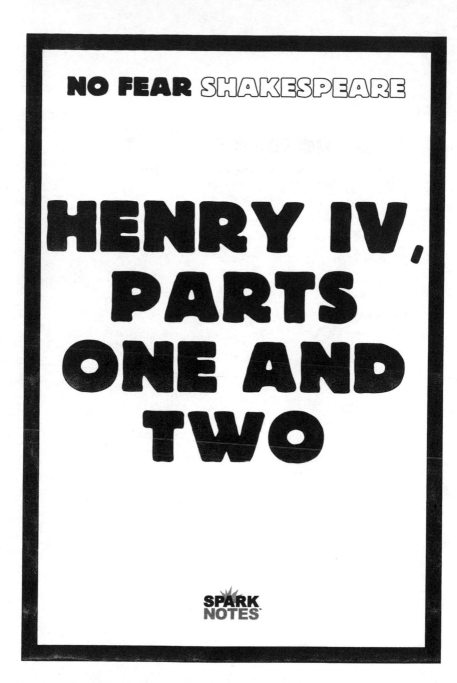

NO FEAR SHAKESPEARE

HENRY IV, PARTS ONE AND TWO

SPARK NOTES

SPARKNOTES is a registered trademark of SparkNotes LLC

The original text and translation for this edition were prepared by John Crowther.

Spark Publishing
120 Fifth Avenue
New York, NY 10011
www.sparknotes.com

12 **SN** 8

Please submit all comments and questions or report errors to www.sparknotes.com/errors

Printed and bound in the United States

ISBN-13: 978-1-4114-0436-6
ISBN-10: 1-4114-0436-X

Library of Congress Cataloging-in-Publication Data

Shakespeare, William, 1564–1616.
  [King Henry IV]
  Henry IV / edited by John Crowther.
    p. cm. — (No fear Shakespeare)
  Summary: Presents the original text of Shakespeare's play side by side
with a modern version, with marginal notes and explanations and full
descriptions of each character.
  ISBN 1-4114-0436-X (alk. paper)
  1. Henry IV, King of England, 1367–1413—Drama. 2. Great
Britain—History—Henry IV, 1399–1413—Drama. I. Crowther, John (John C.)
II. Title. III. Series.
  PR2809.A2C76 2005
  822.3'3—dc22
                                        2005006780

There's matter in these sighs, these profound heaves.
You must translate: 'tis fit we understand them.

(*Hamlet*, 4.1.1–2)

FEAR NOT.

Have you ever found yourself looking at a Shakespeare play, then down at the footnotes, then back at the play, and still not understanding? You know what the individual words mean, but they don't add up. SparkNotes' *No Fear Shakespeare* will help you break through all that. Put the pieces together with our easy-to-read translations. Soon you'll be reading Shakespeare's own words fearlessly—and actually enjoying it.

No Fear Shakespeare puts Shakespeare's language side-by-side with a facing-page translation into modern English—the kind of English people actually speak today. When Shakespeare's words make your head spin, our translation will help you sort out what's happening, who's saying what, and why.

HENRY IV, PART ONE

HENRY IV, PART TWO

NO FEAR SHAKESPEARE

HENRY IV, PART ONE

CHARACTERS

King Henry IV—The ruling King of England; also known as Henry Bolingbroke. When the play opens, King Henry is anxious about the legitimacy and stability of his position. He nurses guilty feelings about having deposed the former King, Richard II, through a civil war (depicted in Shakespeare's *Richard II*). In addition, his reign has not brought an end to internal strife in England, which has now erupted into an even larger, more violent civil war. Finally, the King is vexed by the irresponsible antics of his eldest son, Prince Henry. Regal, proud, and somewhat aloof, King Henry is not the protagonist of the play that bears his name, but he is its historical focus. He gives the play a center of power, though his actions and emotions are largely secondary to the plot.

Henry, Prince of Wales—King Henry IV's son, who will eventually become King Henry V. Prince Henry is sometimes called Harry Monmouth, after the town he was born in, and he is known as Hal to his friends in Eastcheap. Though Prince Henry freely associates with highwaymen, robbers, and whores, he has secret plans to transform himself into a noble prince, and his regal qualities emerge as the play unfolds. Complex and shrewd, Prince Henry is the closest character this play has to a protagonist. However, exactly how we should perceive this simultaneously deceitful and heroic young Prince remains an unresolved question.

Hotspur—The son and heir of the Earl of Northumberland and the nephew of the Earl of Worcester. Though Hotspur's real name is Henry Percy, he is usually referred to by his nickname, which he earned because of his fierceness in battle and hastiness of action. He is a member of the powerful Percy family of the North, which helped bring King Henry IV to power in *Richard II*. When *Henry IV, Part One* opens, the Percy family feels that the new King has forgotten his debt to them. In Shakespeare's account, Hotspur is the same age as Prince Harry and becomes his archrival. Quick-tempered and impatient, Hotspur is preoccupied with the idea of honor and glory, to the exclusion of all other qualities.

Sir John Falstaff—A fat, lecherous, dishonorable old knight between the ages of fifty and sixty-five. Falstaff spends most of his time in the taverns of Eastcheap, a sordid area of London, and seems to make his living as a thief, highwayman, and mooch. He acts as a kind of mentor to Prince Henry, instructing him in the practices of criminals and vagabonds, and is the only member of the Eastcheap gang who can match Henry's sharp wit pun for pun. However, despite their repartee, there is an edge to Falstaff and Prince Henry's relationship. Though Falstaff seems to have real affection for the young Prince, Prince Henry continually insults and pulls pranks on Falstaff, and at the end of *Henry IV, Part Two* he dismisses his old friend completely.

Earl of Westmoreland—A nobleman and military leader, and a close companion and valuable ally to King Henry IV.

Lord John of Lancaster—The younger son of King Henry, and the younger brother of Prince Henry. Lancaster proves himself wise and valiant in battle, despite his youth.

Sir Walter Blunt—A loyal and trusted ally of King Henry IV, and a valuable warrior.

Thomas Percy, Earl of Worcester—Hotspur's uncle. Shrewd and manipulative, Worcester is the mastermind behind the Percy rebellion.

Henry Percy, Earl of Northumberland—Hotspur's father. Northumberland conspires and raises troops on the Percy side, but he claims that he is sick before the Battle of Shrewsbury and does not actually bring his troops into the fray.

Edmund Mortimer, called the Earl of March—A brave warrior, and the brother of Hotspur's wife, Lady Percy. At the beginning of the play, Mortimer has been captured by the Welsh rebel Owen Glendower, and has converted to the rebel cause and married Glendower's daughter. Mortimer has a strong claim to the English throne through Richard II, who was deposed by King Henry IV.

Owen Glendower—The leader of the Welsh rebels and father of Lady Mortimer. Glendower joins with the Percys in their insurrection against King Henry. Well read, English-educated, and highly capable in battle, Glendower is also steeped in the traditional lore of Wales and claims to command great magic. He is mysterious and superstitious and sometimes acts according to prophecies and omens. Some editions refer to Glendower by his Welsh name, Owain Glyndwr.

Lady Percy—Hotspur's wife. A feisty match for her hot-tempered husband, Lady Percy disapproves of Hotspur's military plans.

Lady Mortimer—The daughter of Owen Glendower, and the new wife of Edmund Mortimer. Lady Mortimer only speaks Welsh, so she cannot fully communicate with her beloved husband.

Archibald, Earl of Douglas—The leader of the large Scottish faction rebelling against King Henry. Usually called simply "the Douglas" (a traditional way of referring to a Scottish clan chief), the deadly and fearless Douglas fights on the side of the Percys.

Sir Richard Vernon—A relative and ally of the Earl of Worcester.

The Archbishop of York—The Archbishop, whose given name is Richard Scroop. The Archbishop conspires on the side of the Percys, lending the rebellion his authority as a religious leader.

Ned Poins, Bardolph, and Peto—Criminals and highwaymen. Poins, Bardolph, and Peto are friends of Falstaff and Prince Henry, who drink with them at the Boar's Head Tavern, assist them in highway robbery, and accompany them in war.

Gadshill—Another highwayman friend of Harry, Falstaff, and the rest. Gadshill seems to be nicknamed after the place on the London road—called Gad's Hill—where he has set up many robberies.

Mistress Quickly—Hostess of the Boar's Head Tavern, a seedy dive in Eastcheap, London, where Falstaff and his friends go to drink.

Francis—An assistant drawer, or tavern servant, at the Boar's Head.

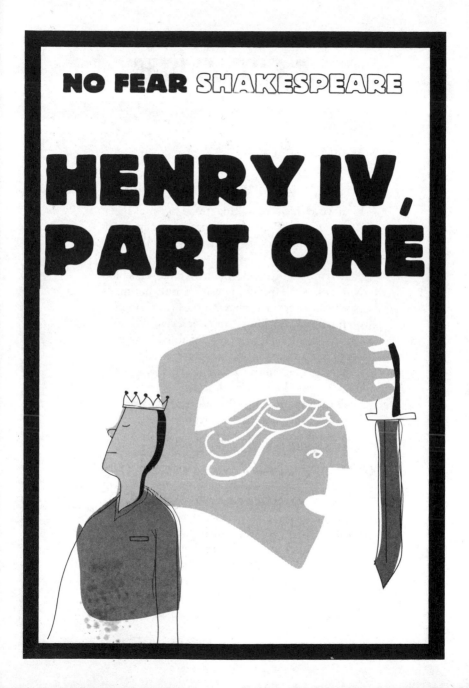

ACT ONE
SCENE 1

Enter the KING, *Lord John of* LANCASTER, *Earl of*
WESTMORELAND, *with others*

KING

So shaken as we are, so wan with care,
Find we a time for frighted peace to pant
And breathe short-winded accents of new broils
To be commenced in strands afar remote.
5   No more the thirsty entrance of this soil
Shall daub her lips with her own children's blood.
Nor more shall trenching war channel her fields,
Nor bruise her flow'rets with the armed hoofs
Of hostile paces. Those opposèd eyes,
10   Which, like the meteors of a troubled heaven,
All of one nature, of one substance bred,
Did lately meet in the intestine shock
And furious close of civil butchery
Shall now, in mutual well-beseeming ranks,
15   March all one way and be no more opposed
Against acquaintance, kindred, and allies.
The edge of war, like an ill-sheathèd knife,
No more shall cut his master. Therefore, friends,
As far as to the sepulcher of Christ—
20   Whose soldier now, under whose blessed cross
We are impressèd and engaged to fight—
Forthwith a power of English shall we levy,
Whose arms were molded in their mothers' womb
To chase these pagans in those holy fields
25   Over whose acres walked those blessèd feet
Which fourteen hundred years ago were nailed
For our advantage on the bitter cross.

ACT ONE

SCENE 1

The KING, *Lord John of* LANCASTER, *the Earl of*
WESTMORELAND, *and others enter.*

KING

Despite how shaken and pale with worry we are, let's
take advantage of this moment of peace to catch our
breath, and as we pant we'll speak about the battles
we'll soon fight in foreign lands. England will no
longer be wet with her own people's blood. War will
no longer damage her fields, and warhorses will no
longer trample her flowers. The soldiers on either side
of this vicious civil war were countrymen and brothers, as similar to one another as shooting stars. They
may have clashed recently, but now they will march
together in beautiful formation, no longer struggling
against family and friend. War is like a mishandled
knife: it can cut its owner, but it will no longer cut us.
My friends, we are now soldiers for Christ, and we take
his blessed cross as our battle flag. We'll raise a new
army of Englishmen and march all the way to the Holy
Land. Our soldiers were born to chase non-believers
from that holy ground touched by Jesus' feet—feet
which, fourteen hundred years ago, were nailed to the
cross for our sins.

But this our purpose now is twelve month old,
And bootless 'tis to tell you we will go.
30   Therefor we meet not now. Then let me hear
Of you, my gentle cousin Westmoreland,
What yesternight our council did decree
In forwarding this dear expedience.

WESTMORELAND
My liege, this haste was hot in question,
35   And many limits of the charge set down
But yesternight: when all athwart there came
A post from Wales loaden with heavy news,
Whose worst was that the noble Mortimer,
Leading the men of Herefordshire to fight
40   Against the irregular and wild Glendower,
Was by the rude hands of that Welshman taken,
A thousand of his people butcherèd,
Upon whose dead corpse there was such misuse,
Such beastly shameless transformation
45   By those Welshwomen done, as may not be
Without much shame retold or spoken of.

KING
It seems then that the tidings of this broil
Brake off our business for the Holy Land.

WESTMORELAND
This matched with other did, my gracious lord.
50   For more uneven and unwelcome news
Came from the north and thus it did import:
On Holy-rood Day, the gallant Hotspur there,
Young Harry Percy, and brave Archibald,
That ever valiant and approvèd Scot,
55   At Holmedon met, where they did spend
A sad and bloody hour—
As by discharge of their artillery
And shape of likelihood the news was told;
For he that brought them, in the very heat

But that's been my plan for a year now, so there's no point in telling you all this again. That's not the issue at hand. So tell me, my noble kinsman Westmoreland, what my royal advisors decided last night about this important undertaking.

WESTMORELAND

Your Highness, there was hot debate about this urgent mission, and many responsibilities had just been assigned when we were suddenly cut off by a messenger with bad news from Wales. The worst of it was that the noble Mortimer, who was leading the men of Herefordshire in battle against that barbarian Glendower, was captured. A thousand of his men have been butchered, their dead corpses desecrated by the Welsh women. The things they did were so horrible that I'm too ashamed to report them.

KING

I suppose this news disrupts our plans to invade the Holy Land.

WESTMORELAND

This and other things, your Highness: even more unsettling and unwelcome news has arrived from the north. On Holy Cross Day, the heroic young Harry Percy—who we know as Hotspur—fought at Holmeden against Archibald, Earl of Douglas, that brave and battle-proven Scotsman. The two of them fought a long and bloody battle there, judging by the way the guns were firing. The messenger who brought the news left when the battle was at its height, so he couldn't say for sure who had won.

60   And pride of their contention did take horse,
        Uncertain of the issue any way.

KING
        Here is a dear, a true-industrious friend,
        Sir Walter Blunt, new lighted from his horse.
        Stained with the variation of each soil
65   Betwixt that Holmedon and this seat of ours,
        And he hath brought us smooth and welcome news.
        The Earl of Douglas is discomfited;
        Ten thousand bold Scots, two-and-twenty knights,
        Balked in their own blood, did Sir Walter see
70   On Holmedon's plains. Of prisoners Hotspur took
        Mordake, Earl of Fife, and eldest son
        To beaten Douglas, and the Earl of Atholl,
        Of Murray, Angus, and Menteith.
        And is not this an honorable spoil?
75   A gallant prize? Ha, cousin, is it not?

WESTMORELAND
        In faith, it is a conquest for a prince to boast of.

KING
        Yea, there thou mak'st me sad, and mak'st me sin
        In envy that my Lord Northumberland
        Should be the father to so blest a son,
80   A son who is the theme of Honor's tongue,
        Amongst a grove the very straightest plant,
        Who is sweet Fortune's minion and her pride;
        Whilst I, by looking on the praise of him,
        See riot and dishonor stain the brow
85   Of my young Harry. O, that it could be proved
        That some night-tripping fairy had exchanged
        In cradle-clothes our children where they lay,
        And called mine "Percy," his "Plantagenet"!
        Then would I have his Harry, and he mine.
90   But let him from my thoughts. What think you, coz,
        Of this young Percy's pride? The prisoners,
        Which he in this adventure hath surprised

KING

My loyal, hard-working friend Sir Walter Blunt has arrived here at court, fresh off his horse and covered with the mud of every town from Holmedon to here. He's brought us very welcome news. The Earl of Douglas has been defeated. Blunt saw ten thousand Scotsmen and twenty-two knights piled up in their own blood on the fields of Holmedon. Hotspur took these men prisoner: Douglas' son Mordake, the Earl of Fife; as well as the Earls of Athol, Murray, Angus, and Menteith. That's a valuable group! A fantastic catch, isn't it, kinsman?

WESTMORELAND

Truly, that's a conquest to make even a prince brag.

KING

Yes, and that makes me sad. Seeing Lord Northumberland with such a blessed son makes me commit the sin of envy. When honor speaks, it speaks about Hotspur. In a grove of trees, Hotspur stands straightest. He is the favorite darling of Fortune. When I see how he is praised, I can only see my own son, Harry, and his reputation for wildness and dishonor. If only it could be proven that a fairy had come to their cradles at night and switched them! Then the Percy family would have my Harry, and we Plantagenets would have Hotspur! But stop thinking about Harry now. Westmoreland, what do you make of young Percy's arrogance? He says he'll keep all the prisoners he captured for himself, and will only send me Mordrake, Earl of Fife.

Prisoners taken in battle were supposed to be turned over to the King so that he could collect ransoms from them. Hotspur's refusal to do this breaks the usual rules and upsets King Henry.

To his own use he keeps, and sends me word
I shall have none but Mordake, Earl of Fife.

WESTMORELAND
95   This is his uncle's teaching. This is Worcester,
Malevolent to you in all aspects,
Which makes him prune himself, and bristle up
The crest of youth against your dignity.

KING
But I have sent for him to answer this.
100   And for this cause awhile we must neglect
Our holy purpose to Jerusalem.
Cousin, on Wednesday next our council we
Will hold at Windsor. So inform the lords.
But come yourself with speed to us again,
105   For more is to be said and to be done
Than out of anger can be utterèd.

WESTMORELAND
I will, my liege.

Exeunt

WESTMORELAND

His uncle Worcester put him up to that. It is just like Worcester to act against you in all ways. He's the one making Hotspur behave like this, flaunting his youth in the face of your dignified age.

KING

I've sent for Hotspur to explain himself. We'll have to postpone the plans for our crusade to Jerusalem. Go tell my advisers that our next meeting will be Wednesday at Windsor. Then hurry back here. There's more to be said and done, but I'm too angry now to speak.

WESTMORELAND

I will, my lord.

They exit.

ACT 1 SCENE 2

Enter HENRY, PRINCE *of Wales, and Sir John* FALSTAFF

FALSTAFF
Now, Hal, what time of day is it, lad?

PRINCE HENRY
Thou art so fat-witted, with drinking of old sack, and
unbuttoning thee after supper, and sleeping upon benches
after noon, that thou hast forgotten to demand that truly
5 which thou wouldst truly know. What a devil hast thou to
do with the time of the day? Unless hours were cups of sack,
and minutes capons, and clocks the tongues of bawds, and
dials the signs of leaping-houses, and the blessed sun
himself a fair hot wench in flame-colored taffeta, I see no
10 reason why thou shouldst be so superfluous to demand the
time of the day.

FALSTAFF
Indeed, you come near me now, Hal, for we that take purses
go by the moon and the seven stars, and not by Phoebus,
he, that wand'ring knight so fair. And I prithee, sweet wag,
15 when thou art king, as God save thy Grace—Majesty, I
should say, for grace thou wilt have none—

PRINCE HENRY
What, none?

FALSTAFF
No, by my troth, not so much as will serve to be prologue to
an egg and butter.

PRINCE HENRY
20 Well, how then? Come, roundly, roundly.

FALSTAFF
Marry, then, sweet wag, when thou art king, let not us that
are squires of the night's body be called thieves of the day's
beauty. Let us be Diana's foresters, gentlemen of the shade,
minions of the moon, and let men say we be men of good
25 government, being governed, as the sea is, by our noble and

ACT 1, SCENE 2

ACT 1, SCENE 2

HENRY, PRINCE *of Wales and Sir John* FALSTAFF *enter.*

FALSTAFF
Hal, what time is it, my boy?

PRINCE HENRY
You are so wasted from drinking booze and loosening your pants after lunch and sleeping on benches all afternoon that you don't even remember how to ask for what you really want to know. What the hell does it matter to you what time it is? Unless hours were glasses of wine, minutes were chickens, clocks were whores' tongues, sundials were whorehouse signs and the sun itself were a hot woman in a flame-colored dress, I don't see any reason why you would need to know the time.

FALSTAFF
Now you're talking, Hal. Thieves like us operate at night, by the moon and stars, and not by the sun. I hope, pretty boy, that when you become king, God save your Grace—or maybe I should just call you "Your Majesty," since you don't have any grace—

PRINCE HENRY
None?

FALSTAFF
No, I swear. Not even enough to say grace before a snack.

PRINCE HENRY
Come on, out with it. Get to the point.

FALSTAFF
Okay then, pretty boy. Whey you become king, don't let those of us who work at night be blamed for wasting daylight by sleeping through it. Give us fancy names: "Servants of the Moon Goddess Diana;" "Gentlemen of Shadows;" "Lunar Laborers." Make

chaste mistress the moon, under whose countenance we
steal.

PRINCE HENRY
Thou sayest well, and it holds well too, for the fortune of us
that are the moon's men doth ebb and flow like the sea,
30   being governed, as the sea is, by the moon. As for proof
now: a purse of gold most resolutely snatched on Monday
night and most dissolutely spent on Tuesday morning, got
with swearing "Lay by" and spent with crying "Bring in";
now in as low an ebb as the foot of the ladder, and by and by
35   in as high a flow as the ridge of the gallows.

FALSTAFF
By the Lord, thou sayest true, lad. And is not my hostess of
the tavern a most sweet wench?

PRINCE HENRY
As the honey of Hybla, my old lad of the castle. And is not
a buff jerkin a most sweet robe of durance?

FALSTAFF
40   How now, how now, mad wag? What, in thy quips and thy
quiddities? What a plague have I to do with a buff jerkin?

PRINCE HENRY
Why, what a pox have I to do with my hostess of the tavern?

people admire us for being well behaved. After all, we're governed by the same force that governs the tides—the pale and cool moon, who lights our way as we sneak around.

PRINCE HENRY

Well said. And you're right—our luck ebbs and flows like the tide, because, like the sea, we're governed by the moon. I'll prove it. Imagine a bag of gold, brilliantly swiped on a Monday night and extravagantly spent on a Tuesday morning. You snatch it, shouting, "Hand it off!" and spend it, calling, "Bring it on!" It's like the gallows: one minute you're at the bottom of the ladder—low tide. The next, you're swinging from the top—high tide!

FALSTAFF

The following banter about the hostess of the tavern depends on puns that suggest she's not only running a legitimate business (the bar), but an illegal one as well (a house of prostitution).

By God that's right, my boy! And by the way, isn't the hostess of the tavern a delicious woman?

PRINCE HENRY

Hybla is a place in Sicily that is famous for its bees and honey.

Sweet as honey from Hybla, you dirty old man. And isn't a sheriff's uniform a pretty durable outfit?

FALSTAFF

What's that supposed to mean, you crazy man? You're in the mood for jokes? Why are you talking to me about a sheriff's uniform?

PRINCE HENRY

Well, why the hell are you asking me about the hostess of the tavern?

FALSTAFF
Well, thou hast called her to a reckoning many a time
and oft.

PRINCE HENRY
45   Did I ever call for thee to pay thy part?

FALSTAFF
No, I'll give thee thy due. Thou hast paid all there.

PRINCE HENRY
Yea, and elsewhere, so far as my coin would stretch, and
where it would not, I have used my credit.

FALSTAFF
Yea, and so used it that were it not here apparent that thou
50   art heir apparent—But I prithee, sweet wag, shall there be
gallows standing in England when thou art king? And
resolution thus fubbed as it is with the rusty curb of old
father Antic the law? Do not thou, when thou art king, hang
a thief.

PRINCE HENRY
55   No, thou shalt.

FALSTAFF
Shall I? O rare! By the Lord, I'll be a brave judge.

PRINCE HENRY
Thou judgest false already: I mean thou shalt have the
hanging of the thieves, and so become a rare hangman.

FALSTAFF
Well, Hal, well, and in some sort it jumps with my humor
60   as well as waiting in the court, I can tell you.

PRINCE HENRY
For obtaining of suits?

FALSTAFF

Shakespeare's line had the added suggestion that Hal has slept with the hostess.

You've asked her for the bill enough times.

PRINCE HENRY

Did I ever ask you to pay for any of it?

FALSTAFF

No. I've got to admit, you've settled with her all by yourself.

PRINCE HENRY

And not just with her, but wherever my cash was good. And when I ran out, I switched to credit.

FALSTAFF

And you've stretched that so far that if it weren't "here apparent" that you're the "heir apparent," your credit wouldn't be worth a thing. But listen, pretty boy. Will England still have hangmen when you're king? And will a thief's courage still be thwarted by that nasty old clown, the law? When you're king, don't hang thieves.

PRINCE HENRY

No. You will.

FALSTAFF

I will? Excellent! By God, I'll be a great judge.

PRINCE HENRY

You've judged wrong already. I mean, you'll be in charge of hanging thieves, and become a superb hangman.

FALSTAFF

All right, Hal. I'll tell you this: in a way, being a hangman agrees with me just as well as hanging around the court.

PRINCE HENRY

suits = petitions

Waiting to get your suits granted?

FALSTAFF
Yea, for obtaining of suits, whereof the hangman hath no
lean wardrobe. 'Sblood, I am as melancholy as a gib cat or
a lugged bear.

PRINCE HENRY
65   Or an old lion, or a lover's lute.

FALSTAFF
Yea, or the drone of a Lincolnshire bagpipe.

PRINCE HENRY
What sayest thou to a hare, or the melancholy of
Moorditch?

FALSTAFF
Thou hast the most unsavory similes, and art indeed the
70   most comparative, rascaliest, sweet young Prince. But,
Hal, I prithee trouble me no more with vanity. I would to
God thou and I knew where a commodity of good names
were to be bought. An old lord of the council rated me the
other day in the street about you, sir, but I marked him not,
75   and yet he talked very wisely, but I regarded him not, and
yet he talked wisely, and in the street, too.

PRINCE HENRY
Thou didst well, for wisdom cries out in the streets and no
man regards it.

FALSTAFF
O, thou hast damnable iteration, and art indeed able to
80   corrupt a saint. Thou hast done much harm upon me, Hal,
God forgive thee for it. Before I knew thee, Hal, I knew
nothing, and now am I, if a man should speak truly, little
better than one of the wicked. I must give over this life, and

FALSTAFF

Exactly. I've got plenty of those, just like the hangman has plenty of suits—the suits he takes off the dead men he hangs.—Damn, I'm as depressed as a tomcat or a dancing bear in chains.

PRINCE HENRY

Or an old lion, or a guitar playing a sad lovesong.

FALSTAFF

Or the wailing of a bagpipe.

PRINCE HENRY

How about a rabbit, or a trip to Moorditch?

In Shakespeare's time it was believed that eating rabbit caused depression. Moorditch was an open ditch that served as London's main sewer channel.

FALSTAFF

You have a knack for foul images. You are the most metaphorical and rascally, sweet young Prince. But Hal, please stop corrupting me with frivolous matters. I wish to God that you and I knew where we could buy a supply of good reputations. The other day, an elderly lord on the King's Council came up to me in the street and lectured me about you, but I didn't pay any attention. He spoke wisely, but I ignored him. But he made sense, and in the street, too.

PRINCE HENRY

You did well. You know the scripture: "Wisdom cries out in the street but no man listens."

FALSTAFF

Oh, you have a wicked talent for wrongly quoting scripture, you really could corrupt a saint. You've deeply harmed me, Hal, and God forgive you for it! Before I met you, I was innocent. And now, if I can speak truly, I'm no better than a sinner. I've got to

I will give it over. By the Lord, an I do not, I am a villain. I'll
85   be damned for never a king's son in Christendom.

PRINCE HENRY
Where shall we take a purse tomorrow, Jack?

FALSTAFF
Zounds, where thou wilt, lad. I'll make one. An I do not,
call me villain and baffle me.

PRINCE HENRY
I see a good amendment of life in thee, from praying to
90   purse-taking.

FALSTAFF
Why, Hal, 'tis my vocation, Hal. 'Tis no sin for a man to
labor in his vocation.

Enter POINS

Poins!—Now shall we know if Gadshill have set a match.
O, if men were to be saved by merit, what hole in hell were
95   hot enough for him? This is the most omnipotent villain
that ever cried "Stand!" to a true man.

PRINCE HENRY
Good morrow, Ned.

POINS
Good morrow, sweet Hal.—What says Monsieur
Remorse? What says Sir John Sack-and-Sugar? Jack, how
100   agrees the devil and thee about thy soul that thou soldest
him on Good Friday last for a cup of Madeira and a cold
capon's leg?

PRINCE HENRY
Sir John stands to his word. The devil shall have his bargain,
for he was never yet a breaker of proverbs. He will give the
105   devil his due.

change my life, and I will change my life, by God. If I don't, I'm an evildoer. I won't be damned, not for any king's son in the universe.

PRINCE HENRY

Where should we go stealing tomorrow, Jack?

FALSTAFF

For God's sake, wherever you want, boy. I'll be one of the gang. If I'm not, call me evildoer and string me up.

PRINCE HENRY

I see you've changed your life, alright. From praying to pursesnatching.

FALSTAFF

It's my calling, Hal. It's no sin for a man to follow his calling.

POINS enters.

Poins! Now we'll find out whether Mr. Gadshill has planned a robbery. If good deeds bring a man to heaven, there's no hell hot enough for Poins. This is the most incredible villain, whoever said "Stick 'em up!" to an honest man.

PRINCE HENRY

Morning, Ned.

POINS

Morning, sweet Hal. What's Mr. Feelbad got to say? What's going on, Sir John, Wino Jack? How's your deal with the devil coming along? You sold him your soul last Good Friday for some cold chicken and a glass of cheap wine, right?

PRINCE HENRY

The devil will get what's coming to him. Sir John's a man of his word, and he never disagrees with a proverb. He will "give the devil his due."

POINS
(to FALSTAFF*)* Then art thou damned for keeping thy word
with the devil.

PRINCE HENRY
Else he had been damned for cozening the devil.

POINS
But, my lads, my lads, tomorrow morning, by four o'clock,
110 early at Gad's Hill, there are pilgrims going to Canterbury
with rich offerings, and traders riding to London with fat
purses. I have vizards for you all. You have horses for
yourselves. Gadshill lies tonight in Rochester. I have
bespoke supper tomorrow night in Eastcheap. We may do
115 it as secure as sleep. If you will go, I will stuff your purses
full of crowns. If you will not, tarry at home and be hanged.

FALSTAFF
Hear ye, Yedward, if I tarry at home and go not, I'll hang
you for going.

POINS
You will, chops?

FALSTAFF
120 Hal, wilt thou make one?

PRINCE HENRY
Who, I rob? I a thief? not I, by my faith.

FALSTAFF
There's neither honesty, manhood, nor good fellowship in
thee, nor thou cam'st not of the blood royal, if thou darest
not stand for ten shillings.

PRINCE HENRY
125 Well then, once in my days I'll be a madcap.

FALSTAFF
Why, that's well said.

PRINCE HENRY
Well, come what will, I'll tarry at home.

POINS

> *(to* FALSTAFF*)* Then you're damned for keeping your word with the devil.

PRINCE HENRY

> His only other choice is to be damned for cheating the devil.

POINS

> But boys, boys! Four o'clock tomorrow morning some pilgrims are going to pass by Gad's Hill. They'll be on their way to Canterbury Cathedral with expensive offerings, and traders will be heading to London with bags of money. I've got masks for you, you've got horses for yourselves. Mr. Gadshill is spending tonight in Rochester, and I've already ordered tomorrow night's dinner in Eastcheap. We could do this in our sleep. If you come, I'll make you rich. If not, stay home and hang yourselves.

FALSTAFF

> Listen, Yedward. If I stay home and don't go, I'll hang you — for going.

POINS

> You will, fatface?

FALSTAFF

> Hal, are you in?

PRINCE HENRY

> Who? Me, a robber? Me, a thief? Not me. No way.

FALSTAFF

> If you don't dare to fight for ten shillings, there's no honesty, manhood, or friendship in you, and you never came from royal blood.

PRINCE HENRY

> Well, okay. For once in my life, I'll be a little crazy.

FALSTAFF

> There you go.

PRINCE HENRY

> Well, you know what? I'll stay home.

FALSTAFF
By the Lord, I'll be a traitor then when thou art king.

PRINCE HENRY
I care not.

POINS
130   Sir John, I prithee, leave the Prince and me alone. I will lay
him down such reasons for this adventure that he shall go.

FALSTAFF
Well, God give thee the spirit of persuasion, and him the
ears of profiting, that what thou speakest may move, and
what he hears may be believed, that the true prince may, for
135   recreation sake, prove a false thief, for the poor abuses of the
time want countenance. Farewell. You shall find me in
Eastcheap.

PRINCE HENRY
Farewell, thou latter spring. Farewell, All-hallown
summer.

Exit FALSTAFF

POINS
140   Now, my good sweet honey lord, ride with us tomorrow. I
have a jest to execute that I cannot manage alone. Falstaff,
Peto, Bardolph, and Gadshill shall rob those men that we
have already waylaid. Yourself and I will not be there. And
when they have the booty, if you and I do not rob them, cut
145   this head off from my shoulders.

PRINCE HENRY
How shall we part with them in setting forth?

POINS
Why, we will set forth before or after them, and appoint
them a place of meeting, wherein it is at our pleasure to fail;
and then will they adventure upon the exploit themselves,
150   which they shall have no sooner achieved but we'll set upon
them.

FALSTAFF

By God, then I'll be a traitor when you become king.

PRINCE HENRY

I don't care.

POINS

Sir John, do me a favor: leave me and the Prince alone. I'll spell out such good reasons for this adventure, he's sure to join.

FALSTAFF

May God give you the power of persuasion and him the good sense to listen, so that what you say will affect him and what he hears will sink in. This way, the true prince will turn into false thief, just for laughs. After all, all the poor, little vices of the age need encouragement. So long; you'll find me in Eastcheap.

PRINCE HENRY

Farewell, you second spring! Farewell, you summer-in-November!

Hal is teasing Falstaff for acting like a teenager, even though he's an old man.

FALSTAFF *exits.*

POINS

Now, my good sweet honey sir, come with us tomorrow. I have an idea for a practical joke, and I can't do it by myself. Falstaff, Peto, Bardolph, and Mr. Gadshill will rob the travelers we're planning to ambush, but you and I won't be there. If you and I don't rob them once they have the loot, then chop off my head!

PRINCE HENRY

But we're all planning to leave together. How will you and I separate ourselves?

POINS

We'll leave before them, or after them. We'll tell them to meet us someplace, but then we won't show up. They'll pull off the robbery by themselves, and the second they've done it, we'll attack them.

PRINCE HENRY
Yea, but 'tis like that they will know us by our horses, by our habits, and by every other appointment to be ourselves.

POINS
Tut, our horses they shall not see; I'll tie them in the wood. Our vizards we will change after we leave them. And, sirrah, I have cases of buckram for the nonce, to immask our noted outward garments.

PRINCE HENRY
Yea, but I doubt they will be too hard for us.

POINS
Well, for two of them, I know them to be as true-bred cowards as ever turned back; and for the third, if he fight longer than he sees reason, I'll forswear arms. The virtue of this jest will be the incomprehensible lies that this same fat rogue will tell us when we meet at supper: how thirty at least he fought with, what wards, what blows, what extremities he endured; and in the reproof of this lies the jest.

PRINCE HENRY
Well, I'll go with thee. Provide us all things necessary and meet me tomorrow night in Eastcheap. There I'll sup. Farewell.

POINS
Farewell, my lord.

Exit POINS

PRINCE HENRY
I know you all, and will awhile uphold
The unyoked humor of your idleness.
Yet herein will I imitate the sun,
Who doth permit the base contagious clouds
To smother up his beauty from the world,
That, when he please again to be himself,
Being wanted, he may be more wondered at
By breaking through the foul and ugly mist

PRINCE HENRY

Sure, but they'll recognize our horses, our clothes, and all our other things.

POINS

Psh! They won't see our horses, because I'll tie them in the forest. We'll put on new masks after we leave them. And, just for this occasion, I've made cloaks out of rough buckram cloth, to cover our regular clothes.

PRINCE HENRY

Okay. But I'm afraid they'll be too tough for us.

POINS

Well, I know that two of them are the biggest cowards who ever turned and ran. As for the third, if he fights even a second longer than is absolutely necessary, I promise to never fight again. The best part about this joke will be listening to the outlandish lies this fat clown will tell when we meet for dinner—how he fought at least thirty men, how he defended himself, how he got hit, what he endured. The funniest part will be when we call him on it.

PRINCE HENRY

Okay. I'll go. Get everything together and meet me in Eastcheap tomorrow. I'll eat there. Farewell.

POINS

Farewell, my lord.

POINS *exits.*

PRINCE HENRY

I understand all of you. For now, I'll put on the rowdy behavior of your good-for-nothing ways. But in this way, I'll be like the sun, who allows the vulgar, corrupting clouds to hide his beauty from the world. Then, when the sun wants to be himself again, he breaks through the foul mists and vapors that seemed to be strangling him.

Of vapors that did seem to strangle him.
If all the year were playing holidays,
180 To sport would be as tedious as to work,
But when they seldom come, they wished for come,
And nothing pleaseth but rare accidents.
So when this loose behavior I throw off
And pay the debt I never promisèd,
185 By how much better than my word I am,
By so much shall I falsify men's hopes;
And, like bright metal on a sullen ground,
My reformation, glitt'ring o'er my fault,
Shall show more goodly and attract more eyes
190 Than that which hath no foil to set it off.
I'll so offend to make offense a skill,
Redeeming time when men think least I will.

Exit

And because people have missed him so much, they are that much more impressed when he finally appears. If every day were a vacation, playing would grow as tedious as working. But when it's rare, it's looked forward to. Nothing is as precious as the unexpected occurrence. So when I throw off this wild behavior and accept the responsibilities of being king—a destiny I didn't choose but was born into— I'll suddenly seem like a far better man. In this way, I'll give everyone the wrong expectation of me. Like a bright metal on a dark background, my reformation will shine even more brilliantly when it's set against my wicked past. I'll be so wild, I'll make wildness an art form, then redeem myself when the world least expects me to.

He exits.

ACT 1, SCENE 3

Enter the KING, NORTHUMBERLAND, WORCESTER, HOTSPUR,
Sir Walter BLUNT, *with others*

KING

My blood hath been too cold and temperate,
Unapt to stir at these indignities,
And you have found me, for accordingly
You tread upon my patience. But be sure
5   I will from henceforth rather be myself,
Mighty and to be feared, than my condition,
Which hath been smooth as oil, soft as young down,
And therefore lost that title of respect
Which the proud soul ne'er pays but to the proud.

WORCESTER

10   Our house, my sovereign liege, little deserves
The scourge of greatness to be used on it,
And that same greatness too which our own hands
Have holp to make so portly.

NORTHUMBERLAND
                                My lord—

KING

Worcester, get thee gone; for I do see
15   Danger and disobedience in thine eye.
O sir, your presence is too bold and peremptory,
And majesty might never yet endure
The moody frontier of a servant brow.
You have good leave to leave us. When we need
20   Your use and counsel, we shall send for you.
                                Exit WORCESTER
(to NORTHUMBERLAND*)* You were about to speak.

ACT 1, SCENE 3

The KING, NORTHUMBERLAND, WORCESTER, HOTSPUR, *Sir Walter* BLUNT *and others enter.*

KING

I've been too calm and even-tempered, unwilling to react angrily to these indignities. You have discovered this, and so you've walked all over my patience. Know this: from now on, I'm going to be my royal self again, powerful and frightening. My natural condition, which was as smooth as oil and soft as feathers, has lost me the respect that powerful people only pay to the similarly powerful.

WORCESTER

Worcester, Northumberland, and Hotspur are all members of the Percy family.

My lord, the Percy family does not deserve to bear the brunt of your anger and power, especially since we helped you become so powerful in the first place.

NORTHUMBERLAND

Your Highness —

KING

Worcester, get out. I see danger and disobedience in your eyes. You carry yourself too boldly and proudly, and royalty should never have to endure a servant's frowning face. You have my permission to leave now. When I need you or your advice, I'll call for you.

WORCESTER *exits.*

(to NORTHUMBERLAND*)* You were about to speak.

NORTHUMBERLAND

Yea, my good lord.
Those prisoners in your Highness' name demanded,
Which Harry Percy here at Holmedon took,
Were, as he says, not with such strength denied
25 As is delivered to your Majesty:
Either envy, therefore, or misprison
Is guilty of this fault, and not my son.

HOTSPUR

My liege, I did deny no prisoners.
But I remember, when the fight was done,
30 When I was dry with rage and extreme toil,
Breathless and faint, leaning upon my sword,
Came there a certain lord, neat, and trimly dressed,
Fresh as a bridegroom, and his chin new reaped
Showed like a stubble land at harvest home.
35 He was perfumèd like a milliner,
And 'twixt his finger and his thumb he held
A pouncet box, which ever and anon
He gave his nose and took 't away again,
Who therewith angry, when it next came there,
40 Took it in snuff; and still he smiled and talked.
And as the soldiers bore dead bodies by,
He called them untaught knaves, unmannerly,
To bring a slovenly unhandsome corse
Betwixt the wind and his nobility.
45 With many holiday and lady terms
He questioned me; amongst the rest demanded
My prisoners in your Majesty's behalf.
I then, all smarting with my wounds being cold,
To be so pestered with a popinjay,
50 Out of my grief and my impatience
Answered neglectingly I know not what—
He should, or he should not; for he made me mad
To see him shine so brisk and smell so sweet
And talk so like a waiting-gentlewoman

NORTHUMBERLAND

Yes, my Lord. The prisoners you asked for, which my son Harry Percy captured at Holmedon, were not kept from you in anger. He's already told you that. Whoever told you my son meant to defy you was either mistaken or trying to make trouble. He's done nothing wrong.

HOTSPUR

Sir, I didn't hold back any prisoners. But I remember this: when the battle ended, I was exhausted with rage and exertion. I was out of breath, dizzy and bent over. All of a sudden a man approached me, neat, clean, and tidily dressed, like a bridegroom. His beard was freshly shaven, like a newly plowed field. He wore fancy cologne and he carried a perfume box, which he kept raising to his nose as he smiled and talked on. Whenever soldiers walked past, bearing dead bodies, he called them rude hoodlums for bringing a foul, disgusting corpse within breathing distance of him. He interrogated me, with his fancy language, and demanded that I give him my prisoners, to be taken on your behalf. There I was, with the cold aggravating all my wounds, being pestered by this idiot. In my grief and impatience, I gave him some kind of answer. I don't even remember what I said—he could take them, or he couldn't.

55 Of guns, and drums, and wounds—God save the mark!—
And telling me the sovereignest thing on earth
Was parmacety for an inward bruise,
And that it was great pity, so it was,
This villanous saltpeter should be digged
60 Out of the bowels of the harmless earth,
Which many a good tall fellow had destroyed
So cowardly, and but for these vile guns
He would himself have been a soldier.
This bald unjointed chat of his, my lord,
65 I answered indirectly, as I said,
And I beseech you, let not his report
Come current for an accusation
Betwixt my love and your high Majesty.

BLUNT
The circumstance considered, good my lord,
70 Whate'er Lord Harry Percy then had said
To such a person and in such a place,
At such a time, with all the rest retold,
May reasonably die and never rise
To do him wrong or any way impeach
75 What then he said, so he unsay it now.

KING
Why, yet he doth deny his prisoners,
But with proviso and exception
That we at our own charge shall ransom straight
His brother-in-law, the foolish Mortimer,
80 Who, on my soul, hath willfully betrayed
The lives of those that he did lead to fight
Against that great magician, damned Glendower,
Whose daughter, as we hear, the Earl of March
Hath lately married. Shall our coffers then
85 Be emptied to redeem a traitor home?
Shall we buy treason and indent with fears
When they have lost and forfeited themselves?
No, on the barren mountains let him starve,

I was so angry, looking at him all shiny and sweet-smelling, and speaking like a squeamish woman about guns and battle drums and wounds—God almighty! —and telling me the best thing for an injury is parmaceti, and that it was a shame that the blameless earth had to be dug up to find saltpeter for the gunpowder, when so many good, brave men had been cowardly destroyed by guns, and that if it hadn't been for those disgusting guns, he would have been a soldier himself. All this trivial, incoherent talk I answered offhandedly, as I've already told you. So I beg you: please don't take his word as evidence that there's anything wrong between you and me, your Majesty.

> *parmaceti = spermaceti, a medicinal ointment derived from fat taken from a sperm whale's head*

BLUNT

Given the circumstances, my lord, whatever Harry Percy may have said to a man like that, in a place and time like that, should be allowed to die and never be spoken of again. It should never be used against Harry in any way, since he has taken it all back now.

KING

But he still won't turn over his prisoners unless he can add these stipulations and exceptions. He wants me, at my own cost, to pay ransom for his brother-in-law, the foolish Mortimer, a man who, on my life, willfully betrayed his own men, whom he had led in fighting against that great magician, the damned Glendower. And now we hear that Mortimer has married Glendower's daughter! Should the treasury be emptied to ransom a traitor? Should I pay for treason, and bargain for a coward, when it was Mortimer who lost himself? No. Let him starve in the wilderness. No man who asks me to spend one penny on that traitor Mortimer can ever be a friend of mine.

90 For I shall never hold that man my friend
 Whose tongue shall ask me for one penny cost
 To ransom home revolted Mortimer.

HOTSPUR
 Revolted Mortimer!
 He never did fall off, my sovereign liege,
 But by the chance of war. To prove that true
95 Needs no more but one tongue for all those wounds,
 Those mouthèd wounds, which valiantly he took
 When on the gentle Severn's sedgy bank
 In single opposition hand to hand
 He did confound the best part of an hour
100 In changing hardiment with great Glendower.
 Three times they breathed, and three times did they drink,
 Upon agreement, of swift Severn's flood,
 Who then, affrighted with their bloody looks,
 Ran fearfully among the trembling reeds
105 And hid his crisp head in the hollow bank,
 Bloodstainèd with these valiant combatants.
 Never did bare and rotten policy
 Color her working with such deadly wounds,
 Nor could the noble Mortimer
110 Receive so many, and all willingly.
 Then let not him be slandered with revolt.

KING
             Thou dost
 belie him, Percy; thou dost belie him.
 He never did encounter with Glendower.
 I tell thee, he durst as well have met the devil alone
115 As Owen Glendower for an enemy.
 Art thou not ashamed? But, sirrah, henceforth
 Let me not hear you speak of Mortimer.
 Send me your prisoners with the speediest means,
 Or you shall hear in such a kind from me
120 As will displease you.—My lord Northumberland,
 We license your departure with your son.—

HOTSPUR

"That traitor Mortimer!" He never faltered, my lord, except through an accident of war. I'll prove it, by speaking about the many wounds he heroically suffered when he spent an hour in brutal hand-to-hand combat against Glendower on the grassy banks of the Severn River. They broke three times from fighting, and they drank three times from the Severn. The river itself was frightened by their horrible looks. Its water became discolored with the blood of these brave fighters, and the Severn ran off, as if to hide itself in the weeds on its banks. Treachery has never used deadly wounds to cover its operations, and Mortimer could never have willingly suffered so many injuries. Do not let him be slandered by calling him a traitor.

KING

You speak wrongly about him, Percy, you speak wrongly! He never fought Glendower. I tell you, he would just as soon dare to meet the devil himself as fight Glendower. Aren't you ashamed of yourself? Don't ever let me hear you speak of Mortimer again. Send me your prisoners as quickly as possible, or you'll hear about it from me, and you won't like what I have to say. Northumberland, I give you and your son permission to leave now.

Send us your prisoners, or you will hear of it.

Exit KING *Henry,* BLUNT, *and train*

HOTSPUR

An if the devil come and roar for them,
I will not send them. I will after straight
125   And tell him so, for I will ease my heart,
Albeit I make a hazard of my head.

NORTHUMBERLAND

What, drunk with choler? stay and pause awhile.
Here comes your uncle.

Enter WORCESTER

HOTSPUR

Speak of Mortimer?
Zounds, I will speak of him, and let my soul
130   Want mercy if I do not join with him.
Yea, on his part I'll empty all these veins
And shed my dear blood drop by drop in the dust,
But I will lift the downtrod Mortimer
As high in the air as this unthankful King,
135   As this ingrate and cankered Bolingbroke.

NORTHUMBERLAND

(to WORCESTER*)* Brother, the King hath made your nephew
        mad.

WORCESTER

Who struck this heat up after I was gone?

HOTSPUR

He will forsooth have all my prisoners,
And when I urged the ransom once again
140   Of my wife's brother, then his cheek looked pale,
And on my face he turned an eye of death,
Trembling even at the name of Mortimer.

Send your prisoners, or you'll hear about it.

KING Henry, BLUNT, and the attendants exit.

HOTSPUR

Even if the devil himself comes screaming for them, I won't send those prisoners. I'm going to go after him and tell him so; it will ease my heart, though it might cost me my head.

NORTHUMBERLAND

What, drunk with anger? Wait a minute. Here comes your uncle.

WORCESTER enters.

HOTSPUR

Talk about Mortimer? God damn, I will talk about him. And damn my soul if I don't join him! I'll empty out my veins for him, and I'll pour my precious blood onto the ground, drop by drop! And I'll lift this put-upon Mortimer as high up as this ungrateful King, this ungenerous, rotten Bolingbroke!

NORTHUMBERLAND

(to WORCESTER) Brother, the King's driven your nephew crazy.

WORCESTER

Who started this trouble after I left?

HOTSPUR

He wants all my prisoners, for God's sake! And when I asked again for him to ransom my brother-in-law, he looked pale, and he shot me a look that could kill. Just the mention of Mortimer's name makes him shake.

WORCESTER
    I cannot blame him. Was not he proclaimed
    By Richard, that dead is, the next of blood?

NORTHUMBERLAND
145   He was; I heard the proclamation.
    And then it was when the unhappy King—
    Whose wrongs in us God pardon!—did set forth
    Upon his Irish expedition;
    From whence he, intercepted, did return
150   To be deposed and shortly murderèd.

WORCESTER
    And for whose death we in the world's wide mouth
    Live scandalized and foully spoken of.

HOTSPUR
    But soft, I pray you. Did King Richard then
    Proclaim my brother Edmund Mortimer
155   Heir to the crown?

NORTHUMBERLAND
                  He did; myself did hear it.

HOTSPUR
    Nay then, I cannot blame his cousin King
    That wished him on the barren mountains starve.
    But shall it be that you that set the crown
    Upon the head of this forgetful man
160   And for his sake wear the detested blot
    Of murderous subornation—shall it be
    That you a world of curses undergo,
    Being the agents or base second means,
    The cords, the ladder, or the hangman rather?
165   O, pardon me that I descend so low
    To show the line and the predicament
    Wherein you range under this subtle King.
    Shall it for shame be spoken in these days,
    Or fill up chronicles in time to come,
170   That men of your nobility and power

WORCESTER

> I don't blame him. Didn't the late King Richard II proclaim that Mortimer should be next in line for the throne?

NORTHUMBERLAND

> He did; I heard the proclamation. That was when the wretched King Richard (may God forgive us for wronging him!) set out to invade Ireland. When that was interrupted, he returned to England, only to be deposed and then murdered.

WORCESTER

> And for our part in his death, the whole world is scandalized by us, and speaks ill of us.

HOTSPUR

> Stop a moment, please. Did King Richard really proclaim that my brother-in-law Edmund Mortimer was next in line for the throne?

NORTHUMBERLAND

> He did. I heard it myself.

HOTSPUR

> Then I can't blame King Henry for wishing for him to starve in the wilderness. But is it right that you—who put the crown on Henry's forgetful head, and who carry the accusations of murder for Henry's sake—should be the target of the world's curses? When you were only accomplices and instruments? Is it right to blame the ropes, the ladder, or the hangman for a man's death? Forgive me for mentioning that you two are like those sordid objects, having been exploited by this conniving King. But will you stand by while people today speak of your shame?

Did gage them both in an unjust behalf
(As both of you, God pardon it, have done)
To put down Richard, that sweet lovely rose,
An plant this thorn, this canker, Bolingbroke?
175   And shall it in more shame be further spoken
That you are fooled, discarded, and shook off
By him for whom these shames you underwent?
No, yet time serves wherein you may redeem
Your banished honors and restore yourselves
180   Into the good thoughts of the world again,
Revenge the jeering and disdain'd contempt
Of this proud King, who studies day and night
To answer all the debt he owes to you
Even with the bloody payment of your deaths.
185   Therefore I say—

WORCESTER
                       Peace, cousin, say no more.
And now I will unclasp a secret book,
And to your quick-conceiving discontents
I'll read you matter deep and dangerous,
As full of peril and adventurous spirit
190   As to o'erwalk a current roaring loud
On the unsteadfast footing of a spear.

HOTSPUR
If he fall in, good night, or sink or swim!
Send danger from the east unto the west,
So honor cross it from the north to south,
195   And let them grapple: O, the blood more stirs
To rouse a lion than to start a hare!

NORTHUMBERLAND
Imagination of some great exploit
Drives him beyond the bounds of patience.

HOTSPUR
By heaven, methinks it were an easy leap
200   To pluck bright honor from the pale-faced moon,
Or dive into the bottom of the deep,

While history books record that men of your nobility
and power dedicated themselves to as unjust a cause
(which, God forgive you, you both did) as the overthrowing of Richard, that sweet lovely rose, and the
planting of this thorn, this weed, Bolingbroke in
Richard's place? Will you listen as people say that you
are fools, and that you've been tossed away by the very
person you shamed yourselves to help? No. There is
still time for you to redeem your reputations and
restore your good names in the eyes of the world. Take
revenge against this King who mocks and scorns you.
He thinks constantly about how to repay you for all
you did—by putting you to death. So I say—

WORCESTER

Quiet, nephew; don't say any more. I have a secret for
you, which is hidden like a book with a lock. I will
open the book and read you a dark, dangerous story
that will appeal to your righteous anger. It's full of
peril and adventure, as risky as walking across a
churning, thundering river while balanced unsteadily
on a spear.

HOTSPUR

If he falls in, then it's all over, whether he sinks or
swims. The honor of the struggle is all that counts, no
matter what the danger is or where it comes from. It
takes more courage to wake a sleeping lion than to
frighten a rabbit!

NORTHUMBERLAND

Dreaming about this heroic exploit is driving him past
his patience.

HOTSPUR

By God, I think it would be easy to jump up and grab
honor off of the moon's pale face, or to dive into the
deepest ocean and pull up honor by its hair.

Where fathom line could never touch the ground,
And pluck up drownèd honor by the locks,
So he that doth redeem her thence might wear
205   Without corrival all her dignities.
But out upon this half-faced fellowship!

WORCESTER
    (to **NORTHUMBERLAND***)* He apprehends a world of figures
        here,
But not the form of what he should attend.—
(to **HOTSPUR***)* Good cousin, give me audience for a while.

HOTSPUR
210   I cry you mercy.

WORCESTER
                        Those same noble Scots
    That are your prisoners—

HOTSPUR
                        I'll keep them all.
By God, he shall not have a Scot of them.
No, if a Scot would save his soul, he shall not.
I'll keep them, by this hand!

WORCESTER
                        You start away
215   And lend no ear unto my purposes:
Those prisoners you shall keep—

HOTSPUR
                        Nay, I will. That's flat!
He said he would not ransom Mortimer,
Forbad my tongue to speak of Mortimer.
But I will find him when he lies asleep,
220   And in his ear I'll hollo "Mortimer."
Nay,
I'll have a starling shall be taught to speak
Nothing but "Mortimer," and give it him
To keep his anger still in motion.

WORCESTER
225   Hear you, cousin, a word.

Then the man who rescues honor can wear her glory alone, without rivals. To hell with sharing the glory!

WORCESTER

(to NORTHUMBERLAND*)* He sees a world built by his imagination, but that world is not the one he should be paying attention to. *(to* HOTSPUR*)* Nephew, listen to me a minute.

HOTSPUR

I beg your pardon.

WORCESTER

These Scotsmen that you've taken prisoner —

HOTSPUR

I'll keep them all. By God, the King won't get a single Scot, even if having a Scot would save his soul! I'll keep them, I swear.

WORCESTER

You're off again and not listening to me. You will get to keep the prisoners —

HOTSPUR

Yes, I will; there's no doubt about it. The King said he would not pay ransom for Mortimer. He forbid me from speaking of Mortimer. But I'll find him when he's sleeping, and I'll shout "Mortimer!" into his ears. No; I'll get a bird and teach it to say nothing but "Mortimer," and I'll give it to the King to anger him forever.

WORCESTER

Listen, nephew, please.

HOTSPUR
All studies here I solemnly defy,
Save how to gall and pinch this Bolingbroke.
And that same sword-and-buckler Prince of Wales—
But that I think his father loves him not
230   And would be glad he met with some mischance—
I would have him poisoned with a pot of ale.

WORCESTER
Farewell, kinsman. I'll talk to you
When you are better tempered to attend.

NORTHUMBERLAND
(to HOTSPUR*)* Why, what a wasp-stung and impatient fool
235   Art thou to break into this woman's mood,
Tying thine ear to no tongue but thine own!

HOTSPUR
Why, look you, I am whipped and scourged with rods,
Nettled and stung with pismires, when I hear
Of this vile politician, Bolingbroke.
240   In Richard's time—what do you call the place?
A plague upon it! It is in Gloucestershire.
'Twas where the madcap duke his uncle kept,
His uncle York; where I first bowed my knee
Unto this king of smiles, this Bolingbroke.
245   'Sblood, when you and he came back from Ravenspurgh.

NORTHUMBERLAND
At Berkley Castle.

HOTSPUR
You say true.
Why, what a candy deal of courtesy
This fawning greyhound then did proffer me:
250   "Look when his infant fortune came to age,"
And "gentle Harry Percy," and "kind cousin."
O, the devil take such cozeners!—God forgive me!
Good uncle, tell your tale. I have done.

HOTSPUR

From now on, all other pursuits I'll cast aside, except for scheming how to aggravate this Bolingbroke and his son, the lowlife Prince of Wales. If it weren't for the fact that I suspect Henry doesn't love his son, and that he'd be glad to see misfortune befall him, I'd poison the Prince's ale.

WORCESTER

Goodbye, nephew. I'll talk to you when you're in a better mood to listen.

NORTHUMBERLAND

(to HOTSPUR) You are an impatient and short-tempered fool to start nattering on like a woman, not listening to any voice but your own!

HOTSPUR

Listen, I feel like I'm being whipped with sticks and stung by ants when I hear about this vile politician, Bolingbroke. When Richard was alive—what is that place called? Damn, it's in Gloucestershire; it's where that crazy duke's uncle lived, his uncle York. It's where I first met this lying Bolingbroke, and bowed to him.—Shoot!—It happened when you and Bolingbroke came back from Ravenspurgh.

NORTHUMBERLAND

At Berkley castle.

HOTSPUR

Right. What great courtesy that flattering dog paid me! "The promise of his childhood has come true," he said. "Gentle Harry Percy," he called me, and "kind kinsman." To hell with liars like him! — I'm sorry. Uncle, go on. I'm done.

WORCESTER
Nay, if you have not, to it again.
255   We will stay your leisure.

HOTSPUR
                                   I have done, i' faith.

WORCESTER
Then once more to your Scottish prisoners:
Deliver them up without their ransom straight,
And make the Douglas' son your only mean
For powers in Scotland, which, for divers reasons
260   Which I shall send you written, be assured
Will easily be granted.—*(to* **NORTHUMBERLAND***)* You,
        my lord,
Your son in Scotland being thus employed,
Shall secretly into the bosom creep
Of that same noble prelate, well beloved,
265   The Archbishop.

HOTSPUR
                        Of York, is it not?

WORCESTER
                                   True; who bears hard
His brother's death at Bristol, the Lord Scroop.
I speak not this in estimation,
As what I think might be, but what I know
Is ruminated, plotted, and set down,
270   And only stays but to behold the face
Of that occasion that shall bring it on.

HOTSPUR
I smell it. Upon my life, it will do well.

NORTHUMBERLAND
Before the game is afoot thou still let'st slip.

HOTSPUR
Why, it cannot choose but be a noble plot.
275   And then the power of Scotland and of York
To join with Mortimer, ha?

WORCESTER

> No, if you're not done yet, keep going. We'll wait until you're ready.

HOTSPUR

> I'm done. I swear.

WORCESTER

> Then go back to your Scottish prisoners. Release them at once, without ransom. Make friends with Douglas, and use his influence to gather an army in Scotland. He'll gladly help you for many reasons, which I'll write you about soon. *(to* NORTHUMBERLAND*)* Now you, sir. While your son is busy in Scotland, you will strike up a close alliance with the Archbishop, that noble, well-beloved churchman.

HOTSPUR

> He is the Archbishop of York, no?

WORCESTER

> Yes, and he's sorely upset about his brother, Lord Scroop, whom Bolingbroke put to death in Bristol. I'm not merely speculating; I'm telling you what I know for a fact has been considered, plotted, and set into motion. They're only waiting now for the right moment to strike.

HOTSPUR

> I get it. And it's good, I bet my life on it!

NORTHUMBERLAND

> Look, you've let your dogs slip off of their leashes before the hunt has even begun.

HOTSPUR

> There's no way this excellent plan won't work. And the armies of Scotland and York will join with Mortimer, right?

WORCESTER
                    And so they shall.

HOTSPUR
        In faith, it is exceedingly well aimed.

WORCESTER
        And 'tis no little reason bids us speed
        To save our heads by raising of a head,
280   For, bear ourselves as even as we can,
        The King will always think him in our debt,
        And think we think ourselves unsatisfied,
        Till he hath found a time to pay us home.
        And see already how he doth begin
285   To make us strangers to his looks of love.

HOTSPUR
        He does, he does. We'll be revenged on him.

WORCESTER
        Cousin, farewell. No further go in this
        Than I by letters shall direct your course.
        When time is ripe, which will be suddenly,
290   I'll steal to Glendower and Lord Mortimer,
        Where you and Douglas and our powers at once,
        As I will fashion it, shall happily meet
        To bear our fortunes in our own strong arms,
        Which now we hold at much uncertainty.

NORTHUMBERLAND
295   Farewell, good brother. We shall thrive, I trust.

HOTSPUR
        Uncle, adieu: O, let the hours be short
        Till fields and blows and groans applaud our sport.

                                                Exeunt

WORCESTER

Yes, they will.

HOTSPUR

I swear, it's extremely well thought out.

WORCESTER

And we've got good reasons to hurry and save ourselves by raising an army. No matter how hard we try to look like everything's fine, the King will always think he owes us for having helped him take the throne, and he'll worry that we don't feel we've been properly compensated. Until he finds a way to pay us for good—by killing us. You can see that he's already begun to distance himself from us.

HOTSPUR

He has, he has. We'll get revenge!

WORCESTER

Nephew, farewell. Don't do any more than I tell you to do in the letters I'll write you. When the time comes, which will be soon, I'll sneak off to Glendower and Mortimer. I'll plan it so that you, Douglas and all our armies will arrive together. Then we can face our future with strength instead of the uncertainty we feel now.

NORTHUMBERLAND

So long, brother. I believe we'll prevail.

HOTSPUR

Good bye, uncle. Oh, I hope it won't be long until battlefields and collisions and groans are witnesses to our game of war!

They exit.

ACT TWO

SCENE 1

Enter a CARRIER *with a lantern in his hand*

FIRST CARRIER
Heigh-ho! An it be not four by the day, I'll be hanged.
Charles's Wain is over the new chimney, and yet our horse
not packed.—What, ostler!

OSTLER
(within) Anon, anon.

FIRST CARRIER
5   I prithee, Tom, beat Cut's saddle. Put a few flocks in the
point. Poor jade is wrung in the withers out of all cess.

Enter another CARRIER

SECOND CARRIER
Peas and beans are as dank here as a dog, and that is the next
way to give poor jades the bots. This house is turned upside
down since Robin ostler died.

FIRST CARRIER
10   Poor fellow never joyed since the price of oats rose. It was
the death of him.

SECOND CARRIER
I think this be the most villanous house in all London road
for fleas. I am stung like a tench.

FIRST CARRIER
Like a tench? By the Mass, there is ne'er a king christen
15   could be better bit than I have been since the first cock.

ACT TWO

SCENE 1

carrier = deliveryman

FIRST CARRIER *enters, holding a lantern.*

FIRST CARRIER

ostler = horse attendant at an inn

I'll be damned if it isn't 4 A.M. already. The Big Dipper has already risen above the chimney, and our horses aren't ready yet. Hey, ostler!

OSTLER

(offstage) Just a second!

FIRST CARRIER

Tom may be the name of either the ostler or the Second Carrier.

Hey, Tom, give the saddle of my horse, Cut, a few whacks to soften it up, and stuff some wool under it— the old nag's got some bad bruises on her shoulders.

SECOND CARRIER *enters.*

SECOND CARRIER

The feed here's as damp as anything. That's a fast way for a horse to get parasites. This stable's upside down since Ostler Robin died.

FIRST CARRIER

Poor guy. Once the price of oats went up, he was never happy again. It killed him.

SECOND CARRIER

This stable's got worse fleas than any in London. I'm stung like a tench.

A tench is a type of fish with markings that look like flea-bites.

FIRST CARRIER

Like a tench? I'm telling you, not even a king could be bitten more than I've been bitten since midnight.

SECOND CARRIER
Why, they will allow us ne'er a jordan, and then we leak in your chimney, and your chamber-lye breeds fleas like a loach.

FIRST CARRIER
What, ostler, come away and be hanged. Come away.

SECOND CARRIER
20   I have a gammon of bacon and two races of ginger to be delivered as far as Charing Cross.

FIRST CARRIER
God's body, the turkeys in my pannier are quite starved.— What, ostler! A plague on thee! Hast thou never an eye in thy head? Canst not hear? An 'twere not as good deed as
25   drink to break the pate on thee, I am a very villain. Come, and be hanged. Hast no faith in thee?

Enter GADSHILL

GADSHILL
Good morrow, carriers. What's o'clock?

FIRST CARRIER
I think it be two o'clock.

GADSHILL
I prithee, lend me thy lantern to see my gelding in the stable.

FIRST CARRIER
30   Nay, by God, soft. I know a trick worth two of that, i' faith.

GADSHILL
(to SECOND CARRIER*)* I pray thee, lend me thine.

SECOND CARRIER
Ay, when, canst tell? "Lend me thy lantern," quoth he. Marry, I'll see thee hanged first.

GADSHILL
Sirrah carrier, what time do you mean to come to London?

SECOND CARRIER

They don't even give us a bathroom. So we pee in the fireplace, and you know that urine breeds fleas like nobody's business.

FIRST CARRIER

Hey, ostler! Come on already, damn you!

SECOND CARRIER

I've got to deliver a ham and some ginger root all the way to Charing Cross.

FIRST CARRIER

God almighty! The turkeys I'm carrying are starving! Hey, Stable-boy! Curse you! Can't you see? Can't you hear? If it isn't a good idea to knock you on the head, I'm a fool. Come on, damn you! Can't we trust you to do your job?

GADSHILL enters.

GADSHILL

Morning, deliverymen. What time is it?

FIRST CARRIER

I think it's two o'clock.

GADSHILL

Let me borrow your lantern so I can check on my horse in the stable.

FIRST CARRIER

No way, by God; just hold on a minute. I know a few tricks like that myself, I swear.

GADSHILL

(to SECOND CARRIER) Please, let me borrow yours.

SECOND CARRIER

Sure, whenever. Whatever you say. "Let me borrow your lantern," he says? Yeah, right. I'll see you dead first.

GADSHILL

Sirrah, what time do you plan to be in London?

sirrah = term of address used for persons of lower social standing

SECOND CARRIER
35   Time enough to go to bed with a candle, I warrant thee.
        Come, neighbour Mugs, we'll call up the gentlemen. They
        will along with company, for they have great charge.

                                              Exeunt CARRIERS

GADSHILL
        What ho, chamberlain!

CHAMBERLAIN
        (within) At hand, quoth pickpurse.

GADSHILL
40   That's even as fair as "at hand, quoth the Chamberlain," for
        thou variest no more from picking of purses than giving
        direction doth from laboring: thou layest the plot how.

        Enter CHAMBERLAIN

CHAMBERLAIN
        Good morrow, Master Gadshill. It holds current that I told
        you yesternight: there's a franklin in the Wild of Kent hath
45   brought three hundred marks with him in gold. I heard him
        tell it to one of his company last night at supper—a kind of
        auditor, one that hath abundance of charge too, God knows
        what. They are up already and call for eggs and butter. They
        will away presently.

GADSHILL
50   Sirrah, if they meet not with Saint Nicholas' clerks, I'll give
        thee this neck.

SECOND CARRIER

> At a reasonable enough time. *(to* FIRST CARRIER*)* Come on, Mugs, old friend. Let's wake up the gentlemen. They want to travel in a group because they're carrying a lot of valuables.

> *Both* CARRIERS *exit.*

GADSHILL

> Hey, chamberlain!

chamberlain = bedroom attendant

CHAMBERLAIN

> *(offstage)* "I'm there for you," as the pickpockets say!

Shakespeare's line apparently references a popular saying of the time.

GADSHILL

> That's as good as saying, "'I'm there for you,' said the chamberlain." You're only as different from a pickpocket as a supervisor is from a worker; you're the one who sets the plans.

The CHAMBERLAIN *enters.*

CHAMBERLAIN

> Morning, Mr. Gadshill. What I told you last night is still true. There's a rich landowner all the way from Kent staying here, and he's got three hundred gold coins with him. I heard him say so to a man at supper last night. That man's some kind of tax collector, and he has plenty of money with him, too. They just woke up and they've ordered breakfast; they'll be leaving soon.

GADSHILL

> Sirrah, if they don't run into some highway robbers today, you can have my neck.

CHAMBERLAIN

No, I'll none of it. I pray thee keep that for the hangman, for
I know thou worshipest Saint Nicholas as truly as a man of
falsehood may.

GADSHILL

55   What talkest thou to me of the hangman? If I hang, I'll
make a fat pair of gallows, for if I hang, old Sir John hangs
with me, and thou knowest he is no starveling. Tut, there
are other Troyans that thou dream'st not of, the which for
sport sake are content to do the profession some grace, that
60   would, if matters should be looked into, for their own credit
sake make all whole. I am joined with no foot-land-rakers,
no long-staff sixpenny strikers, none of these mad
mustachio purple-hued malt-worms, but with nobility and
tranquillity, burgomasters and great oneyers, such as can
65   hold in, such as will strike sooner than speak, and speak
sooner than drink, and drink sooner than pray, and yet,
zounds, I lie, for they pray continually to their saint the
commonwealth, or rather not pray to her but prey on her,
for they ride up and down on her and make her their boots.

CHAMBERLAIN

70   What, the commonwealth their boots? Will she hold out
water in foul way?

GADSHILL

She will, she will. Justice hath liquored her. We steal as in a
castle, cocksure. We have the receipt of fern seed; we walk
invisible.

CHAMBERLAIN

75   Nay, by my faith, I think you are more beholding to the
night than to fern seed for your walking invisible.

GADSHILL

Give me thy hand. Thou shalt have a share in our purchase,
as I am a true man.

CHAMBERLAIN

I don't want it; keep it for the hangman. I know you worship the patron saint of highway robbery, as much as a godless man like you worships anything.

GADSHILL

Why are you taking to me about the hangman? If I hang, I'll make half of a fat pair on the gallows, because if I hang, old Sir John will be hanging right with me—and he's not exactly thin. Please! Our gang has some members you could never guess, and for their own amusement, they're happy to lend the profession of thievery some respect. If we were ever investigated, they would smooth everything over. I've got no wandering highwaymen, no thieves with homemade weapons, no red-faced drunks with crazy mustaches. Only men of calm and noble demeanor for me: magistrates and court officials. Men who can keep a secret; who'd rather smack you than speak, rather speak than drink, and rather drink than pray.—No! That's a lie! They pray all the time to England, their patron saint. Or rather, they don't pray to her; they prey on her. They ride her up and down and then make her their boots.

Gadshill means they plunder England, or take her "booty"; the Chamberlain puns on the words boots/booty.

CHAMBERLAIN

Make her their boots? Why, will she keep their feet dry from muddy water?

GADSHILL

She can, she can. She's been greased with so many bribes that she's waterproof. We thieve in complete safety; we've got a potion that makes us invisible.

CHAMBERLAIN

Oh, I don't think so. It's the dark of night that makes you hard to see, not a secret potion.

GADSHILL

Let's shake hands. You'll get a share of our spoils; I swear on my honor as a true man.

CHAMBERLAIN
　　Nay, rather let me have it as you are a false thief.

GADSHILL
80　　Go to. *Homo* is a common name to all men. Bid the ostler
　　bring my gelding out of the stable. Farewell, you muddy
　　knave.

Exeunt

CHAMBERLAIN

I'd rather have you swear by your reputation as a dishonest thief.

GADSHILL

Whatever. I'm a true man, even if I'm a dishonest thief. Tell the stable-boy to get my horse. Farewell, you fool.

They exit.

ACT 2, SCENE 2

Enter PRINCE HENRY, POINS, BARDOLPH, *and* PETO

POINS
Come, shelter, shelter! I have removed Falstaff's horse, and
he frets like a gummed velvet.

PRINCE HENRY
Stand close.

Exit POINS, BARDOLPH, *and* PETO *exit*

Enter FALSTAFF

FALSTAFF
Poins! Poins, and be hanged! Poins!

PRINCE HENRY
5   Peace, you fat-kidneyed rascal. What a brawling dost thou
keep!

FALSTAFF
Where's Poins, Hal?

PRINCE HENRY
He is walked up to the top of the hill. I'll go seek him.

Exit PRINCE HENRY

FALSTAFF
I am accursed to rob in that thief's company. The rascal
10   hath removed my horse and tied him I know not where. If
I travel but four foot by the square further afoot, I shall
break my wind. Well, I doubt not but to die a fair death for
all this, if I 'scape hanging for killing that rogue. I have
forsworn his company hourly any time this two-and-
15   twenty years, and yet I am bewitched with the rogue's
company. If the rascal hath not given me medicines to make
me love him, I'll be hanged. It could not be else: I have
drunk medicines.—Poins! Hal! A plague upon you both.—
Bardolph! Peto!—I'll starve ere I'll rob a foot further. An
20   'twere not as good a deed as drink to turn true man and to
leave these rogues, I am the veriest varlet that ever chewed

ACT 2, SCENE 2

PRINCE HENRY, POINS, PETO, *and* BARDOLPH *enter.*

POINS

Come on, hide, hide! I stole Falstaff's horse, and he's rubbed the wrong way; he's fraying like cheap velvet.

PRINCE HENRY

Stay hidden.

> POINS, PETO *and* BARDOLPH *exit.*
>
> FALSTAFF *enters.*

FALSTAFF

Poins! Poins, damn you! Poins!

PRINCE HENRY

Quiet, you fat-bellied jerk! What a racket you're making!

FALSTAFF

Where's Poins, Hal?

PRINCE HENRY

He walked up the hill. I'll go find him.

> PRINCE HENRY *exits.*

FALSTAFF

I got a raw deal, to be out robbing with him. He stole my horse and tied him up someplace. If I have to walk even four feet more, I'll be totally out of breath. Still, I bet I'll die a natural death—if I don't get hanged for killing that jerk, that is. Every hour for the past twenty-two years, I've sworn I'd never talk to him again, but I love his company. He must have slipped me a love potion that makes me adore him. Damn, that must be it: I have drunk love potions. Poins! Hal! Drop dead, the both of you! Bardolph! Peto! I'll die if I have to walk another foot. If turning honest and abandoning these jerks weren't the best things I could possibly do for myself, then I'm the worst scoundrel

with a tooth. Eight yards of uneven ground is threescore
and ten miles afoot with me, and the stony-hearted villains
know it well enough. A plague upon it when thieves cannot
25   be true one to another!

They whistle.

Whew!

Enter PRINCE HENRY, POINS, PETO, *and* BARDOLPH

A plague upon you all! Give me my horse, you rogues. Give
me my horse and be hanged!

PRINCE HENRY
      Peace, you fat guts! Lie down, lay thine ear close to the
30   ground, and list if thou canst hear the tread of travelers.

FALSTAFF
      Have you any levers to lift me up again being down?
      'Sblood, I'll not bear mine own flesh so far afoot again for all
      the coin in thy father's Exchequer. What a plague mean you
      to colt me thus?

PRINCE HENRY
35   Thou liest. Thou art not colted; thou art uncolted.

FALSTAFF
      I prithee, good Prince Hal, help me to my horse, good king's
      son.

PRINCE HENRY
      Out, you rogue! Shall I be your ostler?

FALSTAFF
      Hang thyself in thine own heir-apparent garters! If I be
40   ta'en, I'll peach for this. An I have not ballads made on you
      all and sung to filthy tunes, let a cup of sack be my poison—
      when a jest is so forward, and afoot too! I hate it.

that ever lived. Eight yards of rough road is like seventy miles to me, and these hard-hearted crooks know it. It stinks when there's no honor among thieves.

They whistle from offstage.

Whew!

PRINCE HENRY, POINS, PETO, *and* BARDOLPH *enter.*

The hell with you all! Give me my horse, you deadbeats. Give me my horse and the hell with you!

PRINCE HENRY
Shut up, fatso! Lie down, put your ear to the ground, and listen for the footsteps of travelers.

FALSTAFF
Do you have a crane to lift me up again once I'm down? Damn, I wouldn't walk my fat self this far again for all the money in your father's treasury. What are you doing horsing around with me like this?

PRINCE HENRY
You're lying. We can't horse around, because you don't have a horse.

FALSTAFF
Please, my good Hal, help me find my horse, you good king's son.

PRINCE HENRY
Later with that! You want me to be your stable boy?

FALSTAFF
Go drop dead in your own heir-apparent pants. If I'm arrested, I'll rat you out, too. If I don't get them singing dirty songs in the street about you all, let me be poisoned to death with booze. I hate it when a practical joke gets so out of hand—and with me out of a horse, too!

Enter GADSHILL

GADSHILL
Stand.

FALSTAFF
So I do, against my will.

POINS
45 O, 'tis our setter. I know his voice, Bardolph. —What
news?

GADSHILL
Case you, case you. On with your vizards. There's money of
the King's coming down the hill. 'Tis going to the King's
Exchequer.

FALSTAFF
50 You lie, you rogue. 'Tis going to the King's Tavern.

GADSHILL
There's enough to make us all.

FALSTAFF
To be hanged.

PRINCE HENRY
Sirs, you four shall front them in the narrow lane. Ned
Poins and I will walk lower. If they 'scape from your
55 encounter, then they light on us.

PETO
How many be there of them?

GADSHILL
Some eight or ten.

FALSTAFF
Zounds, will they not rob us?

PRINCE HENRY
What, a coward, Sir John Paunch?

FALSTAFF
60 Indeed, I am not John of Gaunt, your grandfather, but yet
no coward, Hal.

GADSHILL *enters.*

GADSHILL

Freeze!

FALSTAFF

I am, and I don't like it.

POINS

Oh, that's the man who planned the whole thing; I recognize his voice, Bardolph.—What's going on?

GADSHILL

Cover your faces, cover your faces. Get your masks on. There's tax money coming down the hill, on its way to the King's treasury.

FALSTAFF

That's a lie, you clown. It's on its way to the king's bank.

GADSHILL

There's enough to make us all rich.

FALSTAFF

Or to get us all hanged.

PRINCE HENRY

Listen, you four confront them in the narrow lane. Ned Poins and I will wait further down. If they get away from you, they'll run right into us.

PETO

How many of them are there?

GADSHILL

About eight or ten.

FALSTAFF

Damn! Won't they rob us?

PRINCE HENRY

What, are you a coward, Sir John Fatstuff?

FALSTAFF

Falstaff puns on the fact that "Gaunt" (Henry's grandfather's name) can also mean "skinny."

Well, I'm certainly not John of Gaunt, your grandfather, but I'm no coward, Hal.

PRINCE HENRY
Well, we leave that to the proof.

POINS
Sirrah Jack, thy horse stands behind the hedge. When thou
needest him, there thou shalt find him. Farewell, and stand
65   fast.

FALSTAFF
Now cannot I strike him, if I should be hanged.

PRINCE HENRY
(aside to POINS*)* Ned, where are our disguises?

POINS
(aside to PRINCE HENRY*)* Here, hard by. Stand close.

Exeunt PRINCE HENRY *and* POINS

FALSTAFF
Now, my masters, happy man be his dole, say I. Every man
70   to his business.

Enter the TRAVELERS

FIRST TRAVELER
Come, neighbor, the boy shall lead our horses down the
hill. We'll walk afoot awhile and ease our legs.

THIEVES
Stand!

TRAVELERS
Jesus bless us!

FALSTAFF
75   Strike! Down with them! Cut the villains' throats! Ah,
whoreson caterpillars, bacon-fed knaves, they hate us
youth. Down with them! Fleece them!

TRAVELERS
O, we are undone, both we and ours forever!

PRINCE HENRY

Well, we'll see about that.

POINS

Jack, sirrah, your horse is there behind the hedge. When you need him, that's where you'll find him. So long, and be brave.

FALSTAFF

I can't hit him. I'd be hanged.

PRINCE HENRY

(to POINS, *so others cannot hear)* Ned, where are our disguises?

POINS

(to PRINCE HENRY*)* They're here, close by. Now hide.

PRINCE HENRY *and* POINS *exit.*

FALSTAFF

Now, men, here's to happy endings. Every man to his station.

The TRAVELERS *enter.*

FIRST TRAVELER

Come on, friend. The boy will lead our horses down the hill while we walk a bit and stretch our legs.

THIEVES

Freeze!

TRAVELERS

Jesus bless us!

FALSTAFF

Hit them! Down with them! Cut their throats! Yahh-hhh! No-good bloodsuckers! Overfed morons! They hate young people like us. Down with them! Rob them blind!

TRAVELERS

Oh! We're done for!

FALSTAFF
Hang, you gorbellied knaves! Are you undone? No, you fat
chuffs. I would your store were here. On, bacons, on! What,
you knaves, young men must live. You are grandjurors, are
you? We'll jure you, faith.

Here they rob them and bind them. Exeunt

Enter PRINCE HENRY *and* POINS

PRINCE HENRY
The thieves have bound the true men. Now could thou and
I rob the thieves and go merrily to London, it would be
argument for a week, laughter for a month, and a good jest
forever.

POINS
Stand close, I hear them coming.

PRINCE HENRY *and* POINS *hide. Enter the thieves again*

FALSTAFF
Come, my masters, let us share, and then to horse before
day. An the Prince and Poins be not two arrant cowards,
there's no equity stirring. There's no more valor in that
Poins than in a wild duck.

As they are sharing, PRINCE HENRY *and* POINS *set upon them.*

PRINCE HENRY
Your money!

POINS
Villains!

They all run away, and FALSTAFF, *after a blow or two, runs
away too, leaving the booty behind them.*

FALSTAFF

Refers to the fact
that only
wealthy men
served on
grand juries

Damn it, you potbellied morons, are you finished?
No, you fat misers. I wish everything you owned were
here. Come on, pigs, come on! What, you idiots!
Young men have to survive. You're Grand Jurors,
aren't you? Well here's some justice for you!

The thieves rob the travelers and tie them up.

They all exit.

PRINCE HENRY *and* POINS *enter.*

PRINCE HENRY

The thieves have tied up the honest men. If you and I
can now rob the robbers and run laughing to London,
we would talk about it for a week, laugh about it for a
month, and it would be a hilarious story forever.

POINS

Get down. I hear them coming.

PRINCE HENRY *and* POINS *hide. The* THIEVES *return.*

FALSTAFF

Come on, boys, let's divide up the spoils and then ride
off before dawn. If the Prince and Poins aren't cowards, there's no justice in the universe. Poins is about
as brave as a duck.

As the thieves split the money, PRINCE HENRY *and* POINS
attack them.

PRINCE HENRY

(in disguise) Give us your money!

POINS

(in disguise) Crooks!

The thieves all run away. FALSTAFF *fights for a moment,
then runs away as well, leaving all of the money behind.*

PRINCE HENRY
Got with much ease. Now merrily to horse.
95   The thieves are all scattered, and possessed with fear
So strongly that they dare not meet each other.
Each takes his fellow for an officer.
Away, good Ned. Falstaff sweats to death,
And lards the lean earth as he walks along.
100   Were 't not for laughing, I should pity him.

POINS
How the fat rogue roared!

Exeunt

PRINCE HENRY

Too easy. Now we ride off happily. The thieves have scattered, and they're so terrified that they don't even want to run into each other—they'll each think that the other guy is an officer! Let's go, Ned. Falstaff is sweating so hard that he's watering the ground as he walks along. If I weren't laughing so hard, I'd actually feel sorry for him.

POINS

How loud that fat rogue screamed!

They exit.

ACT 2, SCENE 3

Enter HOTSPUR *alone, reading a letter*

HOTSPUR
   But, for mine own part, my lord, I could be well contented to
   be there, in respect of the love I bear your house. He could be
   contented; why is he not, then? In respect of the love he
   bears our house—he shows in this he loves his own barn
5 better than he loves our house. Let me see some more. *The*
   purpose you undertake is dangerous. Why, that's certain. 'Tis
   dangerous to take a cold, to sleep, to drink; but I tell you, my
   lord fool, out of this nettle, danger, we pluck this flower,
   safety. *The purpose you undertake is dangerous, the friends*
10 *you have named uncertain, the time itself unsorted, and your*
   whole plot too light for the counterpoise of so great an
   opposition. Say you so, say you so? I say unto you again, you
   are a shallow, cowardly hind, and you lie. What a lack-brain
   is this! By the Lord, our plot is a good plot as ever was laid,
15 our friends true and constant—a good plot, good friends,
   and full of expectation; an excellent plot, very good friends.
   What a frosty-spirited rogue is this! Why, my Lord of York
   commends the plot and the general course of the action.
   Zounds, an I were now by this rascal, I could brain him with
20 his lady's fan. Is there not my father, my uncle, and myself?
   Lord Edmund Mortimer, my Lord of York, and Owen
   Glendower? Is there not besides the Douglas? Have I not all
   their letters to meet me in arms by the ninth of the next
   month, and are they not some of them set forward already?
25 What a pagan rascal is this—an infidel! Ha, you shall see
   now in very sincerity of fear and cold heart, will he to the
   King and lay open all our proceedings. O, I could divide
   myself and go to buffets, for moving such a dish of skim
   milk with so honorable an action! Hang him, let him tell the
30 King. We are prepared. I will set forward tonight.

ACT 2, SCENE 3

HOTSPUR *enters alone, reading a letter.*

HOTSPUR

"As for me, sir, I would be happy to be there because of the love I bear for your family." He would be happy to be here. Well, why isn't he, then? He says he loves my family, but he clearly loves his barn more than our house. I'll read on. "Your plan is dangerous." That's true, and it's also dangerous to catch a cold, to sleep, to drink. But I tell you, my lord fool, we shall pluck a flower of safety from this thorn of danger. "Your plan is dangerous; your allies untrustworthy; your timing poor; and your whole project too weak to counter so powerful an opponent." Is that so? Is that so? I'll say it once again: you are a stupid, cowardly dog, and a liar. What an idiot this is! By God, our plan is as good a plan as ever hatched, our allies loyal and firm. A good plan, good allies, and very promising; it's an excellent plan, very good allies. What a yellowbellied fool this is! Why, the Archbishop of York approves of the plan, and how it's progressing. Damn! If I were with this imbecile right now, I'd break his head open with his wife's fan. Don't we have my father? And my uncle, and me? Edmund Mortimer, York, and Owen Glendower? And besides, don't we have Douglas? Haven't they all sent me letters, promising to meet me with their armies by the ninth of next month? And aren't some of them on their way already? What an unbelievable ass this is! Faithless! Ha! Just watch; he'll run to the King in cold fear and spill our secrets. Oh, I could split myself in two and knock my own self senseless for unfolding this important plan to such a coward. To hell with him! Let him tell the King; we're ready. I'll set off tonight.

Enter his lady, LADY PERCY

How now, Kate? I must leave you within these two hours.

LADY PERCY
O my good lord, why are you thus alone?
For what offense have I this fortnight been
A banished woman from my Harry's bed?
35   Tell me, sweet lord, what is 't that takes from thee
Thy stomach, pleasure, and thy golden sleep?
Why dost thou bend thine eyes upon the earth
And start so often when thou sit'st alone?
Why hast thou lost the fresh blood in thy cheeks
40   And given my treasures and my rights of thee
To thick-eyed musing and curst melancholy?
In thy faint slumbers I by thee have watched,
And heard thee murmur tales of iron wars,
Speak terms of manage to thy bounding steed,
45   Cry "Courage! To the field!" And thou hast talk'd
Of sallies and retires, of trenches, tents,
Of palisadoes, frontiers, parapets,
Of basilisks, of cannon, culverin,
Of prisoners' ransom and of soldiers slain,
50   And all the currents of a heady fight.
Thy spirit within thee hath been so at war,
And thus hath so bestirred thee in thy sleep,
That beads of sweat have stood upon thy brow
Like bubbles in a late-disturbèd stream,
55   And in thy face strange motions have appeared,
Such as we see when men restrain their breath
On some great sudden hest. O, what portents are these?
Some heavy business hath my lord in hand,
And I must know it, else he loves me not.

HOTSPUR
60   What, ho!

His wife, LADY PERCY, *enters.*

What is it, Kate? I must leave you in a few hours.

LADY PERCY

Oh, my good lord, why are you alone like this? What have I done to make my Harry banish me from his bed these past two weeks? Tell me, sweet husband, what has stolen your appetite, your desire, and your sleep? Why do you stare at the ground and jump in your skin when you are sitting alone? Where is the color in your cheeks? Why have you taken all your attention, which should be mine, and given it to this dark mood and terrible sadness? While you sleep so lightly, I've watched you and heard you mumble stories of war. I've heard you give commands to your horse. I've heard you yell, "Courage! To the field!" And you have talked of charges and retreats; of trenches, tents; of fences, ramparts, and walls; of all types of cannon; of prisoners' ransoms and of dead soldiers, and of all the movements of a violent battle. Your soul has also been at war and has disturbed you in your sleep. Beads of sweat have broken out on your forehead, like bubbles in a churning stream. And on your face I've seen strange expressions, like a man who's gulping his breath at an awful, sudden command. Oh, what does all this mean? My lord is contemplating some serious matters, and if he doesn't tell me about them, he surely doesn't love me.

HOTSPUR

You there!

Enter SERVANT

Is Gilliams with the packet gone?

SERVANT
He is, my lord, an hour ago.

HOTSPUR
Hath Butler brought those horses from the sheriff?

SERVANT
One horse, my lord, he brought even now.

HOTSPUR
What horse? A roan, a crop-ear, is it not?

SERVANT
65   It is, my lord.

HOTSPUR
That roan shall be my throne.
Well, I will back him straight. O, Esperance!
Bid Butler lead him forth into the park.

Exit SERVANT

LADY PERCY
But hear you, my lord.

HOTSPUR
What say'st thou, my lady?

LADY PERCY
What is it carries you away?

HOTSPUR
Why, my horse,
70   My love, my horse.

LADY PERCY
Out, you mad-headed ape!
A weasel hath not such a deal of spleen
As you are tossed with. In faith,
I'll know your business, Harry, that I will.
I fear my brother Mortimer doth stir
75   About his title, and hath sent for you
To line his enterprise; but if you go—

A SERVANT *enters.*

Has Gilliams left with my letters?

SERVANT

He has, my lord, an hour ago.

HOTSPUR

Did Butler bring those horses from the sheriff?

SERVANT

He brought one of them just now.

HOTSPUR

Which one? A brown one, right? With its ears clipped?

SERVANT

Yes, my lord.

HOTSPUR

That brown horse will be my throne. I'll mount him in a second. Oh, "Hope is my Comfort!" Tell Butler to walk him out in the fields.

The SERVANT *exits.*

LADY PERCY

Listen, my lord.

HOTSPUR

What is it, my lady?

LADY PERCY

What is it that's got you so carried away?

HOTSPUR

My horse, my love. My horse.

LADY PERCY

Enough, you crazy fool! Not even a weasel is as hot-headed as you are. I swear, I'll find out what you're up to, Harry, I will. I fear that my brother, Mortimer, is making some kind of move over his claim to the throne, and has asked you to help. But if you go—

HOTSPUR
　　—So far afoot, I shall be weary, love.

LADY PERCY
　　Come, come, you paraquito, answer me
　　Directly unto this question that I ask.
80　　In faith, I'll break thy little finger, Harry,
　　An if thou wilt not tell me all things true.

HOTSPUR
　　Away!
　　Away, you trifler. Love, I love thee not.
　　I care not for thee, Kate. This is no world
85　　To play with mammets and to tilt with lips.
　　We must have bloody noses and cracked crowns,
　　And pass them current too.—Gods me, my horse!—
　　What say'st thou, Kate? What would'st thou have with me?

LADY PERCY
　　Do you not love me? Do you not indeed?
90　　Well, do not then, for since you love me not,
　　I will not love myself. Do you not love me?
　　Nay, tell me if you speak in jest or no.

HOTSPUR
　　Come, wilt thou see me ride?
　　And when I am a-horseback, I will swear
95　　I love thee infinitely. But hark you, Kate,
　　I must not have you henceforth question me
　　Whither I go, nor reason whereabout.
　　Whither I must, I must; and to conclude,
　　This evening must I leave you, gentle Kate.
100　　I know you wise, but yet no farther wise
　　Than Harry Percy's wife; constant you are,
　　But yet a woman; and for secrecy
　　No lady closer, for I well believe
　　Thou wilt not utter what thou dost not know,
105　　And so far will I trust thee, gentle Kate.

LADY PERCY
　　How? So far?

HOTSPUR

—such a long way on foot, I'll be tired.

LADY PERCY

Stop it, you little parrot. Answer me straight. I swear, Harry, I'll break your little finger if you don't tell me everything, and the truth, too.

HOTSPUR

Get away from me, you nag! Love? I don't love you. I don't even care about you, Kate. This is no time for playing with dolls and jousting with kisses; we'll have bloody noses and broken heads, and spread them around, too. For God's sake, my horse! What, Kate? What do you want from me?

LADY PERCY

You don't love me? Really, you don't? Well, fine then; don't love me. And since you don't love me, I won't love myself. You don't love me? Seriously, tell me if you're joking or if you mean it.

HOTSPUR

Will you see me off? Once I'm on my horse, I'll swear I love you till the end of time. But listen here, Kate. From now on, I won't have you asking me where I'm going, nor guessing why I'm doing what I'm doing. I must go where I must go. This is final: tonight I must leave you, sweet Kate. I know you are wise, but your wisdom doesn't go further than your role as my wife. You may be able to keep a secret, but you're still a woman; and yet no woman can keep secrets like you, because you cannot reveal what you don't actually know. And that is as far as I will trust you, sweet Kate.

LADY PERCY

Oh really? That far?

HOTSPUR
Not an inch further. But hark you, Kate,
Whither I go, thither shall you go too.
Today will I set forth, tomorrow you.
110   Will this content you, Kate?

LADY PERCY
                                It must, of force.

                                                Exeunt

HOTSPUR

> Not an inch further. But listen here, Kate. Wherever I go, you will go too. I leave today, and tomorrow, you. Will this make you content, Kate?

LADY PERCY

> It must.

They exit.

ACT 2, SCENE 4

Enter PRINCE HENRY *and* POINS

PRINCE HENRY
Ned, prithee, come out of that fat room and lend me thy
hand to laugh a little.

POINS
Where hast been, Hal?

PRINCE HENRY
With three or four loggerheads amongst three or fourscore
5   hogsheads. I have sounded the very bass string of humility.
Sirrah, I am sworn brother to a leash of drawers, and can call
them all by their christen names, as Tom, Dick, and
Francis. They take it already upon their salvation that
though I be but Prince of Wales, yet I am the king of
10   courtesy, and tell me flatly I am no proud jack, like Falstaff,
but a Corinthian, a lad of mettle, a good boy—by the Lord,
so they call me—and when I am King of England, I shall
command all the good lads in Eastcheap. They call drinking
deep "dyeing scarlet," and when you breathe in your
15   watering, they cry "Hem!" and bid you "Play it off!" To
conclude, I am so good a proficient in one quarter of an hour
that I can drink with any tinker in his own language during
my life. I tell thee, Ned, thou hast lost much honor that thou
wert not with me in this action; but, sweet Ned—to sweeten
20   which name of Ned, I give thee this pennyworth of sugar,
clapped even now into my hand by an underskinker, one
that never spake other English in his life than "Eight
shillings and sixpence," and "You are welcome," with this
shrill addition, "Anon, anon, sir.—Score a pint of bastard
25   in the Half-moon," or so. But, Ned, to drive away the time
till Falstaff come, I prithee, do thou stand in some by-room
while I question my puny drawer to what end he gave me
the sugar; and do thou never leave calling "Francis," that

ACT 2, SCENE 4

PRINCE HENRY *and* POINS *enter.*

PRINCE HENRY

Ned, come out of that airless room and help me laugh a bit.

POINS

Where've you been, Hal?

PRINCE HENRY

With three or four knuckleheads and a few dozen kegs of liquor. I've been with the lowest of the low. Sirrah, I've made great friends with these three bartenders, and I'm on a first-name basis with them: Tom, Dick, and Francis. They swear on their souls that, even though I'm only the Prince of Wales, I'm the king of niceness. They say I'm no pompous fool, like Falstaff, but a good sport, a spirited man, a good boy. When I'm King of England, all the good men of Eastcheap will follow me gladly. When you drink deeply, they joke that you have been dyed red; and if you stop for a breath when you're drinking, they yell "Cough!" and they command you to keep going. In fifteen minutes, I got so good at being a drinking companion, I could be at ease with any man over a drink, in any setting. Ned, you didn't do yourself any favors by missing this. But, sweet Ned, I'll sweeten the name Ned with this bit of sugar, given to me by an apprentice drawer who never spoke any English his whole life, except, "That'll be eight shillings and sixpence," and "You're welcome," and also, "Just a second, just a second! Bring a pint of bastard to the Half-Moon room!" But Ned, let's pass the time until Falstaff gets here. Hide in a side room while I ask that little apprentice drawer why he gave me the sugar. Keep calling out his name, Francis, and

drawer = tapster; bartender

bastard = a kind of Spanish wine, mixed with honey

Half-Moon is the name of a room at the inn.

his tale to me may be nothing but "Anon." Step aside, and
30   I'll show thee a precedent.

Exit POINS

POINS
        (within) Francis!
PRINCE HENRY
        Thou art perfect.
POINS
        (within) Francis!

Enter FRANCIS, *a drawer*

FRANCIS
        Anon, anon, sir.—Look down into the Pomgarnet, Ralph.

PRINCE HENRY
35   Come hither, Francis.
FRANCIS
        My lord?
PRINCE HENRY
        How long hast thou to serve, Francis?

FRANCIS
        Forsooth, five years, and as much as to—
POINS
        (within) Francis!
FRANCIS
40   Anon, anon, sir.
PRINCE HENRY
        Five year! By 'r lady, a long lease for the clinking of pewter!
        But, Francis, darest thou be so valiant as to play the coward
        with thy indenture, and show it a fair pair of heels, and run
        from it?
FRANCIS
45   O Lord, sir, I'll be sworn upon all the books in England, I
        could find in my heart—

don't stop, so that all he's able to say is, "Just a second!" Step aside, and I'll give you a taste.

POINS *exits.*

POINS

(offstage) Francis!

PRINCE HENRY

Perfect.

POINS

(offstage) Francis!

FRANCIS, *a drawer, enters.*

FRANCIS

Just a second, sir.—Ralph, make sure everything's okay in the Pomegranate Room!

PRINCE HENRY

Come here, Francis.

FRANCIS

Sir?

PRINCE HENRY

How many more years of your apprenticeship do you have, Francis?

FRANCIS

Truly, five years, which is as long —

POINS

(offstage) Francis!

FRANCIS

Just a second, sir!

PRINCE HENRY

Five years! Wow, that's a long time to be clinking beer mugs. But Francis, are you brave enough to play the coward with your contract? To flash it your heels, as you run away?

FRANCIS

Oh Lord, sir. I'd swear on a stack of Bibles that I'd love to be able to—

POINS
(within) Francis!

FRANCIS
Anon, sir.

PRINCE HENRY
How old art thou, Francis?

FRANCIS
50   Let me see. About Michaelmas next, I shall be—

POINS
(within) Francis!

FRANCIS
Anon, sir. *(to* PRINCE HENRY*)* Pray, stay a little, my lord.

PRINCE HENRY
Nay, but hark you, Francis, for the sugar thou gavest
me, 'twas a pennyworth, was 't not?

FRANCIS
55   O Lord, I would it had been two!

PRINCE HENRY
I will give thee for it a thousand pound. Ask me when thou
wilt, and thou shalt have it.

POINS
(within) Francis!

FRANCIS
Anon, anon.

PRINCE HENRY
60   Anon, Francis? No, Francis, but tomorrow, Francis; or,
Francis, o' Thursday; or indeed, Francis, when thou wilt.
But, Francis—

FRANCIS
My lord?

PRINCE HENRY
Wilt thou rob this leathern jerkin, crystal-button, not-
65   pated, agate-ring, puke-stocking, caddis-garter, smooth-
tongue, Spanish-pouch—

POINS

(offstage) Francis!

FRANCIS

Just a second, sir!

PRINCE HENRY

How old are you, Francis?

FRANCIS

Let's see—at the end of next September, I'll be—

POINS

(offstage) Francis!

FRANCIS

Just a second, sir! (to PRINCE HENRY) Wait here a moment, my lord.

PRINCE HENRY

No, listen to me, Francis. The sugar you gave me was worth about a penny, right?

FRANCIS

Oh lord, I wish I could have given you two pennies' worth!

PRINCE HENRY

I'll give you a thousand pounds for it. Ask for it whenever you want it, and it's yours.

POINS

(offstage) Francis!

FRANCIS

Just a second!

PRINCE HENRY

You want it in a second, Francis? No, Francis. Maybe tomorrow, Francis, or Thursday, Francis, whenever you want it. But, Francis.

FRANCIS

Sir?

PRINCE HENRY

Are you ready to rob this man? This man, with his leather jacket, fashionable crystal buttons, short hair,

Hal is referring to Francis's master, who will be "robbed" if Francis breaks his contract.

FRANCIS
> O Lord, sir, who do you mean?

PRINCE HENRY
> Why, then, your brown bastard is your only drink, for look
> you, Francis, your white canvas doublet will sully. In
> 70   Barbary, sir, it cannot come to so much.

FRANCIS
> What, sir?

POINS
> *(within)* Francis!

PRINCE HENRY
> Away, you rogue! Dost thou not hear them call?

Here they both call him. **FRANCIS** *the drawer stands amazed,*
not knowing which way to go.

Enter **VINTNER**

VINTNER
> What, stand'st thou still and hear'st such a calling? Look to
> 75   the guests within.

> > *Exit* **FRANCIS**

> My lord, old Sir John with half a dozen more are at the door.
> Shall I let them in?

PRINCE HENRY
> Let them alone awhile, and then open the door.

> > *Exit* **VINTNER**

> Poins!

Reenter **POINS**

agate signet ring, dark stockings, ribboned garters, oily speech, Spanish leather pouch—

FRANCIS

Oh Lord, sir, who are you talking about?

PRINCE HENRY

Hal may be trying to confuse Francis, or he may be warning him not to leave his apprenticeship.

Well then, it looks like brown bastard will continue to be your only drink. Because listen, Francis, your white canvas shirt will get stained out there. Even in North Africa, sir, you won't get so much.

FRANCIS

Excuse me, sir?

POINS

(offstage) Francis!

PRINCE HENRY

Get going, you good-for-nothing. Can't you hear people calling you?

POINS *and* **PRINCE HENRY** *both begin to shout "Francis!"* **FRANCIS** *stands there bewildered, not knowing what to do.*

vintner = innkeeper

The **VINTNER** *enters.*

VINTNER

Why are you standing there when people are calling you? Take care of the customers inside!

FRANCIS *exits.*

My lord, old Sir John and a half-dozen others are at the door. Should I let them in?

PRINCE HENRY

Leave them out there for a while, and then open the door.

VINTNER *exits.*

Poins!

POINS *enters.*

POINS

80   Anon, anon, sir.

PRINCE HENRY

Sirrah, Falstaff and the rest of the thieves are at the door.
Shall we be merry?

POINS

As merry as crickets, my lad. But hark you, what cunning
match have you made with this jest of the drawer. Come,
85   what's the issue?

PRINCE HENRY

I am now of all humors that have showed themselves
humors since the old days of Goodman Adam to the pupil
age of this present twelve o'clock at midnight.

Enter FRANCIS

What's o'clock, Francis?

FRANCIS

90   Anon, anon, sir.

Exit FRANCIS

PRINCE HENRY

That ever this fellow should have fewer words than a
parrot, and yet the son of a woman! His industry is upstairs
and downstairs, his eloquence the parcel of a reckoning. I
am not yet of Percy's mind, the Hotspur of the north, he
95   that kills me some six or seven dozen of Scots at a breakfast,
washes his hands, and says to his wife "Fie upon this quiet
life! I want work." "O my sweet Harry," says she, "how
many hast thou killed today?" "Give my roan horse a
drench," says he, and answers "Some fourteen," an hour
100   after. "A trifle, a trifle." I prithee, call in Falstaff. I'll play
Percy, and that damned brawn shall play Dame Mortimer
his wife. *"Rivo!"* says the drunkard. Call in Ribs, call in
Tallow.

POINS

> Just a second, sir!

PRINCE HENRY

> Sirrah, Falstaff and the rest of the thieves are here. Are we ready for a laugh?

POINS

> We'll be happy as crickets, my lad. But listen, what's with this gag you played on the waiter? What's the point?

PRINCE HENRY

> I'm up for anything. Right now, I'm feeling all the moods that anyone has ever felt, from the old days of Adam to this young age, right now, at twelve o'clock midnight.

FRANCIS enters.

> What time is it, Francis?

FRANCIS

> Just a second, sir.

FRANCIS exits.

PRINCE HENRY

> This boy has fewer words than a parrot, but he's actually a person! All he does is run up and down stairs, and the only things he can say are the names of the items on your bill. I'm not yet like Percy, the Hotspur of the North. He kills six or seven dozen Scotsmen before breakfast, washes his hands, and then says to his wife, "To hell with this boring life! I need something to do!" "Oh, my sweet Harry," she says, "How many have you killed today?" "Give my brown horse a dose of medicine," he says. And then about an hour later, he answers her: "About fourteen." Then he says, "That's nothing, nothing." Listen, bring in Falstaff. I'll play Percy, and that damned fat slob will play

Enter FALSTAFF, GADSHILL, PETO, *and* BARDOLPH, *followed
by* FRANCIS *with wine*

POINS
Welcome, Jack. Where hast thou been?

FALSTAFF
105   A plague of all cowards, I say, and a vengeance too! Marry
and amen!—Give me a cup of sack, boy.—Ere I lead this life
long, I'll sew netherstocks and mend them, and foot them
too. A plague of all cowards!—Give me a cup of sack, rogue.
—Is there no virtue extant? *(he drinketh)*

PRINCE HENRY
110   Didst thou never see Titan kiss a dish of butter?—Pitiful-
hearted Titan!—that melted at the sweet tale of the sun's? If
thou didst, then behold that compound.

FALSTAFF
(to FRANCIS*)* You rogue, here's lime in this sack too.—There
is nothing but roguery to be found in villanous man, yet a
115   coward is worse than a cup of sack with lime in it. A
villanous coward! Go thy ways, old Jack. Die when thou
wilt. If manhood, good manhood, be not forgot upon the
face of the earth, then am I a shotten herring. There lives not
three good men unhanged in England, and one of them is
120   fat and grows old, God help the while. A bad world, I say.
I would I were a weaver. I could sing psalms, or anything.
A plague of all cowards, I say still.

his wife, Dame Mortimer. "Bottom's up!" as the drunk says. Bring in the meat, bring in blubber.

FALSTAFF, GADSHILL, BARDOLPH, *and* PETO *enter.* FRANCIS *follows with wine.*

POINS

Welcome, Jack. Where've you been?

FALSTAFF

A curse on all cowards, I say, and revenge on them, too! Amen to that! Give me some wine, boy. I'm not going to keep up this way of life much longer. I'll knit socks, mend them, and fix their feet. A curse on all cowards! Give me a cup of wine, you lowlife! Isn't there any honesty left in this world? *(he drinks)*

PRINCE HENRY

Hal may be referring to the wine melting down Falstaff's throat; he may also be suggesting that Falstaff is hot and sweaty.

Did you ever see the sun kiss a dish of butter? The tender-hearted sun, melting the butter with its sweet words! If you have, then take a look at Falstaff.

FALSTAFF

Lime was added to wine of poor quality to make it sparkle.

(to FRANCIS*)* You bastard! Somebody put lime in my wine! All men are cheaters and schemers, but a coward is worse than a glass of wine with lime in it. A miserable coward! Go on, old Jack, die already. If there's even one real man left on this earth besides me, then I'm as skinny as a herring. In all of England there are only three good men that haven't been put to death, and one of them is fat and growing old. God help us all! It's a bad world, I say. I wish I were a weaver; I could sing psalms while I was sewing. I'll say it again: a curse on all cowards.

PRINCE HENRY
How now, woolsack, what mutter you?

FALSTAFF
A King's son! If I do not beat thee out of thy kingdom with
125   a dagger of lath, and drive all thy subjects afore thee like a
flock of wild geese, I'll never wear hair on my face more.
You, Prince of Wales!

PRINCE HENRY
Why, you whoreson round man, what's the matter?

FALSTAFF
Are not you a coward? Answer me to that—and Poins
130   there?

POINS
Zounds, ye fat paunch, an you call me coward, by the Lord,
I'll stab thee.

FALSTAFF
I call thee coward? I'll see thee damned ere I call thee
coward, but I would give a thousand pound I could run as
135   fast as thou canst. You are straight enough in the shoulders
you care not who sees your back. Call you that backing of
your friends? A plague upon such backing! Give me them
that will face me.—Give me a cup of sack.—I am a rogue if
I drunk today.

PRINCE HENRY
140   O villain, thy lips are scarce wiped since thou drunk'st last.

FALSTAFF
All is one for that. *(he drinketh)* A plague of all cowards, still
say I.

PRINCE HENRY
What's the matter?

FALSTAFF
What's the matter? There be four of us here have ta'en a
145   thousand pound this day morning.

PRINCE HENRY

What's the matter, you sack of wool? What are you muttering about?

FALSTAFF

In medieval morality plays, the character of Vice carried a wooden dagger.

A King's son! If I don't drive you out of the kingdom with a wooden dagger, and send your subjects running before you like a flock of geese, then I'll never grow a beard again. You, Prince of Wales? What a joke!

PRINCE HENRY

You fat son of a whore, what's the matter?

FALSTAFF

Aren't you a coward? Tell me that. And Poins there?

POINS

Dammit, you fat belly. If you call me a coward, I swear, I'll stab you.

FALSTAFF

I call you coward? I'd sooner see you damned than call you a coward, but I tell you; I'd give a thousand pounds to be able to run as fast as you can. You've got good-enough–looking shoulders; you don't care who sees your back! Is that what you call backing up your friends? Damn anyone who backs up like that! I'd rather have a man who faces me. Give me some wine! I'll be damned if I've had anything to drink today.

PRINCE HENRY

Liar! You've barely had time to wipe your lips since your last drink.

FALSTAFF

Whatever. *(he drinks)* A curse on all cowards, I still say.

PRINCE HENRY

What's the matter?

FALSTAFF

What's the matter? There are four of us here who stole a thousand pounds this very morning.

PRINCE HENRY
Where is it, Jack? Where is it?

FALSTAFF
Where is it? Taken from us it is. A hundred upon poor four of us.

PRINCE HENRY
What, a hundred, man?

FALSTAFF
150   I am a rogue if I were not at half-sword with a dozen of them two hours together. I have 'scaped by miracle. I am eight times thrust through the doublet, four through the hose, my buckler cut through and through, my sword hacked like a handsaw. *Ecce signum!* I never dealt better since I was a
155   man. All would not do. A plague of all cowards! *(points to* GADSHILL, PETO *and* BARDOLPH*)* Let them speak. If they speak more or less than truth, they are villains, and the sons of darkness.

PRINCE HENRY
Speak, sirs, how was it?

GADSHILL
160   We four set upon some dozen.

FALSTAFF
Sixteen at least, my lord.

BARDOLPH
And bound them.

PETO
No, no, they were not bound.

FALSTAFF
You rogue, they were bound, every man of them, or I am a
165   Jew else, an Ebrew Jew.

GADSHILL
As we were sharing, some six or seven fresh men set upon us.

FALSTAFF
And unbound the rest, and then come in the other.

PRINCE HENRY

Where is it, Jack? Where is it?

FALSTAFF

Where is it? It was stolen from us. A hundred men against only four of us.

PRINCE HENRY

What, a hundred, man?

FALSTAFF

I'll be damned if I didn't fight with a dozen of them for two straight hours. It's a miracle I managed to get away. They stabbed through my shirt eight times. Four through my pants. My shield's got holes through and through. My sword's as cut up as a hacksaw. Behold the evidence! It was the best fighting I've ever done, but even my all wasn't enough. A curse on all cowards! *(points to* GADSHILL, PETO *and* BARDOLPH*)* Ask these men. If they don't tell you the whole truth, they're liars and devils.

PRINCE HENRY

Tell us, men. What happened?

GADSHILL

The four of us jumped about a dozen—

FALSTAFF

Sixteen at least, my lord.

GADSHILL

And tied them up.

PETO

No, no. We didn't tie them up.

FALSTAFF

You jerk, we did tie them up, every single one of them, or I'm a Jew, a true Hebrew Jew.

GADSHILL

Then, when we were dividing the money, about six or seven other men jumped us—

FALSTAFF

And untied the rest, and then all the others showed up.

PRINCE HENRY
What, fought you with them all?

FALSTAFF
170   All? I know not what you call all, but if I fought not with
fifty of them I am a bunch of radish. If there were not two-
or three-and-fifty upon poor old Jack, then am I no two-
legged creature.

PRINCE HENRY
Pray God you have not murdered some of them.

FALSTAFF
175   Nay, that's past praying for. I have peppered two of them.
Two I am sure I have paid, two rogues in buckram suits. I
tell thee what, Hal, if I tell thee a lie, spit in my face, call me
horse. Thou knowest my old ward. Here I lay, and thus I
bore my point. Four rogues in buckram let drive at me.

PRINCE HENRY
180   What, four? Thou saidst but two even now.

FALSTAFF
Four, Hal, I told thee four.

POINS
Ay, ay, he said four.

FALSTAFF
These four came all afront, and mainly thrust at me. I made
me no more ado, but took all their seven points in my
185   target, thus.

PRINCE HENRY
Seven? Why there were but four even now.

FALSTAFF
In buckram?

POINS
Ay, four in buckram suits.

FALSTAFF
Seven, by these hilts, or I am a villain else.

PRINCE HENRY

What, you fought with all of them?

FALSTAFF

All? I don't know what you mean by "all." But if I didn't fight with fifty of them, I'm a bunch of radishes. If fifty-two or fifty-three of them didn't attack me, then I'm no man.

PRINCE HENRY

I pray to God you didn't kill any of them.

FALSTAFF

Too late for praying now. I made things hot for two of them; two I'm sure I got, two thugs wearing clothes made of buckram cloth. I'll tell you what, Hal: if I'm lying to you, spit in my face and call me a horse. You know my old fighting stance. Here's how I stood, and here's how I handled my sword. Four thugs in buckram came right at me—

PRINCE HENRY

What? Four? You said two a second ago.

FALSTAFF

Four, Hal. I said four.

POINS

That's right. He said four.

FALSTAFF

These four threw everything they had right at me. I made no big fuss of it; I just put up my shield and all seven of their swords hit it.

PRINCE HENRY

Seven? But just now there were only four.

FALSTAFF

Wearing buckram?

POINS

Yes. Four in clothes made of buckram.

FALSTAFF

Seven, I swear on my sword. If not, I'm a liar.

PRINCE HENRY
190   *(aside to* POINS*)* Prithee, let him alone. We shall have more
anon.

FALSTAFF
Dost thou hear me, Hal?

PRINCE HENRY
Ay, and mark thee too, Jack.

FALSTAFF
Do so, for it is worth the listening to. These nine in buckram
195   that I told thee of—

PRINCE HENRY
So, two more already.

FALSTAFF
Their points being broken—

POINS
Down fell their hose.

FALSTAFF
Began to give me ground, but I followed me close, came in
200   foot and hand, and with a thought, seven of the eleven
I paid.

PRINCE HENRY
O monstrous! Eleven buckram men grown out of two!

FALSTAFF
But as the devil would have it, three misbegotten knaves in
Kendal green came at my back, and let drive at me, for it was
205   so dark, Hal, that thou couldst not see thy hand.

PRINCE HENRY
These lies are like their father that begets them, gross as a
mountain, open, palpable. Why, thou claybrained guts,

PRINCE HENRY

(to POINS, *so no one else can hear)* Leave him alone. There'll be more in a minute.

FALSTAFF

Are you listening to me, Hal?

PRINCE HENRY

I'm listening, Jack.

FALSTAFF

Good, because it's worth paying attention to. Anyway, these nine guys in buckram that I told you about—

PRINCE HENRY

So, two more already.

FALSTAFF

Since their points were broken—

POINS

Their stockings fell down.

Falstaff means
points as in
"swords," but the
word can also
mean "stocking
fasteners."

FALSTAFF

They started to run away, but I followed them closely. And as quick as a thought, I finished off seven of the eleven.

PRINCE HENRY

Unbelievable! Eleven buckram men have grown out of two!

FALSTAFF

But as the devil would have it, three wretched bastards wearing green came from behind and ran right at me. It was so dark, Hal, that you couldn't see your hand in front of your face.

PRINCE HENRY

These lies are like the man who tells them: huge as a mountain, obvious, and plain as day. You clay-

thou knotty-pated fool, thou whoreson, obscene, greasy
tallow-catch—

FALSTAFF
210   What, art thou mad? Art thou mad? Is not the truth the
truth?

PRINCE HENRY
Why, how couldst thou know these men in Kendal green,
when it was so dark thou couldst not see thy hand? Come,
tell us your reason. What sayest thou to this?

POINS
215   Come, your reason, Jack, your reason.

FALSTAFF
What, upon compulsion? Zounds, an I were at the
strappado or all the racks in the world, I would not tell you
on compulsion. Give you a reason on compulsion? If
reasons were as plentiful as blackberries, I would give no
220   man a reason upon compulsion, I.

PRINCE HENRY
I'll be no longer guilty of this sin. This sanguine coward,
this bed-presser, this horseback-breaker, this huge hill of
flesh—

FALSTAFF
'Sblood, you starveling, you elfskin, you dried neat's
225   tongue, you bull's pizzle, you stockfish! O, for breath to
utter what is like thee! You tailor's-yard, you sheath, you
bowcase, you vile standing tuck—

PRINCE HENRY
Well, breathe awhile, and then to it again, and when thou
hast tired thyself in base comparisons, hear me speak but
230   this.

POINS
Mark, Jack.

brained fatso, you knuckleheaded fool, you son of a whore, you obscene tub of lard—

FALSTAFF

What are you, crazy? Are you crazy? Isn't the truth the truth?

PRINCE HENRY

Well, how could you know that these men were wearing green when it was so dark you couldn't see your hand in front of your face? Go ahead, tell us. What do you have to say to that?

POINS

Come on, tell us, Jack, go on.

FALSTAFF

What, just because you command me? Dammit, if I were being tortured on all the contraptions in the world, I wouldn't speak just because you commanded. Speak just because you command! If my reasons were as cheap as blackberries, I wouldn't give away my reasons just because I was commanded. Not I.

PRINCE HENRY

I'm not going to put up with this any longer. This red-faced coward, this flattener of mattresses, this breaker of horses' backs, this huge hill of flesh—

FALSTAFF

Dammit! You scarecrow, you skin of an elf, you dried-out ox's tongue, you bull's penis, you salted cod! Oh, I wish I had enough breath to tell you all the things you are! You yardstick, you empty sheath, you case for a violinist's bow, you disgusting erect sword—

PRINCE HENRY

Catch your breath for a moment, then start again. And when you've tired yourself with these awful comparisons, listen to me say just one thing.

POINS

Listen closely, Jack.

PRINCE HENRY
We two saw you four set on four, and bound them and were
masters of their wealth. Mark now how a plain tale shall put
you down. Then did we two set on you four and, with a
235   word, outfaced you from your prize, and have it; yea, and
can show it you here in the house. And, Falstaff, you carried
your guts away as nimbly, with as quick dexterity, and
roared for mercy, and still run and roared, as ever I heard
bull-calf. What a slave art thou to hack thy sword as thou
240   hast done, and then say it was in fight! What trick, what
device, what starting-hole canst thou now find out to hide
thee from this open and apparent shame?

POINS
Come, let's hear, Jack. What trick hast thou now?

FALSTAFF
By the Lord, I knew you as well as he that made you. Why,
245   hear you, my masters, was it for me to kill the heir apparent?
Should I turn upon the true Prince? Why, thou knowest I
am as valiant as Hercules, but beware instinct. The lion will
not touch the true Prince. Instinct is a great matter. I was
now a coward on instinct. I shall think the better of myself,
250   and thee, during my life—I for a valiant lion, and thou for
a true Prince. But, by the Lord, lads, I am glad you have the
money.—Hostess, clap to the doors.—Watch tonight, pray
to-morrow. Gallants, lads, boys, hearts of gold, all the titles
of good fellowship come to you. What, shall we be merry?
255   Shall we have a play extempore?

PRINCE HENRY
Content, and the argument shall be thy running away.

FALSTAFF
Ah, no more of that, Hal, an thou lovest me.

PRINCE HENRY

The two of us saw you four jump four men, tie them up and take their money. Now listen to how the simple truth will shame you. Then the two of us jumped the four of you. And with just a word, we stole your prize from you. Now we have it, and we can show it to you right here in the bar. And Falstaff, you ran away as quickly and as lightfootedly, as a cow from the slaughter, screaming for mercy, as you ran and screamed. What a lowlife you are, to hack up your sword and say it happened in a fight! What outrageous story, what trick, what hiding place can you possibly find to hide you from your open and obvious shame?

POINS

Come on, let's hear it, Jack. What trick have you got now?

FALSTAFF

By God, I knew it was you the whole time, like I was your own father! Listen to me, men: would it be right for me to kill the heir-apparent? Should I have attacked the true Prince? Look, you know I'm as brave as Hercules, but you must listen to your instinct. It's like that old superstition, about how a lion will never attack a true Prince. Instinct is a powerful thing; I was only a coward by instinct. From now on, I'll have to think of myself as a brave lion, and you as a true Prince. But good God, men, I'm glad you have the money. Hostess! Lock the doors; we'll celebrate tonight and pray tomorrow. Gentlemen, lads, boys, hearts of gold—I'll call you every good name I can think of, all at once! Hey! Shall we have some fun? Shall we stage a little play?

Hercules was a Greek hero renowned for his bravery.

PRINCE HENRY

Of course, and the play will be about you running away.

FALSTAFF

Oh, let it go, Hal, if you love me.

Enter MISTRESS QUICKLY

MISTRESS QUICKLY
O Jesu, my lord the Prince!

PRINCE HENRY
How now, my lady the hostess, what sayest thou to me?

MISTRESS QUICKLY
260 Marry, my lord, there is a nobleman of the court at door
would speak with you. He says he comes from your father.

PRINCE HENRY
Give him as much as will make him a royal man and send
him back again to my mother.

FALSTAFF
What manner of man is he?

MISTRESS QUICKLY
265 An old man.

FALSTAFF
What doth Gravity out of his bed at midnight? Shall I give
him his answer?

PRINCE HENRY
Prithee do, Jack.

FALSTAFF
Faith, and I'll send him packing.

          Exit FALSTAFF

PRINCE HENRY
270 Now, sirs. By 'r lady, you fought fair.—So did you, Peto.—
So did you, Bardolph.—You are lions too. You ran away
upon instinct. You will not touch the true Prince. No, fie!

BARDOLPH
Faith, I ran when I saw others run.

PRINCE HENRY
Faith, tell me now in earnest, how came Falstaff's sword so
275 hacked?

MISTRESS QUICKLY *enters.*

MISTRESS QUICKLY

Oh, Jesus—Your Majesty!

PRINCE HENRY

Hello there, my lady the hostess! Do you have something to say to me?

MISTRESS QUICKLY

Indeed, my lord. There's a nobleman from the royal court at the door, and he wants to speak with you. He says your father sent him.

PRINCE HENRY

Give him some coins and send him right back to my mother.

FALSTAFF

What kind of man is he?

MISTRESS QUICKLY

An old man.

FALSTAFF

What is an old man doing out of bed at midnight? Do you want me to talk to him?

PRINCE HENRY

Please do, Jack.

FALSTAFF

Truly, I'll send him on his way.

FALSTAFF *exits.*

PRINCE HENRY

Now, men: by God, you fought well. So did you, Peto, and you, Bardolph. You must be lions, too, since your instinct told you to run away. You wouldn't touch the true Prince; no, indeed!

BARDOLPH

Honestly, I ran when I saw the others run.

PRINCE HENRY

Okay, now tell me the truth. How did Falstaff's sword get broken like that?

PETO

Why, he hacked it with his dagger and said he would swear
truth out of England but he would make you believe it was
done in fight, and persuaded us to do the like.

BARDOLPH

Yea, and to tickle our noses with speargrass to make them
280 bleed, and then to beslubber our garments with it, and
swear it was the blood of true men. I did that I did not this
seven year before: I blushed to hear his monstrous devices.

PRINCE HENRY

O villain, thou stolest a cup of sack eighteen years ago, and
wert taken with the manner, and ever since thou hast
285 blushed extempore. Thou hadst fire and sword on thy side,
and yet thou ran'st away. What instinct hadst thou for it?

BARDOLPH

My lord, do you see these meteors? Do you behold these
exhalations?

PRINCE HENRY

I do.

BARDOLPH

290 What think you they portend?

PRINCE HENRY

Hot livers and cold purses.

BARDOLPH

Choler, my lord, if rightly taken.

PRINCE HENRY

No, if rightly taken, halter.

Enter FALSTAFF

Here comes lean Jack. Here comes bare-bone.—How now,
295 my sweet creature of bombast? How long is 't ago, Jack,
since thou sawest thine own knee?

PETO

> He hacked away at it with his dagger. He said he would swear up and down to make you believe that it happened in a fight, and he made us do the same.

BARDOLPH

> Yes, and he made us rub our noses with rough weeds until they started to bleed, then smear our clothes with the blood and swear that it was from the men we fought. When he told me the crazy things he wanted us to do, I did something I haven't done in seven years: I blushed.

PRINCE HENRY

> Liar! You stole a cup of wine eighteen years ago, got caught in the act, and you've been blushing ever since. You had your fiery-red face and your weapons going for you, but still you ran away. What instinct made you do that?

BARDOLPH

> Sir, do you see these red welts on my face? Do you see these swellings?

PRINCE HENRY

> I do.

BARDOLPH

> What do you think they mean?

PRINCE HENRY

> That your temper is hot and your wallet is empty.

BARDOLPH

> It means anger, sir, you interpret it correctly.

PRINCE HENRY

> It means you'll be hanged if the authorities catch you.

> FALSTAFF *enters.*

> Here comes skinny Jack; here comes the bag of bones. What's going on, now, my sweet windbag? How long has it been, Jack, since you saw your own knees?

FALSTAFF
My own knee? When I was about thy years, Hal, I was not
an eagle's talon in the waist. I could have crept into any
alderman's thumb-ring. A plague of sighing and grief! It
300   blows a man up like a bladder. There's villanous news
abroad. Here was Sir John Bracy from your father. You
must to the court in the morning. That same mad fellow of
the north, Percy, and he of Wales that gave Amamon the
bastinado, and made Lucifer cuckold, and swore the devil
305   his true liegeman upon the cross of a Welsh hook—what a
plague call you him?

POINS
Owen Glendower.

FALSTAFF
Owen, Owen, the same, and his son-in-law Mortimer, and
old Northumberland, and that sprightly Scot of Scots,
310   Douglas, that runs a-horseback up a hill perpendicular—

PRINCE HENRY
He that rides at high speed, and with his pistol kills a
sparrow flying.

FALSTAFF
You have hit it.

PRINCE HENRY
So did he never the sparrow.

FALSTAFF
315   Well, that rascal hath good mettle in him. He will not run.

PRINCE HENRY
Why, what a rascal art thou then to praise him so for
running?

FALSTAFF
A-horseback, you cuckoo, but afoot he will not budge a
foot.

PRINCE HENRY
320   Yes, Jack, upon instinct.

FALSTAFF

My own knees? When I was your age, Hal, my waist was as skinny as an eagle's talon; I could have crawled through a councilman's thumb ring. But damn all that sighing and sadness! It blows a man up like a balloon. There's bad news out there. That was Sir John Bracy, sent by your father. You have to go to court in the morning. Percy, that mad man from up north, and that Welshman who gave Amamon a beating, and stole Lucifer's wife, and made a pact to be the devil's master—what's his name again?

Amamon = the name of a devil

POINS

Oh, Glendower.

FALSTAFF

Owen, Owen, that's the one. And his son-in-law Mortimer, and old Northumberland, and Douglas, that lively Scot of Scots, who can ride a horse straight up a wall—

PRINCE HENRY

The man who can ride at high speeds, then kill a flying sparrow with his pistol.

FALSTAFF

You've hit it; that's him exactly.

PRINCE HENRY

I may have hit it, but Owen never hit the sparrow.

FALSTAFF

Well, that rascal has bravery in him; he won't run away.

PRINCE HENRY

Why, you rascal! You just praised him for running!

FALSTAFF

He'll run on his horse, you cuckoo. But when fighting on foot, he'll never budge.

PRINCE HENRY

Yes he will, Jack. By instinct.

FALSTAFF

I grant you, upon instinct. Well, he is there too, and one Mordake, and a thousand blue-caps more: Worcester is stolen away tonight. Thy father's beard is turned white with the news. You may buy land now as cheap as stinking mackerel.

325

PRINCE HENRY

Why, then, it is like if there come a hot June, and this civil buffeting hold, we shall buy maidenheads as they buy hobnails, by the hundreds.

FALSTAFF

By the Mass, thou sayest true. It is like we shall have good trading that way. But tell me, Hal, art not thou horrible afeard? Thou being heir apparent, could the world pick thee out three such enemies again as that fiend Douglas, that spirit Percy, and that devil Glendower? Art thou not horribly afraid? Doth not thy blood thrill at it?

330

PRINCE HENRY

Not a whit, i' faith; I lack some of thy instinct.

335

FALSTAFF

Well, thou wert be horribly chid tomorrow when thou comest to thy father. If thou love me, practice an answer.

PRINCE HENRY

Do thou stand for my father and examine me upon the particulars of my life.

FALSTAFF

Shall I? Conten. This chair shall be my state, this dagger my scepter, and this cushion my crown.

340

PRINCE HENRY

Thy state is taken for a joined stool, thy golden scepter for a leaden dagger, and thy precious rich crown for a pitiful bald crown.

FALSTAFF

You're right, by instinct. Well, he's there, and a man named Mordake, and a thousand Scottish soldiers besides. Worcester snuck out of London tonight, and your father's hair turned white when he heard. The price of land has dropped as low as a bucket of stinking fish.

PRINCE HENRY

Hal is referring to the common wartime practice of rape.

If that's the case, then when the weather gets hot and the civil war has really broken out, we can buy women's virtues the way other people buy nails: by the hundreds.

FALSTAFF

By God, lad, you tell the truth. We'll probably have good luck in that area. But Hal, aren't you scared? You're the heir apparent. Can you imagine three worse enemies than that demon Douglas, that spirit Percy, and that devil Glendower? Aren't you horribly scared? Isn't your blood running cold at the thought?

PRINCE HENRY

Not in the least, truly: I don't have your instinct.

FALSTAFF

Well, you'll be rebuked horribly when you see your father tomorrow. If you love me, practice a response.

PRINCE HENRY

You pretend to be my father; ask me about the details of my life.

FALSTAFF

Really? Excellent! This chair will be my throne, this dagger my scepter, and this cushion will be my crown.

PRINCE HENRY

Your throne is a wooden stool, your gold scepter is a dagger of lead, and your precious, expensive crown is a lousy bald head.

FALSTAFF

345 Well, an the fire of grace be not quite out of thee, now shalt
thou be moved.—Give me a cup of sack to make my eyes
look red, that it may be thought I have wept, for I must
speak in passion, and I will do it in King Cambyses' vein.

PRINCE HENRY

Well, here is my leg.

FALSTAFF

350 And here is my speech. Stand aside, nobility.

MISTRESS QUICKLY

O Jesu, this is excellent sport, i' faith!

FALSTAFF

Weep not, sweet queen, for trickling tears are vain.

MISTRESS QUICKLY

O the father, how he holds his countenance!

FALSTAFF

For God's sake, lords, convey my tristful queen,
355 For tears do stop the floodgates of her eyes.

MISTRESS QUICKLY

O Jesu, he doth it as like one of these harlotry players as ever
I see.

FALSTAFF

Peace, good pint-pot. Peace, good tickle-brain.— *(to
PRINCE HENRY)* Harry, I do not only marvel where thou
360 spendest thy time, but also how thou art accompanied. For
though the camomile, the more it is trodden on, the faster
it grows, so youth, the more it is wasted, the sooner it wears.
That thou art my son I have partly thy mother's word,
partly my own opinion, but chiefly a villanous trick of thine
365 eye and a foolish-hanging of thy nether lip that doth
warrant me. If then thou be son to me, here lies the point:
why, being son to me, art thou so pointed at? Shall the
blessed sun of heaven prove a micher and eat blackberries?

FALSTAFF

King Cambyses was a character in a play, known for being loud, melodramatic, and over the top. →

If you still have a shred of divine grace in you, you'll be moved by this. Give me some wine to make my eyes bloodshot, so that it looks like I've been crying. I must speak with passion, and I'll do it like King Cambyses.

PRINCE HENRY

Well then, I'll bow to you.

FALSTAFF

And I'll speak to you. Step aside, gentlemen.

MISTRESS QUICKLY

Oh, Jesus! This is an excellent game, truly!

FALSTAFF

Don't cry, sweet queen; your trickling tears do no good.

MISTRESS QUICKLY

Oh Lord, look how well he's keeping it up!

FALSTAFF

For God's sake, gentlemen; take my queen away from here. The floodgates of her eyes are being overwhelmed by her tears.

MISTRESS QUICKLY

My God! He's just as good as those silly old professional actors!

FALSTAFF

Quiet, little ale pot. Quiet, little booze-brain. *(to* PRINCE HENRY*)* Harry, I am not only amazed at where you are spending your time, but whom you're spending it with. They say that stepping on a chamomile plant will make it grow faster. But when it comes to youth, the more it is wasted, the faster is wears away. I know you are my son. Your mother says so, I believe so, and the wicked glint in your eye and foolish expression on your face prove it. If it's true that you are my son, then here is my point: why, since you are my son, do so many people point at you? Should the

370 A question not to be asked. Shall the sun of England prove a thief and take purses? A question to be asked. There is a thing, Harry, which thou hast often heard of, and it is known to many in our land by the name of pitch: this pitch, as ancient writers do report, doth defile; so doth the company thou keepest. For, Harry, now I do not speak to

375 thee, in drink but in tears; not in pleasure, but in passion; not in words only, but in woes also. And yet there is a virtuous man whom I have often noted in thy company, but I know not his name.

PRINCE HENRY
What manner of man, an it like your Majesty?

FALSTAFF
380 A goodly portly man, i' faith, and a corpulent; of a cheerful look, a pleasing eye, and a most noble carriage, and, as I think, his age some fifty, or, by 'r Lady, inclining to three score; and now I remember me, his name is Falstaff. If that man should be lewdly given, he deceiveth me, for, Harry, I

385 see virtue in his looks. If then the tree may be known by the fruit, as the fruit by the tree, then peremptorily I speak it: there is virtue in that Falstaff; him keep with, the rest banish. And tell me now, thou naughty varlet, tell me, where hast thou been this month?

PRINCE HENRY
390 Dost thou speak like a king? Do thou stand for me, and I'll play my father.

FALSTAFF
Depose me? If thou dost it half so gravely, so majestically, both in word and matter, hang me up by the heels for a rabbit-sucker or a poulter's hare.

PRINCE HENRY
395 Well, here I am set.

FALSTAFF
And here I stand. — *(to the others)* Judge, my masters.

blessed sun in heaven waste its time eating blackberries? That is not a question worth asking. Should the son of the king of England become a thief and steal wallets? That is worth asking. Harry, you've heard of a substance known as pitch. Pitch, as the wise men tell us, makes one filthy, and so does the company you keep. Harry, I speak to you not drunk but weeping, not in happiness but in anger, not just in words but also in sadness. And yet, there is a very good and pious man whom I've often seen you with, but I do not know his name.

pitch = sticky tar

PRINCE HENRY

What kind of man, your highness?

FALSTAFF

A stout man, truly; and overweight. He has a cheerful expression, a handsome look, and a noble bearing. I think he is about fifty years old, or perhaps closer to sixty. Now I remember! His name is Falstaff. If that man has a bad character, then I have been fooled. Harry, I see goodness in him. If one can tell a tree by its fruit, and a fruit by its tree, then let me come right out and say this: there is goodness in that Falstaff. Stay with him, but get rid of everyone else. Now tell me, you naughty boy, tell me; where have you been for the past month?

PRINCE HENRY

You think you sound like a king? You play me, and I'll play my father.

FALSTAFF

You're overthrowing me? If you play him even half as well as I did, half as majestically, then hang me up like a rabbit for sale in a butcher shop.

PRINCE HENRY

I'm all set.

FALSTAFF

As am I. *(to the others)* Judge us, everyone.

PRINCE HENRY
Now, Harry, whence come you?

FALSTAFF
My noble lord, from Eastcheap.

PRINCE HENRY
The complaints I hear of thee are grievous.

FALSTAFF
400   'Sblood, my lord, they are false.— *(to the others)* Nay, I'll
tickle you for a young prince, i' faith.

PRINCE HENRY
Swearest thou? Ungracious boy, henceforth ne'er look on
me. Thou art violently carried away from grace. There is a
devil haunts thee in the likeness of an old fat man. A tun of
405   man is thy companion. Why dost thou converse with that
trunk of humors, that bolting-hutch of beastliness, that
swollen parcel of dropsies, that huge bombard of sack, that
stuffed cloakbag of guts, that roasted Manningtree ox with
the pudding in his belly, that reverend Vice, that gray
410   iniquity, that father ruffian, that vanity in years? Wherein
is he good, but to taste sack and drink it? Wherein neat and
cleanly but to carve a capon and eat it? Wherein cunning
but in craft? Wherein crafty but in villany? Wherein
villanous but in all things? Wherein worthy but in nothing?

FALSTAFF
415   I would your Grace would take me with you. Whom means
your Grace?

PRINCE HENRY
That villanous abominable misleader of youth, Falstaff,
that old white-bearded Satan.

FALSTAFF
My lord, the man I know.

PRINCE HENRY
420   I know thou dost.

PRINCE HENRY

Now, Harry, where are you coming from?

FALSTAFF

From Eastcheap, my noble lord.

PRINCE HENRY

The complaints I have heard about you are very serious.

FALSTAFF

For God's sake, my lord, they are lies. *(to the others)* I'll make you laugh by playing a young prince, I truly will.

PRINCE HENRY

Are you swearing, you ungracious boy? From now on, do not even look at me. You have been violently turned away from goodness; there is a devil that haunts you, in the shape of an old, fat man. A ton of man is your companion. Why do you associate with that trunk of bodily fluids, that sifting bin of beastliness, that swollen sack of disease, that huge jug of wine, that stuffed suitcase of guts, that roasted ox crammed with pudding, that ancient Vice, that gray-haired immorality, that father criminal, that aged vanity? What is he good for, besides tasting wine and drinking it? What does he do skillfully, besides carving chickens and eating them? What's he smart about besides schemes? What does he scheme about besides crime? What is he criminal about besides everything? What is he good for besides nothing?

Vice, a familiar character from medieval morality plays, led people into immorality.

FALSTAFF

I wish your highness would help me follow your meaning. Who do you mean, your grace?

PRINCE HENRY

That criminal, loathsome corrupter of youth: Falstaff, that old, white-bearded devil.

FALSTAFF

My lord, I know the man.

PRINCE HENRY

I know you do.

FALSTAFF
But to say I know more harm in him than in myself were to
say more than I know. That he is old, the more the pity; his
white hairs do witness it. But that he is, saving your
reverence, a whoremaster, that I utterly deny. If sack and
425   sugar be a fault, God help the wicked. If to be old and merry
be a sin, then many an old host that I know is damned. If to
be fat be to be hated, then Pharaoh's lean kine are to be
loved. No, my good lord, banish Peto, banish Bardolph,
banish Poins, but for sweet Jack Falstaff, kind Jack Falstaff,
430   true Jack Falstaff, valiant Jack Falstaff, and therefore more
valiant being, as he is old Jack Falstaff, banish not him thy
Harry's company, banish not him thy Harry's company.
Banish plump Jack, and banish all the world.

PRINCE HENRY
I do, I will.

Knocking within. Exeunt BARDOLPH, MISTRESS QUICKLY,
and FRANCIS. *Enter* BARDOLPH, *running*

BARDOLPH
435   O, my lord, my lord, the Sheriff with a most monstrous
watch is at the door.

FALSTAFF
Out, you rogue.—Play out the play. I have much to say in
the behalf of that Falstaff.

Enter MISTRESS QUICKLY

MISTRESS QUICKLY
O Jesu, my lord, my lord—

PRINCE HENRY
440   Heigh, heigh, the devil rides upon a fiddlestick. What's the
matter?

FALSTAFF

But to make me claim that he's any more harmful than I am—well, I can't claim that. Yes he's old, and it's a shame: his white hair proves it. But that he's a—forgive me—pimp? That I absolutely deny. If drinking wine and sugar is a fault, then God forgive us all. If being old and merry is a sin, then I know a lot of old men who are going to hell. If being fat means you should be hated, than we should all love Pharoah's lean cows. No, your highness. Get rid of Peto, get rid of Bardolph, get rid of Poins. But as for sweet Jack Falstaff, kind Jack Falstaff, honest Jack Falstaff, brave Jack Falstaff, and therefore even more brave, given that he is old Jack Falstaff—do not get rid of him. Do not get rid of him. If you get rid of him, you'll be getting rid of the whole world.

In the Bible, Pharoah's dream of seven emaciated cows prophesies famine for Egypt.

PRINCE HENRY

I do. I will.

There are knocks from offstage. MISTRESS QUICKLY, FRANCIS, *and* BARDOLPH *exit.* BARDOLPH *comes back, running.*

BARDOLPH

Oh sir, sir! The Sheriff and a frightening group of officers are at the door.

FALSTAFF

Wait, you ass! We'll finish the play: I have much to say on behalf of that Falstaff.

MISTRESS QUICKLY *enters.*

MISTRESS QUICKLY

Jesus! Sir, sir!

PRINCE HENRY

Well, look here! All this mess over nothing! What's the matter?

MISTRESS QUICKLY
The Sheriff and all the watch are at the door. They are come
to search the house. Shall I let them in?

FALSTAFF
Dost thou hear, Hal? Never call a true piece of gold a
445   counterfeit. Thou art essentially made, without seeming so.

PRINCE HENRY
And thou a natural coward without instinct.

FALSTAFF
I deny your major. If you will deny the Sheriff, so; if not, let
him enter. If I become not a cart as well as another man, a
plague on my bringing up. I hope I shall as soon be
450   strangled with a halter as another.

PRINCE HENRY
Go, hide thee behind the arras. The rest walk up above.—
Now, my masters, for a true face and good conscience.

FALSTAFF
Both which I have had, but their date is out; and therefore
I'll hide me. *(he hides behind the arras)*

Exeunt all but PRINCE HENRY *and* PETO

PRINCE HENRY
455   Call in the Sheriff.

Enter SHERIFF *and the* CARRIER

Now, Master Sheriff, what is your will with me?

MISTRESS QUICKLY

The Sheriff and the officers are at the door. They've come to search the place. Should I let them in?

FALSTAFF

This line is ambiguous; Falstaff may be saying that, though he seems to be a scoundrel, he is a really a good man, and therefore should not be turned over to the watch.

Do you hear that, Hal? Be careful about calling a piece of real gold a counterfeit; you are genuine, even though it may not seem so.

PRINCE HENRY

And you are a genuine coward, with no instinct.

FALSTAFF

I deny that. And if you'll deny the Sheriff, then please do; otherwise, let him in. If I don't look as good on the hangman's cart as any other man, then a curse on my upbringing. I'm as willing to be hanged as any man.

PRINCE HENRY

arras = tapestry hung on a wall

Go, hide behind the arras. The rest of you, go upstairs. Now, my men. Here's wishing for an honest face and a clear conscience.

FALSTAFF

I've had both of those, but their shelf-life has expired. I'd better hide. *(he hides behind the arras)*

Everyone except for PRINCE HENRY *and* PETO *exits.*

PRINCE HENRY

Call in the Sheriff.

The SHERIFF *and a* CARRIER *enter.*

Now, Sheriff, what is it you want from me?

SHERIFF
First pardon me, my lord. A hue and cry
Hath followed certain men unto this house.

PRINCE HENRY
What men?

SHERIFF
460 One of them is well known, my gracious lord,
A gross fat man.

CARRIER
As fat as butter.

PRINCE HENRY
The man, I do assure you is not here,
For I myself at this time have employed him.
465 And, Sheriff, I will engage my word to thee
That I will by tomorrow dinner time
Send him to answer thee or any man
For any thing he shall be charged withal.
And so let me entreat you leave the house.

SHERIFF
470 I will, my lord. There are two gentlemen
Have in this robbery lost three hundred marks.

PRINCE HENRY
It may be so. If he have robbed these men,
He shall be answerable; and so farewell.

SHERIFF
Good night, my noble lord.

PRINCE HENRY
475 I think it is good morrow, is it not?

SHERIFF
Indeed, my lord, I think it be two o'clock.

Exeunt SHERIFF *and* CARRIER

PRINCE HENRY
This oily rascal is known as well as Paul's. Go call him forth.

SHERIFF

First, please forgive me, my lord. A group of citizens followed some criminals into this bar.

PRINCE HENRY

What men?

SHERIFF

One of them is well known, my gracious lord. A huge, fat man.

CARRIER

As fat as butter.

PRINCE HENRY

I promise you, that man isn't here, since he's currently running an errand for me. Sheriff, I give you my word that by lunchtime tomorrow I'll send him to you, or anyone else you need to see. He'll answer to anything he may be accused of. So please, I'd like you to leave this tavern.

SHERIFF

A mark is a unit of currency.

I will, my lord. There are also two gentlemen who, in this robbery, lost three hundred marks.

PRINCE HENRY

It's possible. If he did it, he'll answer for it. And with that, farewell.

SHERIFF

Good night, my noble lord.

PRINCE HENRY

I think it's good morning, isn't it?

SHERIFF

Yes, sir. I think it's two o'clock.

The SHERIFF *and* CARRIER *exit.*

PRINCE HENRY

This oily rascal is as famous as St. Paul's Cathedral. Go, call him out here.

PETO

Falstaff!— *(pulls back the arras)* Fast asleep behind the arras, and snorting like a horse.

PRINCE HENRY

480   Hark, how hard he fetches breath. Search his pockets.

PETO *searcheth his pockets, and findeth certain papers*

What hast thou found?

PETO

Nothing but papers, my lord.

PRINCE HENRY

Let's see what they be. Read them.

PETO

(reads)   *Item, a capon, . . . 2s. 2d.*
485   *Item, sauce, . . . 4d.*
                Item, sack, two gallons, . . . 5s. 8d.
                Item, anchovies and sack after supper, , , , 2s. 6d.
                Item, bread, ob.

PRINCE HENRY

O monstrous! But one halfpennyworth of bread to this
490   intolerable deal of sack! What there is else, keep close. We'll read it at more advantage. There let him sleep till day. I'll to the court in the morning. We must all to the wars, and thy place shall be honorable. I'll procure this fat rogue a charge of foot, and I know his death will be a march of twelve score.
495   The money shall be paid back again with advantage. Be with me betimes in the morning, and so good morrow, Peto.

PETO

Good morrow, good my lord.

                                                    Exeunt

PETO

Falstaff! *(pulls back the arras)* Fast asleep behind the arras, and snoring like a horse.

PRINCE HENRY

Listen, how heavily he breathes! Look in his pockets.

PETO *searches* FALSTAFF'*s pockets and finds some papers.*

What did you find?

PETO

Nothing but some papers, my lord.

PRINCE HENRY

Let's see what they are. Read them.

PETO

(reads) First, a chicken — two shillings and two pence. Second, sauce — four pence. Third, wine, two gallons —five shillings and eight pence. Fourth, anchovies and dessert wine — two shillings and six pence. Fifth, bread — a halfpenny.

PRINCE HENRY

Oh horrible! A halfpenny's worth of bread against this enormous amount of wine? Hang onto everything else you found; we'll read it when we have time. Let him sleep there till tomorrow. I'll go to court in the morning. We're all off to the wars, and you will have honorable positions. I'll put this fat rogue in charge of an infantry company, and a quarter mile's march will be the end of him. The money we stole will be repaid with interest. Meet me early in the morning; and with that, good morning, Peto.

PETO

Good morning, my good lord.

They exit.

ACT THREE
SCENE 1

Enter HOTSPUR, WORCESTER, *Lord* MORTIMER, *and Owen*
GLENDOWER

MORTIMER
>These promises are fair, the parties sure,
>And our induction full of prosperous hope.

HOTSPUR
>Lord Mortimer and cousin Glendower,
>Will you sit down? And Uncle Worcester—
>A plague upon it, I have forgot the map.

5

GLENDOWER
>No, here it is. Sit, cousin Percy
>Sit, good cousin Hotspur, for by that name
>As oft as Lancaster doth speak of you
>His cheek looks pale and with a rising sigh
>He wisheth you in heaven.

10

HOTSPUR
>   And you in hell,
>As oft as he hears Owen Glendower spoke of.

GLENDOWER
>I cannot blame him. At my nativity
>The front of heaven was full of fiery shapes,
>Of burning cressets, and at my birth
>The frame and huge foundation of the earth
>Shaked like a coward.

15

HOTSPUR
>   Why, so it would have done
>At the same season if your mother's cat
>Had but kittened, though yourself had never been born.

GLENDOWER
>I say the earth did shake when I was born.

ACT THREE
SCENE 1

HOTSPUR, WORCESTER, *Lord* MORTIMER, *and Owen* GLENDOWER *enter.*

MORTIMER

These commitments are reliable, our allies are solid, and the beginning of our project bodes well.

HOTSPUR

Lord Mortimer, and kinsman Glendower, won't you please sit? And Uncle Worcester—Dammit! I forgot the map!

GLENDOWER

Here it is. Sit, kinsman Percy. Sit, good cousin Hotspur. For that is the name King Henry calls you, and whenever he says it, he grows pale, and with a sigh he wishes you were in heaven.

HOTSPUR

And you in hell, whenever he hears someone say "Owen Glendower."

GLENDOWER

I don't blame him. The sky was full of fiery meteors and comets when I was conceived, and when I was born, the entire earth shook like a coward.

HOTSPUR

Why, the same thing would have happened if your mother's cat had given birth to kittens that day, whether you'd been born or not.

GLENDOWER

I say there was an earthquake when I was born.

HOTSPUR

20   And I say the earth was not of my mind,
        If you suppose as fearing you it shook.

GLENDOWER

        The heavens were all on fire; the earth did tremble.

HOTSPUR

        O, then the earth shook to see the heavens on fire,
        And not in fear of your nativity.

25   Diseasèd nature oftentimes breaks forth
        In strange eruptions; oft the teeming earth
        Is with a kind of colic pinched and vexed
        By the imprisoning of unruly wind
        Within her womb, which, for enlargement striving,

30   Shakes the old beldam earth and topples down
        Steeples and moss-grown towers. At your birth
        Our grandam earth, having this distemperature,
        In passion shook.

GLENDOWER

                                Cousin, of many men
        I do not bear these crossings. Give me leave

35   To tell you once again that at my birth
        The front of heaven was full of fiery shapes,
        The goats ran from the mountains, and the herds
        Were strangely clamorous to the frighted fields.
        These signs have marked me extraordinary,

40   And all the courses of my life do show
        I am not in the roll of common men.
        Where is he living, clipped in with the sea
        That chides the banks of England, Scotland, Wales,
        Which calls me pupil or hath read to me?

45   And bring him out that is but woman's son
        Can trace me in the tedious ways of art
        And hold me pace in deep experiments.

HOTSPUR

        I think there's no man speaks better Welsh.
        I'll to dinner.

HOTSPUR

And I say that if you think the earth shook because it was afraid of you, then the earth and I do not agree.

GLENDOWER

The heavens were all on fire, and the earth trembled.

HOTSPUR

Oh! Then the earth trembled when it saw the heavens on fire, and not in fear of your birth. When nature is diseased, strange eruptions can break forth. Often, the earth is pinched with a kind of colic, and troubled by gas in her belly. When that gas struggles to be released, it shakes old Mother Earth, bringing down steeples and moss-covered towers. When you were born, our Mother Earth was ill and shook with pain.

GLENDOWER

Kinsman, I don't take this kind of contrary behavior from many people. With your permission, I'll say one more time that when I was born, the heavens were full of shooting stars. The goats ran down from the mountains, and herds of animals stampeded strangely through the fields. These signs marked me as an extraordinary person. All the events of my life prove that I should not be counted with ordinary men. Is there a man who lives anywhere within England, Scotland, or Wales who can say I learned from him, or that he taught me? And bring forward one human who can follow me in the complicated ways of magic, or keep up with me in my obscure experiments.

HOTSPUR

To the English, Welsh often sounded like a barbaric language; Hotspur implies that no one speaks better nonsense then Glendower.

Well, nobody speaks better Welsh. I'm going to lunch.

MORTIMER
50   Peace, cousin Percy. You will make him mad.

GLENDOWER
     I can call spirits from the vasty deep.

HOTSPUR
     Why, so can I, or so can any man,
     But will they come when you do call for them?

GLENDOWER
     Why, I can teach you, cousin, to command the devil.

HOTSPUR
55   And I can teach thee, coz, to shame the devil
     By telling truth. Tell truth and shame the devil.
     If thou have power to raise him, bring him hither,
     And I'll be sworn I have power to shame him hence.
     O, while you live, tell truth and shame the devil!

MORTIMER
60   Come, come, no more of this unprofitable chat.

GLENDOWER
     Three times hath Henry Bolingbroke made head
     Against my power; thrice from the banks of Wye
     And sandy-bottomed Severn have I sent him
     Bootless home and weather-beaten back.

HOTSPUR
65   Home without boots, and in foul weather too!
     How 'scapes he agues, in the devil's name?

GLENDOWER
     Come, here's the map. Shall we divide our right
     According to our threefold order ta'en?

MORTIMER
     The Archdeacon hath divided it
70   Into three limits very equally:
     England, from Trent and Severn hitherto,
     By south and east is to my part assigned;

MORTIMER

Stop now, kinsman Percy. You will upset him.

GLENDOWER

I can summon spirits from the deep ocean.

HOTSPUR

Why, so can I, and so can any other man! But will they come when you summon them?

GLENDOWER

Why, kinsman, I can teach you to command the devil.

HOTSPUR

And I can teach you, kinsman, how to shame the devil—by telling the truth! "Tell the truth and shame the devil," as the old saying goes. If you do have the power to call him up, then bring him here. And I'll swear I have the power to shame him into leaving. Oh, for goodness sake, tell the truth and shame the devil!

MORTIMER

Enough already; stop this useless talking.

GLENDOWER

bootless = unsuccessful →

Three times now, Henry Bolingbroke has raised an army against mine. And three times, I turned him back from the banks of the River Wye, and the sandy-bottomed River Severn. I sent him home, bootless and beaten by foul weather.

HOTSPUR

You sent him home without his boots, and in foul weather? How in the devil's name did he avoid catching fevers?

GLENDOWER

All right, here's the map. Shall we divide up our territories according to our three-way agreement?

MORTIMER

The Archdeacon isn't mentioned anywhere else in the text, but according to the historical chronicle, this meeting took place at the home of the Archdeacon of Bangor. →

The Archdeacon has divided the land into three very equal parts. All of England southeast of the Trent and Severn rivers goes to me.

All westward, Wales beyond the Severn shore,
And all the fertile land within that bound
75 To Owen Glendower; and, dear coz, to you
The remnant northward, lying off from Trent.
And our indentures tripartite are drawn,
Which being sealèd interchangeably—
A business that this night may execute—
80 Tomorrow, cousin Percy, you and I
And my good Lord of Worcester will set forth
To meet your father and the Scottish power,
As is appointed us, at Shrewsbury.
My father Glendower is not ready yet,
85 Not shall we need his help these fourteen days.
(to GLENDOWER*)* Within that space you may have drawn
                together
Your tenants, friends, and neighboring gentlemen.

GLENDOWER
A shorter time shall send me to you, lords,
And in my conduct shall your ladies come,
90 From whom you now must steal and take no leave,
For there will be a world of water shed
Upon the parting of your wives and you.

HOTSPUR
Methinks my moiety, north from Burton here,
In quantity equals not one of yours.
95 See how this river comes me cranking in
And cuts me from the best of all my land
A huge half-moon, a monstrous cantle out.
I'll have the current in this place dammed up,
And here the smug and silver Trent shall run
100 In a new channel, fair and evenly.
It shall not wind with such a deep indent,
To rob me of so rich a bottom here.

GLENDOWER
Not wind? It shall, it must. You see it doth.

All of Wales, and everything west of the Severn—including all the fertile land within those boundaries—goes to Owen Glendower. And, my dear kinsman, you get everything that remains to the north, coming up from the Trent. Our agreement is drawn up in triplicate. We can all sign it tonight, and then, kinsman Percy, tomorrow you, me, and Worcester will set off to meet your father and the Scottish army at Shrewsbury, as planned. My father-in-law Glendower isn't ready yet, but we won't need his army for another two weeks. *(to* GLENDOWER*)* By that time, you will have raised an army of the farmers on your land, your allies, and your neighbors.

GLENDOWER

I'll be ready sooner than that, my lords; and I'll bring your wives along with me. You should sneak away from them now, and leave without saying goodbye. Otherwise, they'll cry an ocean of tears when you leave them.

HOTSPUR

I think my share, north of Burton here, isn't as big as any of yours. Look how this river swoops in. It cuts out a huge chunk of my best land, in the shape of a half-moon. I'll have a dam built. I'll re-route the Trent River so it won't go winding so far into my land and rob me of a fertile valley.

GLENDOWER

It won't go winding? It will. It must. You see that it does.

MORTIMER
Yea, but Mark how he bears his course, and runs me up
105   With like advantage on the other side,
Gelding the opposèd continent as much
As on the other side it takes from you.

WORCESTER
Yea, but a little charge will trench him here
And on this north side win this cape of land,
110   And then he runs straight and even.

HOTSPUR
I'll have it so. A little charge will do it.

GLENDOWER
I'll not have it altered.

HOTSPUR
                        Will not you?

GLENDOWER
No, nor you shall not.

HOTSPUR
                        Who shall say me nay?

GLENDOWER
Why, that will I.

HOTSPUR
115   Let me not understand you, then; speak it in Welsh.

GLENDOWER
I can speak English, lord, as well as you,
For I was trained up in the English court,
Where being but young I framèd to the harp
Many an English ditty lovely well
120   And gave the tongue a helpful ornament—
A virtue that was never seen in you.

HOTSPUR
Marry,
And I am glad of it with all my heart:
I had rather be a kitten and cry "mew"
125   Than one of these same meter balladmongers.

MORTIMER

Yes, but look how the Trent runs its course and winds a similar distance into my share. It cuts out the same amount of land from my side as it does from yours.

WORCESTER

Yes, but a small sum of money will pay to dig a trench, which will reclaim this bit of land on the north side. Then it will run straight along.

HOTSPUR

I'll do that. It will only take a little money.

GLENDOWER

I won't have it changed.

HOTSPUR

You won't?

GLENDOWER

No, and neither will you.

HOTSPUR

Who's going to stop me?

GLENDOWER

Why, I will.

HOTSPUR

Well, say it in Welsh then, so I can't understand you.

GLENDOWER

My lord, I can speak English just as well as you. I was brought up in the English court. There, in my youth, I composed many English songs for the harp, lending the language lovely ornaments of music. That is an accomplishment you have never achieved.

HOTSPUR

Indeed, and my whole heart is glad for that. I'd rather be a kitten and say "meow" than be a courtly balladeer.

I had rather hear a brazen can'stick turned,
Or a dry wheel grate on the axletree,
And that would set my teeth nothing an edge,
Nothing so much as mincing poetry.
130   'Tis like the forced gait of a shuffling nag.

GLENDOWER
Come, you shall have Trent turned.

HOTSPUR
I do not care. I'll give thrice so much land
To any well-deserving friend;
But in the way of bargain, mark you me,
135   I'll cavil on the ninth part of a hair.
Are the indentures drawn? Shall we be gone?

GLENDOWER
The moon shines fair. You may away by night.
I'll haste the writer, and withal
Break with your wives of your departure hence.
140   I am afraid my daughter will run mad,
So much she doteth on her Mortimer.

Exit **GLENDOWER**

MORTIMER
Fie, cousin Percy, how you cross my father!

HOTSPUR
I cannot choose. Sometime he angers me
With telling me of the moldwarp and the ant,
145   Of the dreamer Merlin and his prophecies,
And of a dragon and a finless fish,
A clip-winged griffin and a moulten raven,
A couching lion and a ramping cat,
And such a deal of skimble-skamble stuff
150   As puts me from my faith. I tell you what—
He held me last night at least nine hours
In reckoning up the several devils' names
That were his lackeys. I cried "Hum," and "Well, go to,"
But marked him not a word. O, he is as tedious

I'd rather hear a piece of brass turned on a lathe, or a ungreased wheel grind on its axle. Nothing sets my teeth on edge so as much as finicky poetry; it's like the lurching steps of a lame horse.

GLENDOWER

Fine. Change the Trent's course.

HOTSPUR

I don't care. I'd gladly give away three times as much land to any friend who deserved it. But when it comes to negotiating a deal, mark my words: I'll haggle over the smallest fraction of a hair. Are the agreements drawn up? Are we ready to leave?

GLENDOWER

The moon is bright; you can leave during the night. I'll tell the man writing up our documents to hurry, and I'll tell your wives you're leaving. I'm afraid my daughter will go mad because she loves Mortimer so much.

GLENDOWER *exits.*

MORTIMER

Damn, kinsman Percy! How angry you make my father-in-law!

HOTSPUR

I can't help it. He makes me angry with all his talk. Moles and ants, Merlin and his prophecies, dragons, a fish with no fins, a griffin without wings, a raven without feathers, a crouching lion and a cat rearing up to pounce. He talks so much mumbo-jumbo that I don't know what to believe anymore. I'll tell you this: he kept me awake last night for at least nine hours, listing the names of all the devils that serve him. I said, "Hmm," and, "How interesting," but he didn't hear a word. Oh, he's as tedious as a tired horse or a nagging wife; he's worse than a smoke-filled house.

155 As a tired horse, a railing wife,
Worse than a smoky house: I had rather live
With cheese and garlic in a windmill, far,
Than feed on cates and have him talk to me
In any summerhouse in Christendom.

MORTIMER
160 In faith, he is a worthy gentleman,
Exceedingly well read and profited
In strange concealments, valiant as a lion,
And as wondrous affable, and as bountiful
As mines of India. Shall I tell you, cousin?
165 He holds your temper in a high respect
And curbs himself even of his natural scope
When you come cross his humor. Faith, he does.
I warrant you that man is not alive
Might so have tempted him as you have done
170 Without the taste of danger and reproof.
But do not use it oft, let me entreat you.

WORCESTER
(to HOTSPUR) In faith, my lord, you are too willful-blame,
And, since your coming hither, have done enough
To put him quite beside his patience.
175 You must needs learn, lord, to amend this fault.
Though sometimes it show greatness, courage, blood—
And that's the dearest grace it renders you—
Yet oftentimes it doth present harsh rage,
Defect of manners, want of government,
180 Pride, haughtiness, opinion, and disdain,
The least of which, haunting a nobleman,
Loseth men's hearts and leaves behind a stain
Upon the beauty of all parts besides,
Beguiling them of commendation.

HOTSPUR
185 Well, I am schooled. Good manners be your speed!
Here come our wives, and let us take our leave.

I'd rather live in a windmill and eat nothing but cheese and garlic than in a luxurious home eating delicacies, if it meant I had to listen to him talk.

MORTIMER

Truly, he's a worthy man. He's exceedingly well-read, and proficient in the occult; he's as brave as a lion, incredibly charming, and as generous as the jewel mines of India. And do you know what, cousin? He holds you in great respect. He restrains his temper when you do something to put him in a bad mood. I promise you, there isn't a man alive who could have challenged him as you have, and gotten away without being hurt or punished. But don't try it too often, I beg you.

WORCESTER

(to HOTSPUR) Truly, my lord, you are to blame in your stubbornness. Since you arrived, you have done enough to test his patience. You must learn, sir, to correct this fault. Sometimes it demonstrates greatness, courage, strength—and that honors you. But often it reveals fury, bad manners, lack of self-control, pride, arrogance, conceitedness, and contempt. In a gentlemen, the least of these qualities will make you lose people's affections. It stains your beautiful qualities, making it impossible for them to be noticed.

HOTSPUR

Well, I have had my lesson. May good manners bring you success! Here come our wives; let's say our goodbyes.

Enter GLENDOWER *with the* LADIES PERCY AND MORTIMER

MORTIMER
> This is the deadly spite that angers me:
> My wife can speak no English, I no Welsh.

GLENDOWER
> My daughter weeps; she'll not part with you.
190 > She'll be a soldier too, she'll to the wars.

MORTIMER
> Good father, tell her that she and my aunt Percy
> Shall follow in your conduct speedily.

GLENDOWER *speaks to* THE LADY *in Welsh, and she answers him in the same*

GLENDOWER
> She is desperate here, a peevish self-willed harlotry,
> One that no persuasion can do good upon.

THE LADY *speaks again in Welsh*

MORTIMER
195 > I understand thy looks. That pretty Welsh
> Which thou pourest down from these swelling heavens
> I am too perfect in, and but for shame
> In such a parley should I answer thee.

THE LADY *speaks again in Welsh*

> I understand thy kisses and thou mine,
200 > And that's a feeling disputation;
> But I will never be a truant, love,
> Till I have learned thy language; for thy tongue
> Makes Welsh as sweet as ditties highly penned,

GLENDOWER *enters with the* LADIES PERCY AND MORTIMER.

MORTIMER

> This is the bad luck that angers me: my wife speaks no English, and I speak no Welsh.

GLENDOWER

> My daughter is weeping: she doesn't want to be parted from you. She wants to be a soldier and join you in the war.

MORTIMER

> Father-in-law, tell her that she and Lady Percy will come with you after us.

GLENDOWER *and* THE LADY *speak in Welsh.*

GLENDOWER

> She's desperate now; a cranky, selfish hussy. Nobody can change her mind.

THE LADY *speaks more Welsh.*

MORTIMER

> I understand you by the look on your face. Those pretty Welsh tears streaming from your heavenly eyes I understand perfectly; I'd answer in the same language, if it weren't shameful for a man to cry.

THE LADY *speaks more Welsh.*

> I understand your kisses and you mine; that's a conversation of emotion. I'll study continuously, my love, until I learn your language. Your voice makes Welsh sound as sweet as the most eloquently written songs,

Sung by a fair queen in a summer's bower,
205   With ravishing division, to her lute.

GLENDOWER
Nay, if you melt, then will she run mad.

THE LADY *speaks again in Welsh*

MORTIMER
O, I am ignorance itself in this!

GLENDOWER
She bids you on the wanton rushes lay you down
And rest your gentle head upon her lap,
210   And she will sing the song that pleaseth you
And on your eyelids crown the god of sleep,
Charming your blood with pleasing heaviness,
Making such difference 'twixt wake and sleep
As is the difference betwixt day and night
215   The hour before the heavenly harnessed team
Begins his golden progress in the east.

MORTIMER
With all my heart I'll sit and hear her sing.
By that time will our book, I think, be drawn

GLENDOWER
Do so and those musicians that shall play to you
220   Hang in the air a thousand leagues from hence,
And straight they shall be here. Sit, and attend.

HOTSPUR
Come, Kate, thou art perfect in lying down.
Come, quick, quick, that I may lay my head in thy lap.

LADY PERCY
Go, you giddy goose.

The music plays

sung by a fair queen in a garden of summer flowers, with a gorgeous accompaniment on her a lute.

GLENDOWER

No, if you start to cry, you'll drive her mad.

THE LADY *speaks more Welsh.*

MORTIMER

Oh, I have no idea what she's saying!

GLENDOWER

She wants you to lie down on the rush-covered floor and rest your head in her lap. She'll sing whatever song you like, and she'll lull you to sleep. She'll bewitch you into a pleasant heaviness, halfway between waking and sleeping; like the hour just before the sun begins its golden rise in the east.

MORTIMER

I'll gladly sit and hear her sing. By the time she's done, I think our documents will be prepared.

GLENDOWER

Do so. The musicians who are going to play are now floating in the air a thousand leagues from here. They'll be here shortly; so sit, and listen.

HOTSPUR

Hotspur puns on the slang meanings for "head" ("penis") and "lap" ("vagina").

Kate! You're good at lying down. Come quickly, so that I can put my head in your lap.

LADY PERCY

Stop it, you silly goose.

Music plays.

HOTSPUR
225   Now I perceive the devil understands Welsh,
And 'tis no marvel he is so humorous.
By 'r Lady, he is a good musician.

LADY PERCY
Then should you be nothing but musical, for you are
altogether governed by humors. Lie still, you thief, and
230   hear the lady sing in Welsh.

HOTSPUR
I had rather hear Lady, my brach, howl in Irish.

LADY PERCY
Wouldst thou have thy head broken?

HOTSPUR
No.

LADY PERCY
Then be still.

HOTSPUR
235   Neither; 'tis a woman's fault.

LADY PERCY
Now God help thee!

HOTSPUR
To the Welsh lady's bed.

LADY PERCY
What's that?

HOTSPUR
Peace, she sings.

Here THE LADY *sings a Welsh song*

HOTSPUR
240   Come, Kate, I'll have your song too.

LADY PERCY
Not mine, in good sooth.

HOTSPUR

Now I see that the devil understands Welsh; it's no surprise he's so moody. By God, he's a good musician.

LADY PERCY

Then you should be incredibly musical, for you're the moodiest man alive. Lie still, you thief. Listen to the lady sing in Welsh.

HOTSPUR

I'd rather hear Lady, my dog, howl in Irish.

LADY PERCY

Do you want your head broken in?

HOTSPUR

No.

LADY PERCY

Then be still.

HOTSPUR

Never; that's a womanly trait.

LADY PERCY

Now God help you—

HOTSPUR

Into the Welsh lady's bed!

LADY PERCY

What did you say?

HOTSPUR

Quiet! She's singing.

THE LADY *sings a Welsh song.*

HOTSPUR

Come on, Kate. I want to hear your song, too.

LADY PERCY

Not mine, darn it.

HOTSPUR
Not yours, in good sooth! Heart, you swear like a comfit-
maker's wife! "Not you, in good sooth," and "as true as I
live," and "as God shall mend me," and "as sure as day"—
245   And givest such sarcenet surety for thy oaths
As if thou never walk'st further than Finsbury.
Swear me, Kate, like a lady as thou art,
A good mouth-filling oath, and leave "in sooth,"
And such protest of pepper-gingerbread,
250   To velvet-guards and Sunday citizens.
Come, sing.

LADY PERCY
I will not sing.

HOTSPUR
'Tis the next way to turn tailor, or be red-breast teacher. An
the indentures be drawn, I'll away within these two hours,
255   and so come in when ye will.

Exit HOTSPUR

GLENDOWER
Come, come, Lord Mortimer; you are as slow
As hot Lord Percy is on fire to go.
By this our book is drawn. We'll but seal,
And then to horse immediately.

MORTIMER
With all my heart.

Exeunt

HOTSPUR

Not yours? Darn it? Honestly! You swear like a candymaker's wife. "Not you, darn it." And "I swear on my life," and "God forgive me," and "as plain as day." Your curse words are smooth as silk. You'd think you'd never gone further than Finsbury in your life. Swear like the real lady you are, Kate. Let loose a good mouthful of curses; leave "darn" and such watered-down cursewords to those citizens, trimmed in velvet and wearing their Sunday best. Come on, sing.

LADY PERCY

I will not sing.

HOTSPUR

It's the quickest way to become a tailor; tailors love to sing. Or you could teach songs to birds. If our agreements are drawn up, I'll be gone within two hours; come find me whenever you want.

HOTSPUR exits.

GLENDOWER

Come now, Mortimer. You're as reluctant to leave as Percy is on fire to go. Our agreements are drawn up by now. We'll sign and then go straight to our horses.

MORTIMER

I go with all my heart.

They exit.

ACT 3, SCENE 2

Enter KING, PRINCE HENRY *of Wales, and others*

KING
Lords, give us leave; the Prince of Wales and I
Must have some private conference, but be near at hand,
For we shall presently have need of you.

Exeunt lords

I know not whether God will have it so
5   For some displeasing service I have done,
That, in his secret doom, out of my blood
He'll breed revengement and a scourge for me.
But thou dost in thy passages of life
Make me believe that thou art only marked
10 For the hot vengeance and the rod of heaven
To punish my mistreadings. Tell me else,
Could such inordinate and low desires,
Such poor, such bare, such lewd, such mean attempts,
Such barren pleasures, rude society
15 As thou art matched withal, and grafted to,
Accompany the greatness of thy blood,
And hold their level with thy princely heart?

PRINCE HENRY
So please your Majesty, I would I could
Quit all offenses with as clear excuse
20 As well as I am doubtless I can purge
Myself of many I am charged withal.
Yet such extenuation let me beg
As, in reproof of many tales devised,
which oft the ear of greatness needs must hear,
25 By smiling pickthanks and base newsmongers,
I may for some things true, wherein my youth
Hath faulty wandered and irregular,
Find pardon on my true submission.

ACT 3, SCENE 2

The KING, PRINCE HENRY *of Wales, and others enter.*

KING

Gentlemen, please leave; the Prince of Wales and I must speak in private. But stay close by, for I'll need you in a moment.

The lords exit.

I don't know whether God decided, because of some displeasing crime I have committed, to turn my own flesh and blood into a punisher and a plague upon me. The course of your life has me convinced that you are only meant for one purpose in this world: to be God's vengeance against me for all my misdeeds. Why else would such disorderly and low desires, such poor, such wretched, such lewd, such despicable actions, such wasteful pleasures, and such vulgar company become associated with your high-born self, and call themselves equals with a Prince like you?

PRINCE HENRY

Your majesty, I wish I could be proven innocent of all those accusations, for I can certainly clear myself of many of them. But let me beg one favor of you: if I can demonstrate that I'm not guilty of the false charges of these smiling flatterers and wretched gossips (the kinds of stories that are always told about great men), then you will forgive me when I confess to the youthful indiscretions I actually did commit.

KING
God pardon thee. Yet let me wonder, Harry,
30   At thy affections, which do hold a wing
Quite from the flight of all thy ancestors.
Thy place in council thou hast rudely lost,
Which by thy younger brother is supplied,
And art almost an alien to the hearts
35   Of all the court and princes of my blood.
The hope and expectation of thy time
Is ruined, and the soul of every man
Prophetically doth forethink thy fall.
Had I so lavish of my presence been,
40   So common-hackneyed in the eyes of men,
So stale and cheap to vulgar company,
Opinion, that did help me to the crown,
Had still kept loyal to possession
And left me in reputeless banishment,
45   A fellow of no mark nor likelihood.
By being seldom seen, I could not stir
But like a comet I was wondered at;
That men would tell their children "This is he."
Others would say "Where? Which is Bolingbroke?"
50   And then I stole all courtesy from heaven,
And dressed myself in such humility
That I did pluck allegiance from men's hearts,
Loud shouts and salutations from their mouths,
Even in the presence of the crownèd King.
55   Thus did I keep my person fresh and new,
My presence, like a robe pontifical,
Ne'er seen but wondered at, and so my state,
Seldom but sumptuous, showed like a feast
And won by rareness such solemnity.
60   The skipping King, he ambled up and down
With shallow jesters and rash bavin wits,
Soon kindled and soon burnt; carded his state,
Mingled his royalty with cap'ring fools,

KING

Let God forgive you! But I'm amazed, Harry, at your inclinations, which run completely contrary to those of your ancestors. Your vulgar behavior has cost you your place on my council, a position now held by your younger brother. You have almost completely alienated yourself from the good graces of the courtiers and the other members of the royal family. The hopes of your youth are now ruined; every man, in his heart, thinks he can see your downfall. If I had been so publicly visible, so overly familiar to people, so freely accessible, so cheap and available to the common hordes, then public opinion (which helped me get the crown) would have stayed loyal to King Richard. I would have stayed a banished man, with no reputation and no promise of success. But because I was so rarely seen in public, people were amazed by me when I did appear; they acted as if I were a comet. Men would tell their children, "That's him!" Others would ask, "Where? Which one's Bolingbroke?" I was more gracious than heaven; I acted so modestly that I won the allegiance of their hearts, and the shouts and salutes of their mouths. They even did so when the King himself was present.

This is how I kept myself fresh and new. I was like a priest's ceremonial vestments: rarely seen, but admired. I appeared seldomly, but marvelously, like a feast made all the more impressive by its rarity. Now, ridiculous King Richard pranced about with vapid clowns and superficial wits, quickly lit and just as quickly burnt out. He degraded himself, mingling his royal self with those skipping fools.

Had his great name profanèd with their scorns,
65   And gave his countenance, against his name,
To laugh at gibing boys and stand the push
Of every beardless vain comparative;
Grew a companion to the common streets,
Enfeoffed himself to popularity,
70   That, being daily swallowed by men's eyes,
They surfeited with honey and began
To loathe the taste of sweetness, whereof a little
More than a little is by much too much.
So, when he had occasion to be seen,
75   He was but as the cuckoo is in June,
Heard, not regarded; seen, but with such eyes
As, sick and blunted with community,
Afford no extraordinary gaze
Such as is bent on sunlike majesty
80   When it shines seldom in admiring eyes,
But rather drowsed and hung their eyelids down,
Slept in his face, and rendered such aspect
As cloudy men use to their adversaries,
Being with his presence glutted, gorged, and full.
85   And in that very line, Harry, standest thou,
For thou has lost thy princely privilege
With vile participation. Not an eye
But is aweary of thy common sight,
Save mine, which hath desired to see thee more,
90   Which now doth that I would not have it do,
Make blind itself with foolish tenderness.

PRINCE HENRY
I shall hereafter, my thrice gracious lord,
Be more myself.

KING
                          For all the world
As thou art to this hour was Richard then
95   When I from France set foot at Ravenspurgh,
And even as I was then is Percy now.

His reputation was ruined by their scornful attitudes. He lost face by laughing with those joking boys, and tolerating the rudeness of every smooth-faced, disdainful prankster. He spent his time in common, public places, surrendering himself to the pursuit of popularity. Soon, they saw him every day and it was like overdosing on honey; they began to hate the taste of that sweetness. A little too much is as bad as far too much. Seeing him became as common a sight as a cuckoo in June—heard but not paid attention to; seen, but by eyes so used to seeing that they took it for granted. They didn't look with a special gaze, as they do at the sun when it shines only rarely. Instead, they grew bored, they looked away.

They slept in front of him and watched him dully, the way a sullen man looks at his enemy. They were stuffed, gorged, and full with his presence. And that is just where you stand, Harry. You have lost your princely status by associating with vile criminals: there's not an eye in the kingdom that isn't weary of looking at you. No eyes except mine, that is, which had wished to see more of you; and now they're acting against me, blinding themselves with foolish tears.

PRINCE HENRY

From now on, my very gracious father, I will behave more like myself.

KING

At this moment, you seem just like Richard did when I returned from France to lead the revolt. And just as I was then, Percy seems now.

Now, by my scepter, and my soul to boot,
He hath more worthy interest to the state
Than thou, the shadow of succession.
100   For of no right, nor color like to right,
He doth fill fields with harness in the realm,
Turns head against the lion's armèd jaws,
And, being no more in debt to years than thou,
Leads ancient lords and reverend bishops on
105   To bloody battles and to bruising arms.
What never-dying honor hath he got
Against renownèd Douglas, whose high deeds,
Whose hot incursions and great name in arms,
Holds from all soldiers chief majority
110   And military title capital
Through all the kingdoms that acknowledge Christ.
Thrice hath this Hotspur, Mars in swathling clothes,
This infant warrior, in his enterprises
Discomfited great Douglas, ta'en him once,
115   Enlargèd him, and made a friend of him,
To fill the mouth of deep defiance up
And shake the peace and safety of our throne.
And what say you to this? Percy, Northumberland,
The Archbishop's Grace of York, Douglas, Mortimer,
120   Capitulate against us and are up.
But wherefore do I tell these news to thee?
Why, Harry, do I tell thee of my foes,
Which art my nearest and dearest enemy?
Thou that art like enough, through vassal fear,
125   Base inclination, and the start of spleen,
To fight against me under Percy's pay,
To dog his heels, and curtsy at his frowns,
To show how much thou art degenerate.

PRINCE HENRY
Do not think so. You shall not find it so.
130   And God forgive them that so much have swayed
Your Majesty's good thoughts away from me.

I swear on my scepter and my soul, he has more of a right to the throne than you, you shadowy copy of a king. For without a right to the throne—nor anything even resembling a right—he has filled the kingdom's battlefields with armies. He seeks to lead an army against the King, into the jaws of the lion. And even though he is no older than you are, he leads old statesmen and venerable bishops into bloody battles and violent wars. What lasting honor he won, by beating the renowned Douglas! That man's great exploits, violent invasions, and glorious military reputation had won him praise throughout the Christian world as the most outstanding soldier.

Mars = Roman god of war

And yet Hotspur, this Mars in baby clothes, this infant warrior, has defeated Douglas three times, captured him once, then freed him and made him his ally. Now they have become a huge threat to my throne. And what do you have to say about this? Percy, Northumberland, the Archbishop of York, Douglas, and Mortimer have banded together, and now they are after me. But why am I telling you this?

Why should I tell you about my foes, Harry, when you are my most beloved and most dangerous enemy? With your sycophantic fear, your vulgar inclinations, and your short temper, I wouldn't be surprised if you left me to fight under Percy, following his heels like a dog and bowing to him when he frowns. Just to prove what a degenerate you are.

PRINCE HENRY

Don't think that; that will not happen. God forgive whoever turned you against me like this! I'll redeem myself by beating Percy. And at the end of some

I will redeem all this on Percy's head,
And, in the closing of some glorious day,
Be bold to tell you that I am your son,
135 When I will wear a garment all of blood
And stain my favors in a bloody mask,
Which, washed away, shall scour my shame with it.
And that shall be the day, whene'er it lights,
That this same child of honor and renown,
140 This gallant Hotspur, this all-praisèd knight,
And your unthought-of Harry chance to meet.
For every honor sitting on his helm,
Would they were multitudes, and on my head
My shames redoubled! For the time will come
145 That I shall make this northern youth exchange
His glorious deeds for my indignities.
Percy is but my factor, good my lord,
To engross up glorious deeds on my behalf.
And I will call him to so strict account
150 That he shall render every glory up,
Yea, even the slightest worship of his time,
Or I will tear the reckoning from his heart.
This in the name of God I promise here,
The which if He be pleased I shall perform,
155 I do beseech your Majesty may salve
The long-grown wounds of my intemperance.
If not, the end of life cancels all bands,
And I will die a hundred thousand deaths
Ere break the smallest parcel of this vow.

KING
160 A hundred thousand rebels die in this.
Thou shalt have charge and sovereign trust herein.

Enter BLUNT

glorious victory, I'll come to you and proudly say that I am your son. I will wear a garment made of blood, and my face will be stained by a bloody mask which, when washed away, will clean me of my shame. This will be the day, whenever it happens, that this famous and honored child—this brave Hotspur, this highly praised knight—will meet your disregarded Harry in battle.

I wish that every honor he's earned were multiplied, and that every one of my shames were doubled. For the time will come when I'll make this youth from the north exchange his glorious deeds for my embarrassments. Percy is working for me, my lord. He's collecting glories on my behalf, and I'm going to hold him strictly accountable for them. He'll either have to surrender every last one of those glories to me, no matter how small, or I'll tear them right out of his heart.

This I promise you, in the name of God. And if God allows me to do these things, then I beg you to heal the wound caused by my long years of bad behavior. If not, then my death will cancel all my debts. I would rather die a hundred-thousand deaths than break even the smallest part of this promise.

KING

Through this vow, a hundred-thousand rebels are killed. You will be given a position of command, and absolute trust in this undertaking.

BLUNT *enters.*

How now, good Blunt? Thy looks are full of speed.

BLUNT
So hath the business that I come to speak of.
Lord Mortimer of Scotland hath sent word
165   That Douglas and the English rebels met
The eleventh of this month at Shrewsbury.
A mighty and a fearful head they are,
If promises be kept on every hand,
As ever offered foul play in the state.

KING
170   The Earl of Westmoreland set forth today,
With him my son, Lord John of Lancaster,
For this advertisement is five days old.—
On Wednesday next, Harry, you shall set forward.
On Thursday we ourselves will march. Our meeting
175   Is Bridgenorth. And, Harry, you shall march
Through Gloucestershire; by which account,
Our business valuèd, some twelve days hence
Our general forces at Bridgenorth shall meet.
Our hands are full of business. Let's away.
180   Advantage feeds him fat while men delay.

Exeunt

What's wrong, Blunt? You look like there's an emergency.

BLUNT

There is, which is what I've come to tell you. Lord Mortimer of Scotland sent word that Douglas and the English rebels met at Shrewsbury, on the eleventh of this month. If everyone involved keeps their word, they will have an army as enormous and terrifying as any that ever caused trouble in this kingdom.

KING

We heard this news five days ago. The Earl of Westmoreland left today, along with my son Lord John of Lancaster. Harry, you'll go next Wednesday. On Thursday, I will go myself. We'll meet at Bridgenorth. Harry, you will march through Gloucestershire. Given the amount of time we'll all need, we should come together with our full forces at Bridgenorth twelve days from now. There's a lot to do, so let's go. Our enemies will take advantage if we're slow.

They exit.

ACT 3, SCENE 3

Enter FALSTAFF *and* BARDOLPH

FALSTAFF
Bardolph, am I not fallen away vilely since this last action?
Do I not bate? Do I not dwindle? Why, my skin hangs about
me like an like an old lady's loose gown. I am withered like
an old applejohn. Well, I'll repent, and that suddenly, while
5   I am in some liking. I shall be out of heart shortly, and then
I shall have no strength to repent. An I have not forgotten
what the inside of a church is made of, I am a peppercorn,
a brewer's horse. The inside of a church! Company,
villanous company, hath been the spoil of me.

BARDOLPH
10   Sir John, you are so fretful you cannot live long.

FALSTAFF
Why, there is it. Come sing me a bawdy song, make me
merry. I was as virtuously given as a gentleman need to be,
virtuous enough: swore little; diced not above seven
times—a week; went to a bawdy house once in a quarter—
15   of an hour; paid money that I borrowed, three or four times;
lived well and in good compass; and now I live out of all
order, out of all compass.

BARDOLPH
Why, you are so fat, Sir John, that you must needs be out of
all compass, out of all reasonable compass, Sir John.

FALSTAFF
20   Do thou amend thy face, and I'll amend my life. Thou art
our admiral, thou bearest the lantern in the poop, but 'tis in
the nose of thee. Thou art the knight of the burning lamp.

BARDOLPH
Why, Sir John, my face does you no harm.

ACT 3, SCENE 3

FALSTAFF *and* BARDOLPH *enter.*

FALSTAFF

Bardolph, haven't I shrivelled since our last robbery? Haven't I gotten thin? Aren't I shrinking? My skin is hanging off me like a loose gown on an old lady; I'm puckered like a rotten apple. I'd better repent my sins, and fast, while there's still something left of me. I'll be in bad shape soon, and then I won't have the strength to repent. If I haven't forgotten what the inside of a church looks like, I'm a withered berry, a lame old nag. The inside of a church! The wrong crowd, the wrong crowd has ruined me.

BARDOLPH

Sir John, you complain so much, you're sure not to live much longer.

FALSTAFF

You're absolutely right. Come on then, sing me a dirty song. Make me laugh. I lived my life as properly as a gentleman should. Well, properly enough, anyway. I didn't swear much. I didn't gamble—more than seven days a week. I went to a whorehouse no more than once—every fifteen minutes. I paid my debts—three or four times. I lived well and within reasonable boundaries. And now, I live poorly and out of moderation.

BARDOLPH

You're so fat, Sir John, that you have no choice but to live out of moderation: moderation could not fit you.

FALSTAFF

You fix your face and I'll fix my life. You're like the flagship of our fleet, with a light on its bow—except that your light is in your nose.

BARDOLPH

Why, Sir John, my face isn't hurting you.

FALSTAFF

No, I'll be sworn, I make as good use of it as many a man
25 doth of a death's-head or a *memento mori*. I never see thy
face but I think upon hellfire and Dives that lived in purple,
for there he is in his robes, burning, burning. If thou wert
any way given to virtue, I would swear by thy face. My oath
should be "By this fire, that's God's angel." But thou art
30 altogether given over, and wert indeed, but for the light in
thy face, the son of utter darkness. When thou rannest up
Gadshill in the night to catch my horse, if I did not think
thou hadst been an *ignis fatuus*, or a ball of wildfire, there's
no purchase in money. O, thou art a perpetual triumph, an
35 everlasting bonfire-light! Thou hast saved me a thousand
marks in links and torches, walking with thee in the night
betwixt tavern and tavern: but the sack that thou hast drunk
me would have bought me lights as good cheap at the
dearest chandler's in Europe. I have maintained that
40 salamander of yours with fire any time this two and thirty
years, God reward me for it.

BARDOLPH

'Sblood, I would my face were in your belly!

FALSTAFF

Godamercy, so should I be sure to be heart-burned!

Enter MISTRESS QUICKLY

How now, Dame Partlet the hen, have you enquired yet
45 who picked my pocket?

MISTRESS QUICKLY

Why, Sir John, what do you think, Sir John, do you think I
keep thieves in my house? I have searched, I have enquired,
so has my husband, man by man, boy by boy, servant by
servant. The tithe of a hair was never lost in my house
50 before.

FALSTAFF

No, you're right. I actually get some good from your face: it's like a skull, or a death token. I can't look at your face without thinking of the flames of hell, and Dives from the Bible, who burned eternally. If there were anything pious about you, I could swear oaths on your face. I could say, "Now, by this fire, which is God's angel …" But you're a complete sinner, and if it weren't for the light in your face, you'd be the son of darkness. When you ran up Gadshill at night to find my horse, I could have sworn you were a will-o-the-wisp or a fireball. You're an endless torchlight parade, a permanent bonfire. Walking with you from tavern to tavern at night has saved me a thousand marks in candles and flashlights. But the money I've spent on wine for you would have been enough to buy the most expensive candles in Europe. I've kept that nose of yours burning for thirty-two years, God bless me.

will-o-the-wisp = a natural phenomenon in which lights seem to appear over marshy ground

marks = unit of currency

BARDOLPH

Dammit! I wish my face were in your belly.

a common expression of irritation

FALSTAFF

God have mercy! Then I'd surely have heartburn.

MISTRESS QUICKLY *enters.*

Hello there, Madame Clucking Chicken! Have you figured out yet who picked my pocket?

MISTRESS QUICKLY

Now Sir John, what do you think, Sir John? Do you think I have thieves in my establishment? I've searched, I've asked questions; so has my husband. We've asked every man, boy and servant here. No one's ever lost so much as a fraction of a hair in this tavern before.

FALSTAFF

You lie, hostess. Bardolph was shaved and lost many a hair; and I'll be sworn my pocket was picked. Go to, you are a woman, go.

MISTRESS QUICKLY

Who, I? No; I defy thee! God's light, I was never called so in mine own house before.

FALSTAFF

Go to, I know you well enough.

MISTRESS QUICKLY

No, Sir John, you do not know me, Sir John. I know you, Sir John. You owe me money, Sir John, and now you pick a quarrel to beguile me of it. I bought you a dozen of shirts to your back.

FALSTAFF

Dowlas, filthy dowlas. I have given them away to bakers' wives; they have made bolters of them.

MISTRESS QUICKLY

Now, as I am a true woman, holland of eight shillings an ell. You owe money here besides, Sir John, for your diet and by-drinkings, and money lent you, four and twenty pound.

FALSTAFF

(points at BARDOLPH*)* He had his part of it. Let him pay.

MISTRESS QUICKLY

He? Alas, he is poor. He hath nothing.

FALSTAFF

How, poor? Look upon his face. What call you rich? Let them coin his nose. Let them coin his cheeks. I'll not pay a denier. What, will you make a younker of me? Shall I not take mine case in mine inn but I shall have my pocket picked? I have lost a seal ring of my grandfather's worth forty mark.

MISTRESS QUICKLY

O Jesu, I have heard the Prince tell him, I know not how oft, that that ring was copper!

FALSTAFF

You lie! Bardolph got a shave here, and he lost a lot of hair. And I swear my pocket was picked. To hell with you, you're a woman. To hell with you.

MISTRESS QUICKLY

Who, me? No, I say. By God, I've never been called such a thing in my own tavern before.

FALSTAFF

Oh come on, I know all about you.

MISTRESS QUICKLY

No, Sir John; you don't know me, Sir John. I know you, Sir John. You owe me money, Sir John, and now you're making a fuss so that you can cheat me out of it. I have bought you a dozen shirts to wear.

FALSTAFF

Junk, cheap junk. I gave them away to bakers' wives, to sift flour with.

MISTRESS QUICKLY

I swear, as an honest woman, that they were made of expensive fabric, eight shillings an ell. Besides, you owe me money for food and drink, plus twenty-four pounds I lent you.

ell = measurement of 45 inches

FALSTAFF

(*points at* BARDOLPH) He had some of it. Let him pay.

MISTRESS QUICKLY

Him? He's poor, he has nothing.

FALSTAFF

What? Poor? Look at his face. What do you call rich? They could make coins from his nose, mint his cheeks. I won't pay a denier. You think I'm a rube? What, I can't relax at a tavern without getting my pocket picked? I lost my grandfather's sealing ring, worth forty marks.

denier = a French copper coin, worth very little

MISTRESS QUICKLY

Jesus! I've heard the Prince tell him countless times that ring was only made out of copper.

FALSTAFF
How? The Prince is a jack, a sneak-up. 'Sblood, an he were here, I would cudgel him like a dog if he would say so.

Enter PRINCE HENRY *and* PETO, *marching, and* FALSTAFF *meets them playing on his truncheon like a fife*

How now, lad, is the wind in that door, i' faith? Must we all march?

BARDOLPH
80   Yea, two and two, Newgate fashion.

MISTRESS QUICKLY
My lord, I pray you, hear me.

PRINCE HENRY
What sayest thou, Mistress Quickly? How doth thy husband? I love him well; he is an honest man.

MISTRESS QUICKLY
Good my lord, hear me.

FALSTAFF
85   Prithee, let her alone, and list to me.

PRINCE HENRY
What say'st thou, Jack?

FALSTAFF
The other night I fell asleep here behind the arras, and had my pocket picked. This house is turned bawdy house; they pick pockets.

PRINCE HENRY
90   What didst thou lose, Jack?

FALSTAFF
Wilt thou believe me, Hal, three or four bonds of forty pound apiece, and a seal ring of my grandfather's.

PRINCE HENRY
A trifle, some eightpenny matter.

FALSTAFF

What? The Prince is a bastard, a sneak. Dammit, if he were here and said something like that, I'd beat him like a dog.

PRINCE HENRY *and* PETO *enter, marching like soldiers.* FALSTAFF *joins them, pretending that his cudgel is a fife, or military flute.*

Hey there, lad! Is that what's happening? Are we all going to march?

BARDOLPH

Yes, side by side, like prisoners to the gallows.

MISTRESS QUICKLY

My lord, please, listen to me.

PRINCE HENRY

What is it, Mistress Quickly? How's your husband? I think highly of him; he's an honest man.

MISTRESS QUICKLY

My lord, please listen to me.

FALSTAFF

Forget about her, and listen to me.

PRINCE HENRY

What is it, Jack?

FALSTAFF

The other night I fell asleep here behind the arras and I had my pocket picked. This bar's like a whorehouse: they pick your pockets.

PRINCE HENRY

What did you lose, Jack?

FALSTAFF

Would you believe it, Hal? Three or four I.O.U.'s worth forty pounds each, and my grandfather's sealing ring.

PRINCE HENRY

Junk, not worth more than eight pennies.

MISTRESS QUICKLY
So I told him, my lord, and I said I heard your Grace say so.
95 And, my lord, he speaks most vilely of you, like a foul-
mouthed man as he is;,and said he would cudgel you.

PRINCE HENRY
What, he did not!

MISTRESS QUICKLY
There's neither faith, truth, nor womanhood in me else.

FALSTAFF
There's no more faith in thee than in a stewed prune, nor no
100 more truth in thee than in a drawn fox, and for womanhood,
Maid Marian may be the deputy's wife of the ward to thee.
Go, you thing, go.

MISTRESS QUICKLY
Say, what thing, what thing?

FALSTAFF
What thing! Why, a thing to thank God on.

MISTRESS QUICKLY
105 I am no thing to thank God on, I would thou shouldst know
it! I am an honest man's wife, and, setting thy knighthood
aside, thou art a knave to call me so.

FALSTAFF
Setting thy womanhood aside, thou art a beast to say
otherwise.

MISTRESS QUICKLY
110 Say, what beast, thou knave, thou?

FALSTAFF
What beast? Why, an otter.

PRINCE HENRY
An otter, Sir John. Why an otter?

FALSTAFF
Why, she's neither fish nor flesh; a man knows not where to
have her.

MISTRESS QUICKLY

That's what I said, my lord. And I said I'd heard you say so, and then he said awful things about you, like the foul-mouthed man that he is. He said he'd beat you.

PRINCE HENRY

What? He did?

MISTRESS QUICKLY

If he didn't, I'm not faithful, trustworthy or womanly.

FALSTAFF

You're about as faithful as a whore, as trustworthy as a fox on the run, and—as for womanhood—a man in a dress is the minister's wife compared to you. Get out of here, you thing, get out.

MISTRESS QUICKLY

Thing? What thing?

FALSTAFF

What thing? A thing to say "thank God" for.

MISTRESS QUICKLY

I am not a thing to say "thank God" for, I want you to know; I am an honest man's wife. And ignoring the fact that you are a knight, you are a brute for calling me that.

FALSTAFF

Well, if you ignore the fact that you're a woman, then I suppose that would make you an animal.

MISTRESS QUICKLY

What animal, you brute?

FALSTAFF

What animal? Why, an otter.

PRINCE HENRY

An otter, Sir John? Why an otter?

FALSTAFF

Because she's not quite a fish and not quite a mammal. A man wouldn't know where to put her.

MISTRESS QUICKLY
115   Thou art an unjust man in saying so. Thou or any man
        knows where to have me, thou knave, thou.

PRINCE HENRY
        Thou sayest true, hostess, and he slanders thee most grossly.

MISTRESS QUICKLY
        So he doth you, my lord, and said this other day you owed
        him a thousand pound.

PRINCE HENRY
120   Sirrah, do I owe you a thousand pound?

FALSTAFF
        A thousand pound, Hal? A million. Thy love is worth a
        million; thou owest me thy love.

MISTRESS QUICKLY
        Nay, my lord, he called you "jack," and said he would
        cudgel you.

FALSTAFF
125   Did I, Bardolph?

BARDOLPH
        Indeed, Sir John, you said so.

FALSTAFF
        Yea, if he said my ring was copper.

PRINCE HENRY
        I say 'tis copper. Darest thou be as good as thy word now?

FALSTAFF
        Why, Hal, thou knowest, as thou art but man, I dare, but as
130   thou art Prince, I fear thee as I fear the roaring of a lion's
        whelp.

PRINCE HENRY
        And why not as the lion?

FALSTAFF
        The King is to be feared as the lion. Dost thou think I'll fear
        thee as I fear thy father? Nay, an I do, I pray God my girdle
135   break.

MISTRESS QUICKLY

You're awful for saying so: you or any man would know where to put me, you brute, you!

PRINCE HENRY

You're right, hostess, and he has really insulted you.

MISTRESS QUICKLY

He insulted you, too, my lord. Just the other day, he said you owed him a thousand pounds.

PRINCE HENRY

Sirrah, do I owe you a thousand pounds?

FALSTAFF

A thousand pounds, Hal? A million. Your love is worth a million, and you owe me your love.

MISTRESS QUICKLY

No, sir. He called you a bastard and said he'd beat you.

FALSTAFF

Did I, Bardolph?

BARDOLPH

Indeed, Sir John, you said so.

FALSTAFF

That's right, if he said my ring was junk and made of copper.

PRINCE HENRY

And I do say that it's made of copper. So will you dare keep your word and beat me?

FALSTAFF

Hal, know this: if you were only a man, I would dare. But since you're also a Prince, I'm scared of you, as much as I'm scared by the roar of a lion's cub.

PRINCE HENRY

Why the cub and not the lion?

FALSTAFF

The breaking of a belt was considered bad luck.

Only the King is as frightening as the lion. You think I'm as scared of you as I am of your father? If I am, I pray to God for my belt to break.

PRINCE HENRY
O, if it should, how would thy guts fall about thy knees!
But, sirrah, there's no room for faith, truth, nor honesty in
this bosom of thine. It is all filled up with guts and midriff.
Charge an honest woman with picking thy pocket? Why,
140 thou whoreson, impudent, embossed rascal, if there were
anything in thy pocket but tavern reckonings,
memorandums of bawdy houses, and one poor pennyworth
of sugar candy to make thee long-winded, if thy pocket
were enriched with any other injuries but these, I am a
145 villain. And yet you will stand to it! You will not pocket up
wrong! Art thou not ashamed?

FALSTAFF
Dost thou hear, Hal? Thou knowest in the state of
innocency Adam fell, and what should poor Jack Falstaff do
in the days of villany? Thou seest I have more flesh than
150 another man and therefore more frailty. You confess, then,
you picked my pocket?

PRINCE HENRY
It appears so by the story.

FALSTAFF
Hostess, I forgive thee. Go make ready breakfast, love thy
husband, look to thy servants, cherish thy guests. Thou
155 shalt find me tractable to any honest reason. Thou seest I
am pacified still. Nay, prithee, be gone.
Exit MISTRESS QUICKLY
Now, Hal, to the news at court. For the robbery, lad, how is
that answered?

PRINCE HENRY
O, my sweet beef, I must still be good angel to thee. The
160 money is paid back again.

FALSTAFF
O, I do not like that paying back. 'Tis a double labor.

PRINCE HENRY

Oh, but if it did, your guts would fall down to your knees! Sirrah, there's no room in your chest for trustworthiness, truthfulness, or honesty. It's all filled up with guts and stomach. Accuse an honest woman of picking your pocket? You son of a whore; you rude, bloated cheat. I'll be damned if there was anything in your pocket besides tavern bills, notes about whorehouses, and a penny's worth of candy for energy. If you had anything else in your pockets, then I'm a liar; yet you stand by your lies. You won't even try to hide how bad you are. Aren't you ashamed of yourself?

FALSTAFF

Don't you know, Hal? Adam fell from grace when the world was innocent. What should poor Jack Falstaff do, now that the world is wicked? You see I have more flesh than other men. It follows that I'm more fallible than other men.—So you're confessing to picking my pocket?

PRINCE HENRY

It looks that way.

FALSTAFF

Hostess, I forgive you. Go get breakfast ready; love your husband; tend to your servants; cherish your guests. You'll find me a perfectly reasonable man. See? I'm calm, as always. Now please, get going!

MISTRESS QUICKLY *exits.*

Now Hal, what's the news at court? What ever happened about our robbery?

PRINCE HENRY

I'm your guardian angel again, you fresh piece of meat. The money's been paid back.

FALSTAFF

I don't like that "paying back." It means twice the work!

PRINCE HENRY
　　I am good friends with my father and may do anything.

FALSTAFF
　　Rob me the Exchequer the first thing thou dost, and do it
　　with unwashed hands too.

BARDOLPH
165　　Do, my lord.

PRINCE HENRY
　　I have procured thee, Jack, a charge of foot.

FALSTAFF
　　I would it had been of horse. Where shall I find one that can
　　steal well? O, for a fine thief of the age of two and twenty or
　　thereabouts! I am heinously unprovided. Well, God be
170　　thanked for these rebels. They offend none but the
　　virtuous. I laud them; I praise them.

PRINCE HENRY
　　Bardolph!

BARDOLPH
　　My lord.

PRINCE HENRY
　　Go bear this letter to Lord John of Lancaster,
175　　To my brother John; this to my Lord of Westmoreland.
　　　　　　　　　　　　　　　　　　　Exit BARDOLPH
　　Go, Peto, to horse, to horse, for thou and I have thirty miles
　　to ride yet ere dinner time.
　　　　　　　　　　　　　　　　　　　Exit PETO
　　Jack, meet me tomorrow in the Temple hall
　　At two o'clock in the afternoon;
180　　There shalt thou know thy charge, and there receive
　　Money and order for their furniture.
　　The land is burning. Percy stands on high,
　　And either we or they must lower lie.
　　　　　　　　　　　　　　　　　　　Exit PRINCE HENRY

PRINCE HENRY

My father and I are friends again, and I can do whatever I want.

FALSTAFF

Then rob the treasury right away, and don't even delay long enough to wash your hands.

BARDOLPH

Do it, my lord.

PRINCE HENRY

I have gotten you an infantry company to command, Jack.

FALSTAFF

I wish it were the horse brigade. Where can I recruit a talented crook? Oh, if I only had a gifted thief, about twenty-two years old! I'm terribly lacking in help. Well, thank God for these rebels. The only people they bother are the good people. I like that. I honor and salute them.

PRINCE HENRY

Bardolph!

BARDOLPH

My lord?

PRINCE HENRY

Deliver this letter to Lord John of Lancaster, my brother. Give this one to Westmoreland.

BARDOLPH *exits.*

Peto, get to your horse, get to your horse! You and I have to be thirty miles from here by lunchtime.

PETO *exits.*

Temple Hall is one of the Inns of Court, the London schools of law.

Jack, meet me at Temple Hall at two o'clock tomorrow. You'll get the list of your troops there, plus some money and an order for their equipment. The country is on fire, and Percy's riding high. Either they or we must die.

PRINCE HENRY *exits.*

FALSTAFF
Rare words, brave world!—Hostess, my breakfast,
come.—
185   O, I could wish this tavern were my drum.

Exit

FALSTAFF

Well spoken! What a splendid world! Bring my breakfast, hostess! I wish that I could lead my troops from here!

He exits.

ACT FOUR
SCENE 1

Enter HOTSPUR, WORCESTER, *and* DOUGLAS

HOTSPUR
Well said, my noble Scot. If speaking truth
In this fine age were not thought flattery,
Such attribution should the Douglas have
As not a soldier of this season's stamp
5   Should go so general current through the world.
By God, I cannot flatter. I do defy
The tongues of soothers. But a braver place
In my heart's love hath no man than yourself.
Nay, task me to my word; approve me, lord.

DOUGLAS
10 Thou art the king of honor.
No man so potent breathes upon the ground
But I will beard him.

HOTSPUR
                Do so, and 'tis well.

Enter a MESSENGER *with letters*

What letters hast thou there? *(to* DOUGLAS*)* I can but
    thank you.

MESSENGER
These letters come from your father.

HOTSPUR
15 Letters from him! Why comes he not himself?

MESSENGER
He cannot come, my lord. He is grievous sick.

ACT FOUR
SCENE 1

HOTSPUR, WORCESTER, *and* DOUGLAS *enter.*

HOTSPUR

Well said, you excellent Scotsman. If people these days didn't confuse the truth with flattery, I would praise you highly. No other soldier so newly tested in battle would have gained such a widespread reputation. God knows, I don't flatter: I hate people who give out praise too easily. But you have a place in my heart that no other man has. Make me prove it; try me.

DOUGLAS

You are the most honorable man alive, and if any man challenges that—no matter how powerful—I'll defy him.

HOTSPUR

You do that. Well done.

A MESSENGER *enters with letters.*

What letters have you got there? *(to* DOUGLAS*)* All I can do is thank you.

MESSENGER

These letters come from your father.

HOTSPUR

Letters from him? Why isn't he here in person?

MESSENGER

He can't come, my lord; he's terribly sick.

HOTSPUR
> Zounds, how has he the leisure to be sick
> In such a justling time? Who leads his power?
> Under whose government come they along?

MESSENGER
20
> His letters bear his mind, not I, my lord.

WORCESTER
> I prithee, tell me, doth he keep his bed?

MESSENGER
> He did, my lord, four days ere I set forth,
> And, at the time of my departure thence,
> He was much feared by his physicians.

WORCESTER
25
> I would the state of time had first been whole
> Ere he by sickness had been visited.
> His health was never better worth than now.

HOTSPUR
> Sick now? Droop now? This sickness doth infect
> The very lifeblood of our enterprise.
30
> 'Tis catching hither, even to our camp.
> He writes me here that inward sickness—
> And that his friends by deputation
> Could not so soon be drawn, nor did he think it meet
> To lay so dangerous and dear a trust
35
> On any soul removed but on his own;
> Yet doth he give us bold advertisement
> That with our small conjunction we should on
> To see how fortune is disposed to us,
> For, as he writes, there is no quailing now,
40
> Because the King is certainly possessed
> Of all our purposes. What say you to it?

WORCESTER
> Your father's sickness is a maim to us.

HOTSPUR
> A perilous gash, a very limb lopped off!
> And yet, in faith, it is not. His present want

HOTSPUR

Damn! How can he take the leisure of being sick at such a frantic time? Who's in charge of his army? Who's leading them here?

MESSENGER

His letters will tell you his plans, my lord, not I.

WORCESTER

Pardon me, but is he bedridden?

MESSENGER

He had been, sir, for four days before I left. And on the day I left, his doctors were extremely concerned.

WORCESTER

I wish he'd waited till things were settled before he went and got sick. We've never needed him more than now.

HOTSPUR

Sick now? Faint now? His disease is infecting our entire project. It's spread all the way to here, right to our camp. He writes that some internal illness—and that his allies couldn't be gathered so quickly by one of his deputies. Besides, he didn't think it was appropriate to delegate such a dangerous and important task to someone other than himself. But he also says that we should be bold and press on with our small contingent. For, as he writes, there's no turning back now, since the King surely knows our plans. What do you think?

WORCESTER

Your father's sickness is a serious injury to us.

HOTSPUR

It's a perilous wound, like losing a limb. And yet, truly, it's not that bad; the loss of my father seems

45 Seems more than we shall find it. Were it good
To set the exact wealth of all our states
All at one cast? To set so rich a main
On the nice hazard of one doubtful hour?
It were not good, for therein should we read
50 The very bottom and the soul of hope,
The very list, the very utmost bound
Of all our fortunes.

DOUGLAS
Faith, and so we should, where now remains
A sweet reversion. We may boldly spend
55 Upon the hope of what is to come in.
A comfort of retirement lives in this.

HOTSPUR
A rendezvous, a home to fly unto,
If that the devil and mischance look big
Upon the maidenhead of our affairs.

WORCESTER
60 But yet I would your father had been here.
The quality and hair of our attempt
Brooks no division. It will be thought
By some that know not why he is away
That wisdom, loyalty, and mere dislike
65 Of our proceedings kept the Earl from hence.
And think how such an apprehension
May turn the tide of fearful faction
And breed a kind of question in our cause.
For well you know, we of the off'ring side
70 Must keep aloof from strict arbitrament,
And stop all sight-holes, every loop from whence
The eye of reason may pry in upon us.
This absence of your father's draws a curtain
That shows the ignorant a kind of fear
75 Before not dreamt of.

worse than it is. After all, is it a good idea to bet all our resources on one throw of the dice? Or to gamble such a rich stake on a single hazardous event? No, because that would mean we had reached the end of our hope, and the very limit of our luck.

DOUGLAS

That's right. We have a chance at a rich inheritance; we can take a risk now, based on the promise of success to come. That gives us comfort, something to fall back on.

HOTSPUR

It gives us a refuge, a home we can always run to, in case the devil or misfortune ruins these early plans.

WORCESTER

I still wish your father were here. Our endeavor here won't withstand any division. People who don't realize your father is sick will assume that he knows some kind of secret, or that he is loyal to the King, or that he doesn't approve of how we're handling things. And just imagine how that kind of mistrust could frighten our more timid supporters, and lead them to doubt us. You know very well that the challenger must always avoid careful examination. We must seal every crack, every loophole, which skeptics might look through to see weaknesses. Your father's absence draws the curtains back and reveals frightful things to ignorant people, who had never had a reason to fear before.

HOTSPUR
                              You strain too far.
I rather of his absence make this use:
It lends a luster and more great opinion,
A larger dare, to our great enterprise
Than if the Earl were here, for men must think
80   If we without his help can make a head
To push against a kingdom, with his help
We shall o'erturn it topsy-turvy down.
Yet all goes well, yet all our joints are whole.

DOUGLAS
As heart can think. There is not such a word
85   Spoke of in Scotland as this term of fear.

Enter Sir Richard VERNON

HOTSPUR
My cousin Vernon, welcome, by my soul.

VERNON
Pray God my news be worth a welcome, lord.
The Earl of Westmoreland, seven thousand strong,
Is marching hitherwards, with him Prince John.

HOTSPUR
90   No harm, what more?

VERNON
                              And further I have learned,
The King himself in person is set forth,
Or hitherwards intended speedily,
With strong and mighty preparation.

HOTSPUR
He shall be welcome too. Where is his son,
95   The nimble-footed madcap Prince of Wales,
And his comrades, that daffed the world aside
And bid it pass?

HOTSPUR

You're taking this too far. I'd rather think about his absence this way: it makes us look even better. It makes our great undertaking seem even more daring than it would if Northumberland were here. People will think that if we can raise an army against the King without my father, that once he joins we'll turn the whole kingdom upside down. Everything is fine, we're all in one piece.

DOUGLAS

We're as well off as we could have hoped. In Scotland, we don't even know the meaning of the word fear.

Sir Richard VERNON *enters.*

HOTSPUR

Welcome, kinsman Vernon, from the bottom of my heart.

VERNON

I pray to God that what I have to say is worth welcoming, my lord. The Earl of Westmoreland, with seven thousand men, is marching this way. Prince John is with him.

HOTSPUR

Nothing to be worried about. What else?

VERNON

I've also learned that the King himself is coming this way, or at least plans to very soon, with a huge and powerful force.

HOTSPUR

We'll welcome him too. Where's his son, that sporting, foolhardy Prince of Wales, and his comrades, who don't care about anything?

VERNON
       All furnished, all in arms,
All plumed like estridges that with the wind
Baited like eagles having lately bathed,
100 Glittering in golden coats like images,
As full of spirit as the month of May,
And gorgeous as the sun at midsummer,
Wanton as youthful goats, wild as young bulls.
I saw young Harry with his beaver on,
105 His cuisses on his thighs, gallantly armed
Rise from the ground like feathered Mercury
And vaulted with such ease into his seat
As if an angel dropped down from the clouds,
To turn and wind a fiery Pegasus
110 And witch the world with noble horsemanship.

HOTSPUR
No more, no more! Worse than the sun in March
This praise doth nourish agues. Let them come.
They come like sacrifices in their trim,
And to the fire-eyed maid of smoky war
115 All hot and bleeding will we offer them.
The mailèd Mars shall on his altar sit
Up to the ears in blood. I am on fire
To hear this rich reprisal is so nigh
And yet not ours. Come, let me taste my horse,
120 Who is to bear me like a thunderbolt
Against the bosom of the Prince of Wales.
Harry to Harry shall, hot horse to horse,
Meet and ne'er part till one drop down a corse.
O, that Glendower were come!

VERNON
         There is more news.
125 I learned in Worcester, as I rode along,
He cannot draw his power this fourteen days.

DOUGLAS
That's the worst tidings that I hear of yet.

VERNON

They're all in uniform, all armed. They look like feathered ostriches; like eagles beating their wings after a bath; like statues painted gold. They're as lively as the springtime; as gorgeous as the midsummer sun; as giddy as young goats; as wild as young bulls. I saw young Harry with his helmet on, and armor on his thighs. Armed with powerful weapons, he rose off the ground like the winged god Mercury, and leaped so effortlessly into his saddle, it was as if an angel had dropped out of the sky to ride a fiery Pegasus, and bewitch the world with his incredible horsemanship.

Pegasus = a winged horse, from Greek mythology

HOTSPUR

Stop, stop! This praise of him makes me sicker than the sun on an early spring day. Let them come, like sacrifices in all their finery; we'll offer them, hot and bleeding, to the fire-eyed goddess of smoky war. The war-god Mars will sit on his altar, up to his ears in blood. I am on fire, knowing that this rich prize is so near, and yet still not ours. Come, bring me my horse, who will carry me like a lightning bolt to face the Prince of Wales. Then this Harry will meet that Harry, my horse against his horse; we'll meet and never separate, till one of us falls down as a corpse. Oh, I wish that Glendower were here!

VERNON

I have more news: as I passed through the town of Worcester, I heard that Glendower won't be able to collect his army for two more weeks.

DOUGLAS

That's the worst news I've heard so far.

WORCESTER
Ay, by my faith, that bears a frosty sound.

HOTSPUR
What may the King's whole battle reach unto?

VERNON
130   To thirty thousand.

HOTSPUR
                    Forty let it be.
My father and Glendower being both away,
The powers of us may serve so great a day.
Come, let us take a muster speedily.
Doomsday is near. Die all, die merrily.

DOUGLAS
135   Talk not of dying. I am out of fear
Of death or death's hand for this one half year.

Exeunt

WORCESTER

Yes, truly, that news makes me cold.

HOTSPUR

How many men in the King's army?

VERNON

Thirty thousand.

HOTSPUR

Let it be forty. Even with both my father and Glendower absent, our armies may still be enough to win. Come on, let's gather our troops right now. It's almost doomsday; if we die, we die cheerfully.

DOUGLAS

Don't talk about dying. I won't even worry about dying for the next six months.

They exit.

ACT 4, SCENE 2

Enter FALSTAFF *and* BARDOLPH

FALSTAFF
Bardolph, get thee before to Coventry. Fill me a bottle of
sack. Our soldiers shall march through. We'll to Sutton
Coldfield tonight.

BARDOLPH
Will you give me money, captain?

FALSTAFF
5   Lay out, lay out.

BARDOLPH
This bottle makes an angel.

FALSTAFF
An if it do, take it for thy labor. An if it make twenty, take
. them all. I'll answer the coinage. Bid my lieutenant Peto
meet me at town's end.

BARDOLPH
10   I will, captain. Farewell.

Exit BARDOLPH

FALSTAFF
If I be not ashamed of my soldiers, I am a soused gurnet. I
have misused the King's press damnably. I have got, in
exchange of a hundred and fifty soldiers, three hundred and
odd pounds. I press me none but good householders,
15   yeomen's sons; inquire me out contracted bachelors, such
as had been asked twice on the banns; such a commodity of
warm slaves—as had as lief hear the devil as a drum, such
as fear the report of a caliver worse than a struck fowl or a
hurt wild duck. I pressed me none but such toasts-and-
20   butter, with hearts in their bellies no bigger than pins'

ACT 4, SCENE 2

FALSTAFF *and* BARDOLPH *enter.*

FALSTAFF

Bardolph, go ahead of us to Coventry, and fill me a bottle of wine. Our army will keep marching, and we'll make it to Sutton Coldfield tonight.

BARDOLPH

Will you give me some money, captain?

FALSTAFF

Spend your own.

BARDOLPH

If I buy you this bottle, that makes me an angel.

an angel = several shillings; Bardolph claims he has spent an angel on Falstaff's wine.

FALSTAFF

Well, if this bottle earns you an angel, then keep it for your troubles. If you earn twenty angels, then keep them all; I'm good for it. Tell my lieutenant Peto to meet me at the city limit.

BARDOLPH

I will, captain. Farewell.

BARDOLPH *exits.*

FALSTAFF

If I'm not ashamed of my soldiers, then I'm a pickled fish. I've taken terrible advantage of my position. I've pressed a hundred and fifty soldiers into service, and for that, the treasury has paid me over three hundred pounds. I recruited only well-to-do property owners and rich farmer's sons. I looked for men who were engaged to be married, who were already halfway through their preparations. I found a whole supply of pampered cowards who would rather listen to the devil than a military march; who feared the sound of

heads, and they have bought out their services, and now my whole charge consists of ancients, corporals, lieutenants, gentlemen of companies—slaves as ragged as Lazarus in the painted cloth, where the glutton's dogs licked his sores;

25 and such as indeed were never soldiers, but discarded, unjust servingmen, younger sons to younger brothers, revolted tapsters, and ostlers tradefallen, the cankers of a calm world and a long peace, ten times more dishonorable-ragged than an old feazed ancient; and such have I to fill up

30 the rooms of them that have bought out their services, that you would think that I had a hundred and fifty tattered prodigals lately come from swine-keeping, from eating draff and husks. A mad fellow met me on the way and told me I had unloaded all the gibbets and pressed the dead

35 bodies. No eye hath seen such scarecrows. I'll not march through Coventry with them, that's flat. Nay, and the villains march wide betwixt the legs as if they had gyves on, for indeed I had the most of them out of prison. There's not a shirt and a half in all my company, and the half shirt is two

40 napkins tacked together and thrown over the shoulders like a herald's coat without sleeves; and the shirt, to say the truth, stolen from my host at Saint Albans or the red-nose innkeeper of Daventry. But that's all one; they'll find linen enough on every hedge.

Enter PRINCE HENRY *and Lord* WESTMORELAND

PRINCE HENRY
45   How now, blown Jack? How now, quilt?

gunfire more than a wounded bird or a maimed duck might. I recruited only the soft-hearted, who each had as much courage as could fit on a pin head and bribed me to avoid fighting. So now, my battalion is made up of flag bearers, corporals, lieutenants, and crooks as ragged as Lazarus in those paintings where the dogs are licking the sores on his body. I have men who've never been soldiers: servants dismissed for their dishonesty; youngest sons with no hope of an inheritance; runaway apprentice bartenders; unemployed stable boys. When the world is calm and peaceful, these men are blisters on society. They're ten times more ragged than an old, tattered flag, and they're the kind of men I have to replace the ones who bribed me. You'd think I had a hundred and fifty men who'd just come from pig farming, who eat scraps and garbage. One madman saw us on the march and told me that it looked as if I'd unloaded all the gallows and drafted all the dead bodies. No one's ever seen such a group of scarecrows. I'm not going to march through Coventry with them tonight, that's for sure. They march with their legs wide apart, as though they had chains on their ankles. Which makes sense, since I drafted most of them out of jails. There's only a shirt and a half in the whole group, and the half-shirt is really just two napkins sewn together and thrown over the shoulders like a cape. And the whole shirt, to tell the truth, was stolen from a tavern owner in St. Alban's, or maybe that drunken innkeeper in Daventry. But that doesn't matter. They'll be able to steal plenty of clothing from the hedges, where the washers hang the laundry out to dry.

> In the Bible, Jesus raises Lazarus from the dead.

PRINCE HENRY *and Lord* **WESTMORELAND** *enter.*

PRINCE HENRY
What's up, swollen Jack! What's up, quilt?

> A "jack" was also a quilted jacket.

FALSTAFF
What, Hal, how now, mad wag? What a devil dost thou in
Warwickshire?—My good Lord of Westmoreland, I cry
you mercy: I thought your Honor had already been at
Shrewsbury.

WESTMORELAND
50   Faith, Sir John, 'tis more than time that I were there and you
too, but my powers are there already. The King, I can tell
you, looks for us all. We must away all night.

FALSTAFF
Tut, never fear me. I am as vigilant as a cat to steal cream.

PRINCE HENRY
I think to steal cream indeed, for thy theft hath already
55   made thee butter. But tell me, Jack, whose fellows are these
that come after?

FALSTAFF
Mine, Hal, mine.

PRINCE HENRY
I did never see such pitiful rascals.

FALSTAFF
Tut, tut, good enough to toss; food for powder, food for
60   powder. They'll fill a pit as well as better. Tush, man,
mortal men, mortal men.

WESTMORELAND
Ay, but, Sir John, methinks they are exceeding poor and
bare, too beggarly.

FALSTAFF
Faith, for their poverty, I know not where they had that, and
65   for their bareness, I am sure they never learned that of me.

PRINCE HENRY
No, I'll be sworn, unless you call three fingers in the ribs
bare. But, sirrah, make haste. Percy is already in the field.
                              Exit PRINCE.

FALSTAFF

Hello there, Hal, you crazy boy! What in the devil's name are you doing in Warwickshire? And Lord Westmoreland, I beg your pardon. I thought you were already at Shrewsbury.

WESTMORELAND

You're right, Sir John; it's about time I got there, and you, too. But my army's already there. The King is waiting for us, so we must march all night.

FALSTAFF

Don't worry about me. I'm as focused as a cat looking for cream to steal.

PRINCE HENRY

Steal cream is right—you've stolen so much that it's turned you into butter. But tell me, Jack, whose soldiers are those?

FALSTAFF

Mine, Hal, mine.

PRINCE HENRY

I never saw such pitiful-looking losers.

FALSTAFF

Now, now: they're good enough to die. Cannon fodder, cannon fodder—they'll fill a mass grave as well as better men would. They're just men, just men.

WESTMORELAND

Maybe so, Sir John, but I think they look terribly poor and bare; they look like beggars.

FALSTAFF

Well, I don't know where they got their poverty, but their bareness—or their bare-bonedness—well, they didn't get that from me.

PRINCE HENRY

That's for sure. Unless you think several inches of fat over your ribs makes you "bare-boned." But hurry up, sirrah: Percy is already at the battlefield.

PERCY *exits.*

FALSTAFF
What, is the King encamped?

WESTMORELAND
He is, Sir John. I fear we shall stay too long.

FALSTAFF
                                                    Well,
70   To the latter end of a fray and the beginning of a feast
Fits a dull fighter and a keen guest.

Exeunt

FALSTAFF

What, has the King already made camp?

WESTMORELAND

He has, Sir John: I'm afraid we may be too late.

FALSTAFF

Well, a hungry guest arrives early for a feast, but a poor soldier arrives late to a battle.

They exit.

ACT 4, SCENE 3

Enter HOTSPUR, WORCESTER, DOUGLAS, *and* VERNON

HOTSPUR
We'll fight with him tonight.

WORCESTER
                                    It may not be.

DOUGLAS
You give him then advantage.

VERNON
                                    Not a whit.

HOTSPUR
Why say you so? Looks he not for supply?

VERNON
So do we.

HOTSPUR
5   His is certain; ours is doubtful.

WORCESTER
Good cousin, be advised. Stir not tonight.

VERNON
(to HOTSPUR*)* Do not, my lord.

DOUGLAS
                                    You do not counsel well.
You speak it out of fear and cold heart.

VERNON
Do me no slander, Douglas. By my life
10   (And I dare well maintain it with my life),
If well-respected honor bid me on,
I hold as little counsel with weak fear
As you, my lord, or any Scot that this day lives.
Let it be seen tomorrow in the battle
15   Which of us fears.

DOUGLAS
                                    Yea, or tonight.

ACT 4, SCENE 3

HOTSPUR, WORCESTER, DOUGLAS, *and* VERNON *enter.*

HOTSPUR

We'll fight him tonight.

WORCESTER

We can't do that.

DOUGLAS

Then you're giving him the advantage.

VERNON

Not in the least.

HOTSPUR

Why do you say that? Doesn't he have backup coming?

VERNON

So do we.

HOTSPUR

His is guaranteed. Ours isn't.

WORCESTER

Nephew, I'm telling you. Don't start the fighting tonight.

VERNON

(to HOTSPUR*)* Don't, my lord.

DOUGLAS

You're giving poor advice, based on fear and cowardice.

VERNON

Don't slander me, Douglas. I swear on my life—and I'll prove it with my life—that if I'm roused to fight through thoughtful, careful consideration, I'm just as unafraid as you, my lord, or any Scotsman alive. In tomorrow's battle, we'll see which one of us is afraid.

DOUGLAS

Fine. Or tonight.

VERNON
Content.

HOTSPUR
Tonight, say I.

VERNON
Come, come it nay not be. I wonder much,
Being men of such great leading as you are,
20   That you foresee not what impediments
Drag back our expedition. Certain horse
Of my cousin Vernon's are not yet come up.
Your Uncle Worcester's horse came but today,
And now their pride and mettle is asleep,
25   Their courage with hard labor tame and dull,
That not a horse is half the half of himself.

HOTSPUR
So are the horses of the enemy
In general journey-bated and brought low.
The better part of ours are full of rest.

WORCESTER
30   The number of the King exceedeth ours.
For God's sake, cousin, stay till all come in.

The trumpet sounds a parley

Enter BLUNT

BLUNT
I come with gracious offers from the King,
If you vouchsafe me hearing and respect.

HOTSPUR
Welcome, Sir Walter Blunt, and would to God
35   You were of our determination.
Some of us love you well, and even those some
Envy your great deservings and good name
Because you are not of our quality
But stand against us like an enemy.

VERNON

That's enough.

HOTSPUR

Tonight, I say.

VERNON

Come on, we can't do that. I wonder how—being the great leaders you are—you cannot see the problems we're facing. My cousin has yet to arrive with his horses, and your Uncle Worcester's troops only arrived today. Their spirit and their bravery is asleep; their courage is dulled and tamed by the hard journey. They don't have even a quarter of their usual strength.

HOTSPUR

The enemy's horses are tired from the journey as well. The majority of ours are well-rested.

WORCESTER

But the King has more men then we do. For God's sake, nephew, wait until everyone arrives.

A trumpet announces the approach of an envoy.

BLUNT enters.

BLUNT

I'm here with a generous offer from the King, if you'll listen to me and treat me with respect.

HOTSPUR

Welcome, Sir Walter Blunt. I wish to God you were on our side. Many of us think very highly of you, though we begrudge you your honor and reputation, since you fight on the enemy's side.

BLUNT

40   And God defend but still I should stand so,
      So long as out of limit and true rule
      You stand against anointed majesty.
      But to my charge. The king hath sent to know
      The nature of your griefs, and whereupon
45   You conjure from the breast of civil peace
      Such bold hostility, teaching his duteous land
      Audacious cruelty. If that the king
      Have any way your good deserts forgot,
      Which he confesseth to be manifold,
50   He bids you name your griefs, and with all speed
      You shall have your desires with interest
      And pardon absolute for yourself and these
      Herein misled by your suggestion.

HOTSPUR

      The king is kind, and well we know the king
55   Knows at what time to promise, when to pay.
      My father and my uncle and myself
      Did give him that same royalty he wears,
      And when he was not six-and-twenty strong,
      Sick in the world's regard, wretched and low,
60   A poor unminded outlaw sneaking home,
      My father gave him welcome to the shore;
      And when he heard him swear and vow to God
      He came but to be Duke of Lancaster,
      To sue his livery, and beg his peace,
65   With tears of innocency and terms of zeal,
      My father, in kind heart and pity moved,
      Swore him assistance and performed it too.
      Now when the lords and barons of the realm
      Perceived Northumberland did lean to him,
70   The more and less came in with cap and knee,
      Met him in boroughs, cities, villages,
      Attended him on bridges, stood in lanes,
      Laid gifts before him, proffered him their oaths,

BLUNT

And I hope to God I always will, so long as you over-step the bounds of allegiance and duty by standing against the anointed King. But let me get to the point. The King sent me to learn your complaints, and to find out why you are stirring up warfare in a time of peace, and spreading violent dissent throughout his loyal country. If the King has somehow overlooked one of your deserving acts—which, he admits, there are many—he asks you to name your complaints. He'll meet your demands, with interest, as quickly as possible, and grant an absolute pardon to you and everyone who has followed your mistaken lead.

HOTSPUR

That's kind of the King. We know all too well about the promises the King makes, and the ways he keeps his word. My father, my uncle, and I put that crown on his head. And when he had barely twenty-six men supporting him, when no one cared about him, when he was wretched and low, a poor, forsaken criminal trying to sneak home, my father welcomed him. When he swore an oath to God, weeping and speaking passionately, that he had come back to England only to reclaim his father's title and make peace with King Richard, my father took pity on him, swore to help him and did so.

When the country's most important men saw that Northumberland was on his side, they came to see Henry, and bowed down to him. They met him in towns, cities, villages; they waited for him on bridges, stood in the streets, lay gifts before him, swore their loyalty, pledged the support of their sons, followed

Gave him their heirs as pages, followed him
75   Even at the heels in golden multitudes.
He presently, as greatness knows itself,
Steps me a little higher than his vow
Made to my father while his blood was poor
Upon the naked shore at Ravenspurgh,
80   And now forsooth takes on him to reform
Some certain edicts and some strait decrees
That lie too heavy on the commonwealth,
Cries out upon abuses, seems to weep
Over his country's wrongs, and by this face,
85   This seeming brow of justice, did he win
The hearts of all that he did angle for,
Proceeded further—cut me off the heads
Of all the favourites that the absent King
In deputation left behind him here
90   When he was personal in the Irish war.

BLUNT
Tut, I came not to hear this.

HOTSPUR
                                   Then to the point.
In short time after, he deposed the King,
Soon after that deprived him of his life
And, in the neck of that, tasked the whole state.
95   To make that worse, suffered his kinsman March
(Who is, if every owner were well placed,
Indeed his king) to be engaged in Wales,
There without ransom to lie forfeited,
Disgraced me in my happy victories,
100   Sought to entrap me by intelligence,
Rated mine uncle from the council board,
In rage dismissed my father from the court,
Broke oath on oath, committed wrong on wrong,
And in conclusion drove us to seek out
105   This head of safety, and withal to pry

him like servants. Soon enough, he began to understand his power. He overstepped the promise he'd made to my father at Ravenspurgh, when his blood was still humble. And then, suddenly, he took it upon himself to reform certain laws and strict decrees that weighed too heavily on the kingdom. He made angry speeches about the abuses we were suffering, and seemed to weep over the country's problems.

And with this face, this mask of righteousness, he won everyone's hearts. Then he went even further, and cut off the heads of all of Richard's deputies, who stayed behind to run the country while Richard was waging war in Ireland.

BLUNT

I didn't come here to listen to this.

HOTSPUR

Then I'll get to the point. A little while later, he overthrew King Richard. Soon after that, he killed him. And right after that, he raised taxes on everyone. To make matters worse, he allowed his kinsman Mortimer—who by rights ought to be the king—to be imprisoned in Wales, and remain there without ransom. He tried to use my victories to disgrace me, and tried to trap me with spies. He dismissed my uncle from his royal Council, threw my father out of the royal court, broke promise after promise, and committed crime after crime. In conclusion, he forced us to raise this army for our own safety, and to question his claim on the crown, which we believe is too flimsy to stand.

Into his title, the which we find
Too indirect for long continuance.

BLUNT
Shall I return this answer to the King?

HOTSPUR
Not so, Sir Walter. We'll withdraw awhile.
110   Go to the King, and let there be impawned
Some surety for a safe return again,
And in the morning early shall my uncle
Bring him our purposes. And so farewell.

BLUNT
I would you would accept of grace and love.

HOTSPUR
115   And maybe so we shall.

BLUNT
                    Pray God you do.

Exeunt

BLUNT

Should I bring this answer to the King?

HOTSPUR

No, Sir Walter. We'll stand down for a while. Go to the King. My uncle will bring him our demands early in the morning, provided that you arrange for a guarantee that he'll be allowed to return safely. And so, farewell.

BLUNT

I wish you would accept the King's offer of kindness and love.

HOTSPUR

Perhaps we will.

BLUNT

I pray to God you do.

They exit.

ACT 4, SCENE 4

Enter the ARCHBISHOP *of York and* SIR MICHAEL

ARCHBISHOP
Hie, good Sir Michael, bear this sealèd brief
With winged haste to the Lord Marshal,
This to my cousin Scroop, and all the rest
To whom they are directed. If you knew
5   How much they do import, you would make haste.

SIR MICHAEL
My good lord, I guess their tenor.

ARCHBISHOP
Like enough you do.
Tomorrow, good Sir Michael, is a day
Wherein the fortune of ten thousand men
10   Must bide the touch. For, sir, at Shrewsbury,
As I am truly given to understand,
The King with mighty and quick-raisèd power
Meets with Lord Harry. And I fear, Sir Michael,
What with the sickness of Northumberland,
15   Whose power was in the first proportion,
And what with Owen Glendower's absence thence,
Who with them was a rated sinew too
And comes not in, o'er-ruled by prophecies,
I fear the power of Percy is too weak
20   To wage an instant trial with the King.

SIR MICHAEL
Why, my good lord, you need not fear.
There is Douglas and Lord Mortimer.

ARCHBISHOP
No, Mortimer is not there.

SIR MICHAEL
But there is Mordake, Vernon, Lord Harry Percy,
25   And there is my Lord of Worcester and a head
Of gallant warriors, noble gentlemen.

ACT 4, SCENE 4

The ARCHBISHOP *of York and* SIR MICHAEL *enter.*

ARCHBISHOP

Hurry, Sir Michael, bring this sealed letter as fast as you can to the Lord Marshal. Bring this one to Scroop, and all the rest to whom they are addressed. If you knew how important they were, you would hurry.

SIR MICHAEL

My good lord, I can guess what they say.

ARCHBISHOP

I'm sure you can. Tomorrow, Sir Michael, ten thousand men will try their luck. I'm told that at Shrewsbury, the King—with a huge and quickly assembled army—will fight Harry Percy. I'm afraid, Michael, that without Northumberland, whose army was the largest of all, and without Owen Glendower, who was also being counted on but is absent because his horoscope told him to stay away, I'm afraid that Percy's army will be too weak to fight the King right now.

SIR MICHAEL

Don't worry, sir. Douglas and Mortimer are there.

ARCHBISHOP

No, Mortimer isn't there.

SIR MICHAEL

But Mordake is there, and Vernon, and Harry Percy, and Worcester and a slew of brave warriors and excellent men.

ARCHBISHOP
And so there is. But yet the King hath drawn
The special head of all the land together:
The Prince of Wales, Lord John of Lancaster,
30   The noble Westmoreland, and warlike Blunt,
And many more corrivals and dear men
Of estimation and command in arms.

SIR MICHAEL
Doubt not, my lord, they shall be well opposed.

ARCHBISHOP
I hope no less, yet needful 'tis to fear;
35   And to prevent the worst, Sir Michael, speed.
For if Lord Percy thrive not, ere the King
Dismiss his power, he means to visit us,
For he hath heard of our confederacy,
And 'tis but wisdom to make strong against him:
40   Therefore make haste. I must go write again
To other friends. And so farewell, Sir Michael.

Exeunt

ARCHBISHOP

That's correct. But the King has pulled together the best men in the country: the Prince of Wales, Lord John of Lancaster, the noble Westmoreland, warlike Blunt, and many other acquaintances and valuable men of good reputation, with great skill in battle.

SIR MICHAEL

No doubt they will face great opposition.

ARCHBISHOP

I hope so, but still I'm afraid. Now hurry, Sir Michael, to prevent an absolute disaster. For if Percy doesn't prevail, the King will come after us before he disbands his army. He's heard that we're part of the rebellion, so we'd be wise to prepare against him. Now hurry. I have to go write to more friends. Farewell, Sir Michael.

They exit.

ACT FIVE
SCENE 1

Enter the KING, PRINCE HENRY *of Wales, Lord John of*
LANCASTER, *Earl of* WESTMORELAND, BLUNT, *and* FALSTAFF

KING

How bloodily the sun begins to peer
Above yon busky hill. The day looks pale
At his distemp'rature.

PRINCE HENRY

              The southern wind
Doth play the trumpet to his purposes,
5   And by his hollow whistling in the leaves
Foretells a tempest and a blust'ring day.

KING

Then with the losers let it sympathize,
For nothing can seem foul to those that win.

The trumpet sounds. Enter WORCESTER *and* VERNON

How now, my Lord of Worcester? 'Tis not well
10   That you and I should meet upon such terms
As now we meet. You have deceived our trust
And made us doff our easy robes of peace
To crush our old limbs in ungentle steel.
This is not well, my lord; this is not well.
15   What say you to it? Will you again unknit
This curlish knot of all-abhorrèd war
And move in that obedient orb again
Where you did give a fair and natural light,
And be no more an exhaled meteor,
20   A prodigy of fear and a portent
Of broachèd mischief to the unborn times?

ACT FIVE
SCENE 1

The KING, PRINCE HENRY *of Wales, Lord John of* LANCASTER, *Earl of* WESTMORELAND, *Sir Walter* BLUNT, *and* FALSTAFF *enter.*

KING

How bloody the sun looks as it peers over that massive hill. The day looks pale—it must be sick to see the sun in such a mood.

PRINCE HENRY

The southern wind is playing its trumpet, to announce to the world what the sun means. And judging by the whistling leaves, it's going to be a stormy, windy day.

KING

Then let it take the losers' side. To winners, nothing seems unpleasant.

A trumpet sounds. WORCESTER *and* VERNON *enter.*

Hello there, my lord of Worcester! It isn't right that you and I are meeting under these circumstances. You have betrayed my trust. You forced me to put aside my comfortable peacetime clothing and instead have made me crush my old body into hard, military armor. That isn't right, sir, that isn't right. What do you have to say about it? Will you untie this ill-tempered knot of hateful war? Will you return to my loyalty? When you circled me, your King, in your obedient orbit, you shone beautifully and naturally. Now you blaze like a comet: a fearful omen, and a signal that evil will be released into the future.

WORCESTER
    Hear me, my liege:
    For mine own part I could be well content
    To entertain the lag end of my life
25   With quiet hours. For I do protest
    I have not sought the day of this dislike.

KING
    You have not sought it. How comes it then?

FALSTAFF
    Rebellion lay in his way, and he found it.

PRINCE HENRY
    Peace, chewet, peace.

WORCESTER
30   *(to the* **KING***)* It pleased your Majesty to turn your looks
    Of favour from myself and all our house;
    And yet I must remember you, my lord,
    We were the first and dearest of your friends.
    For you my staff of office did I break
35   In Richard's time, and posted day and night
    To meet you on the way, and kiss your hand
    When yet you were in place and in account
    Nothing so strong and fortunate as I.
    It was myself, my brother, and his son
40   That brought you home and boldly did outdare
    The dangers of the time. You swore to us,
    And you did swear that oath at Doncaster,
    That you did nothing purpose 'gainst the state,
    Nor claim no further than your new-fall'n right,
45   The seat of Gaunt, dukedom of Lancaster.
    To this we swore our aid. But in short space
    It rained down fortune show'ring on your head,
    And such a flood of greatness fell on you—
    What with our help, what with the absent King,
50   What with the injuries of a wanton time,
    The seeming sufferances that you had borne,

WORCESTER

Listen, my lord. For me, I would love nothing more than to spend my old age in peace and quiet. I protest: I did not seek out this day of aggression.

KING

You did not seek it? Then how did it come here?

FALSTAFF

Rebellion was standing in front of him, and he bumped into it.

PRINCE HENRY

Quiet, you chatterer, quiet!

WORCESTER

(to the KING*)* Your Highness chose to turn your back on me and my family. I must remind you, sir, that we were your first and dearest friends. For you, I quit my position under Richard, and ran day and night to meet you on the road and kiss your hand. At that time, you were far less powerful than I was. But my brother, his son, and I brought you home and ignored the danger. At Doncaster you swore an oath to us that you were not going to challenge the King; all you wanted was your late father's estate, the dukedom of Lancaster, and in this we promised to help you.

But soon, good luck began to pour on you like rain, and a flood of greatness fell upon you. You had a swarm of advantages: you had our assistance; and the King had been away so long; and the country was suffering under violence; and you seemed to have been so grievously wronged; and difficult winds were keeping

And the contrarious winds that held the King
So long in his unlucky Irish wars
That all in England did repute him dead—
55   And from this swarm of fair advantages
You took occasion to be quickly wooed
To gripe the general sway into your hand,
Forget your oath to us at Doncaster;
And being fed by us, you used us so
60   As that ungentle gull, the cuckoo's bird,
Useth the sparrow—did oppress our nest,
Grew by our feeding to so great a bulk
That even our love durst not come near your sight
For fear of swallowing; but with nimble wing
65   We were enforced for safety sake to fly
Out of sight and raise this present head,
Whereby we stand opposèd by such means
As you yourself have forged against yourself
By unkind usage, dangerous countenance,
70   And violation of all faith and troth
Sworn to us in your younger enterprise.

KING

These things indeed you have articulate,
Proclaimed at market crosses, read in churches,
To face the garment of rebellion
75   With some fine color that may please the eye
Of fickle changelings and poor discontents,
Which gape and rub the elbow at the news
Of hurlyburly innovation.
And never yet did insurrection want
80   Such water colors to impaint his cause,
Nor moody beggars starving for a time
Of pellmell havoc and confusion.

PRINCE HENRY

In both your armies there is many a soul
Shall pay full dearly for this encounter
85   If once they join in trial. Tell your nephew,

Richard so long in those unlucky Irish wars, people thought he was dead. You seized the opportunity, and used the general feeling to your advantage. You forgot the oath you swore to us at Doncaster.

We nourished you, but you used us, like the cuckoo bird uses the sparrow: you settled in our nest, ate our food, and as you grew, you crowded us out. We loved you, but we couldn't even come near you, for fear that you'd swallow us up. For our own safety, we were forced to run away and secretly raise this army. And now we stand with it, armed with powers that you yourself have caused to stand against you. You treated us poorly, you looked at us with anger, and you broke the faith and trust you swore to us when you were younger.

KING

You've said all this already. You've announced it in marketplaces, given sermons on it in churches. You've tried to make rebellion look pleasant in the eyes of all the fickle turncoats and poor malcontents, who laugh and clap eagerly at the news that a revolution is coming. But rebellion always trades in these kinds of thin excuses, and never lacks angry beggars, desperate for mayhem and chaos.

PRINCE HENRY

Both our armies are full of men who will make the ultimate sacrifice in this battle, once it starts. Tell your nephew that the Prince of Wales joins the whole world

The Prince of Wales doth join with all the world
In praise of Henry Percy. By my hopes,
This present enterprise set off his head,
I do not think a braver gentleman,
90   More active-valiant, or more valiant-young,
More daring or more bold, is now alive
To grace this latter age with noble deeds.
For my part, I may speak it to my shame,
I have a truant been to chivalry,
95   And so I hear he doth account me too.
Yet this before my father's majesty:
I am content that he shall take the odds
Of his great name and estimation,
And will, to save the blood on either side,
100   Try fortune with him in a single fight.

KING
And, Prince of Wales, so dare we venture thee,
Albeit considerations infinite
Do make against it.—No, good Worcester, no,
We love our people well, even those we love
105   That are misled upon your cousin's part.
And, will they take the offer of our grace,
Both he and they and you, yea, every man
Shall be my friend again, and I'll be his.
So tell your cousin, and bring me word
110   What he will do. But if he will not yield,
Rebuke and dread correction wait on us,
And they shall do their office. So begone.
We will not now be troubled with reply.
We offer fair. Take it advisedly.

Exeunt WORCESTER *and* VERNON

PRINCE HENRY
115   It will not be accepted, on my life.
The Douglas and the Hotspur both together
Are confident against the world in arms.

in praising Henry Percy. Except for his current endeavor, I don't think there's a man alive who is braver, more heroic, more daring, or more bold.

As for me, I'm ashamed to admit that I've shirked my responsibilities. I hear that he agrees with me on that point. And yet—and I say this in front of my father— in order to avoid casualties on both sides, I want to challenge him in hand-to-hand combat. And I'm content to admit that, based on his good name and reputation, he's the favorite to win.

KING

Prince of Wales, I'd support that idea, except that there are countless reasons why I shouldn't. No, Worcester, no. I love my subjects, even those who have mistakenly followed your nephew's lead. If they accept our pardon, then he, you, and they will all be my friends again, and I'll be theirs. Tell your nephew this, and bring back his answer.

But if he doesn't surrender, he will be rebuked and harshly punished. So, be gone. I don't want to hear anymore from you now. I offer a fair deal; I advise you to accept it.

WORCESTER *and* VERNON *exit.*

PRINCE HENRY

He won't accept. I'll bet my life on it. Douglas and Hotspur are convinced that they could take on the whole world together.

KING
Hence, therefore, every leader to his charge,
For on their answer will we set on them,
120 And God befriend us as our cause is just.

Exeunt all but PRINCE HENRY *and* FALSTAFF

FALSTAFF
Hal, if thou see me down in the battle and bestride me, so;
'tis a point of friendship.

PRINCE HENRY
Nothing but a colossus can do thee that friendship.
Say thy prayers, and farewell.

FALSTAFF
125 I would 'twere bedtime, Hal, and all well.

PRINCE HENRY
Why, thou owest God a death.

Exit PRINCE HENRY

FALSTAFF
'Tis not due yet. I would be loath to pay Him before His
day. What need I be so forward with Him that calls not on
me? Well, 'tis no matter. Honour pricks me on. Yea, but
130 how if honor prick me off when I come on? How then? Can
honor set to a leg? no. Or an arm? no. Or take away the grief
of a wound? No. Honor hath no skill in surgery, then? No.
What is honor? A word. What is in that word "honor"?
What is that "honor"? Air. A trim reckoning. Who hath it?
135 He that died o' Wednesday. Doth he feel it? No. Doth he
hear it? No. 'Tis insensible, then? Yea, to the dead. But will
it not live with the living? No. Why? Detraction will not
suffer it. Therefore, I'll none of it. Honor is a mere
scutcheon. And so ends my catechism.

Exit

KING

> Then everyone get to their battalions. As soon as they respond, we'll attack. May God be with us. Our cause is just!

Everyone exits except PRINCE HENRY *and* FALSTAFF.

FALSTAFF

> Hal, if you see me fall in battle, stand over me, like this. It would be an act of friendship.

PRINCE HENRY

> Only a giant could do you that friendship. Say your prayers, and farewell.

FALSTAFF

> I wish it were bedtime, Hal, and everything were okay.

PRINCE HENRY

> But you owe God a death.

PRINCE HENRY *exits.*

FALSTAFF

catechism = a series of questions and answers that tests students' understanding of Christian principles

> It's not due yet. I'd hate to pay him before the due date. Why should I be so eager to pay him before he even asks for it? Well, it doesn't matter: honor spurs me on. Yeah, but what if honor spurs me off once I'm on, and picks me out to die? What happens then? Can honor set a broken leg? No. Or an arm? No. Can it make a wound stop hurting? No. Honor can't perform surgery, then? No. What is honor? A word. What is in that word, "honor?" What is that "honor?" Air. Quite a bargain! Who has it? A guy who died last Wednesday. Does he feel it? No. Does he hear it? No. It can't be detected, then? Right—not by the dead, anyway. But won't it live with the living? No. Why? Slander won't allow it. That's why I don't want any part of it. Honor is nothing more than a gravestone, and that concludes my catechism.

He exits.

ACT 5, SCENE 2

Enter WORCESTER *and Sir Richard* VERNON

WORCESTER
O no, my nephew must not know, Sir Richard,
The liberal and kind offer of the King.

VERNON
'Twere best he did.

WORCESTER
                              Then are we all undone.
It is not possible, it cannot be
5   The King should keep his word in loving us.
He will suspect us still and find a time
To punish this offense in other faults.
Suspicion all our lives shall be stuck full of eyes,
For treason is but trusted like the fox,
10 Who, never so tame, so cherished and locked up,
Will have a wild trick of his ancestors.
Look how we can, or sad or merrily,
Interpretation will misquote our looks,
And we shall feed like oxen at a stall,
15 The better cherished still the nearer death.
My nephew's trespass may be well forgot;
It hath the excuse of youth and heat of blood,
And an adopted name of privilege—
A hairbrained Hotspur governed by a spleen:
20 All his offenses live upon my head
And on his father's. We did train him on,
And, his corruption being ta'en from us,
We as the spring of all shall pay for all.
Therefore, good cousin, let not Harry know
25 In any case the offer of the King.

VERNON
Deliver what you will; I'll say 'tis so.

ACT 5, SCENE 2

WORCESTER *and Sir Richard* VERNON *enter.*

WORCESTER

Oh no, Sir Richard, my nephew cannot be told about the generous and kind offer the King made.

VERNON

But he should be told.

WORCESTER

It will be the end of all of us! There is absolutely no way that the King will keep his word and trust us again. He will always be wary of us. He'll find other reasons to punish us for this rebellion. For the rest of our lives he and his loyalists will look on us with suspicion. Treason is like a fox: you can tame it, care for it, and put it in a cage, but it will always have the wild instincts it inherited from its ancestors. No matter how we look—sad or happy—people will interpret our looks in the worst possible light. We'll be like oxen in a stall: the better they're fed, the closer they are to being slaughtered.

My nephew's disloyalty might be forgiven: his young age and hot temper will excuse it. Plus, his nickname gives him permission: Hotspur the Harebrain, always flaring up. All his offenses will be blamed on me and his father. After all, we encouraged him, and since we taught him to be angry at the King, we'll pay for it. So cousin, don't by any means let Harry know what the King offered.

VERNON

Tell him what you want, and I'll back you up.

Enter HOTSPUR *and* DOUGLAS

Here comes your cousin.

HOTSPUR

My uncle is returned.
Deliver up my Lord of Westmoreland.—
Uncle, what news?

WORCESTER

30   The King will bid you battle presently.

DOUGLAS

Defy him by the Lord of Westmoreland.

HOTSPUR

Lord Douglas, go you and tell him so.

DOUGLAS

Marry, and shall, and very willingly.

Exit DOUGLAS

WORCESTER

There is no seeming mercy in the King.

HOTSPUR

35   Did you beg any? God forbid!

WORCESTER

I told him gently of our grievances,
Of his oath-breaking, which he mended thus
By now forswearing that he is forsworn.
He calls us "rebels," "traitors," and will scourge
40   With haughty arms this hateful name in us.

Enter DOUGLAS

DOUGLAS

Arm, gentlemen, to arms. For I have thrown
A brave defiance in King Henry's teeth,
And Westmoreland, that was engaged, did bear it,
Which cannot choose but bring him quickly on.

WORCESTER

45   The Prince of Wales stepped forth before the King,
And, nephew, challenged you to single fight.

HOTSPUR *and* DOUGLAS *enter.*

Here comes your nephew.

HOTSPUR

My uncle's back. Free Westmoreland, his hostage. Uncle, what's happening?

WORCESTER

The King will beckon you to battle shortly.

DOUGLAS

Have Westmoreland deliver your message of defiance.

HOTSPUR

Douglas, go tell him to do that.

DOUGLAS

Indeed, I will, and gladly.

DOUGLAS *exits.*

WORCESTER

The King doesn't appear willing to forgive us.

HOTSPUR

Did you ask him to? God forbid!

WORCESTER

I politely told him what our issues were. I accused him of breaking his promise to us, and here's how he answered: he lied about the fact that he lied. He called us rebels, traitors, and said he'd punish us with his mighty army.

DOUGLAS *enters.*

DOUGLAS

Get your weapons, gentlemen, get your weapons! I sent King Henry a brave and defiant message, and Westmoreland, who was our hostage, will deliver it. This will surely bring the battle on immediately.

WORCESTER

The Prince of Wales stepped forward, nephew, and challenged you to a one-on-one fight.

HOTSPUR
O, would the quarrel lay upon our heads,
And that no man might draw short breath today
But I and Harry Monmouth! Tell me, tell me,
50   How showed his tasking? Seemed it in contempt?

VERNON
No, by my soul. I never in my life
Did hear a challenge urged more modestly,
Unless a brother should a brother dare
To gentle exercise and proof of arms.
55   He gave you all the duties of a man,
Trimmed up your praises with a princely tongue,
Spoke your deservings like a chronicle,
Making you ever better than his praise
By still dispraising praise valued in you,
60   And, which became him like a prince indeed,
He made a blushing cital of himself,
And chid his truant youth with such a grace
As if he mastered there a double spirit
Of teaching and of learning instantly.
65   There did he pause: but let me tell the world:
If he outlive the envy of this day,
England did never owe so sweet a hope,
So much misconstrued in his wantonness.

HOTSPUR
Cousin, I think thou art enamorèd
70   On his follies. Never did I hear
Of any Prince so wild a liberty.
But be he as he will, yet once ere night
I will embrace him with a soldier's arm,
That he shall shrink under my courtesy.—
75   Arm, arm with speed, and, fellows, soldiers, friends,
Better consider what you have to do
Than I that have not well the gift of tongue
Can lift your blood up with persuasion.

HOTSPUR

Monmouth is the town in Wales where Hal was born.

Oh, I wish the whole battle were between us, and that the only people who would lose their breath today would be me and Harry Monmouth! Tell me, tell me, what was the tone of his challenge? Did he show contempt for me?

VERNON

No, I swear; I never heard a challenge issued more gracefully. It was like a brother asking a brother to a little friendly competition. He paid you all due respect, and he summed up your good qualities in the most princely language. He spoke of how deserving you are, as though he were your biographer. He claimed you were even above praise, for simple praise could never measure up to your true merits. And he gave a modest account of himself, as well, which made him seem like a true prince indeed. He berated himself for having behaved wildly, but he said this so gracefully that he sounded like a teacher giving a lesson and a student learning one at the same time. There he stopped, but let me say this: if he survives this battle, then England never had a sweeter hope, nor one so misunderstood in his recklessness.

HOTSPUR

I think you've been charmed by his foolishness. I've never heard of a Prince who was so wild and loose. But however he wants to seem, before night falls I will embrace him with these soldier's arms, and he will tremble at my affection.

Get ready, get ready quickly! And friends, partners, soldiers, take a moment to think for yourselves about what you have to do. I'm not a good enough speaker to motivate you.

Enter a MESSENGER

MESSENGER
   My lord, here are letters for you.

HOTSPUR
80   I cannot read them now.—
   O gentlemen, the time of life is short;
   To spend that shortness basely were too long
   If life did ride upon a dial's point,
   Still ending at the arrival of an hour.
85   An if we live, we live to tread on kings;
   If die, brave death, when princes die with us.
   Now, for our consciences, the arms are fair
   When the intent of bearing them is just.

Enter another MESSENGER

SECOND MESSENGER
   My lord, prepare. The King comes on apace.

HOTSPUR
90   I thank him that he cuts me from my tale,
   For I profess not talking. Only this:
   Let each man do his best. And here draw I a sword,
   Whose temper I intend to stain
   With the best blood that I can meet withal
95   In the adventure of this perilous day.
   Now, Esperance! Percy! And set on.
   Sound all the lofty instruments of war,
   And by that music let us all embrace,
   For, heaven to earth, some of us never shall
100   A second time do such a courtesy.

Here they embrace. The trumpets sound.

                                                        Exeunt

A MESSENGER *enters.*

MESSENGER

My lord, I have some letters for you.

HOTSPUR

I can't read them now. Oh, gentlemen, life is short. But if you spend that brief time shamefully, you are wasting your time: even if life lasted only an hour, it would still be too long. If we live, it will be in triumph over kings. If we die, it will be a glorious death, since princes will die with us. As for our consciences, our battle is fair: it's right to bear arms when the cause is just.

Another MESSENGER *enters.*

SECOND MESSENGER

My lord, get ready. The King has launched his attack.

HOTSPUR

I thank him for cutting off my speech, since I have no talent for speaking. Only one more thing: each man should do his best, and with that I will draw my sword. On this dangerous day, I intend to stain it with the best blood I can find. "Hope is my comfort!" Percy! Let's go! Sound all the imposing instruments of battle, and let's embrace one another to the tune of that music. For, by heaven, some of us will never be able to do that again.

They embrace. The trumpets sound.

They exit.

ACT 5, SCENE 3

The KING *enters with his power and they cross the stage.*
Alarum to the battle.

Then enter DOUGLAS *and Sir Walter* BLUNT, *disguised as*
the KING

BLUNT
What is thy name that in the battle thus
Thou crossest me? What honor dost thou seek
Upon my head?

DOUGLAS
Know then, my name is Douglas,
5   And I do haunt thee in the battle thus
Because some tell me that thou art a king.

BLUNT
They tell thee true.

DOUGLAS
The Lord of Stafford dear today hath bought
Thy likeness, for instead of thee, King Harry,
10   This sword hath ended him. So shall it thee,
Unless thou yield thee as my prisoner.

BLUNT
I was not born a yielder, thou proud Scot,
And thou shalt find a king that will revenge
Lord Stafford's death.

They fight. DOUGLAS *kills* BLUNT. *Enter* HOTSPUR

HOTSPUR
15   O Douglas, hadst thou fought at Holmedon thus,
I never had triumphed upon a Scot.

DOUGLAS
All's done, all's won; here breathless lies the King.

ACT 5, SCENE 3

The KING *crosses the stage with his army. The trumpets sound the call to battle.*

DOUGLAS *and Sir Walter* BLUNT *enter.* BLUNT *is disguised as the* KING.

BLUNT

What is your name—you, who are attacking me like this? What honor do you think you'll get by fighting me?

DOUGLAS

My name is Douglas, and I'm haunting you in this battle because they tell me you are a king.

BLUNT

They tell you the truth.

DOUGLAS

Today, Lord Stafford paid for resembling you so well, for instead of you, King Harry, my sword killed him. Now it will kill you, unless you surrender as my prisoner.

BLUNT

I was not born to surrender, you arrogant Scotsman. You're about to see a king take revenge for Stafford's death.

They fight. DOUGLAS *kills* BLUNT. HOTSPUR *enters.*

HOTSPUR

Oh, Douglas! If you'd fought like this at Holmedon, I would never have been able to beat you.

DOUGLAS

It's over, we've won: here's the King, dead.

HOTSPUR
Where?

DOUGLAS
Here.

HOTSPUR
20   This, Douglas? No, I know this face full well.
A gallant knight he was; his name was Blunt,
Semblably furnished like the King himself.

DOUGLAS
(to BLUNT*)* A fool go with thy soul whither it goes!
A borrowed title hast thou bought too dear.
25   Why didst thou tell me that thou wert a king?

HOTSPUR
The King hath many marching in his coats.

DOUGLAS
Now, by my sword, I will kill all his coats.
I'll murder all his wardrobe, piece by piece,
Until I meet the King.

HOTSPUR
                                        Up and away!
30   Our soldiers stand full fairly for the day.

Exeunt

Alarum. Enter FALSTAFF *alone.*

FALSTAFF
Though I could 'scape shot-free at London, I fear the shot
here. Here's no scoring but upon the pate.—Soft, who are
you? Sir Walter Blunt. There's honor for you. Here's no
vanity. I am as hot as molten lead, and as heavy too. God
35   keep lead out of me; I need no more weight than mine own
bowels. I have led my ragamuffins where they are peppered.
There's not three of my hundred and fifty left alive, and
they are for the town's end, to beg during life. But who
comes here?

HOTSPUR

Where?

DOUGLAS

Here.

HOTSPUR

This, Douglas? No. I know this man: he was a brave knight, by the name of Blunt; he is disguised as the King.

DOUGLAS

(to BLUNT*)* Wherever your soul is off to now, let it carry the name of fool! You paid too much for that borrowed title. Why did you tell me you were a king?

HOTSPUR

The King has many men on the battlefield disguised in his uniform.

DOUGLAS

Now, I swear on my sword, I'll kill all his uniforms! I'll murder every item of his clothing, one piece at a time, until I find the King himself.

HOTSPUR

Get going! Our side looks like it will win today.

They exit.

The trumpets play a call to arms. FALSTAFF *enters, alone.*

FALSTAFF

escape shot-free
= leave without
paying the bill

I could always escape shot-free in London, but I'm scared of getting shot out here. Here, you take it on the head. Wait a minute—who's this? Sir Walter Blunt! There's honor for you, but no vanity! I'm as hot as molten lead, and as heavy, too; so God keep the lead out of me. I don't need any lead bullets in my belly—my own guts are heavy enough. My army of ragged bums has been massacred. Not even three of my hundred-fifty troops are still alive, and the ones who are have run away, to panhandle in the streets. Who's coming?

Enter PRINCE HENRY

PRINCE HENRY
40   What, stand'st thou idle here? Lend me thy sword.
     Many a nobleman lies stark and stiff
     Under the hoofs of vaunting enemies,
     Whose deaths are yet unrevenged. I prithee,
     Lend me thy sword.

FALSTAFF
45   O Hal, I prithee, give me leave to breathe awhile. Turk
     Gregory never did such deeds in arms as I have done this
     day. I have paid Percy; I have made him sure.

PRINCE HENRY
     He is indeed, and living to kill thee.
     I prithee, lend me thy sword.

FALSTAFF
50   Nay, before God, Hal, if Percy be alive, thou gett'st not my
     sword; but take my pistol, if thou wilt.

PRINCE HENRY
     Give it to me. What, is it in the case?

FALSTAFF
     Ay, Hal, 'tis hot, 'tis hot. There's that will sack a city.
     (PRINCE HENRY *draws it out and finds it to be a bottle of sack*)

PRINCE HENRY
55   What, is it a time to jest and dally now?

     He throws the bottle at him.
                                          Exit PRINCE HENRY

FALSTAFF
     Well, if Percy be alive, I'll pierce him. If he do come in my
     way, so; if he do not, if I come in his willingly, let him make
     a carbonado of me. I like not such grinning honor as Sir
     Walter hath. Give me life, which if I can save, so: if not,
60   honor comes unlooked for, and there's an end.
                                          Exit

PRINCE HENRY *enters.*

PRINCE HENRY

What, are you standing here doing nothing? Give me your sword. Many good men are lying cold and dead on the ground, with the enemy's horses galloping over them. Their deaths have not been revenged. Come, give me your sword.

FALSTAFF

Oh, Hal, please, give me a moment to catch my breath. No one has ever fought as heroically as I did today. I've killed Percy, I've made him safe.

PRINCE HENRY

You're right; he's safe, and now he's coming to kill you. Now please, give me your sword.

FALSTAFF

No, Hal, I swear to God! If Percy's alive, you're not taking my sword. But you can have my gun, if you want.

PRINCE HENRY

Give it to me. Is it in its holster?

FALSTAFF

"Sack" is a pun, meaning both "ransack" and a kind of white wine.

Yup. It's hot, hot; it could sack a city. *(PRINCE HENRY opens the holster and finds a bottle of white wine)*

PRINCE HENRY

Is this a time to joke and fool around?

He throws the bottle at FALSTAFF.

PRINCE HENRY *exits.*

FALSTAFF

If Percy's alive, I'll pierce him. If he runs into me, fine. If he doesn't run into me, but I run into him, let him slice me like a butcher. I don't want the kind of honor Sir Walter has: give me life. If I manage to save my life, fine. If not, I'll have honor that I never looked for, and that'll be that.

He exits.

ACT 5, SCENE 4

Alarum. Excursions. Enter the KING, PRINCE HENRY, *Lord John of* LANCASTER, *and the Earl of* WESTMORELAND

KING
 I prithee, Harry, withdraw thyself. Thou bleedest too much.
 Lord John of Lancaster, go you with him.

LANCASTER
 Not I, my lord, unless I did bleed too.

PRINCE HENRY
 I beseech your Majesty, make up,
5 Lest your retirement do amaze your friends.

KING
 I will do so.—My Lord of Westmoreland,
 Lead him to his tent.

WESTMORELAND
 Come, my lord, I'll lead you to your tent.

PRINCE HENRY
 Lead me, my lord? I do not need your help,
10 And God forbid a shallow scratch should drive
 The Prince of Wales from such a field as this,
 Where stained nobility lies trodden on,
 And rebels' arms triumph in massacres.

LANCASTER
 We breathe too long. Come, cousin Westmoreland,
15 Our duty this way lies. For God's sake, come.

Exeunt Lord John of LANCASTER *and* WESTMORELAND

PRINCE HENRY
 By God, thou hast deceived me, Lancaster.
 I did not think thee lord of such a spirit.
 Before, I loved thee as a brother, John,
 But now, I do respect thee as my soul.

ACT 5, SCENE 4

Trumpets sound battle calls. Soldiers skirmish. The
KING, PRINCE HENRY, *injured and bleeding, Lord John*
of LANCASTER, *and* WESTMORELAND *enter.*

KING

Please, Harry, get out of here: you're bleeding too
heavily. John of Lancaster, go with him.

LANCASTER

I won't leave, my lord, unless I am bleeding too.

PRINCE HENRY

I beg your highness, advance. Your army will lose
heart if it sees you falling back.

KING

I will. My Lord of Westmoreland, take him to his tent.

WESTMORELAND

(to PRINCE HENRY*)* Come, my lord. I'll lead you to
your tent.

PRINCE HENRY

Lead me, my lord? I don't need your help. God forbid
that a shallow scratch could make the Prince of Wales
retreat from a battlefield like this one, where great
men are falling and being trampled upon, and rebels
are triumphing in their massacres!

LANCASTER

We've stopped for too long. Come, Westmoreland.
We have work to do. For God's sake, come on!

LANCASTER *and* WESTMORELAND *exit.*

PRINCE HENRY

By God, you have deceived me, Lancaster. I didn't
think you were that brave. Before, I loved you as a
brother; now, I respect you as my soulmate.

KING
20   I saw him hold Lord Percy at the point
      With lustier maintenance than I did look for
      Of such an ungrown warrior.

PRINCE HENRY
      O, this boy lends mettle to us all.

Exit

Enter DOUGLAS

DOUGLAS
      Another king! they grow like Hydra's heads.—
25   I am the Douglas, fatal to all those
      That wear those colors on them. What art thou
      That counterfeit'st the person of a king?

KING
      The King himself, who, Douglas, grieves at heart,
      So many of his shadows thou hast met
30   And not the very king. I have two boys
      Seek Percy and thyself about the field,
      But, seeing thou fall'st on me so luckily,
      I will assay thee. And defend thyself.

DOUGLAS
      I fear thou art another counterfeit,
35   And yet, in faith, thou bear'st thee like a king.
      But mine I am sure thou art, whoe'er thou be,
      And thus I win thee.

They fight. The KING *being in danger, enter* PRINCE HENRY *of Wales*

PRINCE HENRY
      Hold up thy head, vile Scot, or thou art like
      Never to hold it up again. The spirits
40   Of valiant Shirley, Stafford, Blunt are in my arms.
      It is the Prince of Wales that threatens thee,
      Who never promiseth but he means to pay.

KING

> He had Percy cornered, and he carried himself more bravely than I would have expected of such a young warrior.

PRINCE HENRY

> Oh, this boy lends us all courage!

> *PRINCE HENRY exits.*

> *DOUGLAS enters.*

DOUGLAS

> Another king! The more of them we kill, the more of them spring up. I am Douglas, and I bring death to everyone wearing that uniform. Who are you, disguised as a king?

KING

> The King himself. And it pains me, Douglas, that you ran into so many of my shadows, and not me. I have two sons on the field, looking for Percy and for you. But, since you were lucky enough to come upon me, I'll fight you myself. Defend yourself.

DOUGLAS

> I fear that you're another fake; and yet, you bear yourself like a king. Whoever you are, you're mine, and I'll defeat you.

> *They fight. The KING begins to lose. PRINCE HENRY of Wales enters.*

PRINCE HENRY

> Look at me, you nasty Scotsman, or you'll never look at anything again. I have the spirits of brave Shirley, Stafford, and Blunt in me. It is the Prince of Wales who threatens you, and I never make promises I cannot keep.

They fight. DOUGLAS *flieth*

Cheerly, my lord. How fares your Grace?
Sir Nicholas Gawsey hath for succor sent,
45   And so hath Clifton. I'll to Clifton straight.

KING

Stay, and breathe awhile.
Thou hast redeemed thy lost opinion
And showed thou mak'st some tender of my life
In this fair rescue thou hast brought to me.

PRINCE HENRY

50   O God, they did me too much injury
That ever said I hearkened for your death.
If it were so, I might have let alone
The insulting hand of Douglas over you,
Which would have been as speedy in your end
55   As all the poisonous potions in the world,
And saved the treacherous labor of your son.

KING

Make up to Clifton. I'll to Sir Nicholas Gawsey.

Exit the KING

Enter HOTSPUR

HOTSPUR

If I mistake not, thou art Harry Monmouth.

PRINCE HENRY

Thou speak'st as if I would deny my name.

HOTSPUR

60   My name is Harry Percy.

PRINCE HENRY

Why, then I see
A very valiant rebel of the name.
I am the Prince of Wales; and think not, Percy,
To share with me in glory any more.
Two stars keep not their motion in one sphere,

They fight. DOUGLAS *runs away.*

Cheer up, father. How are you? Sir Nicholas Gawsey called for reinforcements, and so has Clifton. I'm going to Clifton right now.

KING

Wait, and breathe for a moment. You have redeemed your bad reputation, and show that you care something for me, by rescuing me like this.

PRINCE HENRY

Oh God! Anyone who ever said I wished for you to die did me a terrible wrong. If I wanted that, I would have let Douglas continue his attack. That would have killed you faster than any dose of poison, and it would have saved me the trouble of treachery.

KING

Go to Clifton; I'll go to Sir Nicholas Gawsey.

The KING *exits.*

HOTSPUR *enters.*

HOTSPUR

If I'm not mistaken, you're Harry Monmouth.

PRINCE HENRY

You make it sound as if I'd deny it.

HOTSPUR

My name is Harry Percy.

PRINCE HENRY

Why then, I'm looking at a very brave rebel by that name. I am the Prince of Wales, and don't think, Percy, that you can share in my glory any longer. There isn't enough room for two stars in the same orbit; England cannot handle a double reign, Harry Percy and the Prince of Wales ruling at once.

65   Nor can one England brook a double reign,
            Of Harry Percy and the Prince of Wales.

HOTSPUR
            Nor shall it, Harry, for the hour is come
            To end the one of us, and would to God
            Thy name in arms were now as great as mine.

PRINCE HENRY
70   I'll make it greater ere I part from thee,
            And all the budding honors on thy crest
            I'll crop, to make a garland for my head.

HOTSPUR
            I can no longer brook thy vanities.

They fight

Enter FALSTAFF

FALSTAFF
            Well said, Hal! To it Hal! Nay, you shall find no boys' play
75   here, I can tell you.

Enter DOUGLAS. *He fighteth with* FALSTAFF, *who falls down as if he were dead.*

                                    Exit DOUGLAS

PRINCE HENRY *killeth* HOTSPUR

HOTSPUR
            O Harry, thou hast robbed me of my youth.
            I better brook the loss of brittle life
            Than those proud titles thou hast won of me.
80   They wound my thoughts worse than thy sword my flesh.
            But thoughts, the slave of life, and life, time's fool,
            And time, that takes survey of all the world,
            Must have a stop. O, I could prophesy,
            But that the earthy and cold hand of death

HOTSPUR

> It won't have to, Harry, for the time has come for one of us to die. I only wish that you had as great a reputation in warfare as I do.

PRINCE HENRY

> My reputation will be greater by the time we part. I'll take all the flowers of honor from your helmet, and turn them into a garland for myself.

HOTSPUR

> I can't stand your arrogance any longer.

They fight.

FALSTAFF *enters.*

FALSTAFF

> Well said, Hal! Go for it, Hal! This isn't child's play, I'll tell you that much!

DOUGLAS *returns and fights with* **FALSTAFF**, *who falls down and plays dead.*

> **DOUGLAS** *exits.*

PRINCE HENRY *kills* **HOTSPUR**.

HOTSPUR

> Oh, Harry, you've taken away my youth. I can handle the loss of my fragile life, but not the loss of all the honors you have won from me: that loss wounds my thoughts more than your sword wounds my flesh. But thought depends on life, and life depends on time, and time, which watches over the whole world, must stop eventually. Oh, I could make prophecies, but the cold

85 Lies on my tongue. No, Percy, thou art dust,
    And food for— *(he dies)*

PRINCE HENRY
    For worms, brave Percy. Fare thee well, great heart.
    Ill-weaved ambition, how much art thou shrunk!
    When that this body did contain a spirit,
90 A kingdom for it was too small a bound,
    But now two paces of the vilest earth
    Is room enough. This earth that bears thee dead
    Bears not alive so stout a gentleman.
    If thou wert sensible of courtesy,
95 I should not make so dear a show of zeal.
    But let my favors hide thy mangled face;
    And even in thy behalf I'll thank myself
    For doing these fair rites of tenderness.
    Adieu, and take thy praise with thee to heaven.
100 Thy ignominy sleep with thee in the grave,
    But not remembered in thy epitaph.

    He spieth FALSTAFF *on the ground*

    What, old acquaintance, could not all this flesh
    Keep in a little life? Poor Jack, farewell.
    I could have better spared a better man.
105 O, I should have a heavy miss of thee
    If I were much in love with vanity.
    Death hath not struck so fat a deer today,
    Though many dearer in this bloody fray.
    Emboweled will I see thee by and by;
110 Till then in blood by noble Percy lie.

                            Exit PRINCE HENRY

    FALSTAFF *riseth up*

FALSTAFF
    Emboweled? If thou embowel me today, I'll give you leave
    to powder me and eat me too tomorrow. 'Sblood, 'twas time

hand of death is stopping my tongue. No, Percy. You are dust, and food for—*(he dies)*

PRINCE HENRY

For worms, brave Percy. Farewell, brave soul. Your ambition, aimed at evil, ends—look at how withered it has become. When this body contained a soul, an entire kingdom was too small to hold it. But now, two paces of wretched earth is plenty of room. The ground that you lie dead upon doesn't have a single living man upon it as brave as you. If you could hear me, I wouldn't praise you so lavishly. But let me cover your battered face with part of my uniform. I'll thank myself on your behalf for doing these rites of respect.

Adieu, and take my praise of you to heaven. Let your disgraces sleep with you in the grave, and let them be kept off your tombstone!

He sees FALSTAFF *lying on the ground.*

What? My old friend? Couldn't all this flesh hold onto a little life? Poor Jack, farewell. I would rather have lost a more valuable soldier. If I were in love with vanity, I'd really miss you.

embowelled = disemboweled, in order to be embalmed

Death hasn't taken anyone as fat today, though it has taken many better men in this vicious battle. I'll have you embowelled soon; till then, lie here in blood, by the great Percy.

PRINCE HENRY *exits.*

FALSTAFF *stands up.*

FALSTAFF

Embowelled? If you cut me open today, I'll let you pickle me and eat me tomorrow. Damn! I had to fake

to counterfeit, or that hot termagant Scot had paid me scot
and lot too. Counterfeit? I lie. I am no counterfeit. To die is
115   to be a counterfeit, for he is but the counterfeit of a man who
hath not the life of a man; but to counterfeit dying when a
man thereby liveth is to be no counterfeit, but the true and
perfect image of life indeed. The better part of valor is
discretion, in the which better part I have saved my life.
120   Zounds, I am afraid of this gunpowder Percy, though he be
dead. How if he should counterfeit too and rise? By my
faith, I am afraid he would prove the better counterfeit.
Therefore I'll make him sure, yea, and I'll swear I killed
him. Why may not he rise as well as I? Nothing confutes me
125   but eyes, and nobody sees me. Therefore, sirrah, *(stabs the
body)* with a new wound in your thigh, come you along with
me. *(he takes up* HOTSPUR *on his back)*

Enter PRINCE HENRY *and Lord John of* LANCASTER

PRINCE HENRY
Come, brother John. Full bravely hast thou fleshed
Thy maiden sword.

LANCASTER
                          But soft, whom have we here?
130   Did you not tell me this fat man was dead?

PRINCE HENRY
I did; I saw him dead,
Breathless and bleeding on the ground.—Art thou alive?
Or is it fantasy that plays upon our eyesight?
I prithee, speak. We will not trust our eyes
135   Without our ears. Thou art not what thou seem'st.

FALSTAFF
No, that's certain. I am not a double man. But if I be not
Jack Falstaff, then am I a jack. There is Percy. If your father
will do me any honor, so; if not, let him kill the next Percy
himself. I look to be either earl or duke, I can assure you.

being dead, or that raging rebel of a Scotsman would have ended me. Fake? No, I tell a lie: I'm not a faker. To die is to be a faker, because a dead body is an imitation of a living one. But to fake being dead, in order to stay alive, that's no kind of faking. That's the truest kind of living there is. Bravery is mostly about precaution; I'm careful, and it saved my life. Damn, I'm scared of this bombshell Percy, even though he's dead. What if he's faking, too, and he gets up? I swear, he'd be the better faker. Therefore, I'll make sure he's dead; in fact, I'll swear that I killed him. Why couldn't he just get up, like I did? Only a witness could stop me, and there are no witnesses here. Therefore, sirrah, *(stabs the body)* you're coming with me—complete with a new wound in your thigh. *(he throws* HOTSPUR*'s body over his shoulder)*

PRINCE HENRY *and Lord John of* LANCASTER *enter.*

PRINCE HENRY

John, my brother, you've bravely proven yourself in this, your first battle.

LANCASTER

Wait! Who do we have here? Didn't you say this fat man was dead?

PRINCE HENRY

I did. I saw him dead on the ground, bleeding and not breathing. Are you alive? Or is this some kind of dream, playing with our sight? Talk to us. We won't trust our eyes without our ears. You aren't what you seem to be.

FALSTAFF

That's for sure. I'm not a double man. But if I'm not Jack Falstaff, then I'm a crook. Here's Percy. If the king will honor me for this, fine. If not, let him kill the

PRINCE HENRY
140   Why, Percy I killed myself, and saw thee dead.

FALSTAFF
    Didst thou? Lord, Lord, how this world is given to lying. I
    grant you, I was down and out of breath, and so was he, but
    we rose both at an instant and fought a long hour by
    Shrewsbury clock. If I may be believed, so; if not, let them
145   that should reward valor bear the sin upon their own heads.
    I'll take it upon my death, I gave him this wound in the
    thigh. If the man were alive and would deny it, zounds, I
    would make him eat a piece of my sword.

LANCASTER
    This is the strangest tale that ever I heard.

PRINCE HENRY
150   This is the strangest fellow, brother John.—
    Come, bring your luggage nobly on your back.
    For my part, if a lie may do thee grace,
    I'll gild it with the happiest terms I have.

    A retreat is sounded

    The trumpet sounds retreat; the day is ours.
155   Come, brother, let us to the highest of the field
    To see what friends are living, who are dead.

    Exeunt PRINCE HENRY *and Lord John of* LANCASTER

FALSTAFF
    I'll follow, as they say, for reward. He that rewards me, God
    reward him. If I do grow great, I'll grow less, for I'll purge
    and leave sack and live cleanly as a nobleman should do.
                                          Exit

next Percy himself. I expect to me made an earl or a Duke for this, I'll tell you that much.

PRINCE HENRY

Why, I killed Percy myself and I saw you dead.

FALSTAFF

You did? Lord, Lord, how people love to lie! I admit I had fallen and was out of breath, and so was he. But we both stood up at the same time and fought for a long hour. If I am to be believed, fine. If I'm not believed, then the guilt will lie with the people who are supposed to reward bravery. I swear on my life, I gave him this gash in the leg. Damn, if he were alive and said I didn't, I'd shove my sword down his throat.

LANCASTER

This is the strangest story I've ever heard.

PRINCE HENRY

This is the strangest man, John. All right then, display your prize on your back. As far as I'm concerned, if lying will help you out, I'll decorate your lie as prettily as I can.

A trumpet blows a call of retreat.

A trumpet is blowing retreat: we've won. Come on, brother. Let's get to high ground and see which of our friends are alive, and which are dead.

PRINCE HENRY and Lord John of LANCASTER exit.

FALSTAFF

I'll follow them and claim my reward. May God reward whoever rewards me. If I grow into a great man, I'll grow thinner: I'll go on a diet, quit drinking, and live properly, like a great man should.

He exits.

ACT 5, SCENE 5

The trumpets sound. Enter the KING, PRINCE HENRY, *Lord John of* LANCASTER, *Earl of* WESTMORELAND, *with* WORCESTER *and* VERNON *prisoners*

KING
Thus ever did rebellion find rebuke.—
Ill-spirited Worcester, did not we send grace,
Pardon, and terms of love to all of you?
And wouldst thou turn our offers contrary,
5   Misuse the tenor of thy kinsman's trust?
Three knights upon our party slain today,
A noble earl ,and many a creature else
Had been alive this hour,
If like a Christian thou hadst truly borne
10   Betwixt our armies true intelligence.

WORCESTER
What I have done my safety urged me to.
And I embrace this fortune patiently,
Since not to be avoided it falls on me.

KING
Bear Worcester to the death, and Vernon too.
15   Other offenders we will pause upon.

Exeunt WORCESTER *and* VERNON *under guard*

How goes the field?

PRINCE HENRY
The noble Scot, Lord Douglas, when he saw
The fortune of the day quite turned from him,
The noble Percy slain, and all his men
20   Upon the foot of fear, fled with the rest,
And, falling from a hill, he was so bruised
That the pursuers took him. At my tent

ACT 5, SCENE 5

Trumpets sound. The KING, PRINCE HENRY, *Lord John of* LANCASTER, *and* WESTMORELAND *enter, with* WORCESTER *and* VERNON *as prisoners.*

KING

This is how rebellions always end—defeated. Evil-spirited Worcester! Didn't I offer kindness, forgiveness and friendship to all of you? And you pretended that I did the opposite? Your relatives and friends trusted you, yet you lied to them? Three of our knights who were killed today, a noble earl, and many other men might have been alive right now if you had been a decent man and reported truthfully on the negotiations between our two armies.

WORCESTER

I did what I had to do for the sake of my own well-being. I accept my fate patiently, since there's no way I can avoid it.

KING

Put Worcester to death, and Vernon too: I'll wait a while before I decide what to do about the others.

WORCESTER *and* VERNON *are escorted away by guards.*

What's happening on the battlefield?

PRINCE HENRY

When that brave Scotsman, Lord Douglas, saw that things were turning against him, that Percy had been killed, and that his men were fleeing in terror, he ran away too. He fell down a hill and was so badly injured that our men were able to capture him. He's being held prisoner at my tent.

The Douglas is, and I beseech your Grace
I may dispose of him.

KING

                    With all my heart.

PRINCE HENRY

25   Then, brother John of Lancaster, to you
This honorable bounty shall belong.
Go to the Douglas, and deliver him
Up to his pleasure, ransomless and free.
His valor shown upon our crests today
30   Hath taught us how to cherish such high deeds,
Even in the bosom of our adversaries.

LANCASTER

I thank your Grace for this high courtesy,
Which I shall give away immediately.

KING

Then this remains, that we divide our power.
35   You, son John, and my cousin Westmoreland,
Towards York shall bend you with your dearest speed
To meet Northumberland and the prelate Scroop,
Who, as we hear, are busily in arms.
Myself and you, son Harry, will towards Wales
40   To fight with Glendower and the Earl of March.
Rebellion in this land shall lose his sway,
Meeting the check of such another day.
And since this business so fair is done,
Let us not leave till all our own be won.

                               Exeunt

I ask your highness to let me decide what to do with him.

KING

With all my heart.

PRINCE HENRY

Brother, John of Lancaster, I'm going to give you the honor of this generous act. Go to Douglas and set him free, with no ransom due. Let him do whatever he wants. His brave fighting against us today should be valued, even though he was our enemy.

LANCASTER

Thank you for giving me this honor. I'll take care of it immediately.

KING

All that's left is for us to split up our armies. You, my son John, and you, Westmoreland, head towards York as quickly as you can. Confront Northumberland and that churchman the Archbishop, who, I gather, are raising armies against us. You and I, Harry my son, will head for Wales to fight Glendower and Mortimer. The rebellion in this land will break apart once it meets battles like the one we fought today. And since we have accomplished our business so well, let's not quit until everything has been won.

They exit.

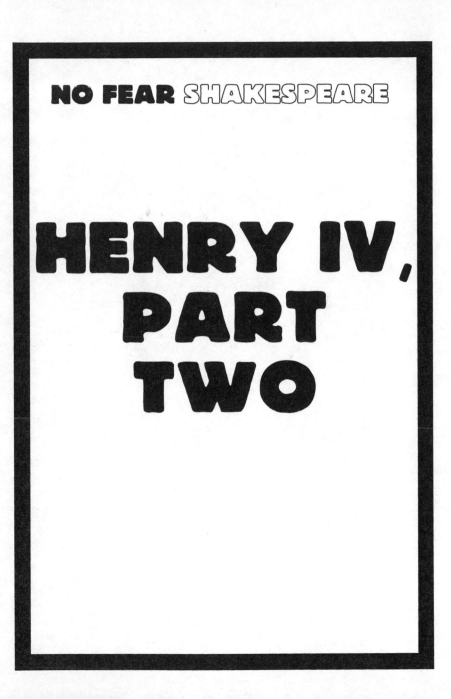

NO FEAR SHAKESPEARE

HENRY IV, PART TWO

CHARACTERS

King Henry IV—The reigning King of England, and the father of Prince Henry. His health declines throughout the play, due in part to his anxiety about civil insurrection and the fate of his seemingly irresponsible heir, Prince Henry.

Henry, Prince of Wales—The heir to the English throne. Prince Henry, or Harry, is known as Hal to Falstaff and his friends. Upon his father's death, he becomes King Henry V. He is the play's main protagonist, and his transformation from a youthful hell-raiser into the dignified King Henry V is one of the major psychological developments of the play.

Prince John, Duke of Lancaster; Humphrey, Duke of Gloucester; and **Thomas, Duke of Clarence**—Sons of King Henry IV and younger brothers of Prince Henry.

The Lord Chief Justice—The most powerful official of the law in England. Level-headed, perceptive, and intelligent, he is a close advisor to King Henry IV. He also becomes an advisor and father figure to Prince Henry after the King's death and Prince Henry's subsequent coronation.

Earl of Warwick, Earl of Surrey, Earl of Westmoreland, Harcourt, Sir John Blunt—Noblemen; King Henry IV's allies and advisors.

Sir John Falstaff—A fat, jovial, aging knight. Falstaff is a cheat and a liar, and the butt of many jokes and pranks. However, he seems well loved by his friends, especially the prostitute Doll Tearsheet. An incredibly popular character on the Elizabethan stage, Falstaff is Prince Henry's long-time mentor and close friend. However, as Prince Henry prepares himself for kingship by shedding his disreputable past, his relationship with Falstaff becomes increasingly strained.

Page—A boy whom Prince Henry has assigned to serve Falstaff. The page carries Falstaff's sword and runs his errands, and soon begins to imitate Falstaff in his insolence and disrespectfulness.

Poins, Peto, Bardolph—Friends of Falstaff and Prince Henry. Former crooks and highwaymen, these men have, like Falstaff, gained money and prestige since the Battle of Shrewsbury. Poins is the smartest of the three, and the closest to Henry. Bardolph, an incorrigible drunkard, has a bright red nose and welts all over his face.

Ancient Pistol—An army ensign (*ancient* meant "ensign" in Elizabethan English). Pistol serves under Falstaff and is extremely aggressive and belligerent.

Mouldy, Shadow, Wart, Feeble, and **Bullcalf**—Army recruits whom Falstaff inspects in Gloucestershire. Only Shadow, Wart, and Feeble go with Falstaff to the war; the others manage to bribe their way out.

Archbishop of York—A powerful northern clergyman who helps lead the rebellion against King Henry IV.

Mowbray and **Hastings**—Two lords who conspire with the Archbishop of York to overthrow King Henry IV.

Henry Percy, Earl of Northumberland—Usually called Northumberland, but sometimes called Percy. A powerful northern nobleman whose brother, the Earl of Worcester, and son Hotspur have recently been killed in battle against King Henry IV.

Hotspur—Dead before the play begins, but often referred to in its early scenes. Hotspur was Northumberland's son and a key leader in the rebellion against the King. In *King Henry IV, Part One*, the quick-tempered warrior Hotspur was a discernible contrast to the self-indulgent Prince Henry.

Lady Northumberland—Wife of the Earl of Northumberland.

Lady Percy—Hotspur's widow.

Lord Bardolph—An ally of Northumberland. Lord Bardolph is not to be confused with Bardolph, Falstaff's drunken associate.

Owen Glendower—The mysterious and influential leader of the Welsh rebellion. Glendower is a key figure in *Henry IV, Part One*, though his character never appears in *Part Two*.

Mistress Quickly—Proprietress of the Boar's Head Tavern in Eastcheap, London. She has a dim wit but a good heart.

Doll Tearsheet—Falstaff's favorite prostitute and a friend of Mistress Quickly. Doll Tearsheet seems both fiercer and smarter than most of the law officers in Eastcheap, and she also seems to have a deep and abiding affection for Falstaff.

Fang and **Snare**—Incompetent officers of the law whom Mistress Quickly calls upon to arrest Falstaff.

Justice Shallow and **Justice Silence**—Middle-class country landowners, and justices of the peace (minor local law officers). These two cousins live up to their names: Justice Shallow talks endlessly about trivial topics, while Justice Silence barely ever opens his mouth—except to sing rowdy songs when he gets drunk. Shallow is an old friend of Falstaff's from law school.

Davy—A household servant of Justice Shallow.

Travers—Northumberland's servant.

Master Gower—A messenger from the King, to the Lord Chief Justice.

Morton—A messenger from Shrewsbury, to Northumberland.

Sir John Coleville—A rebel, captured by Falstaff.

Rumor and **Epilogue**—Presenters who deliver the opening and concluding speeches, respectively. Rumor is the personification of rumor and gossip, and wears a costume painted with tongues.

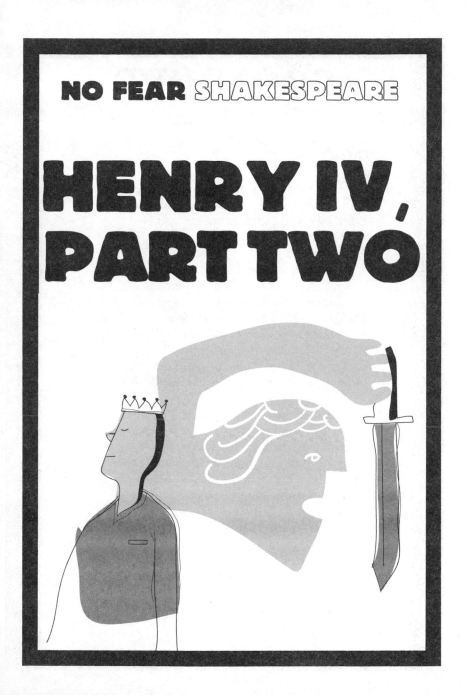

PROLOGUE

Enter RUMOR *all painted with tongues*

RUMOR

Open your ears, for which of you will stop
The vent of hearing when loud Rumor speaks?
I, from the orient to the drooping west,
Making the wind my post-horse, still unfold
5   The acts commenced on this ball of earth.
Upon my tongues continual slanders ride,
The which in every language I pronounce,
Stuffing the ears of men with false reports.
I speak of peace while covert enmity
10   Under the smile of safety wounds the world.
And who but Rumor, who but only I,
Make fearful musters and prepared defense,
Whiles the big year, swoll'n with some other grief,
Is thought with child by the stern tyrant war,
15   And no such matter? Rumor is a pipe
Blown by surmises, jealousies, conjectures,
And of so easy and so plain a stop
That the blunt monster with uncounted heads,
The still-discordant wav'ring multitude,
20   Can play upon it. But what need I thus
My well-known body to anatomize
Among my household? Why is Rumor here?
I run before King Harry's victory,
Who in a bloody field by Shrewsbury
25   Hath beaten down young Hotspur and his troops,
Quenching the flame of bold rebellion
Even with the rebels' blood. But what mean I
To speak so true at first? My office is
To noise abroad that Harry Monmouth fell

PROLOGUE

RUMOR *enters, wearing a costume covered with painted tongues.*

RUMOR

Open your ears! For who could possibly block them when loud Rumor speaks? I make the wind my horse, and ride it from the Orient in the east to the place where the sun sets in the west, describing the events taking place in the world. I continually tell lies and I tell them in every language, stuffing men's ears with falsehoods. I say that things are peaceful when, in reality, concealed hatred is at work, hidden behind smiles of good will.

And who but Rumor—who besides me—can make armies prepare anxious defenses, when in fact the world is uneasy for other reasons and there's no war coming at all? Rumor is like a flute. Guesswork, suspicion, and speculation are the breath that makes it sound, and it's so easy to play that even the common masses—that dim monster with innumerable heads, forever clamoring and wavering—can play it. But why should I describe myself in such detail to the one group of people who knows exactly what falsehood is all about: a theater audience? Why am I here?

King Henry has won the war, and at Shrewsbury, he ended the rebellion against him by defeating Hotspur and his allies, quenching the fire of revolt with the rebels' own blood. But what am I doing, telling you the truth up front? My job is to spread word that Hotspur in his fury killed Prince Hal, and that Douglas killed the King. I've spread this rumor through all

30 Under the wrath of noble Hotspur's sword,
And that the King before the Douglas' rage
Stooped his anointed head as low as death.
This have I rumored through the peasant towns
Between that royal field of Shrewsbury
35 And this worm-eaten hold of ragged stone,
Where Hotspur's father, old Northumberland,
Lies crafty-sick. The posts come tiring on,
And not a man of them brings other news
Than they have learnt of me. From Rumor's tongues
40 They bring smooth comforts false, worse than true wrongs.

Exit

the peasant villages from Shrewsbury to the place where I now stand: in front of the worm-eaten, dilapidated castle of Northumberland, Hotspur's father, who lies within and pretends to be sick.

The messengers are coming hot and heavy, and every single one of them will report nothing but what he's heard from me. Straight from Rumor, they bring pretty tales of false comfort, which are far worse than truthful news of misfortune.

RUMOR *exits.*

ACT ONE
SCENE 1

Enter LORD BARDOLPH

LORD BARDOLPH
Who keeps the gate here, ho?

Enter the PORTER

Where is the Earl?

PORTER
What shall I say you are?

LORD BARDOLPH
Tell thou the Earl
That the Lord Bardolph doth attend him here.

PORTER
His lordship is walked forth into the orchard.
Please it your Honor knock but at the gate
And he himself will answer.

Enter NORTHUMBERLAND

LORD BARDOLPH
Here comes the Earl.
Exit PORTER

NORTHUMBERLAND
What news, Lord Bardolph? Every minute now
Should be the father of some stratagem.
The times are wild. Contention, like a horse
Full of high feeding, madly hath broke loose
And bears down all before him.

ACT ONE
SCENE 1

LORD BARDOLPH *enters.*

LORD BARDOLPH
Hello? Who's the doorman around here?

The PORTER *opens the door.*

(to the PORTER*)* Where's the Earl?

PORTER
Who shall I say you are?

LORD BARDOLPH
Tell the Earl that the Lord Bardolph is here to see him.

PORTER
His lordship is out walking in the orchard. If you don't mind, knock at the orchard gate and he'll answer it himself.

NORTHUMBERLAND *enters from another side of the stage.*

LORD BARDOLPH
Here comes the Earl.

The PORTER *exits.*

NORTHUMBERLAND
What's the news, Lord Bardolph? Every minute, new violence erupts; it is a wild time. Conflict is like a horse, fed with too much rich food: it has broken out uncontrollably, and tramples everyone who stands before it.

LORD BARDOLPH

                              Noble Earl,
    I bring you certain news from Shrewsbury.

NORTHUMBERLAND
    Good, an God will!

LORD BARDOLPH
    As good as heart can wish.
15 The King is almost wounded to the death,
    And, in the fortune of my lord your son,
    Prince Harry slain outright; and both the Blunts
    Killed by the hand of Douglas; young Prince John
    And Westmoreland and Stafford fled the field;
20 And Harry Monmouth's brawn, the hulk Sir John,
    Is prisoner to your son. O, such a day,
    So fought, so followed, and so fairly won,
    Came not till now to dignify the times
    Since Caesar's fortunes.

NORTHUMBERLAND
                              How is this derived?
25 Saw you the field? Came you from Shrewsbury?

LORD BARDOLPH
    I spake with one, my lord, that came from thence,
    A gentleman well bred and of good name,
    That freely rendered me these news for true.

NORTHUMBERLAND
    Here comes my servant Travers, who I sent
30 On Tuesday last to listen after news.

        Enter TRAVERS

LORD BARDOLPH
    My lord, I overrode him on the way;
    And he is furnished with no certainties
    More than he haply may retail from me.

NORTHUMBERLAND
    Now, Travers, what good tidings comes with you?

LORD BARDOLPH

Noble Earl, I have reliable news from Shrewsbury.

NORTHUMBERLAND

Good news, God willing.

LORD BARDOLPH

As good as one could wish for. The King has been wounded and is near death. And, thanks to your son's luck, Prince Harry has been killed. Douglas killed both Lords Blunt. Prince John of Lancaster, Westmoreland, and Stafford fled the battlefield. And your son captured that hulking Sir John Falstaff, Prince Harry's fattened pig. Oh, there hasn't been a battle so well fought or a victory so well won since the days of Julius Caesar! It brings honor to our times.

NORTHUMBERLAND

How do you know all this? Did you see the battlefield? Did you come from Shrewsbury?

LORD BARDOLPH

I talked with someone, my lord, who was coming from there. He was a gentleman, with good breeding and a good reputation. He swore that all this was the truth.

NORTHUMBERLAND

Here comes my servant, Travers. I sent him last Tuesday to find out what was happening.

TRAVERS *enters.*

LORD BARDOLPH

Sir, I passed him on my way here. He doesn't know anything more than what I told him.

NORTHUMBERLAND

Now Travers, what good news do you have?

TRAVERS
35   My lord, Sir John Umfrevile turned me back
        With joyful tidings and, being better horsed,
        Outrode me. After him came spurring hard
        A gentleman, almost forspent with speed,
        That stopp'd by me to breathe his bloodied horse.
40   He asked the way to Chester, and of him
        I did demand what news from Shrewsbury.
        He told me that rebellion had bad luck
        And that young Harry Percy's spur was cold.
        With that he gave his able horse the head
45   And, bending forward, struck his armèd heels
        Against the panting sides of his poor jade
        Up to the rowel-head, and starting so
        He seemed in running to devour the way,
        Staying no longer question.

NORTHUMBERLAND
                                        Ha? Again:
50   Said he young Harry Percy's spur was cold?
        Of Hotspur, Coldspur? That rebellion
        Had met ill luck?

LORD BARDOLPH
                        My lord, I'll tell you what:
        If my young lord your son have not the day,
        Upon mine honor, for a silken point
55   I'll give my barony. Never talk of it.

NORTHUMBERLAND
        Why should that gentleman that rode by Travers
        Give then such instances of loss?

LORD BARDOLPH
                                        Who, he?
        He was some hilding fellow that had stolen
        The horse he rode on and, upon my life,
60   Spoke at a venture. Look, here comes more news.

        Enter MORTON

TRAVERS

Many critics believe that the "Sir John Umfrevile" in Shakespeare's text is a textual error, an accidental leftover from an early draft, and that Travers is actually referring to Bardolph.

Sir, Lord Bardolph told me happy news and I turned around, to come back here. But he had a faster horse, so he passed me and got here first. Another man came after him, riding hard. He was nearly exhausted from going so fast, and he stopped to give his bleeding horse a break. He asked me for directions to Chester, and I demanded to hear news from Shrewsbury. He said that the rebels had been beaten, and that Harry Percy's spur was cold. Then he took off on his horse, leaned forward in his saddle, and jammed his heels into the animal's side so hard that they almost disappeared. He rode so fast he seemed to be devouring the highway. He didn't stay around to answer any of my questions.

NORTHUMBERLAND

What? Say that again: he said that Harry Percy's spur was cold? Hotspur is now "Coldspur?" That the rebels had bad luck?

LORD BARDOLPH

My lord, I'll tell you what—if your son hasn't won, on my honor, I'll exchange all my land for a lace to tie stockings with; don't even say such a thing.

NORTHUMBERLAND

But why would that gentleman who rode past Travers describe such examples of loss?

LORD BARDOLPH

Who, him? He was some insignificant nobody who stole the horse he was riding and, I bet my life, was just talking nonsense. Look, here comes another messenger.

MORTON *enters.*

NORTHUMBERLAND
    Yea, this man's brow, like to a title leaf,
    Foretells the nature of a tragic volume.
    So looks the strand whereon the imperious flood
    Hath left a witness'd usurpation.—
65   Say, Morton, didst thou come from Shrewsbury?

MORTON
    I ran from Shrewsbury, my noble lord,
    Where hateful death put on his ugliest mask
    To fright our party.

NORTHUMBERLAND
    How doth my son and brother?
70   Thou tremblest, and the whiteness in thy cheek
    Is apter than thy tongue to tell thy errand.
    Even such a man, so faint, so spiritless,
    So dull, so dead in look, so woebegone,
    Drew Priam's curtain in the dead of night,
75   And would have told him half his Troy was burnt;
    But Priam found the fire ere he his tongue,
    And I my Percy's death ere thou report'st it.
    This thou wouldst say, "Your son did thus and thus;
    Your brother thus; so fought the noble Douglas"—
80   Stopping my greedy ear with their bold deeds.
    But in the end, to stop my ear indeed,
    Thou hast a sigh to blow away this praise,
    Ending with "Brother, son, and all are dead."

MORTON
    Douglas is living, and your brother yet,
85   But for my lord your son—

NORTHUMBERLAND
                    Why, he is dead.
    See what a ready tongue suspicion hath!
    He that but fears the thing he would not know
    Hath, by instinct, knowledge from others' eyes
    That what he feared is chancèd. Yet speak, Morton.
90   Tell thou an earl his divination lies,

NORTHUMBERLAND

Yes. And the look on his face is like the title page of a book: it hints at the tragic story within. His brow is lined with furrows, like a beach after a wild flood. Morton, did you come from Shrewsbury?

MORTON

I ran from Shrewsbury, my noble lord. Death was there, frightening our side with his ugliest mask.

NORTHUMBERLAND

How are my son and my brother? You're trembling, and the paleness of your face is more likely to convey your news than your tongue. This is like that old story about the burning of Troy. A man like you—faint, lifeless, dull, deadly-looking, sad—woke King Priam in the dead of night to tell him that half the city of Troy had been burned down. But Priam saw the fire before this man could speak, and I can see my Percy's death before you report it. You're going to tell me, "Your son did such-and-such; your brother did this; the noble Douglas fought like so." You'll stuff my greedy ears with stories of their bold deeds. But in the end, you'll stop my ears forever with a sigh that blows away all your words of praise. You will end your story by saying, "Your brother, your son, everyone–dead."

MORTON

Douglas is alive, and so is your brother, for now. But as for your son, my lord—

NORTHUMBERLAND

Why, he is dead. My suspicion is so quick to speak! When a man fears something, and doesn't want to know the truth, he can still tell when that thing has happened; by instinct, he can read it in another man's eyes. But speak, Morton. Tell me, who am an earl, that

And I will take it as a sweet disgrace
And make thee rich for doing me such wrong.

MORTON
You are too great to be by me gainsaid,
Your spirit is too true, your fears too certain.

NORTHUMBERLAND
95   Yet, for all this, say not that Percy's dead.
I see a strange confession in thine eye.
Thou shak'st thy head and hold'st it fear or sin
To speak a truth. If he be slain, say so.
The tongue offends not that reports his death;
100   And he doth sin that doth belie the dead,
Not he which says the dead is not alive.
Yet the first bringer of unwelcome news
Hath but a losing office, and his tongue
Sounds ever after as a sullen bell
105   Remembered tolling a departing friend.

LORD BARDOLPH
I cannot think, my lord, your son is dead.

MORTON
I am sorry I should force you to believe
That which I would to God I had not seen,
But these mine eyes saw him in bloody state,
110   Rend'ring faint quittance, wearied and outbreathed,
To Harry Monmouth; whose swift wrath beat down
The never-daunted Percy to the earth,
From whence with life he never more sprung up.
In few, his death, whose spirit lent a fire
115   Even to the dullest peasant in his camp,
Being bruited once, took fire and heat away
From the best tempered courage in his troops;
For from his metal was his party steeled,
Which, once in him abated, all the rest
120   Turned on themselves, like dull and heavy lead.
And as the thing that's heavy in itself
Upon enforcement flies with greatest speed,

I have no talent for prophecy. I'll take it as a pleasant insult, and I'll pay you richly for doing me that wrong.

MORTON

You are too great a man to be slandered by me. Your instinct is correct; your fears are true.

NORTHUMBERLAND

But despite all this, don't say that Percy's dead. I can see a strange sort of confession in your eyes. You shake your head; you're afraid to tell the truth, or you think it would be sinful. If he's been killed, say so. The man who reports a death doesn't offend with that report. To lie about the dead is a sin, but it is no sin to say that a dead man is not alive. It's a losing situation, being the first man to bring unwelcome news. That man's voice sounds forever like a sad bell, and it will always be remembered for tolling the death of a friend.

LORD BARDOLPH

My lord, I cannot believe your son is dead.

MORTON

I'm sorry that I must force you to believe this, when I wish to God that I hadn't seen it myself. But I saw him, in his bloody state, with my own eyes. He was barely able to fight back, exhausted and out of breath. Harry Monmouth's swift fury beat the unflinching Percy down to the ground, and once he was there, Percy never rose again. To be brief, Percy's spirit inspired the entire army, down to the dullest peasant. When the news got out that he had been killed, it took the fire and courage away from even the bravest soldiers. Percy's metal steeled the whole army; when they learned that he had been blunted, they bent and warped like dull, heavy lead.

And just as a heavy object gains momentum once it's pushed into motion, our army, made heavy by

So did our men, heavy in Hotspur's loss,
Lend to this weight such lightness with their fear
125   That arrows fled not swifter toward their aim
Than did our soldiers, aiming at their safety,
Fly from the field. Then was the noble Worcester
Too soon ta'en prisoner; and that furious Scot,
The bloody Douglas, whose well-laboring sword
130   Had three times slain th'appearance of the King,
Gan vail his stomach and did grace the shame
Of those that turned their backs and in his flight,
Stumbling in fear, was took. The sum of all
Is that the King hath won and hath sent out
135   A speedy power to encounter you, my lord,
Under the conduct of young Lancaster
And Westmoreland. This is the news at full.

NORTHUMBERLAND
For this I shall have time enough to mourn.
In poison there is physic, and these news,
140   Having been well, that would have made me sick,
Being sick, have in some measure made me well.
And as the wretch whose fever-weakened joints,
Like strengthless hinges, buckle under life,
Impatient of his fit, breaks like a fire
145   Out of his keeper's arms, even so my limbs,
Weakened with grief, being now enraged with grief,
Are thrice themselves. Hence therefore, thou nice crutch.
A scaly gauntlet now with joints of steel
Must glove this hand. And hence, thou sickly coif.
150   Thou art a guard too wanton for the head
Which princes, fleshed with conquest, aim to hit.
Now bind my brows with iron, and approach
The ragged'st hour that time and spite dare bring
To frown upon th'enraged Northumberland.
155   Let heaven kiss earth! Now let not Nature's hand
Keep the wild flood confined. Let order die,
And let this world no longer be a stage

Hotspur's death, suddenly started moving fast—faster than arrows flying toward a target—but they flew toward safety, not toward the battle. Soon, Worcester, that furious Scotsman, was captured. The warlike Douglas, who killed three enemies disguised as King Henry, began to lose courage: he ran away as well, lending his authority to the shameful retreat. But running in fear, he stumbled and was captured.

The bottom line is that King Henry has won. He's sent a speedy force after you, sir, led by young John of Lancaster and Westmoreland. That is the whole story.

NORTHUMBERLAND

There will be time to mourn for this. Sometimes poison can be a kind of medicine: this news, which would have made me sick had I been well, has, because I am sick, made me well. A dying man—his joints weakened by fever, dangling like useless hinges and crumpling under the man's own weight—will sometimes be stuck with a fit of impatience, causing him to burst out of his caretaker's arms. My limbs are like that now; once weakened by grief, they're now enraged by grief, and are three times as powerful as they were before. Away from me, you unmanly crutch! Chain mail armor will cover my hands now. Away from me, you invalid's cap! You are too fanciful a helmet for this head which is now the target of kings, grown arrogant with their victories. Wrap my head in iron, and then attack me with the roughest things that destiny and hatred will dare to bring upon me in my rage. Let the sky come crashing down! Let the ocean overflow the shores! Let law and order die! And let the world no longer be a stage for a long, drawn-out struggle: let the

       To feed contention in a lingering act;
       But let one spirit of the firstborn Cain
160   Reign in all bosoms, that, each heart being set
       On bloody courses, the rude scene may end,
       And darkness be the burier of the dead.

LORD BARDOLPH
       This strainèd passion doth you wrong, my lord.

MORTON
       Sweet Earl, divorce not wisdom from your honor.
165   The lives of all your loving complices
       Lean on your health, the which, if you give o'er
       To stormy passion, must perforce decay.
       You cast th' event of war, my noble lord,
       And summed the account of chance before you said
170   "Let us make head." It was your presurmise
       That, in the dole of blows your son might drop.
       You knew he walked o'er perils on an edge,
       More likely to fall in than to get o'er.
       You were advised his flesh was capable
175   Of wounds and scars, and that his forward spirit
       Would lift him where most trade of danger ranged.
       Yet did you say "Go forth," and none of this,
       Though strongly apprehended, could restrain
       The stiff-borne action. What hath then befall'n,
180   Or what did this bold enterprise brought forth,
       More than that being which was like to be?

LORD BARDOLPH
       We all that are engagèd to this loss
       Knew that we ventured on such dangerous seas
       That if we wrought out life, 'twas ten to one;
185   And yet we ventured, for the gain proposed
       Choked the respect of likely peril feared;

spirit of Cain, who committed the first murder against his brother Abel, live in every heart. If every heart is a murderer's heart, this violent play will end, and darkness will shroud the corpses.

LORD BARDOLPH

This extreme passion is bad for you, sir.

MORTON

Gentle Earl, don't abandon your wisdom. All your allies are depending on you and your well-being. If you allow yourself to indulge in this kind of stormy emotion, your health will deteriorate even further. Before you said, "Let's raise an army," you calculated how the war might end, and you thought carefully about the likeliness of a victory. You knew from the beginning that, once the fighting started, your son might die. You knew that he was treading danger-ously, as if on the edge of a precipice: you knew he was more likely to fall over than make it across. You were warned that your son was made of flesh and blood, and that it was possible he'd get hurt. You were warned that his temper and hot-headedness would push him into the most dangerous situations. But you still said, "Go forward." None of this consideration, even though it was clearly understood, could stop the stub-born course of events. So what happened here? What has been the result of this brave undertaking? Only this: precisely what was likely to happen in the first place.

LORD BARDOLPH

We all knew that we were venturing into dangerous waters. We knew the odds were ten to one that we would come out alive, and yet we ventured forward anyway. The potential reward of winning outweighed the fear of our probable loss. We lost this time, but let's try again. Come, we'll all go for it, body and soul.

And since we are o'erset, venture again.
Come, we will all put forth, body and goods.

MORTON
'Tis more than time.—And, my most noble lord,
190   I hear for certain, and do speak the truth:
The gentle Archbishop of York is up
With well-appointed powers. He is a man
Who with a double surety binds his followers.
My lord your son had only but the corpse,
195   But shadows and the shows of men, to fight;
For that same word "rebellion" did divide
The action of their bodies from their souls,
And they did fight with queasiness, constrained,
As men drink potions, that their weapons only
200   Seemed on our side. But, for their spirits and souls,
This word "rebellion," it had froze them up
As fish are in a pond. But now the Bishop
Turns insurrection to religion.
Supposed sincere and holy in his thoughts,
205   He's followed both with body and with mind,
And doth enlarge his rising with the blood
Of fair King Richard, scraped from Pomfret stones;
Derives from heaven his quarrel and his cause;
Tells them he doth bestride a bleeding land,
210   Gasping for life under great Bolingbroke;
And more and less do flock to follow him.

NORTHUMBERLAND
I knew of this before, but, to speak truth,
This present grief had wiped it from my mind.
Go in with me and counsel every man
215   The aptest way for safety and revenge.
Get posts and letters, and make friends with speed.
Never so few, and never yet more need.

Exeunt

MORTON

It is the appropriate time. Good sir, I hear for certain, and I tell you truthfully, that the Archbishop of York has raised a powerful army. He motivates his men with both his earthly and his spiritual powers. My lord, your son commanded only his soldiers' bodies. The word "rebellion" frightened them, separating their bodies from their hearts. It caused them to fight timidly, hesitantly, as though they were taking medicine: their weapons seemed to be on our side, but their spirits and souls were frozen, like fish in an icy pond. But now, the Archbishop turns our rebellion into a religious cause. Everyone believes he's a righteous and holy man, and they follow him not only in body but also in mind. He enhances his cause by preaching about the blood of good King Richard, which was spilled at Pomfret Castle. The Archbishop claims that he derives his authority from heaven; tells the men that the whole country is bleeding, gasping for life under the terrible leadership of Bolingbroke. And so men from every walk of life flock like sheep to follow him.

NORTHUMBERLAND

I knew all this, but to tell you the truth, this terrible grief had pushed it out of my thoughts. Come inside; I want to hear everyone's ideas on the best way to defend ourselves and enact our revenge. Send out messengers and letters, and make new allies quickly. Our numbers have never been smaller, but there's never been more need for what we have to do.

They exit.

ACT 1, SCENE 2

Enter Sir John FALSTAFF, *with his* PAGE *bearing his sword and buckler*

FALSTAFF
Sirrah, you giant, what says the doctor to my water?

PAGE
He said, sir, the water itself was a good healthy water, but, for the party that owed it, he might have more diseases than he knew for.

FALSTAFF
5   Men of all sorts take a pride to gird at me. The brain of this foolish-compounded clay, man, is not able to invent anything that tends to laughter more than I invent, or is invented on me. I am not only witty in myself, but the cause that wit is in other men. I do here walk before thee like a sow
10   that hath overwhelmed all her litter but one. If the Prince put thee into my service for any other reason than to set me off, why then I have no judgment. Thou whoreson mandrake, thou art fitter to be worn in my cap than to wait at my heels. I was never manned with an agate till now, but
15   I will inset you neither in gold nor silver, but in vile apparel, and send you back again to your master for a jewel. The juvenal, the Prince your master, whose chin is not yet fledge—I will sooner have a beard grow in the palm of my hand than he shall get one off his cheek, and yet he will not
20   stick to say his face is a face royal. God may finish it when He will. 'Tis not a hair amiss yet. He may keep it still at a face royal, for a barber shall never earn sixpence out of it, and yet he'll be crowing as if he had writ man ever since his father was a bachelor. He may keep his own grace, but he's
25   almost out of mine, I can assure him. What said Master

ACT 1, SCENE 2

Sir John **FALSTAFF** *enters with his* **PAGE**, *who carries a sword and shield.*

page = young
servant

FALSTAFF

Sirrah = term of
address for a
person of lower
social rank

Sirrah, you giant, what did the doctor say about my urine?

Falstaff is mocking the page for being so small.

PAGE

He said that the urine itself was good, healthy urine, but that the man who owned it probably had more diseases than he could tell.

FALSTAFF

All kinds of people make it a matter of pride to heckle me. No man—that foolishly assembled lump of clay—could ever invent something quite as funny as I seem to be to other people. I'm not only witty on my own, but I bring out wit in other people. Look at the two of us, walking here: I look like a sow that's smothered all of her baby pigs, except for you. If the Prince sent you to serve me for any other reason than to irritate me, I'm a fool. You weedy little son of a bitch: you're so tiny that you should be a decoration on my hat, not a servant at my feet. I've never had a servant before who was as tiny as a ring stone. But I won't set you in a gold or silver ring; I'll wrap you in rags and send you back to your master, to be used as a jewel—that youth, the Prince your master, whose chin is still lacking a beard. Why, I'll grow a beard in the palm of my hand before he'll have one that he can shave off his face. And yet, this doesn't stop him from claiming that he has a face for royalty. Well, God will give him a beard whenever he chooses to—there's not a hair out of place yet. It's a good thing the Prince's face is a royal, because a barber will never earn a coin from

Falstaff puns on the fact that a "royal" was a kind of coin, stamped with the king's face.

Dommelton about the satin for my short cloak and my
slops?

PAGE

He said, sir, you should procure him better assurance than
Bardolph. He would not take his band and yours. He liked
30   not the security.

FALSTAFF

Let him be damned like the glutton! Pray God his tongue be
hotter! A whoreson Achitophel, a rascally yea-forsooth
knave, to bear a gentleman in hand and then stand upon
security! The whoreson smoothy-pates do now wear
35   nothing but high shoes and bunches of keys at their girdles;
and if a man is through with them in honest taking up, then
they must stand upon security. I had as lief they would put
ratsbane in my mouth as offer to stop it with "security." I
looked he should have sent me two-and-twenty yards of
40   satin, as I am a true knight, and he sends me "security."
Well, he may sleep in security, for he hath the horn of
abundance, and the lightness of his wife shines through it,
and yet cannot he see though he have his own lantern to
light him. Where's Bardolph?

PAGE

45   He's gone into Smithfield to buy your Worship a horse.

FALSTAFF

I bought him in Paul's, and he'll buy me a horse in
Smithfield. An I could get me but a wife in the stews, I were
manned, horsed, and wived.

shaving it. And still, the Prince brags that he's been a full-grown man since before he was born. He can keep that title, for all I care; I have no affection for him now, I can assure him. What did Master Dommelton say about the satin for my cape and baggy trousers?

PAGE

He said that you have to give him a better guarantee of payment than just saying Bardolph was good for it. He wouldn't accept Bardolph's promise or yours; he felt that neither should be trusted.

FALSTAFF

Damn him to hell then, just like Dives in the Bible—the rich glutton who rejected the beggar Lazarus! And may Dommelton burn even hotter! He's a son-of-a-bitch traitor! A two-faced liar, who smiles and says "Yes sir, that'll be fine" to my face, and then demands a guarantee of payment! These bastard shopkeepers, with their fashionable short haircuts, and fancy shoes, and their fat key chains on their belts—you make an agreement to put something on credit, and then they throw a "guarantee of payment" at you. I would rather eat rat poison than guarantee my payment. I expected him to send me twenty-two yards of satin, and instead he sends me a "guarantee of payment." Well, let him guarantee himself a good night's sleep. After all, his wife's in somebody else's bed, so why not? She's practically shining a spotlight on her adultery, but he's so clueless he can't even tell. Where's Bardolph?

PAGE

He went to Smithfield to buy you a horse, sir.

FALSTAFF

Unemployed men waited at St. Paul's Cathedral to be hired for short-term jobs. The nearby Smithfield was a livestock market; horses bought there were considered cheap nags.

I bought Bardolph at St. Paul's Cathedral, and he's buying me a horse in Smithfield. Now if he could just find me a wife in a whorehouse, I'd be fully stocked with high-quality servants, horses, and wives.

Enter the Lord CHIEF JUSTICE *and* SERVANT

PAGE
Sir, here comes the nobleman that committed the Prince for
striking him about Bardolph.

FALSTAFF
Wait close. I will not see him.

CHIEF JUSTICE
What's he that goes there?

SERVANT
Falstaff, an 't please your Lordship.

CHIEF JUSTICE
He that was in question for the robbery?

SERVANT
He, my lord; but he hath since done good service at
Shrewsbury, and, as I hear, is now going with some charge
to the Lord John of Lancaster.

CHIEF JUSTICE
What, to York? Call him back again.

SERVANT
Sir John Falstaff!

FALSTAFF
Boy, tell him I am deaf.

PAGE
You must speak louder. My master is deaf.

CHIEF JUSTICE
I am sure he is, to the hearing of any thing good.—Go pluck
him by the elbow. I must speak with him.

SERVANT
Sir John!

FALSTAFF
What, a young knave and begging? Is there not wars? Is
there not employment? Doth not the King lack subjects?
Do not the rebels need soldiers? Though it be a shame to be
on any side but one, it is worse shame to beg than to be on

The Lord CHIEF JUSTICE *and his* SERVANT *enter.*

PAGE

Sir, here comes the man who put the Prince in jail for hitting him during that argument about Bardolph.

FALSTAFF

Hide; I don't want to talk to him.

CHIEF JUSTICE

Who is that man?

SERVANT

Falstaff, if it please you, sir.

CHIEF JUSTICE

The man who was a suspect in that robbery?

SERVANT

That's the one. But he did good work in the Battle of Shrewsbury, and I hear he's taking some soldiers to help Lord John of Lancaster.

CHIEF JUSTICE

Where, to York? Tell him to come here.

SERVANT

Sir John Falstaff!

FALSTAFF

Boy, tell him I'm deaf.

PAGE

You have to speak up; my master is deaf.

CHIEF JUSTICE

I'm sure he is, when anything good's being said. Go, tap him on the shoulder. I must speak with him.

SERVANT

Sir John!

FALSTAFF

What? A young troublemaker? A beggar? Isn't there a war on? Isn't there work to do? Doesn't the King need subjects? Don't the rebels need soldiers? Though it's shameful to be on any side but the King's, it's even more shameful to be an idle beggar than a

70   the worst side, were it worse than the name of rebellion can
        tell how to make it.

SERVANT
        You mistake me, sir.

FALSTAFF
        Why sir, did I say you were an honest man? Setting my
        knighthood and my soldiership aside, I had lied in my
        throat if I had said so.

75   **SERVANT**
        I pray you, sir, then set your knighthood and our
        soldiership aside, and give me leave to tell you, you lie in
        your throat if you say I am any other than an honest man.

FALSTAFF
        I give thee leave to tell me so? I lay aside that which grows
        to me? If thou gett'st any leave of me, hang me; if thou tak'st
80   leave, thou wert better be hanged. You hunt counter.
        Hence! Avaunt!

SERVANT
        Sir, my lord would speak with you.

CHIEF JUSTICE
        Sir John Falstaff, a word with you.

FALSTAFF
        My good lord. God give your Lordship good time of the
85   day. I am glad to see your Lordship abroad. I heard say your
        Lordship was sick: I hope your Lordship goes abroad by
        advice. Your Lordship, though not clean past your youth,
        have yet some smack of an ague in you, some relish of the
        saltness of time in you, and I most humbly beseech your
90   Lordship to have a reverent care of your health.

CHIEF JUSTICE
        Sir John, I sent for you before your expedition to
        Shrewsbury.

FALSTAFF
        An 't please your Lordship, I hear his Majesty is returned
        with some discomfort from Wales.

soldier on the wrong side—even if the rebellion were more despicable than the word "rebellion" already leads me to believe.

SERVANT

You're mistaken, sir.

FALSTAFF

Why is that? Did I say you were an honest man? Because, setting aside the fact that I'm knight and a soldier, I'd be nothing but a liar if I said that.

SERVANT

Then please, sir, set aside your knighthood and your soldiership and let me tell you that you're a deliberate liar, if you say I'm anything other than an honest man.

FALSTAFF

Should I allow you to say that? Should I set aside something that's mine by right? If I allow you anything, hang me. If you allow yourself, hang you. You're running in the wrong direction: get out of here! Go!

SERVANT

Sir, my master wants to speak with you.

CHIEF JUSTICE

Sir John Falstaff, I'd like a word with you.

FALSTAFF

My good sir! God grant you a good day! It's great to see you out and about: I'd heard you were sick. I hope your doctor knows you're out. Though you're not entirely past your youth, your lordship, you have a touch of age in you, a touch of the passage of time, and I must humbly urge you to take good care of your health.

CHIEF JUSTICE

Sir John, I sent for you to come see me before you left for Shrewsbury.

FALSTAFF

If you don't mind my saying so, I hear the King is back from Wales and it didn't go so well.

CHIEF JUSTICE
95   I talk not of his Majesty. You would not come when I sent for
        you.

FALSTAFF
        And I hear, moreover, his Highness is fallen into this same
        whoreson apoplexy.

CHIEF JUSTICE
        Well, God mend him. I pray you let me speak with you.

FALSTAFF
100   This apoplexy, as I take it, is a kind of lethargy, an 't please
        your Lordship, a kind of sleeping in the blood, a whoreson
        tingling.

CHIEF JUSTICE
        What tell you me of it? Be it as it is.

FALSTAFF
        It hath its original from much grief, from study, and
105   perturbation of the brain. I have read the cause of his effects
        in Galen. It is a kind of deafness.

CHIEF JUSTICE
        I think you are fallen into the disease, for you hear not what
        I say to you.

FALSTAFF
        Very well, my lord, very well. Rather, an 't please you, it is
110   the disease of not listening, the malady of not marking, that
        I am troubled withal.

CHIEF JUSTICE
        To punish you by the heels would amend the attention of
        your ears, and I care not if I do become your physician.

FALSTAFF
        I am as poor as Job, my lord, but not so patient. Your
115   Lordship may minister the potion of imprisonment to me
        in respect of poverty, but how should I be your patient to
        follow your prescriptions, the wise may make some dram of
        a scruple, or indeed a scruple itself.

CHIEF JUSTICE

I'm not talking about the King. You didn't come when I sent for you.

FALSTAFF

And I also hear that the King has fallen into a terrible paralysis.

CHIEF JUSTICE

Well, God give him a speedy recovery. Please, let me speak with you.

FALSTAFF

His paralysis is, as I understand it, a kind of lethargy, if it please you. It's a sleepiness in the blood, a nasty tingling.

CHIEF JUSTICE

Why are you telling me this? Let it be.

FALSTAFF

It comes from heavy sadness; from too much reading, and too much thinking. I read about it in the reference books: it's a kind of deafness.

CHIEF JUSTICE

I think you must have that disease as well, because you're not hearing a word I'm saying.

FALSTAFF

Very likely, my lord, very likely. But actually, sir, I have the not-listening disease; I have the not-paying-attention sickness.

CHIEF JUSTICE

The cure for that illness would be to put you in shackles, and I wouldn't mind being your doctor.

FALSTAFF

In the Bible, Job patiently withstood a series of hardships set on him by God.

I may be as poor as Job, but I'm not as patient. You may be able to throw me in jail because of my poverty, but some people might have slight reservations about that.

CHIEF JUSTICE
I sent for you, when there were matters against you for your
120 life, to come speak with me.

FALSTAFF
As I was then advised by my learned counsel in the laws of
this land-service, I did not come.

CHIEF JUSTICE
Well, the truth is, Sir John, you live in great infamy.

FALSTAFF
He that buckles him in my belt cannot live in less.

CHIEF JUSTICE
125 Your means are very slender, and your waste is great.

FALSTAFF
I would it were otherwise. I would my means were greater
and my waist slender.

CHIEF JUSTICE
You have misled the youthful Prince.

FALSTAFF
The young Prince hath misled me. I am the fellow with the
130 great belly, and he my dog.

CHIEF JUSTICE
Well, I am loath to gall a new-healed wound. Your day's
service at Shrewsbury hath a little gilded over your night's
exploit on Gad's Hill. You may thank th' unquiet time for
your quiet o'erposting that action.

FALSTAFF
135 My lord.

CHIEF JUSTICE
But since all is well, keep it so. Wake not a sleeping wolf.

CHIEF JUSTICE

I sent for you to come speak with me. There were charges against you that might have earned you the death penalty.

FALSTAFF

I was advised that, since I was working for the army at the time, I shouldn't go.

CHIEF JUSTICE

The truth is, Sir John, that you are massively notorious.

FALSTAFF

Anybody who wears a belt this big couldn't be anything less than massive.

CHIEF JUSTICE

Your bank account is thin, and yet you put it to huge waste.

FALSTAFF

I wish it were the other way around: that my bank account were huge and my waist were thin.

CHIEF JUSTICE

You've misled the young Prince.

FALSTAFF

The young Prince has misled me. I'm the man with the big belly, and he's the dog who walks in front of me.

CHIEF JUSTICE

Well, I'd rather not open up a wound that's just healed. The good work you did at Shrewsbury has made up a little for the bad thing you did at Gad's Hill. You can thank the rebellion for helping you get away with that terrible deed.

The robbery at Gad's Hill occurs in Henry IV, Part One.

FALSTAFF

Really?

CHIEF JUSTICE

But since things are calm now, let's keep them that way. We won't wake a sleeping wolf.

FALSTAFF
To wake a wolf is as bad as to smell a fox.

CHIEF JUSTICE
What, you are as a candle, the better part burnt out.

FALSTAFF
A wassail candle, my lord, all tallow. If I did say of wax, my
140   growth would approve the truth.

CHIEF JUSTICE
There is not a white hair on your face but should have his
effect of gravity.

FALSTAFF
His effect of gravy, gravy, gravy.

CHIEF JUSTICE
You follow the young Prince up and down like his ill angel.

FALSTAFF
145   Not so, my lord. Your ill angel is light, but I hope he that
looks upon me will take me without weighing. And yet in
some respects I grant I cannot go. I cannot tell. Virtue is of
so little regard in these costermongers' times that true valor
is turned bear-herd; pregnancy is made a tapster, and hath
150   his quick wit wasted in giving reckonings. All the other gifts
appurtenant to man, as the malice of this age shapes them,
are not worth a gooseberry. You that are old consider not the
capacities of us that are young. You do measure the heat of
our livers with the bitterness of your galls, and we that are
155   in the vaward of our youth, I must confess, are wags too.

CHIEF JUSTICE
Do you set down your name in the scroll of youth, that are
written down old with all the characters of age? Have you
not a moist eye, a dry hand, a yellow cheek, a white beard,

FALSTAFF

smell a fox = be suspicious

To wake a wolf is as bad as to smell a fox.

CHIEF JUSTICE

What? You're like a candle, half burned out.

FALSTAFF

Maybe, if I were a big, fat holiday candle made of animal fat. But you'd be better off saying that I'm a wax candle: I keep "waxing" larger and larger.

CHIEF JUSTICE

Your gray beard should be a sign that you're a man of gravity.

FALSTAFF

I'm a man of gravy, gravy, gravy.

CHIEF JUSTICE

You follow the young Prince everywhere, like a false angel on his shoulder.

FALSTAFF

angel = a kind of coin; angels were often trimmed of some of their metal; a defective angel could be distinguished from a proper by weighing it on a scale.

That's not so, my lord. False angels are light, and anyone can see without having to weigh me that I'm too heavy. But I don't know; in some ways, you're right. I'm not for these times. Virtue counts for so little in this commercial world of ours. True courage is worthless; it's only used by animal trainers in the bear-baiting rings. Intelligence is good for nobody but bartenders, who waste their wits totaling up tavern bills. In these mean-spirited days, man's best qualities aren't worth a thing. You older folks don't value us young people. You measure our fiery passion according to your melancholic bitterness. And I have to tell you, those of us who are highly advanced in our youth, we're spirited as well as young.

CHIEF JUSTICE

You'd add your name to the list of the young? You, who have age written all over you? Don't you have mucus in your eyes? Dry skin? Jaundice? A white

a decreasing leg, an increasing belly? Is not your voice
160   broken, your wind short, your chin double, your wit single,
and every part about you blasted with antiquity? And will
you yet call yourself young? Fie, fie, fie, Sir John.

FALSTAFF
My lord, I was born about three of the clock in the
afternoon, with a white head and something a round belly.
165   For my voice, I have lost it with halloing and singing of
anthems. To approve my youth further, I will not. The
truth is, I am only old in judgment and understanding. And
he that will caper with me for a thousand marks, let him
lend me the money, and have at him! For the box of the ear
170   that the Prince gave you, he gave it like a rude prince, and
you took it like a sensible lord. I have checked him for it, and
the young lion repents. Marry, not in ashes and sackcloth,
but in new silk and old sack.

CHIEF JUSTICE
Well, God send the Prince a better companion.

FALSTAFF
175   God send the companion a better prince. I cannot rid my
hands of him.

CHIEF JUSTICE
Well, the King hath severed you and Prince Harry. I hear
you are going with Lord John of Lancaster against the
Archbishop and the Earl of Northumberland.

FALSTAFF
180   Yea, I thank your pretty sweet wit for it. But look you pray,
all you that kiss my Lady Peace at home, that our armies
join not in a hot day, for, by the Lord, I take but two shirts
out with me, and I mean not to sweat extraordinarily. If it be
a hot day and I brandish anything but a bottle, I would I
185   might never spit white again. There is not a dangerous
action can peep out his head but I am thrust upon it. Well,

beard? An arthritic leg? A growing belly? Isn't your voice scratchy? Your breath short? Your chin doubled? Your last wit abandoned? Isn't every part of you devastated by age? And still you call yourself young? Shame on you, Sir John.

FALSTAFF

Sir, I was born around three o'clock in the afternoon, with a white head and a bit of a round belly. As for my scratchy voice, I lost it through shouting and singing loud songs. But I won't try to prove how young I am any longer. I have only one trait of old age, and that is wisdom. If somebody wants to challenge me to a dance contest for a thousand-mark wager, let him hand me the money and off we go. Now, as for the fact that the Prince hit you on the head, he did it like a rude prince and you took it like a sensible gentleman. I reprimanded him for it, and he repents. He's not wearing the traditional sackcloth and ashes, for sure, but he's repenting in silk cloth and wine.

mark = unit of currency

CHIEF JUSTICE

May God send the Prince a better friend!

FALSTAFF

May God send the friend a better prince! I can't get him off my hands!

CHIEF JUSTICE

Well, the King has separated you and Prince Harry. I hear you're going with John of Lancaster to go fight Northumberland and the Archbishop.

FALSTAFF

Yes, and thanks for reminding me. I hope that all of you who stay home, safe and sound, will say a prayer that we soldiers don't end up in some hot battle. For, by the Lord, I've only packed two shirts, and I don't want to sweat too much. If things get hot and I pull out any other weapon besides a bottle, I'll never drink wine again. I get sent out on every dangerous assign-

I cannot last ever. But it was always yet the trick of our
English nation, if they have a good thing, to make it too
common. If ye will needs say I am an old man, you should
190   give me rest. I would to God my name were not so terrible
to the enemy as it is. I were better to be eaten to death with
a rust than to be scoured to nothing with perpetual motion.

CHIEF JUSTICE
Well, be honest, be honest; and God bless your expedition!

FALSTAFF
Will your Lordship lend me a thousand pound to furnish
195   me forth?

CHIEF JUSTICE
Not a penny, not a penny. You are too impatient to bear
crosses. Fare you well. Commend me to my cousin
Westmoreland.

Exeunt CHIEF JUSTICE *and* SERVANT

FALSTAFF
If I do, fillip me with a three-man beetle. A man can no
200   more separate age and covetousness than he can part young
limbs and lechery; but the gout galls the one, and the pox
pinches the other, and so both the degrees prevent my
curses.—Boy!

PAGE
Sir.

FALSTAFF
205   What money is in my purse?

PAGE
Seven groats and two pence.

FALSTAFF
I can get no remedy against this consumption of the purse.
Borrowing only lingers and lingers it out, but the disease is
incurable. Go bear this letter to my Lord of Lancaster, this
210   to the Prince, this to the Earl of Westmoreland; and this to
old Mistress Ursula, whom I have weekly sworn to marry

ment that comes up. Well, I can't live forever. That's the thing about the English: when they have something good, they use it continually. If you're going to insist that I'm an old man, then let me rest. I wish to God the enemy weren't as scared of me as they are: I'd rather sit and rust than be worn out by all this work.

CHIEF JUSTICE

Well, stay honest, stay honest. God bless your undertaking.

FALSTAFF

Could your lordship lend me a thousand pounds for some equipment I need?

CHIEF JUSTICE

Not a penny, not a penny: you're too impatient to endure adversity. Farewell; give my regards to my kinsman Westmoreland.

The **CHIEF JUSTICE** *and his* **SERVANT** *exit.*

FALSTAFF

If I do, hit me with a sledgehammer. Old age and greed go together like youth and lust. Gout afflicts one and syphilis plagues the other, so there's no point in me cursing either the old or the young: they're both cursed already. Boy!

PAGE

Sir?

FALSTAFF

How much money's in my wallet?

PAGE

About seven groats and two pence.

groat = coin worth four pence

FALSTAFF

There no way to cure the illness that's making my wallet waste away; borrowing makes it live a little longer, but the disease is incurable. Bring this letter to Lord John of Lancaster, this one to the Prince, this one to Westmoreland, and this one to Madame Ursula. I've

since I perceived the first white hair on my chin. About it.
You know where to find me.

Exit PAGE

A pox of this gout! Or, a gout of this pox, for the one or the
other plays the rogue with my great toe. 'Tis no matter if I
do halt. I have the wars for my color, and my pension shall
seem the more reasonable. A good wit will make use of
anything. I will turn diseases to commodity.

Exit

215

promised to marry her every single week since I got my first gray hair. Get going: you know where I'll be.

The PAGE *exits.*

Damn this gout! Or damn this syphilis! One of them is really messing up my big toe. Oh well, it doesn't matter if I limp. I can blame it on the war, and that will help justify my disability payments. A sharp brain can turn any problem to its advantage. I'll turn my diseases into cash.

He exits.

ACT 1, SCENE 3

Enter the ARCHBISHOP *of York, Thomas* MOWBRAY *the Earl Marshal, Lord* HASTINGS, *and* LORD BARDOLPH

ARCHBISHOP
Thus have you heard our cause and known our means,
And, my most noble friends, I pray you all
Speak plainly your opinions of our hopes.
And first, Lord Marshal, what say you to it?

MOWBRAY
5   I well allow the occasion of our arms,
But gladly would be better satisfied
How in our means we should advance ourselves
To look with forehead bold and big enough
Upon the power and puissance of the King.

HASTINGS
10   Our present musters grow upon the file
To five-and-twenty thousand men of choice,
And our supplies live largely in the hope
Of great Northumberland, whose bosom burns
With an incensèd fire of injuries.

LORD BARDOLPH
15   The question then, Lord Hastings, standeth thus:
Whether our present five-and-twenty thousand
May hold up head without Northumberland.

HASTINGS
With him we may.

LORD BARDOLPH
                 Yea, marry, there's the point.
But if without him we be thought too feeble,
20   My judgment is we should not step too far
Till we had his assistance by the hand.
For in a theme so bloody-faced as this,
Conjecture, expectation, and surmise
Of aids incertain should not be admitted.

ACT 1, SCENE 3

The ARCHBISHOP *of York, Thomas* MOWBRAY *the Earl Marshal, Lord* HASTINGS *and* LORD BARDOLPH *enter.*

ARCHBISHOP

So that's what we're fighting for, and that's the kind of support we have. Now please, my noble friends, tell me frankly if you think we have a chance. First you, Marshal Mowbray. What do you say?

MOWBRAY

I absolutely agree with our reasons for fighting. But given our resources, I'd feel better if I knew how we're going to grow bold and strong enough to defeat this mighty and powerful King.

HASTINGS

Our army has grown to twenty-five thousand good men. Our reinforcements are coming with Northumberland, and his heart burns with anger over all he's lost.

LORD BARDOLPH

Then, Lord Hastings, this is the question: can our twenty-five thousand get the job done without Northumberland?

HASTINGS

With him, we can.

LORD BARDOLPH

Yes, exactly, and that's the point. If we're too weak without him, then I don't think we should advance until we know that his help is guaranteed. In a fight as bloody as this one, we need to be certain about the status of our supporters: we can't rely on conjecture, hope, and guesswork when aid isn't guaranteed.

ARCHBISHOP

25 'Tis very true, Lord Bardolph; for indeed
It was young Hotspur's cause at Shrewsbury.

LORD BARDOLPH

It was, my lord; who lined himself with hope,
Eating the air on promise of supply,
Flatt'ring himself in project of a power
30 Much smaller than the smallest of his thoughts,
And so, with great imagination
Proper to madmen, led his powers to death
And, winking, leapt into destruction.

HASTINGS

But, by your leave, it never yet did hurt
35 To lay down likelihoods and forms of hope.

LORD BARDOLPH

Yes, if this present quality of war—
Indeed the instant action, a cause on foot—
Lives so in hope, as in an early spring
We see the appearing buds, which to prove fruit
40 Hope gives not so much warrant as despair
That frosts will bite them. When we mean to build,
We first survey the plot, then draw the model,
And when we see the figure of the house,
Then must we rate the cost of the erection,
45 Which if we find outweighs ability,
What do we then but draw anew the model
In fewer offices, or at last desist
To build at all? Much more in this great work,
Which is almost to pluck a kingdom down
50 And set another up, should we survey
The plot of situation and the model,
Consent upon a sure foundation,
Question surveyors, know our own estate,
How able such a work to undergo,
55 To weigh against his opposite. Or else

ARCHBISHOP

That's right, Lord Bardolph. That's what happened to young Hotspur at Shrewsbury.

LORD BARDOLPH

That's true, my lord. Hotspur fortified himself with nothing but hope, and mistook empty words as a true promise of reinforcements. He imagined that a huge army was coming to his aid, but what actually arrived turned out to be even smaller than the smallest of his fantasies. And so, with daydreams that could only belong to a madman, he closed his eyes and leaped into destruction.

HASTINGS

But, begging your pardon, there's no harm in making guesses and hopeful strategies.

LORD BARDOLPH

Yes, there is. Presently, our armies are already in motion, but putting our hope in them is as ridiculous as expecting that early spring buds will produce fruit: at that time of year, buds are more likely to be killed by frost than to bloom. When we want to put up a building, first we survey the land, and then we draw up a set of plans. Then we calculate the cost, and if we can't afford it, we revise the plans with fewer rooms, or we decide not to build at all. In the great task we're attempting—the taking down of one kingdom, and the building of another—we have even more reason to evaluate the land and the plans. We must be certain that the foundation is sound, that the engineer is skilled. We must know precisely what we can afford, how ready and able we are, and we must consider the opposing arguments.

We fortify in paper and in figures,
Using the names of men instead of men,
Like one that draws the model of a house
Beyond his power to build it, who, half through,
60 Gives o'er and leaves his part-created cost
A naked subject to the weeping clouds
And waste for churlish winter's tyranny.

HASTINGS
Grant that our hopes, yet likely of fair birth,
Should be stillborn and that we now possessed
65 The utmost man of expectation,
I think we are a body strong enough,
Even as we are, to equal with the King.

LORD BARDOLPH
What, is the King but five-and-twenty-thousand?

HASTINGS
To us no more, nay, not so much, Lord Bardolph,
70 For his divisions, as the times do brawl,
Are in three heads: one power against the French,
And one against Glendower; perforce a third
Must take up us. So is the unfirm King
In three divided, and his coffers sound
75 With hollow poverty and emptiness.

ARCHBISHOP
That he should draw his several strengths together
And come against us in full puissance
Need not be dreaded.

HASTINGS
                        If he should do so,
He leaves his back unarmed, the French and Welsh
80 Baying him at the heels. Never fear that.

LORD BARDOLPH
Who is it like should lead his forces hither?

Otherwise, it becomes a meaningless exercise: papers and numbers, and names of men rather than real, live men. That's like drawing up plans for a house you can't possibly afford, building half of it, and then abandoning the partly-built structure to be ruined by the elements.

HASTINGS

Let's suppose that everything we're hoping for fails to materialize, and the army we have now is as big as it's going to get. I still think that, even in this condition, we're a match for the King.

LORD BARDOLPH

Why? Does the King only have twenty-five thousand men?

HASTINGS

The King isn't facing us with any more than that—in fact, he doesn't even have that many, Lord Bardolph. This is a time of war, and the King's had to divide his army into three sections. One division is fighting the French; one's fighting Glendower. That leaves a third of his army to fight against us. The King is weak and divided into three, and the coffers of his treasury echo with the sounds of hollow poverty and emptiness.

ARCHBISHOP

There's no reason to fear that he will pull all three divisions together and confront us with his full strength.

HASTINGS

If he did that, he'd be vulnerable at the rear, and the French and the Welsh would be at his heels. He would never let that happen.

LORD BARDOLPH

Who's going to lead his troops against us?

HASTINGS
>The Duke of Lancaster and Westmoreland;
>Against the Welsh, himself and Harry Monmouth;
>But who is substituted against the French
>I have no certain notice.

85

ARCHBISHOP
>   Let us on,
>And publish the occasion of our arms.
>The commonwealth is sick of their own choice.
>Their over-greedy love hath surfeited.
>An habitation giddy and unsure

90
>Hath he that buildeth on the vulgar heart.
>O thou fond many, with what loud applause
>Didst thou beat heaven with blessing Bolingbroke
>Before he was what thou wouldst have him be.
>And being now trimmed in thine own desires,

95
>Thou, beastly feeder, art so full of him
>That thou provok'st thyself to cast him up.
>So, so, thou common dog, didst thou disgorge
>Thy glutton bosom of the royal Richard,
>And now thou wouldst eat thy dead vomit up

100
>And howl'st to find it. What trust is in these times?
>They that, when Richard lived, would have him die
>Are now become enamored on his grave.
>Thou, that threw'st dust upon his goodly head
>When through proud London he came sighing on

105
>After th' admired heels of Bolingbroke,
>Criest now "O earth, yield us that King again,
>And take thou this!" O thoughts of men accursed!
>Past and to come seems best; things present, worst.

MOWBRAY
>Shall we go draw our numbers and set on?

HASTINGS
110
>We are time's subjects, and time bids begone.
>   *Exeunt*

HASTINGS

> The Duke of Lancaster and Westmoreland. The King and Harry Monmouth will fight against the Welsh. I don't know for sure who is in charge of the fight against the French.

ARCHBISHOP

> Let's continue. We'll publicly proclaim the reasons we're fighting. The people are sick of the leadership they themselves supported. They were greedy for it, but now they have overfed. When you build your foundation on the public's love, you build on shaky and unsure ground. Oh, you foolish masses! You shouted your love for Bolingbroke to the skies, before you knew what he'd turn into. Now that you're dressed in the things you desired, you monstrous devourer, you're so full of Bolingbroke that you're ready to vomit him up. This, you vulgar dog, is just how you emptied your gluttonous stomach of King Richard; and now you want to eat up your dead vomit, and you howl trying to find it. What can you count on in this world? The very people who wanted Richard dead when he was alive are now in love with his corpse. The very people who threw garbage on his noble head when he marched through London in shame behind the admired Bolingbroke are now saying, "Oh Earth, return that King, and take this one!" Curses on men's thoughts! Only the past and the future appeal to them; whatever they have right now they despise.

MOWBRAY

> Should we gather our troops and press forward?

HASTINGS

> Time is our commander, and time proposes we be on our way.

> *They exit.*

ACT TWO

SCENE 1

Enter MISTRESS QUICKLY, *with two officers;* FANG *with her and* SNARE *following*

MISTRESS QUICKLY
    Master Fang, have you entered the action?

FANG
    It is entered.

MISTRESS QUICKLY
    Where's your yeoman? Is 't a lusty yeoman? Will a' stand to 't?

FANG
5   Sirrah! Where's Snare?

MISTRESS QUICKLY
    O Lord, ay, good Master Snare.

SNARE
    Here, here.

FANG
    Snare, we must arrest Sir John Falstaff.

MISTRESS QUICKLY
    Yea, good Master Snare, I have entered him and all.

SNARE
10   It may chance cost some of us our lives, for he will stab.

MISTRESS QUICKLY
    Alas the day, take heed of him. He stabbed me in mine own house, and that most beastly, in good faith. He cares not what mischief he does. If his weapon be out, he will foin like any devil. He will spare neither man, woman, nor child.

FANG
15   If I can close with him, I care not for his thrust.

ACT TWO
SCENE 1

MISTRESS QUICKLY *enters with Sheriff* FANG. *Deputy*
SNARE *follows.*

MISTRESS QUICKLY

Master Fang, have you filed the lawsuit?

FANG

It's filed.

MISTRESS QUICKLY

Where's your deputy? Is he a strong deputy? Will he
rise to the occasion?

FANG

Sirrah, where's Snare?

MISTRESS QUICKLY

Oh my goodness! Master Snare!

SNARE

Here, here.

FANG

Snare, we've got to arrest Sir John Falstaff.

MISTRESS QUICKLY

Yes, good Master Snare. I've filed the suit against him
and everything.

SNARE

It could cost some of us our lives: he'll stab.

MISTRESS QUICKLY

Oh my goodness! Watch out for him: he stabbed me in
my own house, and it was nasty. I swear, he doesn't
care what trouble he causes. Once he's got his weapon
out, he'll thrust it like the devil. He won't spare man,
woman, or child.

FANG

If I can get close to him, I won't worry about his
thrusting.

MISTRESS QUICKLY
No, nor I neither. I'll be at your elbow.

FANG
An I but fist him once, an he come but within my view—

MISTRESS QUICKLY
I am undone by his going. I warrant you, he's an infinitive
thing upon my score. Good Master Fang, hold him sure.
20   Good Master Snare, let him not 'scape. He comes
continuantly to Pie Corner, saving your manhoods, to buy
a saddle, and he is indited to dinner to the Lubber's Head in
Lumbert Street, to Master Smooth's the silkman. I pray
you, since my exion is entered, and my case so openly
25   known to the world, let him be brought in to his answer. A
hundred mark is a long one for a poor lone woman to bear,
and I have borne, and borne, and borne, and have been
fubbed off, and fubbed off, and fubbed off from this day to
that day, that it is a shame to be thought on. There is no
30   honesty in such dealing, unless a woman should be made an
ass and a beast to bear every knave's wrong. Yonder he
comes, and that errant malmsey-nose knave, Bardolph,
with him. Do your offices, do your offices, Master Fang and
Master Snare, do me, do me, do me your offices.

Enter FALSTAFF, BARDOLPH, *and* PAGE

FALSTAFF
35   How now! Whose mare's dead? What's the matter?

FANG
Sir John, I arrest you at the suit of Mistress Quickly.

MISTRESS QUICKLY

Me neither. I'll be right next to you.

FANG

If I can grab him once, if he just comes within my grasp—

MISTRESS QUICKLY

I'm bankrupt from his never paying. He's run up an infinitive bill with me. Catch him, Master Fang! Don't let him get away, Master Snare! He's always going to Pie Corner—sorry to mention it—to buy a saddle. And every day he gets indited to lunch with Master Smooth the silk seller, at the Leopard's Head on Lumbert Street. Please bring him to justice. I've been entered—I mean, my lawsuit's been entered at court, and the whole world knows how easy I am—I mean how easy it was for him to rip me off. A hundred marks is a lot for a poor, solitary woman to take. And I've taken it, and taken it, and taken it. And I've been fobbed off and fobbed off and fobbed off, day in and day out. It's horrible to even think about. That's a terrible way to treat people, unless you think that every woman should be made an ass and an animal, and that she should be opened to every jerk's molestation. Here he comes, with that notorious wine-faced crook, Bardolph. Do me a favor and do me your jobs, Master Fang and Master Snare. Do me! Do me! Do me a favor and do me your jobs!

> i.e., "he's run up a bill as big as infinity." Mistress Quickly has a tendency to comically mangle her phrases.

> Pie Corner was a market known for cook's shops, horses, and sex. "Saddle" is a pun on female genitalia.

> indited = invited

> mark = unit of currency

FALSTAFF, *his* PAGE, *and* BARDOLPH *enter.*

FALSTAFF

What's going on? Whose horse died? What's the matter?

FANG

Sir John, you're under arrest for charges brought by Mistress Quickly.

FALSTAFF
Away, varlets!—Draw, Bardolph. Cut me off the villain's
head. Throw the quean in the channel.

MISTRESS QUICKLY
Throw me in the channel? I'll throw thee in the channel.
40   Wilt thou, wilt thou, thou bastardly rogue?—Murder,
murder!—Ah, thou honeysuckle villain, wilt thou kill
God's officers and the King's? Ah, thou honeyseed rogue,
thou art a honeyseed, a man-queller, and a woman-queller.

FALSTAFF
Keep them off, Bardolph.

FANG
45   A rescue, a rescue!

MISTRESS QUICKLY
Good people, bring a rescue or two.— *(to* **FALSTAFF***)* Thou
wot, wot thou? Thou wot, wot ta? Do, do, thou rogue. Do,
thou hempseed.

FALSTAFF
Away, you scullion, you rampallion, you fustilarian! I'll
50   tickle your catastrophe.

Enter the Lord **CHIEF JUSTICE** *and his men*

CHIEF JUSTICE
What is the matter? Keep the peace here, ho!

MISTRESS QUICKLY
Good my lord, be good to me. I beseech you stand to me.

CHIEF JUSTICE
How now, Sir John? What, are you brawling here?
Doth this become your place, your time, and business?
55   You should have been well on your way to York.—
(to **FANG***)* Stand from him, fellow: wherefore hang'st thou
upon him?

FALSTAFF

Get out of here, you crooks! Draw your sword, Bardolph. Cut off this rascal's head, and throw this whore in the gutter.

MISTRESS QUICKLY

Throw me in the gutter? I'll throw you in the gutter. You will? You will? You bastardly cheat! Murder! Murder! Oh, you honeysuckle criminal! You're going to kill God's sheriffs, and the King's? Oh, you honey-seed creep! You're a honey-seed, a man-killer, and a woman-killer.

honeysuckle, honey-seed, hemp-seed = homicidal, homicide

FALSTAFF

Keep them off me, Bardolph.

FANG

An escape! An escape!

MISTRESS QUICKLY

Somebody, bring an escape or two! *(to FALSTAFF)* You will, will you? You will, will you? Go ahead, go ahead, you scoundrel! You hemp-seed!

Mistress Quickly mistakes Fang's warning as a request for "escapes."

FALSTAFF

Get off, you serving wench! You ruffian! You fat old hag! I'll beat you on the backside!

The Lord CHIEF JUSTICE *and his men enter.*

CHIEF JUSTICE

What's the matter? Let's have some order here!

MISTRESS QUICKLY

Good sir, be good to me. I beg you, stand up for me.

CHIEF JUSTICE

Well if it isn't Sir John! Are you making trouble here? Is this appropriate for a man of your position, your age, and your responsibilities? You should be well on your way to York by now. *(to FANG)* Get off him, man. Why are you holding him?

MISTRESS QUICKLY
O my most worshipful lord, an 't please your Grace, I am a
poor widow of Eastcheap, and he is arrested at my suit.

CHIEF JUSTICE
For what sum?

MISTRESS QUICKLY
60   It is more than for some, my lord; it is for all I have. He hath
eaten me out of house and home. He hath put all my substance
into that fat belly of his. *(to* FALSTAFF*)* But I will have some
of it out again, or I will ride thee o' nights like the mare.

FALSTAFF
I think I am as like to ride the mare if I have any vantage of
65   ground to get up.

CHIEF JUSTICE
How comes this, Sir John? Fie, what man of good temper
would endure this tempest of exclamation? Are you not
ashamed to enforce a poor widow to so rough a course to
come by her own?

FALSTAFF
70   *(to* MISTRESS QUICKLY*)* What is the gross sum that I owe thee?

MISTRESS QUICKLY
Marry, if thou wert an honest man, thyself and the money
too. Thou didst swear to me upon a parcel-gilt goblet,
sitting in my Dolphin chamber at the round table by a sea-
coal fire, upon Wednesday in Wheeson week, when the
75   Prince broke thy head for liking his father to a singing-man
of Windsor, thou didst swear to me then, as I was washing
thy wound, to marry me and make me my lady thy wife.
Canst thou deny it? Did not goodwife Keech, the butcher's
wife, come in then and call me Gossip Quickly, coming in
80   to borrow a mess of vinegar; telling us she had a good dish
of prawns, whereby thou didst desire to eat some, whereby
I told thee they were ill for a green wound? And didst thou
not, when she was gone downstairs, desire me to be no more

MISTRESS QUICKLY

Oh, most excellent lord, begging your pardon: I'm a poor Eastcheap widow, and he's arrested on charges I brought against him.

CHIEF JUSTICE

What sum does he owe you?

MISTRESS QUICKLY

It's more than some, sir: it's all, all that I have. He's eaten me out of house and home. He's put everything I own into that fat belly of his. *(to* FALSTAFF*)* But I'll get some of it back again, or I'll ride you all night like a bad dream.

FALSTAFF

I think I might just ride you, if I get the chance to mount you.

CHIEF JUSTICE

What is this, Sir John? Damn! How could any decent man put up with this storm of screaming and cursing? Aren't you ashamed to force a poor widow to take these extreme measures simply to get what's hers?

FALSTAFF

(to MISTRESS QUICKLY*)* What's the total I owe you?

MISTRESS QUICKLY

My goodness! If you were an honest man, you'd give yourself to me, as well as the money. You swore to me—over a gold-plated wine goblet, in the Dolphin Room in my tavern, at the round table, next to the fire, on the Wednesday seven weeks after Easter, when the Prince swung at your head for claiming his father was a fake—you swore, while I was cleaning your wounds, to marry me and make me a proper lady and your wife. Can you deny it? Didn't Mrs. Baconfat, the butcher's wife, come into the room then and ask to borrow some vinegar, saying that she had some good prawns—and you wanted to eat some, and I told you that it was a bad idea, to eat shrimp when you had a fresh wound—and

85 so familiarity with such poor people, saying that ere long
they should call me madam? And didst thou not kiss me
and bid me fetch thee thirty shillings? I put thee now to thy
book-oath. Deny it if thou canst.

FALSTAFF
My lord, this is a poor mad soul, and she says up and down
the town that her eldest son is like you. She hath been in
90 good case, and the truth is, poverty hath distracted her. But,
for these foolish officers, I beseech you I may have redress
against them.

CHIEF JUSTICE
Sir John, Sir John, I am well acquainted with your manner
of wrenching the true cause the false way. It is not a
95 confident brow, nor the throng of words that come with
such more than impudent sauciness from you, can thrust
me from a level consideration. You have, as it appears to me,
practiced upon the easy-yielding spirit of this woman, and
made her serve your uses both in purse and in person.

MISTRESS QUICKLY
100 Yea, in truth, my lord.

CHIEF JUSTICE
Pray thee, peace.— *(to* FALSTAFF*)* Pay her the debt you owe
her, and unpay the villany you have done her. The one you
may do with sterling money, and the other with current
repentance.

FALSTAFF
105 My lord, I will not undergo this sneap without reply. You
call honorable boldness "impudent sauciness." If a man
will make curtsy and say nothing, he is virtuous. No, my
lord, my humble duty remembered, I will not be your
suitor. I say to you, I do desire deliverance from these
110 officers, being upon hasty employment in the King's affairs.

shillings = unit of currency

when she left, didn't you tell me to stop being friends with low types like her, because before long we'd be married and I'd be a proper lady? And didn't you kiss me and tell me to lend you thirty shillings? Put your hand on the bible and deny it, if you dare.

FALSTAFF

Sir, this is a poor, insane soul. She's been saying all over town that her oldest son looks just like you. She was once rich, but poverty has driven her crazy. Now, as for these two foolish officers, I would like to press charges against them.

CHIEF JUSTICE

Sir John, Sir John. I know too well how you are accustomed to turning the truth into a big lie. But neither your confident demeanor nor the storm of words that accompanies your insolent disrespect will sway me from making a just consideration. As far as I can see, you've taken advantage of this trusting woman, and you've made her give you cash and other favors.

MISTRESS QUICKLY

Yes, truthfully, sir.

CHIEF JUSTICE

Quiet, please. *(to* **FALSTAFF***)* Pay her what you owe her, and undo the wrongdoings you've done to her. You can do the first with money, and the second with a sincere apology.

FALSTAFF

Sir, I will not put up with this snub without a reply. You call my brave, honorable dealings insolent disrespect. Does a man have to stand here, silent and bowing, to be a virtuous man? No, sir. With all due respect, I won't bow down to you. I say that I want to be set free by these officers, seeing as I have urgent work to do for the King.

CHIEF JUSTICE
You speak as having power to do wrong; but answer in th'
effect of your reputation, and satisfy this poor woman.

FALSTAFF
Come hither, hostess.

FALSTAFF *takes* MISTRESS QUICKLY *aside*

Enter GOWER

CHIEF JUSTICE
Now, Master Gower, what news?

GOWER
115 The King, my lord, and Harry Prince of Wales
Are near at hand. The rest the paper tells.

FALSTAFF
As I am a gentleman!

MISTRESS QUICKLY
Faith, you said so before.

FALSTAFF
As I am a gentleman. Come. No more words of it.

MISTRESS QUICKLY
120 By this heavenly ground I tread on, I must be fain to pawn
both my plate and the tapestry of my dining chambers.

FALSTAFF
Glasses, glasses, is the only drinking. And for thy walls, a
pretty slight drollery, or the story of the Prodigal or the
German hunting in waterwork is worth a thousand of these
125 bed-hangers and these fly-bitten tapestries. Let it be ten
pound, if thou canst. Come, an 'twere not for thy humors,
there's not a better wench in England. Go wash thy face,
and draw the action. Come, thou must not be in this humor
with me. Dost not know me? Come, come, I know thou
130 wast set on to this.

CHIEF JUSTICE

You talk as though you have permission to break the law. But act appropriately to your status: satisfy this poor woman.

FALSTAFF

Come here, hostess.

FALSTAFF *takes* MISTRESS QUICKLY *aside.*

GOWER *enters.*

CHIEF JUSTICE

Master Gower, what's going on?

GOWER

My lord, the King and Harry Prince of Wales are nearby. This letter will tell you the rest.

FALSTAFF

On my honor.

MISTRESS QUICKLY

Honestly, that's what you said before.

FALSTAFF

On my honor. Come, let's not talk about it anymore.

MISTRESS QUICKLY

By heaven above and below, I'll have to pawn my good china and the tapestries in my dining rooms.

FALSTAFF

It's not such a big deal. Glass is the only good thing to drink out of anyway. And as for the walls, something pretty and comical—or a depiction of the prodigal son; or maybe one of those German hunting scenes, painted on the wall to look like a tapestry—why, those are worth a thousand of those bed curtains and moth-eaten tapestries. Let me borrow just ten pounds, all right? Come on—other than your moodiness, you're the best wench in England. Go wash your face and withdraw the lawsuit. Come on—don't be this way

The Biblical tale of the prodigal son, who wastes his inheritance before contritely returning to his father's house, was a popular subject for wall decorations.

MISTRESS QUICKLY
Pray thee, Sir John, let it be but twenty nobles. I' faith, I am
loath to pawn my plate, so God save me, la.

FALSTAFF
Let it alone. I'll make other shift. You'll be a fool still.

MISTRESS QUICKLY
Well, you shall have it, though I pawn my gown. I hope
135   you'll come to supper. You'll pay me all together?

FALSTAFF
Will I live? *(to* BARDOLPH*)* Go with her, with her. Hook on,
hook on.

MISTRESS QUICKLY
Will you have Doll Tearsheet meet you at supper?

FALSTAFF
No more words. Let's have her.
                              Exeunt MISTRESS QUICKLY, FANG, SNARE,
                                         BARDOLPH, *and the* PAGE

CHIEF JUSTICE
140   I have heard better news.

FALSTAFF
What's the news, my good lord?

CHIEF JUSTICE
Where lay the King last night?

GOWER
At Basingstoke, my lord.

FALSTAFF
I hope, my lord, all's well. What is the news, my lord?

CHIEF JUSTICE
145   Come all his forces back?

with me. Don't you know me? Come, come, I know somebody put you up to this.

MISTRESS QUICKLY

noble = unit of currency; twenty nobles = approximately six pounds

Please, Sir John, let's call it twenty nobles. I don't want to have to pawn my china, in God's name!

FALSTAFF

All right, forget it. I'll figure something else out. You'll always be a fool.

MISTRESS QUICKLY

All right, I'll lend it to you, even if I have to pawn my clothes. I hope you'll have dinner here tonight. You'll pay me the full amount then?

FALSTAFF

Will I live? *(to* BARDOLPH*)* Go, stick with her, stick with her. Don't let her out of your sight.

MISTRESS QUICKLY

Do you want Doll Tearsheet to meet you at dinner?

FALSTAFF

No more talking. Let's have her.

> MISTRESS QUICKLY, BARDOLPH, *the* PAGE, FANG, *and* SNARE *exit.*

CHIEF JUSTICE

I've heard better news.

FALSTAFF

What's the news, my lord?

CHIEF JUSTICE

Where did the King spend last night?

GOWER

At Basingstoke, sir.

FALSTAFF

I hope everything's okay, sir. What's the news?

CHIEF JUSTICE

And his armies have come back?

GOWER
No; fifteen hundred foot, five hundred horse
Are marched up to my Lord of Lancaster
Against Northumberland and the Archbishop.

FALSTAFF
Comes the King back from Wales, my noble lord?

CHIEF JUSTICE
150   You shall have letters of me presently.
Come. Go along with me, good Master Gower.

FALSTAFF
My lord!

CHIEF JUSTICE
What's the matter?

FALSTAFF
Master Gower, shall I entreat you with me to dinner?

GOWER
155   I must wait upon my good lord here. I thank you, good Sir
John.

CHIEF JUSTICE
Sir John, you loiter here too long, being you are to take
soldiers up in counties as you go.

FALSTAFF
Will you sup with me, Master Gower?

CHIEF JUSTICE
160   What foolish master taught you these manners, Sir John?

FALSTAFF
Master Gower, if they become me not, he was a fool that
taught them me.—This is the right fencing grace, my lord:
tap for tap, and so part fair.

CHIEF JUSTICE
Now the Lord lighten thee. Thou art a great fool.

Exeunt

GOWER

> No. Fifteen hundred infantrymen and five hundred horsemen are marching to meet Lord Lancaster, to fight against Northumberland and the Archbishop.

FALSTAFF

> Is the King back from Wales, my noble lord?

CHIEF JUSTICE

> I'll give you some letters shortly. Come with me, Master Gower.

FALSTAFF

> Sir!

CHIEF JUSTICE

> What's the matter?

FALSTAFF

> Master Gower, would you like to join me for lunch?

GOWER

> I have to attend to this noble man right here. But thank you, Sir John.

CHIEF JUSTICE

> Sir John, you've been loitering here too long. You have to recruit soldiers in the counties you pass through on your way north.

FALSTAFF

> Will you join me for supper, then, Master Gower?

CHIEF JUSTICE

> What foolish teacher taught you these manners, Sir John?

FALSTAFF

Falstaff is referencing an earlier part of the scene, when the Chief Justice similarly ignored Falstaff.

> Master Gower, if my manners are inappropriate, I must have indeed been taught by a fool. That's how the game is played—tit for tat, and game over.

CHIEF JUSTICE

> God help you! You are a great fool.

> *They exit.*

ACT 2, SCENE 2

Enter PRINCE HENRY *and* POINS

PRINCE HENRY
Before God, I am exceeding weary.

POINS
Is 't come to that? I had thought weariness durst not have
attached one of so high blood.

PRINCE HENRY
Faith, it does me; though it discolors the complexion of my
5   greatness to acknowledge it. Doth it not show vilely in me
to desire small beer?

POINS
Why, a prince should not be so loosely studied as to
remember so weak a composition.

PRINCE HENRY
Belike then my appetite was not princely got, for, by my
10   troth, I do now remember the poor creature small beer. But
indeed these humble considerations make me out of love
with my greatness. What a disgrace is it to me to remember
thy name, or to know thy face tomorrow, or to take note how
many pair of silk stockings thou hast—with these, and
15   those that were thy peach-colored ones—or to bear the
inventory of thy shirts, as, one for superfluity and another
for use. But that the tennis-court keeper knows better than
I, for it is a low ebb of linen with thee when thou keepest not
racket there, as thou hast not done a great while, because the
20   rest of the low countries have made a shift to eat up thy
holland; and God knows whether those that bawl out the
ruins of thy linen shall inherit His kingdom; but the
midwives say the children are not in the fault, whereupon
the   world   increases   and   kindreds   are   mightily
25   strengthened.

ACT 2, SCENE 2

PRINCE HENRY *and* POINS *enter.*

PRINCE HENRY

I swear to God, I'm exceedingly tired.

POINS

Really? I would have thought that weariness wouldn't dare afflict someone as highly born as you.

PRINCE HENRY

small beer =
a kind of weak,
thin beer

Well, it afflicts me, although saying so dims my nobility somewhat. Does it make me seem coarse and common to say that I'd love a small beer?

POINS

A prince shouldn't be vulgarly inclined toward things like small beer.

PRINCE HENRY

Then I suppose don't have a prince's appetite, because right now all I can think about is small beer. But it's true: all these everyday considerations distance me from my own nobility. It's disgraceful that I should be familiar with a man like you! To know your name, your face, and your wardrobe so intimately that I know that you have two pairs of stockings: the ones you're wearing now, and those peach-colored ones. I even know how many shirts you have: one to wear, and one extra. But then, the keeper of the tennis courts knows your wardrobe better than I do, for when you've run out of clean shirts, you don't show up to play. And you haven't played in a while, because the whore houses have eaten all the rest of your money, which you'd otherwise use to buy more shirts. God only knows whether all the crying brats you've fathered will make it to heaven. But then, the midwives say that babies don't bear the sins of the parents.

POINS
How ill it follows, after you have labored so hard, you should talk so idly! Tell me, how many good young princes would do so, their fathers being so sick as yours at this time is?

PRINCE HENRY
Shall I tell thee one thing, Poins?

POINS
30   Yes, faith, and let it be an excellent good thing.

PRINCE HENRY
It shall serve among wits of no higher breeding than thine.

POINS
Go to. I stand the push of your one thing that you will tell.

PRINCE HENRY
Marry, I tell thee it is not meet that I should be sad, now my father is sick—albeit I could tell thee, as to one it pleases me,
35   for fault of a better, to call my friend, I could be sad, and sad indeed too.

POINS
Very hardly, upon such a subject.

PRINCE HENRY
By this hand, thou thinkest me as far in the devil's book as thou and Falstaff for obduracy and persistency. Let the end
40   try the man. But I tell thee, my heart bleeds inwardly that my father is so sick: and keeping such vile company as thou art hath in reason taken from me all ostentation of sorrow.

POINS
The reason?

PRINCE HENRY
What wouldst thou think of me if I should weep?

That's how the population increases, and families are strengthened.

POINS

It seems wrong, after all your hard work in battle, that you should be spending your time now in idle chatter. How many other princes would behave like this if their fathers were as sick as yours?

PRINCE HENRY

Can I tell you something, Poins?

POINS

Sure; and make sure it's an excellent thing.

PRINCE HENRY

It'll be fine, for people who aren't any smarter than you are.

POINS

Go ahead. I'm can take whatever you have to say.

PRINCE HENRY

Here it is, then. It's not seemly for me to be sad over my father's illness. But I could tell you—as a person who, for lack of anyone else, I'm pleased to call my friend—that I could be sad. I could be very sad, indeed.

POINS

It would be difficult to feel that way over a thing like this.

PRINCE HENRY

I swear, you must think that I'm as sinful as you and Falstaff are, and as stubborn and persistent. We'll see about that. But I'm telling you: my heart is bleeding for my father, and for his illness. But because I'm hanging out with lowlifes like you, I can't show how sorrowful I am.

POINS

Why?

PRINCE HENRY

What would you think of me if I started crying?

POINS

45   I would think thee a most princely hypocrite.

PRINCE HENRY

It would be every man's thought, and thou art a blessed
fellow to think as every man thinks. Never a man's thought
in the world keeps the roadway better than thine. Every
man would think me an hypocrite indeed. And what accites
50   your most worshipful thought to think so?

POINS

Why, because you have been so lewd and so much engraffed
to Falstaff.

PRINCE HENRY

And to thee.

POINS

By this light, I am well spoke on. I can hear it with my own
55   ears. The worst that they can say of me is that I am a second
brother, and that I am a proper fellow of my hands; and
those two things, I confess, I cannot help. By the Mass, here
comes Bardolph.

Enter BARDOLPH *and the* PAGE

PRINCE HENRY

And the boy that I gave Falstaff. He had him from me
60   Christian, and look if the fat villain have not transformed
him ape.

BARDOLPH

God save your Grace.

PRINCE HENRY

And yours, most noble Bardolph.

POINS

(to BARDOLPH*)* Come, you virtuous ass, you bashful fool,
65   must you be blushing? Wherefore blush you now? What a
maidenly man-at-arms are you become! Is 't such a matter
to get a pottle-pot's maidenhead?

POINS

I would think you're a royal hypocrite.

PRINCE HENRY

That's what everyone would be thinking. And what's great about you is that you think just the way everyone else does: nobody sticks to popular opinion quite as well as you. Everyone would think I was a hypocrite, indeed. And, your honor, what makes you think that?

POINS

Because you've behaved so badly, and because you're so attached to Falstaff.

PRINCE HENRY

And to you.

POINS

Honestly, people think highly of me; I hear their praises with my own ears. The worst thing they can say about me is that, as a younger brother, I've had no inheritance from my family, and that I'm a good fighter. And I can't help either of those things. By God, here comes Bardolph.

BARDOLPH *and the* PAGE *enter.*

PRINCE HENRY

And the boy who I sent to work for Falstaff. He was a normal boy when I sent him, and now look: the fat bastard's turned him into an ape.

Possibly, Falstaff has dressed his page in a ridiculous outfit.

BARDOLPH

God save your grace!

PRINCE HENRY

And yours, most noble Bardolph!

POINS

Poins and the page are joking about Bardolph's face, which is red from drinking.

(to BARDOLPH*)* Come on, you principled ass, you timid fool! Why are you blushing? What a womanly solider you are! Is it that big a deal to deflower a two-quart tankard of ale?

PAGE
> He calls me e'en now, my lord, through a red lattice, and I
> could discern no part of his face from the window. At last I
> 70 spied his eyes, and methought he had made two holes in the
> ale-wife's new petticoat and so peeped through.

PRINCE HENRY
> Has not the boy profited?

BARDOLPH
> Away, you whoreson upright rabbit, away!

PAGE
> Away, you rascally Althea's dream, away!

PRINCE HENRY
> 75 Instruct us, boy. What dream, boy?

PAGE
> Marry, my lord, Althea dreamt she was delivered of a
> firebrand, and therefore I call him her dream.

PRINCE HENRY
> A crown's worth of good interpretation. There 'tis, boy.

POINS
> O, that this good blossom could be kept from cankers! Well,
> 80 there is sixpence to preserve thee.

BARDOLPH
> An you do not make him hanged among you, the gallows
> shall have wrong.

PRINCE HENRY
> And how doth thy master, Bardolph?

BARDOLPH
> Well, my good lord. He heard of your Grace's coming to
> 85 town. There's a letter for you.

POINS
> Delivered with good respect. And how doth the Martlemas
> your master?

BARDOLPH
> In bodily health, sir.

PAGE

> Just now he called to me from behind a red window
> shade, and I couldn't tell his face from the curtain!
> Finally I saw his eyes, and I thought he'd made two
> holes in a whore's skirt and peeped through them!

PRINCE HENRY

> This kid's learned a lot from Falstaff, hasn't he?

BARDOLPH

> Get out of here, you little rabbit! Get out!

PAGE

> You get out, you rotten Althea's dream!

PRINCE HENRY

> What dream, boy? Tell us.

PAGE

> Sir, Althea dreamed she gave birth to a red-hot iron.
> That's why I call him her dream; he's all red in the face.

PRINCE HENRY

crown = kind
of coin

> That joke's worth a crown! Here you go, boy.

POINS

> I wish this wholesome little flower could be kept away
> from disease. Well, here's a sixpence for you.

BARDOLPH

> If between the three of you this boy doesn't end up
> hanged, the gallows will be cheated.

PRINCE HENRY

> How's your master Falstaff doing, Bardolph?

BARDOLPH

> Fine, sir. He heard you were coming to town. Here's a
> letter for you.

POINS

> Delivered very respectfully. How is that fattened calf,
> your boss?

BARDOLPH

> His body's healthy, sir.

POINS

90 Marry, the immortal part needs a physician, but that moves
not him. Though that be sick, it dies not.

PRINCE HENRY

(reads to himself) I do allow this wen to be as familiar with
me as my dog, and he holds his place, for look you how be
writes. *(he hands the letter to* **POINS***)*

POINS

(reads) John Falstaff, knight. Every man must know that as
95 oft as he has occasion to name himself, even like those that
are kin to the King, for they never prick their finger but they
say, "There's some of the King's blood spilt." "How comes
that?" says he that takes upon him not to conceive. The
answer is as ready as a borrower's cap: "I am the King's poor
100 cousin, sir."

PRINCE HENRY

Nay, they will be kin to us, or they will fetch it from
Japheth. But to the letter. *(takes the letter and reads) Sir John
Falstaff, knight, to the son of the King nearest his father,
Harry Prince of Wales, greeting.*

POINS

105 Why, this is a certificate.

PRINCE HENRY

Peace! *(reads) I will imitate the honorable Romans in brevity.*

POINS

He sure means brevity in breath, short-winded.

PRINCE HENRY

*(reads) I commend me to thee, I commend thee, and I leave
thee. Be not too familiar with Poins, for he misuses thy favors
110 so much that he swears thou art to marry his sister Nell.
Repent at idle times as thou mayest, and so, farewell. Thine*

POINS

That's right, it's just his immortal soul that needs a doctor. But he doesn't care. His soul may be sick, but it won't die.

PRINCE HENRY

(reads to himself) I allow this wart to be as familiar with me as my dog, and he holds onto his privileged position. Listen to how he writes. *(he hands the letter to* **POINS***)*

POINS

(reads) "John Falstaff, knight"—he always throws that title around, every chance he gets. It's like people who are related to the King: every time they get a tiny cut, they say, "Some of the King's blood has been spilled." Then someone pretends not to get it, and asks, "How do you mean?" The answer comes faster than a beggar can whip out his cap: "I'm the King's poor relative."

PRINCE HENRY

Right. They all say they're related to us, even if they have to trace the family tree all the way back to Japhet, the common ancestor of all Europeans. But back to the letter. *(takes the letter and reads)* "Sir John Falstaff—knight to the son of the King, nearest to his father, Harry Prince of Wales—sends his greetings."

POINS

Listen to that. It sounds like a contract.

PRINCE HENRY

Quiet! *(reads)* "I will copy the Romans in shortness."

POINS

He must mean shortness of breath, and wheezing.

PRINCE HENRY

(reads) "I salute myself, I salute you, and I'm done. Don't get too close to Poins. He takes such rampant advantage of your kindness that he swears you will marry his sister Nell. Confess your sins when you

by yea and no, which is as much as to say, as thou usest him,
Jack Falstaff with my familiars, John with my brothers and
sisters, and Sir John with all Europe.

POINS

115   My lord, I'll steep this letter in sack and make him eat it.

PRINCE HENRY

That's to make him eat twenty of his words. But do you use
me thus, Ned? Must I marry your sister?

POINS

God send the wench no worse fortune! But I never said so.

PRINCE HENRY

Well, thus we play the fools with the time, and the spirits of
120   the wise sit in the clouds and mock us. *(to* **BARDOLPH***)* Is
your master here in London?

BARDOLPH
Yea, my lord.

PRINCE HENRY
Where sups he? Doth the old boar feed in the old frank?

BARDOLPH
At the old place, my lord, in Eastcheap.

PRINCE HENRY
125   What company?

PAGE
Ephesians, my lord, of the old church.

PRINCE HENRY
Sup any women with him?

PAGE
None, my lord, but old Mistress Quickly and Mistress Doll
Tearsheet.

PRINCE HENRY
130   What pagan may that be?

have the time; and with that, farewell. Yours up and down (which is to say, in whatever way you feel like), I remain Jack Falstaff to my friends, John to my brothers and sisters, and Sir John to all Europe."

POINS

Sir, I'll soak this letter in wine and shove it down his throat.

PRINCE HENRY

That would be making him eat twenty of his words. But are you taking advantage of me like he says, Ned? Must I marry your sister?

POINS

It would be her lucky day if you did. But I never said that.

PRINCE HENRY

Well, we're wasting time, and the angels in heaven are mocking us. *(to* BARDOLPH*)* Is your boss here in London?

BARDOLPH

Yes, my lord.

PRINCE HENRY

Where's he eating tonight? Is the old pig eating in the old sty?

BARDOLPH

At the old place, my lord. In Eastcheap.

PRINCE HENRY

Who's with him?

PAGE

The usual old characters.

PRINCE HENRY

Are any women eating with him?

PAGE

No women sir. Just old Mistress Quickly and Mistress Doll Tearsheet.

PRINCE HENRY

What heathen is that?

PAGE
A proper gentlewoman, sir, and a kinswoman of my master's.

PRINCE HENRY
Even such kin as the parish heifers are to the town bull.—
Shall we steal upon them, Ned, at supper?

POINS
135   I am your shadow, my lord. I'll follow you.

PRINCE HENRY
Sirrah—you, boy—and Bardolph, no word to your master
that I am yet come to town. *(gives them money)* There's for
your silence.

BARDOLPH
I have no tongue, sir.

PAGE
140   And for mine, sir, I will govern it.

PRINCE HENRY
Fare you well. Go.

Exeunt BARDOLPH *and* PAGE

This Doll Tearsheet should be some road.

POINS
I warrant you, as common as the way between Saint Alban's
and London.

PRINCE HENRY
145   How might we see Falstaff bestow himself tonight in his
true colors, and not ourselves be seen?

POINS
Put on two leathern jerkins and aprons, and wait upon him
at his table as drawers.

PRINCE HENRY
From a god to a bull: a heavy decension. It was Jove's case.
150   From a prince to a 'prentice: a low transformation that shall
be mine, for in everything the purpose must weigh with the
folly. Follow me, Ned.

Exeunt

PAGE

A proper lady, sir, and my master's relative.

PRINCE HENRY

Exactly the kind of relative as the country cows are to the town bull. Ned, should we spy on them as they eat supper?

POINS

I'm after you like a shadow, my lord: I'll follow you.

PRINCE HENRY

Sirrah, you boy, and you, Bardolph—don't tell your master that I'm back in town. *(gives them money)* This is for your silence.

BARDOLPH

I have no tongue to speak with, sir.

PAGE

As for my tongue, I'll manage it.

PRINCE HENRY

Farewell to you both; go now.

road = slang for "common prostitute"

BARDOLPH *and the* PAGE *exit.*

This Doll Tearsheet must be some road.

POINS

Truly, she's as well-traveled as the highway to London.

PRINCE HENRY

How can we see Falstaff behave like his true self tonight, and yet not be detected ourselves?

POINS

We'll put on leather jackets and aprons and wait upon him as bartenders.

PRINCE HENRY

Should a God disguise himself as a bull? That's quite a degradation. Well, Jove did it. And should a prince disguise himself as an apprentice bartender and transform into something so lowly? Yes, I will: in every undertaking, the ends must match the means. Follow me, Ned.

The Roman god Jove disguised himself as a white bull to carry away the maiden Europa

They exit.

ACT 2, SCENE 3

Enter NORTHUMBERLAND, LADY NORTHUMBERLAND, *and*
LADY PERCY

NORTHUMBERLAND
I pray thee, loving wife and gentle daughter,
Give even way unto my rough affairs.
Put not you on the visage of the times
And be, like them, to Percy troublesome.

LADY NORTHUMBERLAND
5   I have given over. I will speak no more.
Do what you will; your wisdom be your guide.

NORTHUMBERLAND
Alas, sweet wife, my honor is at pawn,
And, but my going, nothing can redeem it.

LADY PERCY
O yet, for God's sake, go not to these wars.
10 The time was, father, that you broke your word,
When you were more endeared to it than now,
When your own Percy, when my heart's dear Harry,
Threw many a northward look to see his father
Bring up his powers; but he did long in vain.
15 Who then persuaded you to stay at home?
There were two honors lost, yours and your son's.
For yours, the God of heaven brighten it.
For his, it stuck upon him as the sun
In the gray vault of heaven, and by his light
20 Did all the chivalry of England move
To do brave acts. He was indeed the glass
Wherein the noble youth did dress themselves.
He had no legs that practiced not his gait;
And speaking thick, which nature made his blemish,
25 Became the accents of the valiant;
For those that could speak low and tardily
Would turn their own perfection to abuse

ACT 2, SCENE 3

NORTHUMBERLAND, LADY NORTHUMBERLAND, *and*
LADY PERCY *enter.*

NORTHUMBERLAND

Please, my loving wife and sweet daughter-in-law,
support me in my difficult tasks. Don't let the grim-
ness of these days be reflected in your faces; don't add
to Percy's troubles.

LADY NORTHUMBERLAND

I give up; I won't say any more. Do what you want.
Let your wisdom guide you.

NORTHUMBERLAND

For goodness sake, sweet wife, my honor is at stake.
Nothing can redeem it except my going.

LADY PERCY

For God's sake, don't go to these wars! Father-in-law,
you once broke your word when you had better reason
to keep it than you do now. Your own son Percy—my
heart's beloved Harry—looked northward again and
again, hoping to see his father coming with an army.
But he hoped in vain. Who persuaded you to stay
home that time? Two honors were lost in that battle:
yours, and your son's. As for yours, I hope God will
make it shine again. As for Harry's honor, it clung to
him like the sun in a pale blue sky, and by its light
every knight in England was moved to act bravely. He
was the mirror in which noble youths dressed themselves. All men copied his way of walking, except
those who had no legs.

And talking loudly and quickly—the one flaw nature
had given him—became the speech pattern for all
brave men. Those who spoke softly and slowly would
corrupt their proper speech, just to seem more like

To seem like him. So that in speech, in gait,
In diet, in affections of delight,
30   In military rules, humors of blood,
He was the mark and glass, copy and book,
That fashioned others. And him—O wondrous him!
O miracle of men!—him did you leave,
Second to none, unseconded by you,
35   To look upon the hideous god of war
In disadvantage, to abide a field
Where nothing but the sound of Hotspur's name
Did seem defensible. So you left him.
Never, O never, do his ghost the wrong
40   To hold your honor more precise and nice
With others than with him. Let them alone.
The Marshal and the Archbishop are strong.
Had my sweet Harry had but half their numbers,
Today might I, hanging on Hotspur's neck,
45   Have talked of Monmouth's grave.

NORTHUMBERLAND
                                    Beshrew your heart,
Fair daughter, you do draw my spirits from me
With new lamenting ancient oversights.
But I must go and meet with danger there,
Or it will seek me in another place
50   And find me worse provided.

LADY NORTHUMBERLAND
                                    Oh, fly to Scotland
Till that the nobles and the armèd commons
Have of their puissance made a little taste.

LADY PERCY
If they get ground and vantage of the King,
Then join you with them like a rib of steel
55   To make strength stronger; but, for all our loves,
First let them try themselves. So did your son;
He was so suffered. So came I a widow,
And never shall have length of life enough

Harry. In speech, bearing, and diet; in inclinations toward pleasure, in military actions, and in moods, he was the target, mirror, example, and rulebook that other men followed. And him—Oh wondrous him! Oh miracle of men!—you left him! The best man in the world, unsupported by you, faced the hideous god of war from a position of weakness. His only defense was the sound of his own name, and that is how you left him.

Never insult his memory by letting your honor count more with strangers than with him. Leave them alone: Marshal Mowbray and the Archbishop are strong. If my darling Harry had had half their army, I might be hanging on his neck today, talking about Prince Hal's grave.

NORTHUMBERLAND

For goodness sake, pretty daughter-in-law. You take me out of myself, reminding me again of these past mistakes. But I must go and face danger there or danger will find me somewhere else, where I will be less prepared.

LADY NORTHUMBERLAND

Oh, run to Scotland until these noblemen and their armies have skirmished against the king.

LADY PERCY

If they make any headway against the King, then join them, and like a steel rod make their strength even stronger. But in the name of the love you feel for us, let them begin on their own. That's how your son fought. You allowed him to do that, and that's how I became a widow. If I spend the rest of my life pouring tears on

To rain upon remembrance with mine eyes
60   That it may grow and sprout as high as heaven
For recordation to my noble husband.

NORTHUMBERLAND
Come, come, go in with me. 'Tis with my mind
As with the tide swelled up unto his height,
That makes a still-stand, running neither way.
65   Fain would I go to meet the Archbishop,
But many thousand reasons hold me back.
I will resolve for Scotland. There am I
Till time and vantage crave my company.

Exeunt

the plant of remembrance, it will never grow tall enough to pay proper tribute to my extraordinary husband.

NORTHUMBERLAND

Come. Come. Go inside with me. My thoughts are like the ocean at high tide—neither coming in nor going out, seeming to stand still. I want to go join the Archbishop, but many thousands of reasons are holding me back. I'll go to Scotland and wait there till events unfold and my help is called for.

They exit.

ACT 2, SCENE 4

Enter two DRAWERS

FRANCIS
What the devil hast thou brought there—applejohns?
Thou knowest Sir John cannot endure an applejohn.

SECOND DRAWER
Mass, thou sayest true. The Prince once set a dish of
applejohns before him and told him there were five more Sir
5   Johns and, putting off his hat, said "I will now take my leave
of these six dry, round, old, withered knights." It angered
him to the heart. But he hath forgot that.

FRANCIS
Why then, cover, and set them down, and see if thou canst
find out Sneak's noise. Mistress Tearsheet would fain hear
10   some music.

Enter THIRD DRAWER

THIRD DRAWER
Dispatch: the room where they supped is too hot. They'll
come in straight.

FRANCIS
Sirrah, here will be the Prince and Master Poins anon, and
they will put on two of our jerkins and aprons, and Sir John
15   must not know of it. Bardolph hath brought word.

THIRD DRAWER
By the Mass, here will be old utis. It will be an excellent
stratagem.

SECOND DRAWER
I'll see if I can find out Sneak.
                                        FRANCIS *and* THE DRAWERS *exit*

ACT 2, SCENE 4

Two DRAWERS *enter.*

FRANCIS

*apple johns = a
variety of apple,
eaten once the
fruit is shriveled*

What the hell have you got there? Apple johns? You
know Sir John can't stand apple johns.

SECOND DRAWER

Damn, you're right. One day the Prince put a plate of
apple-johns in front of Falstaff and said, "Here are
five more Sir Johns." Then the Prince took off his hat
and said, "I'm now going to bid farewell to these six
dry, round, old, withered knights." It angered Sir
John deeply, but he got over it.

FRANCIS

Well then, put the table cloth on and set the dish
down. Go see if you can find Sneak's band of musicians. Mistress Tearsheet wants to hear some music.

Enter THIRD DRAWER

THIRD DRAWER

Hurry! The room they ate in was too hot, and they'll
be here any minute.

FRANCIS

Sirrah, the Prince and Poins will be here soon. They're
going to put on a couple of our jackets and aprons. Sir
John can't know it's them. Bardolph came and told me.

THIRD DRAWER

Well, there's going to be hilarity here! What a great
scheme!

SECOND DRAWER

I'll see if I can find Sneak.

The DRAWERS *exit.*

Enter MISTRESS QUICKLY *and* DOLL TEARSHEET

MISTRESS QUICKLY
I' faith, sweetheart, methinks now you are in an excellent
20   good temperality. Your pulsidge beats as extraordinarily as
heart would desire, and your color, I warrant you, is as red
as any rose, in good truth, la. But, i' faith, you have drunk
too much canaries, and that's a marvellous searching wine,
and it perfumes the blood ere one can say "What's this?"
25   How do you now?

DOLL TEARSHEET
Better than I was. Hem.

MISTRESS QUICKLY
Why, that's well said. A good heart's worth gold.
Lo, here comes Sir John.

Enter FALSTAFF

FALSTAFF
(sings) When Arthur first in court—Empty the jordan. *(sings)*
30   *And was a worthy king*—How now, Mistress Doll?

MISTRESS QUICKLY
Sick of a calm, yea, good faith.

FALSTAFF
So is all her sect. An they be once in a calm, they are sick.

DOLL TEARSHEET
A pox damn you, muddy rascal. Is that all the comfort you
give me?

FALSTAFF
35   You make fat rascals, Mistress Doll.

MISTRESS QUICKLY *and* DOLL TEARSHEET *enter.*

MISTRESS QUICKLY

temporality = temper; pulsidge = pulse

I swear, sweetheart, you seem to be in a great temporality. Your pulsidge is beating as strongly as you could want, and your color is as red as a rose; truly! But seriously, I do think you've drank too much of that sweet wine from the Canary Islands—it's a mighty powerful drink, and it'll get into your blood faster than you can say, "What's this?" How are you feeling now?

DOLL TEARSHEET

Better than I was before. *(she coughs or belches)*

MISTRESS QUICKLY

Well said! A healthy heart is worth its weight in gold. Look, here comes Sir John.

FALSTAFF *enters.*

FALSTAFF

The lyrics are from a popular ballad of the time, "Sir Lancelot du Lake."

(singing) "When Arthur first in court"—somebody empty the chamber pot! "And was a worthy king"—how are you, Mistress Doll?

MISTRESS QUICKLY

qualm = nausea, or a fainting spell

She's sick of a qualm, she is.

FALSTAFF

That's how all the women in her profession are. As soon as they're calm—and not in someone's bed—they get sick.

DOLL TEARSHEET

You stupid bastard. Is this how you make me feel better?

FALSTAFF

You make fat bastards, Mistress Doll.

DOLL TEARSHEET
I make them? Gluttony and diseases make them; I make
them not.

FALSTAFF
If the cook help to make the gluttony, you help to make the
diseases, Doll. We catch of you, Doll, we catch of you.
40   Grant that, my poor virtue, grant that.

DOLL TEARSHEET
Yea, joy, our chains and our jewels.

FALSTAFF
Your broaches, pearls, and ouches—for to serve bravely is
to come halting off, you know; to come off the breach with
his pike bent bravely, and to surgery bravely, to venture
45   upon the charged chambers bravely—

DOLL TEARSHEET
Hang yourself, you muddy conger, hang yourself!

MISTRESS QUICKLY
By my troth, this is the old fashion. You two never meet but
you fall to some discord. You are both, i' good truth, as
rheumatic as two dry toasts. You cannot one bear with
50   another's confirmities. What the good-year! One must
bear, and that must be you. You are the weaker vessel, as
they say, the emptier vessel.

DOLL TEARSHEET
Can a weak empty vessel bear such a huge full hogshead?
There's a whole merchant's venture of Bourdeaux stuff in
55   him. You have not seen a hulk better stuffed in the hold. —
Come, I'll be friends with thee, Jack. Thou art going to the

DOLL TEARSHEET

> I make them fat? Gluttony and disease will make men fat; I have nothing to do with it.

FALSTAFF

> Well, cooks help create gluttony, by making and selling food—the object of gluttony. And you help create diseases, Doll. We catch them from you, Doll, we catch them from you: admit it.

DOLL TEARSHEET

> Sure, sweetheart. You catch us by the chains and the jewels, and then you steal them from us.

FALSTAFF

This might be a line from a ballad. "Ouches," in the original Shakespearean line, meant both "gem, brooch, or buckle" and "sore." Falstaff jokes that the "jewels" men get from Doll are the sores of a venereal disease.

> "Your brooches, pearls, and gems"—We fight bravely and then come away limping. We retreat from the breach in the wall with our weapons bravely bent. We head off to the doctor, bravely. And then we charge into the loaded chambers again, bravely.

Falstaff describes a bout of venereal disease as a military battle.

DOLL TEARSHEET

> Drop dead, you filthy eel. Drop dead!

MISTRESS QUICKLY

In Shakespeare's line, Mistress Quickly mistakenly uses "rheumatic" for "choleric" (i.e., irritable) and "confirmities" for "infirmities."

> I swear, this is how it always is. You two even see each other without fighting. You're as hot as dry toast, you can't stand each other's bad qualities. Good grief! But one of you has to bear the burden, and that's you, Doll. You're the weaker sex, the empty vessel.

DOLL TEARSHEET

> Can a weak, empty vessel bear the burden of such a huge, full barrel? There's a whole merchant's stock of Bordeaux wine in him; you've never seen a ship with a fuller cargo hold. Come, Jack, I'll be friends with

wars, and whether I shall ever see thee again or no, there is
nobody cares.

Enter FIRST DRAWER

FIRST DRAWER
Sir, Ancient Pistol's below and would speak with you.

DOLL TEARSHEET
60   Hang him, swaggering rascal! Let him not come hither. It
is the foul-mouthed'st rogue in England.

MISTRESS QUICKLY
If he swagger, let him not come here. No, by my faith, I must
live among my neighbors. I'll no swaggerers: I am in good
name and fame with the very best. Shut the door. There
65   comes no swaggerers here. I have not lived all this while to
have swaggering now. Shut the door, I pray you.

FALSTAFF
Dost thou hear, hostess?

MISTRESS QUICKLY
Pray you pacify yourself, Sir John. There comes no
swaggerers here.

FALSTAFF
70   Dost thou hear? It is mine ancient.

MISTRESS QUICKLY
Tilly-vally, Sir John, ne'er tell me. And your ancient
swaggerer comes not in my doors. I was before Master
Tisick, the debuty t' other day, and, as he said to me—'twas
no longer ago than Wednesday last, i' good faith—
75   "Neighbour Quickly," says he—Master Dumb, our
minister, was by then—"Neighbour Quickly," says he,
"receive those that are civil, for," said he, "you are in an ill
name." Now he said so, I can tell whereupon. "For," says
he, "you are an honest woman, and well thought on.
80   Therefore take heed what guests you receive. Receive,"

you. You're going off to war, and whether or not I ever
see you again—well, who cares.

*drawers = those
who serve drinks*

The **FIRST DRAWER** *enters.*

FIRST DRAWER

Sir, Ensign Pistol's downstairs. He wants to talk with
you.

DOLL TEARSHEET

Let him drop dead, that hot-tempered jerk! Don't let
him in: he's got the foulest mouth in England.

MISTRESS QUICKLY

If he's going to make trouble, don't let him in. No way;
I have my neighbors to think about. I'll have no troublemakers here. I've got my good reputation to watch
out for. Shut the doors; no troublemakers are getting
in here. I haven't lived this long to have trouble now.
Shut the doors, please.

FALSTAFF

Do you hear, hostess?

MISTRESS QUICKLY

Please, be quiet a second, Sir John. No troublemakers
are coming in here.

FALSTAFF

Didn't you hear? It's my ensign.

MISTRESS QUICKLY

Oh fiddlesticks, Sir John, I don't want to hear it. Your
Ensign Troublemaker is not coming in here. I talked
to Master Tisick, the deputy, the other day. And he
said to me—it couldn't have been longer ago than last
Wednesday—"I swear, neighbor Quickly," he said.
(Master Dumbe, the minister, was here at the time.)
"Neighbor Quickly," he said, "only let in people who
are well behaved, because," he said, "your reputation
is suffering." He said that, and I'll tell you why.
"You're an honest woman, and people think highly of

says he, "no swaggering companions." There comes none
here. You would bless you to hear what he said. No, I'll no
swaggerers.

FALSTAFF

He's no swaggerer, hostess, a tame cheater, i' faith. You may
85   stroke him as gently as a puppy greyhound. He'll not
swagger with a Barbary hen if her feathers turn back in any
show of resistance.—Call him up, drawer.

Exit **FIRST DRAWER**

MISTRESS QUICKLY

"Cheater," call you him? I will bar no honest man my
house, nor no cheater, but I do not love swaggering. By my
90   troth, I am the worse when one says "swagger." Feel,
masters, how I shake; look you, I warrant you.

DOLL TEARSHEET

So you do, hostess.

MISTRESS QUICKLY

Do I? Yea, in very truth, do I, an 'twere an aspen leaf. I
cannot abide swaggerers.

Enter **PISTOL**, **BARDOLPH**, *and the* **PAGE**

PISTOL

95   God save you, Sir John.

FALSTAFF

Welcome, Ancient Pistol. Here, Pistol, I charge you with a
cup of sack. Do you discharge upon mine hostess.

you. So think about who you let in. Don't let in," he said, "any troublemakers." And none are getting in. You'd be lucky if you heard what he said. No way, no troublemakers.

FALSTAFF

He's not a troublemaker, hostess. He's a harmless cheater; you can pet him like a little puppy. He wouldn't even start a fight with a guinea-hen, if her feathers stood up in annoyance. Get him up here, drawer.

FIRST DRAWER *exits.*

MISTRESS QUICKLY

> *Mistress Quickly misunderstands "cheater" as "escheator," a type of royal treasury officer.*

You call him a cheater? I won't keep an honest man out of this bar, so I won't keep a cheater out, either. But I don't like troublemakers, I swear. I get sick when I hear the word, "troublemaker." Feel, masters: I'm shaking. Look, I'm telling you.

DOLL TEARSHEET

You are shaking.

MISTRESS QUICKLY

I am?—I am! I swear, I'm shaking like a big tree leaf. I can't stand troublemakers.

PISTOL, BARDOLPH, *and the* PAGE *enter.*

PISTOL

Good to see you, Sir John!

FALSTAFF

> *Falstaff "charges", or toasts Pistol, and asks him to toast Mistress Quickly in return. A pistol is also "charged," or loaded, with bullets, and "discharged" when it is fired.*

Welcome, Ensign Pistol. Here, Pistol. I charge you with a glass of wine. Now discharge on the hostess.

PISTOL
> I will discharge upon her, Sir John, with two bullets.

FALSTAFF
> She is pistol-proof. Sir, you shall not hardly offend her.

MISTRESS QUICKLY
100 > Come, I'll drink no proofs nor no bullets. I'll drink no more
> than will do me good, for no man's pleasure, I.

PISTOL
> Then to you, Mistress Dorothy! I will charge you.

DOLL TEARSHEET
> Charge me! I scorn you, scurvy companion. What, you
> poor, base, rascally, cheating lack-linen mate! Away, you
105 > mouldy rogue, away! I am meat for your master.

PISTOL
> I know you, Mistress Dorothy.

DOLL TEARSHEET
> Away, you cutpurse rascal, you filthy bung, away! By this
> wine, I'll thrust my knife in your mouldy chaps an you play
> the saucy cuttle with me. Away, you bottle-ale rascal, you
110 > basket-hilt stale juggler, you. Since when, I pray you, sir?
> God's light, with two points on your shoulder? Much!

PISTOL
> God let me not live, but I will murder your ruff for this.

FALSTAFF
> No more, Pistol. I would not have you go off here.
> Discharge yourself of our company, Pistol.

MISTRESS QUICKLY
115 > No, good Captain Pistol, not here, sweet captain.

DOLL TEARSHEET
> Captain? Thou abominable damned cheater, art thou not
> ashamed to be called captain? An captains were of my
> mind, they would truncheon you out for taking their names
> upon you before you have earned them. You a captain? You

PISTOL

I'll unload two big bullets on her, Sir John.

bullets = testicles

FALSTAFF

She's Pistol-proof, sir. You'll hardly be able to injure her.

MISTRESS QUICKLY

I won't have any proofs or any bullets. I won't drink any more than I feel like, not for any man.

PISTOL

Then here's to you, Mistress. Dorothy, I'll charge you.

DOLL TEARSHEET

Charge me? Get lost, you sick jerk. What? You broke, rude, scheming, cheating, shirtless fool! Get away from me, you moldy bastard, away! I'm meant for your betters.

PISTOL

I know you, Mistress Dorothy.

DOLL TEARSHEET

Get away, you pickpocket rascal! You dirty thief, away! I swear on this wine, I'll stick a knife in your rotten cheeks if you keep abusing me like this. Out, you boozy rascal! You imposter of a solider! Since when are you a soldier, I ask you? With two armor tags on your shoulder? I'm sure!

PISTOL

I'll strangle your neck for that, or I'll die trying.

FALSTAFF

Hold it, Pistol. I don't want you to go off here. Discharge someplace else, Pistol.

MISTRESS QUICKLY

No, good Captain Pistol. Not here, sweet captain.

DOLL TEARSHEET

Captain? You horrible, damned liar, aren't you ashamed to be called "captain"? If captains shared my opinions, they'd beat you for taking their rank without earning it. You, a captain? You bastard, for what? For

120   slave, for what? For tearing a poor whore's ruff in a bawdy
house? He a captain! Hang him, rogue. He lives upon
mouldy stewed prunes and dried cakes. A captain? God's
light, these villains will make the word as odious as the word
"occupy," which was an excellent good word before it was
125   ill sorted. Therefore captains had need look to 't.

BARDOLPH
Pray thee go down, good ancient.

FALSTAFF
Hark thee hither, Mistress Doll.

PISTOL
Not I. I tell thee what, Corporal Bardolph, I could tear her.
I'll be revenged of her.

PAGE
130   Pray thee go down.

PISTOL
I'll see her damned first to Pluto's damnèd lake, by this
hand, to th' infernal deep with Erebus and tortures vile
also. Hold hook and line, say I. Down, down, dogs! Down,
Fates! Have we not Hiren here?

MISTRESS QUICKLY
135   Good Captain Peesell, be quiet. 'Tis very late, i' faith. I
beseek you now, aggravate your choler.

PISTOL
These be good humors indeed. Shall pack-horses
And hollow pampered jades of Asia, which cannot go but
thirty mile a day,
140   Compare with Caesars and with cannibals, and Troyant
Greeks? Nay, rather damn them with King
Cerberus, and let the welkin roar. Shall we fall foul
for toys?

tearing a poor whore's clothes in a whorehouse? Him, a captain? Let him drop dead, the rogue! He lives off the moldy food you find in brothels. A captain? For God's sake! Men like him will make the word "captain" as nasty as the word "occupy," which was a fine word before it got corrupted. Captains had better watch out.

occupy = slang for "copulate"

BARDOLPH

Please, calm down, good ensign.

FALSTAFF

Listen here, Mistress Doll.

PISTOL

Not me. I'll tell you what, Corporal Bardolph, I could tear her. I'll get revenge on her.

PAGE

Please, calm down!

PISTOL

I'll see her damned first. To the waters of hell, I swear, to the endless deep, with chaos and vile tortures. Hold onto that pole, I say. Down, down, dogs! Down, fates! Here's my sword!

MISTRESS QUICKLY

Captain Pisser, be quiet! It's late. I beg of you, stop being angry!

PISTOL

From here until he exits, Pistol's language is strange and heightened. He continually makes garbled references to classical plays and poems that would have been familiar to Shakespeare's audience.

Now we're talking! Are we going to let old nags and pampered horses (who can't manage more than a few miles a day) be compared with kings, and generals, and mythic heroes? No! Damn them to hell, and let the storms rage! Should we fight over nothing?

MISTRESS QUICKLY
By my troth, captain, these are very bitter words.

BARDOLPH
145   Begone, good ancient. This will grow to a brawl anon.

PISTOL
Die men like dogs! Give crowns like pins! Have we not
Hiren here?

MISTRESS QUICKLY
O' my word, captain, there's none such here. What the
good-year, do you think I would deny her? For God's sake,
150   be quiet.

PISTOL
Then feed and be fat, my fair Calipolis. Come, give 's some
sack. *Si fortune me tormente, sperato me contento.* Fear we
broadsides? No, let the fiend give fire. Give me some sack,
and, sweetheart, lie thou there. *(lays down his sword)* Come
155   we to full points here? And are etceteras nothing?

FALSTAFF
Pistol, I would be quiet.

PISTOL
Sweet knight, I kiss thy neaf. What, we have seen the seven
stars.

DOLL TEARSHEET
For God's sake, thrust him downstairs. I cannot endure
160   such a fustian rascal.

PISTOL
"Thrust him downstairs"? Know we not Galloway nags?

FALSTAFF
Quoit him down, Bardolph, like a shove-groat shilling.
Nay, an he do nothing but speak nothing, he shall be
nothing here.

MISTRESS QUICKLY

My goodness, captain! Those are strong words!

BARDOLPH

You should go now, ensign. This is going to get out of control in a minute.

PISTOL

Let men die like dogs! Give away kings' crowns like they're nothing! Isn't this a sword we have here?

MISTRESS QUICKLY

My word of honor, captain, there's no such thing here! For goodness sake! Do you think I'd say she's not if she were? For God's sake, be quiet!

Mistress Quickly mishears the word "Hiren" as a woman's name.

PISTOL

Then eat and grow fat, my sweet lady! Come, bring me some wine. *Si fortuna me tormente, sperato me contento.* Are we scared of an attack? No! Let the devil open fire. Give me some wine, and darling, lie there. *(he lays his sword down)* Is the party over? What about the rest of it, the et ceteras?

"If fortune torments me, hope contents me." Pistol's motto is a garbled mix of French, Spanish and Italian.

et ceteras = slang for "vaginas"

FALSTAFF

Pistol, I'd be quiet if I were you.

PISTOL

Sweet knight, I kiss your fist. Look! It's so late—we can see the Big Dipper out.

DOLL TEARSHEET

For God's sake, throw him down the stairs. I can't stand such a worthless jerk.

PISTOL

Throw him down the stairs? Don't we know a common prostitute when we see one?

FALSTAFF

Toss him down, Bardolph, like a coin on a game board. He does nothing but talk a bunch of nothing, so he's going to count for nothing here.

BARDOLPH

165   Come, get you downstairs.

PISTOL

What! shall we have incision? Shall we imbrue? *(snatches up his sword)* Then death rock me asleep, abridge my doleful days. Why then, let grievous, ghastly, gaping wounds untwine the Sisters Three. Come, Atropos, I say.

MISTRESS QUICKLY

170   Here's goodly stuff toward!

FALSTAFF

Give me my rapier, boy.

DOLL TEARSHEET

I pray thee, Jack, I pray thee do not draw.

FALSTAFF

Get you downstairs. *(drawing and driving* PISTOL *out)*

MISTRESS QUICKLY

Here's a goodly tumult. I'll forswear keeping house afore
175   I'll be in these tirrits and frights. So, murder, I warrant now. Alas, alas, put up your naked weapons, put up your naked weapons.

Exeunt PISTOL *pursued by* BARDOLPH

DOLL TEARSHEET

I pray thee, Jack, be quiet. The rascal's gone. Ah, you whoreson little valiant villain, you.

MISTRESS QUICKLY

180   Are you not hurt i' the groin? Methought he made a shrewd thrust at your belly.

Enter BARDOLPH

FALSTAFF

Have you turned him out o' doors?

BARDOLPH

Come on. Get downstairs.

PISTOL

In Greek and Roman mythology, the Three Fates spun threads representing the life of each human being; Atropos, the third sister, cut the thread when life was finished.

What? Is there going to be cutting now? Shall we be soaked in blood? *(he grabs his sword)* Then let death sing me a lullaby; let him end my melancholy days! Let grievous, ghastly, gaping wounds unravel the thread of my life, spun by those three sisters of fate! Come, Atropos, cut off my thread!

MISTRESS QUICKLY

This ought to be good.

FALSTAFF

Give me my sword, boy.

DOLL TEARSHEET

Please, Jack, please; don't fight!

FALSTAFF

Get downstairs! *(he draws his sword and chases* PISTOL*)*

MISTRESS QUICKLY

This is going to be some fight! I would sooner close this bar than put up with terrors and fits. It's murder, I swear! Oh my! Oh my! Put away your naked weapons! Put away your naked weapons!

PISTOL *exits, pursued by* BARDOLPH.

DOLL TEARSHEET

Please, Jack, calm down; the jerk's gone. Oh you son-of-a-bitch, brave little bastard, you!

MISTRESS QUICKLY

Did he hurt you in the groin? I thought he got in a good shot at your belly.

BARDOLPH *enters.*

FALSTAFF

Did you kick him out of here?

BARDOLPH
Yea, sir. The rascal's drunk. You have hurt him, sir, i' the
shoulder.

FALSTAFF
185   A rascal to brave me!

DOLL TEARSHEET
Ah, you sweet little rogue, you. Alas, poor ape, how thou
sweat'st! Come, let me wipe thy face. Come on, you
whoreson chops. Ah, rogue, i' faith, I love thee. Thou art as
valorous as Hector of Troy, worth five of Agamemnon, and
190   ten times better than the Nine Worthies. Ah, villain!

FALSTAFF
Ah, rascally slave! I will toss the rogue in a blanket.

DOLL TEARSHEET
Do, an thou darest for thy heart. An thou dost, I'll canvass
thee between a pair of sheets.

Enter musicians

PAGE
The music is come, sir.

FALSTAFF
195   Let them play.—Play, sirs.—Sit on my knee, Doll. A rascal
bragging slave! The rogue fled from me like quicksilver.

DOLL TEARSHEET
I' faith, and thou followed'st him like a church. Thou
whoreson little tidy Bartholomew boar-pig, when wilt thou
leave fighting a-days and foining a-nights and begin to
200   patch up thine old body for heaven?

Enter, behind, PRINCE HENRY *and* POINS, *disguised as
drawers*

BARDOLPH

Yup! The jerk's drunk. You hurt his shoulder.

FALSTAFF

That jerk! How dare he challenge me!

DOLL TEARSHEET

Oh, you sweet little rogue, you! Oh my, you poor monkey, you're sweating! Come, let me wipe your face. Come on, you fat bastard. Oh, you rogue! I swear, I love you. You're as brave as Hector of Troy, you're worth five Agamemnons, and you're ten times better than the nine wonders of the world! Oh, you villain!

Hector of Troy and Agamemnon were great heroes of the Trojan War.

FALSTAFF

The no-good jerk! I'll wrap the rogue in a blanket, the way they punish cowards.

DOLL TEARSHEET

Do it, if you dare. If you do, I'll toss you between a pair of sheets!

The musicians enter.

PAGE

The music is here, sir.

FALSTAFF

Let them play. Play, sirs. Sit on my knee, Doll. A no-good, bragging jerk! The fool ran from me like quicksilver.

DOLL TEARSHEET

Truly, and you chased him like a church—slowly. You rotten little fat roasting pig! When will you stop fighting all day and thrusting all night, and start to get your body ready for its final resting place?

Unseen, **PRINCE HENRY** *and* **POINS** *enter, disguised as drawers.*

FALSTAFF
Peace, good Doll. Do not speak like a death's-head; do not bid me remember mine end.

DOLL TEARSHEET
Sirrah, what humor's the Prince of?

FALSTAFF
A good shallow young fellow, he would have made a good
205   pantler; he would a' chipped bread well.

DOLL TEARSHEET
They say Poins has a good wit.

FALSTAFF
He a good wit? Hang him, baboon. His wit's as thick as Tewksbury mustard. There's no more conceit in him than is in a mallet.

DOLL TEARSHEET
210   Why does the Prince love him so then?

FALSTAFF
Because their legs are both of a bigness, and he plays at quoits well, and eats conger and fennel, and drinks off candles' ends for flap-dragons, and rides the wild mare with the boys, and jumps upon joint stools, and swears with a
215   good grace, and wears his boots very smooth, like unto the sign of the Leg, and breeds no bate with telling of discreet stories, and such other gambol faculties he has that show a weak mind and an able body, for the which the Prince admits him; for the Prince himself is such another. The
220   weight of a hair will turn the scales between their avoirdupois.

FALSTAFF

death's-head =
a skull, used as
a reminder of
one's mortality

Quiet, Doll. Don't talk like a death's-head. Don't make me think of my own end.

DOLL TEARSHEET

Sirrah, what's the Prince like?

Directors must decide if Doll sees Hal and Poins and sets Falstaff up, or if she doesn't see them and happens to ask these questions innocently.

FALSTAFF

He's a shallow youngster. He would have made a good pantry servant: he would have been great at trimming the crusts off bread.

DOLL TEARSHEET

They say Poins is smart.

FALSTAFF

Him, smart? Hang him, he's a baboon! He's as thick as mustard, and no smarter than a sledgehammer.

DOLL TEARSHEET

Then why does the Prince love him?

FALSTAFF

Because their legs are the same size, and he likes to play the game of quoits and eat fatty foods; and he'll play drinking games, like dropping burning candle ends into his drinks. He plays on the see-saw with the boys, and pulls crazy stunts, and curses nicely. And his boots fit nice and smooth, just like the ones painted on the shoe store's signs. And he doesn't cause trouble by spilling secrets. He has all kinds of qualities associated with weak minds and healthy bodies, and that's why the Prince keeps him around: because the Prince

PRINCE HENRY
(to POINS*)* Would not this nave of a wheel have his ears cut off?

POINS
Let's beat him before his whore.

PRINCE HENRY
Look whe'er the withered elder hath not his poll clawed like
225   a parrot.

POINS
Is it not strange that desire should so many years outlive
performance?

FALSTAFF
Kiss me, Doll.

PRINCE HENRY
Saturn and Venus this year in conjunction! What says th'
230   almanac to that?

POINS
And look whether the fiery trigon, his man, be not lisping
to his master's old tables, his notebook, his counsel keeper.

FALSTAFF
(to DOLL*)* Thou dost give me flattering busses.

DOLL TEARSHEET
By my troth, I kiss thee with a most constant heart.

FALSTAFF
235   I am old, I am old.

DOLL TEARSHEET
I love thee better than I love e'er a scurvy young boy of them
all.

FALSTAFF
What stuff wilt have a kirtle of? I shall receive money o'
Thursday; shalt have a cap tomorrow. A merry song!

is exactly the same. There's not a hair's difference between the two of them.

PRINCE HENRY

(to POINS) We should cut this fatso's ears off.

POINS

Let's beat him in front of his whore.

PRINCE HENRY

Look at that old geezer having his head scratched like a parrot.

Possibly, Doll is playing with Falstaff's hair.

POINS

Isn't it odd that desire lasts so much longer than the ability to perform?

FALSTAFF

Kiss me, Doll.

PRINCE HENRY

Saturn and Venus must be aligned this year! What do you think the astrological tables have to say about that?

Saturn was the planet of old age, Venus the planet of love and desire.

POINS

And look. That fiery-faced Bardolph is whispering sweet nothings to Quickly, his master's old confidante.

FALSTAFF

(to DOLL) You flatter me with your kisses.

DOLL TEARSHEET

I swear, my kisses are heartfelt.

FALSTAFF

I'm old. I'm old.

DOLL TEARSHEET

I love you more than I could love any ridiculous young man in the world.

FALSTAFF

What fabric do you want a new skirt made out of? I'll get paid on Thursday, so you'll get a new hat tomor-

240   Come, it grows late. We'll to bed. Thou 'lt forget me when
         I am gone.

DOLL TEARSHEET
         By my troth, thou 'lt set me a-weeping an thou sayest so.
         Prove that ever I dress myself handsome till thy return.
         Well, harken a' th' end.

FALSTAFF
245   Some sack, Francis.

PRINCE HENRY AND POINS
         Anon, anon, sir.

         Coming forward

FALSTAFF
         Ha? A bastard son of the King's?—And art not thou
         Poins his brother?

PRINCE HENRY
         Why, thou globe of sinful continents, what a life dost thou
250   lead?

FALSTAFF
         A better than thou. I am a gentleman. Thou art a drawer.

PRINCE HENRY
         Very true, sir, and I come to draw you out by the ears.

MISTRESS QUICKLY
         O, the Lord preserve thy good Grace! By my troth,
         welcome to London. Now the Lord bless that sweet face of
255   thine. O Jesu, are you come from Wales?

FALSTAFF
         Thou whoreson mad compound of majesty, *(indicating*
         DOLL*)* by this light flesh and corrupt blood, thou art
         welcome.

DOLL TEARSHEET
         How? You fat fool, I scorn you.

row. Let's have a happy song. It's getting late; let's go
to bed. You'll forget me when I'm gone.

DOLL TEARSHEET

I swear, you'll make me cry if you talk like that. I won't
wear any beautiful clothing till you return. Well, we'll
see what happens.

FALSTAFF

Some wine, Francis.

PRINCE HENRY AND POINS

Right away, sir!

PRINCE HENRY *and* POINS *reveal themselves.*

FALSTAFF

What! A bastard son of the King? And aren't you
Poins, his brother?

PRINCE HENRY

Your globe, covered with continents of sin! What kind
of life are you leading?

FALSTAFF

A better life than you. I'm a gentleman and you're just
a drawer.

PRINCE HENRY

That's right, sir. And I'm going to draw you out of this
room by the ears.

MISTRESS QUICKLY

Oh, may God bless you, sir. I swear, welcome to London. God bless that sweet face of yours! Oh Jesus!
Have you come from Wales?

FALSTAFF

You son of a bitch, you insane block of royalty! *(indi-
cating* DOLL*)* I swear on this piece of weak flesh and
corrupt blood that you're welcome here!

DOLL TEARSHEET

What? You fat fool! The hell with you!

POINS

260   My lord, he will drive you out of your revenge and turn all
to a merriment, if you take not the heat.

PRINCE HENRY

You whoreson candle-mine, you how vilely did you speak
of me even now before this honest, virtuous, civil
gentlewoman!

MISTRESS QUICKLY

265   God's blessing of your good heart, and so she is, by my troth.

FALSTAFF

Didst thou hear me?

PRINCE HENRY

Yea, and you knew me, as you did when you ran away by
Gad's Hill. You knew I was at your back, and spoke it on
purpose to try my patience.

FALSTAFF

270   No, no, no; not so. I did not think thou wast within hearing.

PRINCE HENRY

I shall drive you, then, to confess the wilfull abuse, and then
I know how to handle you.

FALSTAFF

No abuse, Hal, o' mine honor, no abuse.

PRINCE HENRY

Not to dispraise me and call me pantier and bread-chipper
275   and I know not what?

FALSTAFF

No abuse, Hal.

POINS

No abuse?

FALSTAFF

No abuse, Ned, i' th' world, honest Ned, none. I dispraised
him before the wicked, that the wicked might not fall in love
280   with thee; in which doing, I have done the part of a careful
friend and a true subject, and thy father is to give me thanks

POINS

> My lord, if you don't strike while the iron's hot, he'll turn everything into a joke and rob you of your chance for revenge.

PRINCE HENRY

> You son of a whore, you giant piece of candle wax, you said such horrible things about me just now, in front of this honest, upstanding and well-behaved lady.

MISTRESS QUICKLY

> May God bless your good heart! She is all that, I swear.

FALSTAFF

> Did you hear me?

PRINCE HENRY

> Yes. And you knew I was there, right? It's just like when you ran away at Gad's Hill: you knew I was the one who beat you, and you made up some story just to irritate me.

The incident at Gad's Hill occurs in Act Two of Henry IV, Part One.

FALSTAFF

> No, no, no. Not at all. I had no idea you were there.

PRINCE HENRY

> Then I'm going to make you confess that you deliberately slandered me. And then I'll know what to do next.

FALSTAFF

> No slander, Hal. On my honor, no slander.

PRINCE HENRY

> No? To malign me, and call me a pantry servant and a bread-trimmer, and I don't know what else?

FALSTAFF

> No slander, Hal.

POINS

> No slander?

FALSTAFF

> No slander, Ned, in the world, honest Ned, none. I maligned him only to the wicked, so that the wicked wouldn't fall in love with him. And by doing that, I've acted like a good friend and loyal subject, and your

for it. No abuse, Hal.—None, Ned, none. No, faith, boys, none.

PRINCE HENRY
See now whether pure fear and entire cowardice doth not
285   make thee wrong this virtuous gentlewoman to close with
us. Is she of the wicked, is thine hostess here of the wicked,
or is thy boy of the wicked, or honest Bardolph, whose zeal
burns in his nose, of the wicked?

POINS
Answer, thou dead elm, answer.

FALSTAFF
290   The fiend hath pricked down Bardolph irrecoverable, and
his face is Lucifer's privy kitchen, where he doth nothing
but roast malt-worms. For the boy, there is a good angel
about him, but the devil outbids him too.

PRINCE HENRY
For the women?

FALSTAFF
295   For one of them, she's in hell already and burns poor souls.
For the other, I owe her money, and whether she be damned
for that I know not.

MISTRESS QUICKLY
No, I warrant you.

FALSTAFF
No, I think thou art not; I think thou art quit for that.
300   Marry, there is another indictment upon thee for suffering
flesh to be eaten in thy house contrary to the law, for the
which I think thou wilt howl.

MISTRESS QUICKLY
All vitlars do so. What's a joint of mutton or two in a whole
Lent?

PRINCE HENRY
305   You, gentlewoman.

DOLL TEARSHEET
What says your Grace?

father should thank me for it. No slander, Hal, none,
Ned. No, truly boys, none.

PRINCE HENRY

Now your absolute fear and utter cowardliness has
made you wrong this good lady in order to make peace
with us. Is she wicked? Is this hostess here wicked? Is
your boy here wicked? Or honest Bardolph, whose
piety burns in his face? Is he wicked?

POINS

Answer, you withered old trunk, answer.

FALSTAFF

The devil has marked Bardolph as long gone, and his
face is Lucifer's kitchen, where only drunks are
served. As for the boy, he may have a good spirit on
one shoulder, but the devil on the other is stronger.

PRINCE HENRY

And the women?

FALSTAFF

One of them is in hell already, where she gets poor
souls hot. As for the other, I owe her money. If she's
damned for that, I have no idea.

MISTRESS QUICKLY

I'm not, I promise you that.

FALSTAFF

No, I think you're not. I think you've been excused for
that. But there's another charge against you. You serve
flesh in this place, and that's against the law. You're
going to hell for that.

MISTRESS QUICKLY

Everybody who serves food does that. What's wrong
with a bite or two of meat during Lent?

PRINCE HENRY

You, good lady—

DOLL TEARSHEET

What is it, gracious sir?

FALSTAFF
His grace says that which his flesh rebels against.

Knocking within

MISTRESS QUICKLY
Who knocks so loud at door? Look to th' door there, Francis.

Enter PETO

PRINCE HENRY
Peto, how now, what news?

PETO
310   The King your father is at Westminster,
And there are twenty weak and wearied posts
Come from the north, and as I came along
I met and overtook a dozen captains,
Bareheaded, sweating, knocking at the taverns
315   And asking everyone for Sir John Falstaff.

PRINCE HENRY
By heaven, Poins, I feel me much to blame
So idly to profane the precious time
When tempest of commotion, like the south
Borne with black vapour, doth begin to melt
320   And drop upon our bare unармèd heads.—
Give me my sword and cloak.—Falstaff, good night.

Exeunt PRINCE HENRY, POINS, PETO
and BARDOLPH

FALSTAFF
Now comes in the sweetest morsel of the night, and we must
hence and leave it unpicked.

Knocking within

More knocking at the door?

FALSTAFF

He may speak to you graciously, but his body feels otherwise.

Knocking is heard offstage.

MISTRESS QUICKLY

Who's knocking so loudly on the door? Francis, go see.

PETO *enters.*

PRINCE HENRY

Peto, how are you? What's going on?

PETO

Your father the King is in Westminster. Twenty exhausted messengers have arrived from the north. And, on my way here, I met a dozen captains, hustling and working hard, knocking on the door of every tavern and searching for Sir John Falstaff.

PRINCE HENRY

My God, Poins, I feel terrible wasting precious time on this idleness when a huge black storm is brewing, soon to open up on our bare, vulnerable heads. Give me my coat and my sword. Good night, Falstaff.

PRINCE HENRY, **POINS**, **PETO**, *and* **BARDOLPH** *exit.*

FALSTAFF

Now's the sweetest part of the night, and we have to leave without enjoying it.

Knocking is heard offstage.

More knocking!

Enter BARDOLPH

325   How now, what's the matter?

BARDOLPH
        You must away to court, sir, presently.
        A dozen captains stay at door for you.

FALSTAFF
        (to the PAGE*)* Pay the musicians, sirrah.—Farewell,
        hostess.—Farewell, Doll. You see, my good wenches, how
330   men of merit are sought after. The undeserver may sleep
        when the man of action is called on. Farewell, good
        wenches. If I be not sent away post, I will see you again ere
        I go.

DOLL TEARSHEET
        I cannot speak. If my heart be not ready to burst—well,
335   sweet Jack, have a care of thyself.

FALSTAFF
        Farewell, farewell.
                    Exeunt FALSTAFF, BARDOLPH, PAGE, *and musicians*

MISTRESS QUICKLY
        Well, fare thee well. I have known thee these twenty-nine
        years, come peascod time, but an honester and truer-
        hearted man—well, fare thee well.

BARDOLPH
340   *(within)* Mistress Tearsheet!

MISTRESS QUICKLY
        What's the matter?

BARDOLPH
        (within) Bid Mistress Tearsheet come to my master.

MISTRESS QUICKLY
        O, run, Doll, run, run, good Doll. Come.—She comes
        blubbered.—Yea! Will you come, Doll?
                                                    Exeunt

BARDOLPH *enters.*

What's going on? What's the matter?

BARDOLPH

You have to go to the royal court immediately, sir. A dozen captains are at the door waiting for you.

FALSTAFF

(to the PAGE*)* Pay the musicians, Sirrah. Goodbye, waitress. Goodbye, Doll. See, wenches, how wanted we valuable men are? The good-for-nothing may sleep when the man of action is needed. Farewell, good wenches. If I'm not sent away immediately, I'll come see you again before I go.

DOLL TEARSHEET

I can't speak; my heart is ready to burst. Well, sweet Jack, take care of yourself.

FALSTAFF

Farewell, farewell.

FALSTAFF *and* BARDOLPH *exit.*

MISTRESS QUICKLY

Well, goodbye. I've known you twenty-nine years this June. But a more honest, more good-hearted man—well, fare you well.

BARDOLPH

(offstage) Mistress Tearsheet!

MISTRESS QUICKLY

What's the matter?

BARDOLPH

(offstage) Mistress Tearsheet, come to my master.

MISTRESS QUICKLY

O, run, Doll, run; run, good Doll. Come.—She's coming, all crying and blubbering.—Will you come, Doll?

They exit.

ACT THREE

SCENE 1

Enter KING *Henry in his nightgown, with a page*

KING

Go call the Earls of Surrey and of Warwick;
But, ere they come, bid them o'erread these letters
And well consider of them. Make good speed.

Exit page

How many thousand of my poorest subjects
5   Are at this hour asleep! O sleep, O gentle sleep,
Nature's soft nurse, how have I frighted thee,
That thou no more wilt weigh my eyelids down
And steep my senses in forgetfulness?
Why rather, sleep, liest thou in smoky cribs,
10 Upon uneasy pallets stretching thee
And hushed with buzzing night-flies to thy slumber,
Than in the perfumed chambers of the great,
Under the canopies of costly state,
And lull'd with sound of sweetest melody?
15 O thou dull god, why liest thou with the vile
In loathsome beds and leavest the kingly couch
A watch-case or a common 'larum bell?
Wilt thou upon the high and giddy mast
Seal up the shipboy's eyes, and rock his brains
20 In cradle of the rude imperious surge
And in the visitation of the winds,
Who take the ruffian billows by the top,
Curling their monstrous heads and hanging them
With deafening clamor in the slippery clouds
25 That with the hurly death itself awakes?
Canst thou, O partial sleep, give thy repose
To the wet sea-boy in an hour so rude,

ACT THREE

SCENE 1

KING *Henry enters, wearing his nightgown. A page follows.*

KING

Call the earls of Surrey and Warwick. Tell them to read over these letters before they come, and to think carefully about them. Hurry.

The page exits.

Thousands of even my poorest subjects are sleeping right now. Oh sleep! Oh sweet sleep, nature's gentle healer, what have I done to frighten you? You won't weigh down my eyelids anymore, or dull my mind to make me forget. Sleep, why do you lie in filthy hovels, stretched out on uncomfortable cots, where insects' buzzing is the lullaby? Why don't you lie in the sweet-smelling bedrooms of kings, under opulent canopies, lulled with soft and beautiful music? You drowsy god, why do you lie with the common people in their loathsome beds, leaving the royal bed lonely like a sentry post, or a bell tower?

Will you even close the eyes of a ship boy, high up on the whirling mast, and rock him gently in a cradle made of rough, tossing seas and howling winds—winds which take the waves and, curling them over, crashes them through the air with such a deafening noise that they wake death itself? Can you, oh unfair sleep, give rest to a drenched little sailor in the midst of such roughness, and yet deny it to a king?

And, in the calmest and most stillest night,
With all appliances and means to boot,
30   Deny it to a king? Then, happy low, lie down.
Uneasy lies the head that wears a crown.

Enter WARWICK *and* SURREY

WARWICK
Many good morrows to your Majesty.

KING
Is it good morrow, lords?

WARWICK
'Tis one o'clock, and past.

KING
35   Why then, good morrow to you all, my lords.
Have you read o'er the letter that I sent you?

WARWICK
We have, my liege.

KING
Then you perceive the body of our kingdom
How foul it is, what rank diseases grow
40   And with what danger near the heart of it.

WARWICK
It is but as a body yet distempered,
Which to his former strength may be restored
With good advice and little medicine.
My Lord Northumberland will soon be cooled.

KING
45   O God, that one might read the book of fate
And see the revolution of the times
Make mountains level, and the continent,
Weary of solid firmness, melt itself
Into the sea, and other times to see
50   The beachy girdle of the ocean
Too wide for Neptune's hips; how chance's mocks
And changes fill the cup of alteration

A king on the calmest, stillest night, with everything available for sleep? Then, you happy commoners, put yourselves to bed. The head that wears the crown sleeps uneasily.

WARWICK *and* SURREY *enter.*

WARWICK

Good morning, your highness.

KING

Is it morning, lords?

WARWICK

It's after one o'clock.

KING

Well, then, good morning to you all, my lords. Have you read the letters I sent you?

WARWICK

We have, your highness.

KING

Then you can tell how sick the kingdom is. There are serious diseases spreading through its body, very near its heart.

WARWICK

The body's only out of sorts. It can be brought back to full health through good care and some medicine. Northumberland will soon be suppressed.

KING

Oh God! If only we could read the book of destiny! We'd see how time changes everything, bringing mountains low and melting the land—which is tired of being solid and firm—into the sea. We'd see how the beach is sometimes too wide for even the tide to conquer. We'd see how blind luck can make mockeries of men, and how change can affect you in countless ways.

With divers liquors! O, if this were seen,
The happiest youth, viewing his progress through,
55   What perils past, what crosses to ensue,
Would shut the book, and sit him down and die.
'Tis not ten years gone
Since Richard and Northumberland, great friends,
Did feast together, and in two years after
60   Were they at wars. It is but eight years since
This Percy was the man nearest my soul,
Who like a brother toiled in my affairs
And laid his love and life under my foot,
Yea, for my sake, even to the eyes of Richard
65   Gave him defiance. But which of you was by—
(to WARWICK*)* You, cousin Nevil, as I may remember—
When Richard, with his eye brimful of tears,
Then checked and rated by Northumberland,
Did speak these words, now proved a prophecy?
70   "Northumberland, thou ladder by the which
My cousin Bolingbroke ascends my throne"—
Though then, God knows, I had no such intent,
But that necessity so bowed the state
That I and greatness were compelled to kiss—
75   "The time shall come," thus did he follow it,
"The time will come that foul sin, gathering head,
Shall break into corruption"—so went on,
Foretelling this same time's condition
And the division of our amity.

WARWICK
80   There is a history in all men's lives
Figuring the nature of the times deceased,
The which observed, a man may prophesy,
With a near aim, of the main chance of things
As yet not come to life, which in their seeds
85   And weak beginnings lie intreasurèd.
Such things become the hatch and brood of time,
And by the necessary form of this,

If even the happiest youth could read this book, he'd look at the course of his life—the dangers he's endured, the challenges that still lie ahead—and he'd shut that book, sit down and die. It was less than ten years ago that Richard and Northumberland loved each other. Then two years later, they were at war. Just eight years ago, Northumberland was the man closest to my heart. Like a brother, he devoted himself to me, dedicating both life and limb to my cause. He even challenged Richard on my behalf. But which of you was there—

I think it was you, Warwick—when Richard, his eyes brimming with tears because of Northumberland's rebellion, spoke these words that now seem prophetic: "Northumberland, you are the ladder that Bolingbroke has climbed to get to the throne." Although, God knows, it wasn't my intention then to become king. But the country needed it so badly, I was forced to rise up and become great. "The time will come," Richard continued, "when this terrible sin, growing in size, will break out into corruption." That's how he went on. He predicted our current condition, and the collapse of our alliances.

WARWICK

There is a chronicle for every man's life, which shows what happened to him in times now past. If you study that chronicle, you can prophecy what lies ahead with some accuracy. The seeds of things to come are buried in the things that have already happened. These seeds grow, and become the children of time.

King Richard might create a perfect guess
That great Northumberland, then false to him,
90   Would of that seed grow to a greater falseness,
Which should not find a ground to root upon
Unless on you.

KING

Are these things then necessities?
Then let us meet them like necessities.
95   And that same word even now cries out on us.
They say the Bishop and Northumberland
Are fifty thousand strong.

WARWICK

It cannot be, my lord.
Rumor doth double, like the voice and echo,
100   The numbers of the feared. Please it your Grace
To go to bed. Upon my soul, my lord,
The powers that you already have sent forth
Shall bring this prize in very easily.
To comfort you the more, I have received
105   A certain instance that Glendower is dead.
Your Majesty hath been this fortnight ill,
And these unseasoned hours perforce must add
Unto your sickness.

KING

                              I will take your counsel.
And were these inward wars once out of hand,
110   We would, dear lords, unto the Holy Land.

                                                    Exeunt

King Richard could look at the pattern of what had gone before and predict perfectly that Northumberland's betrayal—then still a seed—would someday grow larger, if it could find suitable soil to root in. And you're the only soil it could have found.

KING

Were these things necessary, then? Then we'll treat them like necessities, even though the very word "necessities" cries out against us. They say the Archbishop and Northumberland have fifty thousand men in their army.

WARWICK

That can't be, my lord. Rumor, like an echo, doubles the size of our enemy's army. Please, your highness, go to bed. I swear on my soul that the army you've already sent out can win this battle easily. And here's more good news: I've heard for sure that Glendower is dead. You've been ill for two weeks now, your majesty. Keeping such irregular hours will surely make things worse.

KING

I'll listen to your advice. And once we've got this civil war in hand, we will, my friends, march to the Holy Land.

They exit.

ACT 3, SCENE 2

Enter Justice SHALLOW *and Justice* SILENCE, *with* MOULDY,
SHADOW, WART, FEEBLE, BULLCALF, *and a servant or two*

SHALLOW
Come on, come on, come on. Give me your hand, sir, give
me your hand, sir. An early stirrer, by the rood. And how
doth my good cousin Silence?

SILENCE
Good morrow, good cousin Shallow.

SHALLOW
5   And how doth my cousin your bedfellow? And your fairest
daughter and mine, my goddaughter Ellen?

SILENCE
Alas, a black ousel, cousin Shallow.

SHALLOW
By yea and no, sir. I dare say my cousin William is become
a good scholar. He is at Oxford still, is he not?

SILENCE
10   Indeed, sir, to my cost.

SHALLOW
He must then to the Inns o' Court shortly. I was once of
Clement's Inn, where I think they will talk of mad Shallow
yet.

SILENCE
You were called "Lusty Shallow" then, cousin.

SHALLOW
15   By the Mass, I was called anything, and I would have done
anything indeed too, and roundly too. There was I, and
little John Doit of Staffordshire, and black George Barnes,
and Francis Pickbone, and Will Squele, a Cotswold man.
You had not four such swinge-bucklers in all the Inns o'

ACT 3, SCENE 2

Justice SHALLOW *and Justice* SILENCE *enter. They are followed by* MOULDY, SHADOW, WART, FEEBLE, BULLCALF, *and a servant or two.*

SHALLOW

Come on, come on, come on, sir. Shake my hand, sir, shake my hand. You're an early riser, I swear. How are you, cousin Silence?

SILENCE

Good morning, cousin Shallow.

SHALLOW

And how's my cousin, your wife? And your prettiest daughter, my fair god-daughter Ellen?

SILENCE

I'm afraid she's got dark hair, cousin Shallow!

Dark hair was considered unattractive.

SHALLOW

By gum, I bet William's become a real scholar. He's still at Oxford, right?

SILENCE

He sure is, and I'm the one who's paying for it.

SHALLOW

He'll be going to law school soon. I studied law at Clement's Inn, where I think they still talk about crazy old Shallow.

The Inns of Court are London legal colleges.

SILENCE

You were known as lusty Shallow back then, cousin.

SHALLOW

I was known as anything, I swear. And I would have done anything too, and all the way, too. I was there, and little John Doit from Staffordshire, and black-haired George Barnes, and Francis Pickbone, and Will Squele, from the Cotswolds. Since then, no law

20 Court again. And I may say to you, we knew where the bona robas were and had the best of them all at commandment. Then was Jack Falstaff, now Sir John, a boy, and page to Thomas Mowbray, Duke of Norfolk.

SILENCE

25 This Sir John, cousin, that comes hither anon about soldiers?

SHALLOW

The same Sir John, the very same. I see him break Scoggin's head at the court gate, when he was a crack not thus high; and the very same day did I fight with one Sampson Stockfish, a fruiterer, behind Grey's Inn. Jesu, Jesu, the

30 mad days that I have spent! And to see how many of my old acquaintance are dead.

SILENCE

We shall all follow, cousin.

SHADOW

Certain, 'tis certain; very sure, very sure. Death, as the Psalmist saith, is certain to all. All shall die. How a good

35 yoke of bullocks at Stamford Fair?

SILENCE

By my troth, cousin, I was not there.

SHALLOW

Death is certain. Is old Dooble of your town living yet?

SILENCE

Dead, sir.

SHALLOW

Jesu, Jesu, dead! He drew a good bow, and dead? He shot a

40 fine shoot. John o' Gaunt loved him well, and betted much money on his head. Dead! He would have clapped i' th' clout at twelve score, and carried you a forehand shaft a

college in the world has seen four swashbucklers like us. And let me tell you this: we knew where to find the highest-quality whores, and the best of them were at our beck and call. At that time, Jack Falstaff, now Sir John, was just a boy. He worked as a page for Thomas Mowbray, the Duke of Norfolk.

SILENCE

Do you mean the same Sir John that's coming here soon to recruit soldiers?

SHALLOW

The same Sir John, the very same. I saw him beat Skogan upon the head when he was a little tyke, not this high. The same day, I had a fight with a guy named Sampson Stockfish. He sold fruit behind Gray's Inn. Jesus, Jesus! I've had some crazy times! To think that so many of my old pals are dead!

SILENCE

We'll all follow them, cousin.

SHALLOW

Right you are, very right. That's for sure, that's for sure. Death, as the Psalms say, is certain. Everyone dies. How much are they getting for good young bulls at the Stamford county fair?

SILENCE

Truly, I wasn't there.

SHALLOW

Death is certain. Is old Double from your hometown still alive?

SILENCE

Dead, sir.

SHALLOW

Jesus, Jesus, dead! He was a good archer, and dead! He could fire one heck of a shot. John of Gaunt loved him, and used to wager on his shooting. Dead! He could hit a target from two hundred and forty yards, and he could shoot a straight arrow two hundred and

fourteen and fourteen and a half, that it would have done a
man's heart good to see. How a score of ewes now?

SILENCE
45   Thereafter as they be, a score of good ewes may be worth ten
pounds.

SHALLOW
And is old Dooble dead?

SILENCE
Here come two of Sir John Falstaff's men, as I think.

Enter BARDOLPH *and one with him*

SHALLOW
Good morrow, honest gentlemen.

BARDOLPH
50   I beseech you, which is Justice Shallow?

SHALLOW
I am Robert Shallow, sir, a poor esquire of this county and
one of the King's justices of the peace. What is your good
pleasure with me?

BARDOLPH
My captain, sir, commends him to you, my captain, Sir
55   John Falstaff, a tall gentleman, by heaven, and a most
gallant leader.

SHALLOW
He greets me well, sir. I knew him a good backsword man.
How doth the good knight? May I ask how my lady his wife
doth?

BARDOLPH
60   Sir, pardon. A soldier is better accommodated than with a
wife.

SHALLOW
It is well said, in faith, sir, and it is well said indeed too.
"Better accommodated." It is good, yea, indeed, is it. Good

eighty yards—maybe even two hundred and ninety. That was something to see. How much are they getting for twenty ewes?

SILENCE

Depends on the quality. Twenty good ewes could be worth ten pounds.

SHALLOW

And old Double's dead?

SILENCE

Here come two of Sir John Falstaff's men, I think.

BARDOLPH and another man enter.

BARDOLPH

Good morning, gentlemen. If you don't mind, which of you is Judge Shallow?

SHALLOW

I'm Robert Shallow, sir, a poor landowner in this county, and one of the King's justices of the peace. How can I help you?

BARDOLPH

My captain sends his regards. My captain, Sir John Falstaff. He's a valiant gentleman, I swear, and a brave leader.

SHALLOW

It's great to hear from him. I knew him to be a good fencer. How's the good knight doing? And, if you don't mind my asking, how's his wife?

BARDOLPH

I beg your pardon, sir. A soldier has no need for a wife; he is well enough accommodated.

SHALLOW

Well said, I swear, sir. Well said. "Well enough accommodated!" That's good. That's very good.

65 phrases are surely, and ever were, very commendable.
"Accommodated." It comes of *accommodo.* Very good, a
good phrase.

BARDOLPH

Pardon, sir; I have heard the word—"phrase" call you it?
By this day, I know not the phrase, but I will maintain the
word with my sword to be a soldierlike word, and a word of
70 exceeding good command, by heaven. "Accommodated,"
that is when a man is, as they say, accommodated, or when
a man is being whereby he may be thought to be
accommodated, which is an excellent thing.

Enter FALSTAFF

SHALLOW

It is very just. Look, here comes good Sir John.—Give me
75 your good hand, give me your Worship's good hand. By my
troth, you like well and bear your years very well. Welcome,
good Sir John.

FALSTAFF

I am glad to see you well, good Master Robert Shallow.—
Master Sure-card, as I think?

SHALLOW

80 No, Sir John. It is my cousin Silence, in commission with me.

FALSTAFF

Good Master Silence, it well befits you should be of the
peace.

SILENCE

Your good Worship is welcome.

FALSTAFF

Fie, this is hot weather, gentlemen. Have you provided me
85 here half a dozen sufficient men?

Good turns of phrase deserve to be praised. "Accommodated!" It comes from the Latin, *"accommodo."* Very good. That's a good turn of phrase.

BARDOLPH

Excuse me, sir. I've heard the word. You call it a turn of phrase? I don't know anything about phrases, but I'll fight for the word. It's a good, soldier-like word; a word with many uses, to be sure. "Accommodated." You can say that a man is accommodated when he has been furnished with supplies. And you can also say that a man is being accommodated when he's, you know, *being accommodated.* Which is an excellent thing.

Bardolph here gives "being accommodated" a sexual connotation.

FALSTAFF *enters.*

SHALLOW

It certainly is. Look, here comes good Sir John. Let me shake your hand; let me shake your hand, sir. I swear, you look good, like you haven't aged a day. Welcome, good Sir John.

FALSTAFF

I'm glad to see you're well, Master Robert Shallow. And this is Master Surecard, isn't it?

SHALLOW

No, Sir John. It's my cousin Silence. Like me, he's also a justice of the peace.

FALSTAFF

Master Silence. Your name suits a justice of "the peace."

SILENCE

Welcome, sir.

FALSTAFF

Damn! It's hot out, gentlemen. Have you found half a dozen able-bodied men for me?

SHALLOW
Marry, have we, sir. Will you sit?

FALSTAFF
Let me see them, I beseech you.

SHALLOW
Where's the roll? Where's the roll? Where's the roll? Let me
see, let me see, let me see. So, so, so, so, so. So, so. Yea,
90   marry, sir.—Rafe Mouldy!—Let them appear as I call, let
them do so, let them do so. Let me see, where is Mouldy?

MOULDY
Here, an it please you.

SHALLOW
What think you, Sir John? A good-limbed fellow; young,
strong, and of good friends.

FALSTAFF
95   Is thy name Mouldy?

MOULDY
Yea, an 't please you.

FALSTAFF
'Tis the more time thou wert used.

SHALLOW
Ha, ha, ha, most excellent, i' faith! Things that are mouldy
lack use. Very singular good, in faith. Well said, Sir John,
100   very well said.

FALSTAFF
Prick him.

MOULDY
I was pricked well enough before, an you could have let me
alone. My old dame will be undone now for one to do her
husbandry and her drudgery. You need not to have pricked
105   me. There are other men fitter to go out than I.

SHALLOW

Yes sir, we have. Won't you sit?

FALSTAFF

Let me see them, please.

SHALLOW

Where's the list? Where's the list? Where's the list? Let's see, let's see, let's see. Right, right. Yes, sir: Ralph Mouldy! Let them come when I call. Let them do that, let them do that. Let's see. Where's Mouldy?

MOULDY

Here, sir.

SHALLOW

What do you think, Sir John? He's got good muscles. Young, strong, and well-connected.

FALSTAFF

Are you Mouldy?

MOULDY

Yes, sir.

FALSTAFF

Well then, it's about time you were put to use.

SHALLOW

Ha, ha, ha! Excellent, I swear! Things that don't get used enough do indeed become moldy. Good one, I swear. Well said, Sir John, very well said.

FALSTAFF

Prick him.

i.e., mark his name on the list

MOULDY

I've already been pricked well enough, thanks. You could have left me alone. My old lady's in trouble now: she won't have anyone to do her husbandry or her housework. You didn't have to prick me; there are abler men than me.

pricked = annoyed; "prick" is also slang for "penis"; Mouldy puns that he has already been supplied with one.

husbandry = farm work; a husband's sexual duties

FALSTAFF
Go to. Peace, Mouldy. You shall go. Mouldy, it is time you
were spent.

MOULDY
Spent?

SHALLOW
Peace, fellow, peace. Stand aside. Know you where you
are?—For th' other, Sir John. Let me see.—Simon Shadow!

FALSTAFF
Yea, marry, let me have him to sit under. He's like to be a
cold soldier.

SHALLOW
Where's Shadow?

SHADOW
Here, sir.

FALSTAFF
Shadow, whose son art thou?

SHADOW
My mother's son, sir.

FALSTAFF
Thy mother's son! Like enough, and thy father's shadow. So
the son of the female is the shadow of the male. It is often so,
indeed, but much of the father's substance.

SHALLOW
Do you like him, Sir John?

FALSTAFF
Shadow will serve for summer. Prick him, for we have a
number of shadows to fill up the muster book.

SHALLOW
Thomas Wart!

FALSTAFF
Where's he?

110

115

120

ACT 3, SCENE 2

NO FEAR SHAKESPEARE

FALSTAFF

That's enough; quiet, Mouldy. You're going. Mouldy, it's time you were put to use.

MOLDY

Put to use?

SHALLOW

Quiet, man, quiet. Step aside. Don't you know where you are? Now the next, Sir John. Let's see. Simon Shadow!

FALSTAFF

Now you're talking. I'd like to sit under him. He'll be a cool soldier.

SHALLOW

Where's Shadow?

SHADOW

Here, sir.

FALSTAFF

Shadow, whose son are you?

SHADOW

My mother's son, sir.

FALSTAFF

Your mother's son? Probably, and you got your father's name. The woman's son is a portrait of the father; yes, that's usually the case, though the son is little more than a dim copy, without any of the father's true substance.

SHALLOW

Do you like him, Sir John?

FALSTAFF

shadows = fake names of nonexistent people

Shadow will be useful in the summer. Prick him, too. We'll need him, for there are a lot of shadows filling up this roster.

SHALLOW

Thomas Wart!

FALSTAFF

Where's he?

WART
125   Here, sir.

FALSTAFF
Is thy name Wart?

WART
Yea, sir.

FALSTAFF
Thou art a very ragged wart.

SHALLOW
Shall I prick him down, Sir John?

FALSTAFF
130   It were superfluous, for his apparel is built upon his back,
and the whole frame stands upon pins. Prick him no more.

SHALLOW
Ha, ha, ha. You can do it, sir, you can do it. I commend you
well.—Francis Feeble!

FEEBLE
Here, sir.

FALSTAFF
135   What trade art thou, Feeble?

FEEBLE
A woman's tailor, sir.

SHALLOW
Shall I prick him, sir?

FALSTAFF
You may, but if he had been a man's tailor, he'd ha' pricked
you.—Wilt thou make as many holes in an enemy's battle
140   as thou hast done in a woman's petticoat?

FEEBLE
I will do my good will, sir. You can have no more.

FALSTAFF
Well said, good woman's tailor, well said, courageous
Feeble. Thou wilt be as valiant as the wrathful dove or most

WART

Here, sir.

FALSTAFF

Is your name Wart?

WART

Yup.

FALSTAFF

You're a pretty ragged wart.

SHALLOW

Should I prick him on the list, Sir John?

FALSTAFF

Not necessary. For look: his clothing is just a bunch of pieces sewn together, and his whole body rests on legs as skinny as pins. He's been pricked enough by pins and needles—don't prick him anymore.

SHALLOW

Ha, ha, ha! You are funny, sir. You are funny. I've got to hand it to you. Francis Feeble!

FEEBLE

Here, sir.

FALSTAFF

What kind of work do you do, Feeble?

FEEBLE

I'm a woman's tailor, sir.

SHALLOW

Should I prick him, sir?

FALSTAFF

You might as well. But if he had been a man's tailor, he would have already pricked you with his pins. Will you make as many holes in the enemy's armor as you have in women's underwear?

FEEBLE

I'll do my best, sir. I can't do any more.

FALSTAFF

Well said, good woman's tailor! Well said, courageous Feeble! You'll be as brave as the angriest dove or the

magnanimous mouse.—Prick the woman's tailor well,
145   Master Shallow, deep, Master Shallow.

FEEBLE
I would Wart might have gone, sir.

FALSTAFF
I would thou wert a man's tailor, that thou mightst mend
him and make him fit to go. I cannot put him to a private
soldier that is the leader of so many thousands. Let that
150   suffice, most forcible Feeble.

FEEBLE
It shall suffice, sir.

FALSTAFF
I am bound to thee, reverend Feeble.—Who is next?

SHALLOW
Peter Bullcalf o' th' green.

FALSTAFF
Yea, marry, let's see Bullcalf.

BULLCALF
155   Here, sir.

FALSTAFF
Fore God, a likely fellow. Come, prick me Bullcalf till he
roar again.

BULLCALF
O Lord, good my lord captain—

FALSTAFF
What, dost thou roar before thou art pricked?

BULLCALF
160   O Lord, sir, I am a diseased man.

FALSTAFF
What disease hast thou?

BULLCALF
A whoreson cold, sir, a cough, sir, which I caught with
ringing in the King's affairs upon his coronation day, sir.

most valiant mouse. Prick the woman's tailor. A big one, Master Shallow; a deep one, Master Shallow.

FEEBLE

I wish Wart were going, sir.

FALSTAFF

And I wish you were a man's tailor. You could have mended his clothes and made him fit to go. I can't make him a private soldier when he's already the leader of thousands—of lice, that is. But never mind, oh forcible Feeble.

FEEBLE

Never mind, sir.

FALSTAFF

I like you, good Feeble. Who's next?

SHALLOW

Peter Bullcalf from the village green!

FALSTAFF

Oh yeah. Let's see Bullcalf.

BULLCALF

Here, sir!

FALSTAFF

My God! What a great man! Prick Bullcalf until he shouts again.

BULLCALF

Oh Lord! My lord, good Captain—

FALSTAFF

What, you're yelling before you've even been pricked?

BULLCALF

Oh Lord, sir! I'm a sick man.

FALSTAFF

What disease do you have?

BULLCALF

A nasty cold, sir. A cough, sir. I caught it when I was ringing the church bells in honor of the King's coronation.

FALSTAFF

165   Come, thou shalt go to the wars in a gown. We will have away thy cold, and I will take such order that my friends shall ring for thee.— *(to* SHALLOW*)* Is here all?

SHALLOW

     Here is two more called than your number. You must have but four here, sir, and so I pray you go in with me to dinner.

FALSTAFF

170   Come, I will go drink with you, but I cannot tarry dinner. I am glad to see you, by my troth, Master Shallow.

SHALLOW

     O, Sir John, do you remember since we lay all night in the windmill in Saint George's Field?

FALSTAFF

     No more of that, good Master Shallow, no more of that.

SHALLOW

     Ha, 'twas a merry night. And is Jane Nightwork alive?

FALSTAFF

175   She lives, Master Shallow.

SHALLOW

     She never could away with me.

FALSTAFF

     Never, never; she would always say she could not abide Master Shallow.

SHALLOW

     By the Mass, I could anger her to th' heart. She was then a

180   bona roba. Doth she hold her own well?

FALSTAFF

     Old, old, Master Shallow.

SHALLOW

     Nay, she must be old. She cannot choose but be old. Certain, she's old, and had Robin Nightwork by old Nightwork before I came to Clement's Inn.

FALSTAFF

Then you'll go to war in a dressing gown. We'll get rid of your cold, and I'll give orders for some of my men to ring the bells for you while you're away. *(to* SHALLOW*)* Is this everybody?

SHALLOW

We've got two more here than you need. You can have four, sir. Now, come inside and eat lunch with me.

FALSTAFF

I'll have a drink with you, but I can't stay to eat. But I'm truly glad to see you, Master Shallow.

SHALLOW

Oh, Sir John, do you remember the time we spent all night in the windmill in St. George's field?

FALSTAFF

Don't go there, Master Shallow. Don't go there.

SHALLOW

Ha! That was a fun night. Is Jane Nightwork still alive?

FALSTAFF

She's alive, Master Shallow.

SHALLOW

She never could stand me.

FALSTAFF

Never, never. She always said she couldn't stand Master Shallow.

SHALLOW

Truly, I could anger her to the core. She was a good-looking wench then. Does she still look good?

FALSTAFF

Old, old, Master Shallow.

SHALLOW

Well, she must be old. She's got no choice but to be old. Of course she's old. She gave birth to Robin Nightwork, the son of old man Nightwork, before I even got to Clement's Inn.

SILENCE
185   That's fifty-five year ago.

SHALLOW
           Ha, cousin Silence, that thou hadst seen that that this
           knight and I have seen!—Ha, Sir John, said I well?

FALSTAFF
           We have heard the chimes at midnight, Master Shallow.

SHALLOW
           That we have, that we have, that we have. In faith, Sir John,
190   we have. Our watchword was "Hem, boys." Come, let's to
           dinner; come, let's to dinner. Jesus, the days that we have
           seen! Come, come.
                              Exeunt FALSTAFF, SHALLOW, *and* SILENCE

BULLCALF
           Good Master Corporate Bardolph, stand my friend, and
           here's four Harry ten-shillings in French crowns for you.
195   In very truth, sir, I had as lief be hanged, sir, as go. And yet,
           for mine own part, sir, I do not care, but rather because I am
           unwilling, and, for mine own part, have a desire to stay
           with my friends. Else, sir, I did not care, for mine own part,
           so much.

BARDOLPH
200   Go to. Stand aside.

MOULDY
           And, good Master Corporal Captain, for my old dame's
           sake, stand my friend. She has nobody to do anything about
           her when I am gone, and she is old and cannot help herself:
           You shall have forty, sir.

BARDOLPH
205   Go to. Stand aside.

FEEBLE
           By my troth, I care not. A man can die but once. We owe
           God a death. I'll ne'er bear a base mind. An 't be my
           destiny, so; an 't be not, so. No man's too good to serve 's

SILENCE

That's fifty-five years ago.

SHALLOW

Ha, cousin Silence, if only you'd seen what this knight and I have seen! Ha! Am I right, Sir John?

FALSTAFF

We've seen the clock strike midnight, Master Shallow.

SHALLOW

We sure have, we sure have, we sure have. I swear, Sir John, we sure have. Our slogan was "Down the hatch, boys!" Come, let's have lunch, let's have lunch. Jesus, the things we've seen! Come, come.

FALSTAFF, SHALLOW, *and* SILENCE *exit.*

BULLCALF

Bullcalf's mistake for "corporal"

A "Harry ten shilling" was a ten-shilling coin minted during the reign of Henry VII; by Shakespeare's time, they were each worth about five shillings.

Good Master Corporate Bardolph, be my friend. Here are some French crowns for you, worth four Harry ten shillings. I'm telling you, sir, I'd just as soon be hanged as go fight. It's not that I care about my well-being. It's just that I'm not willing to go, and further-more, I'd like to stay here with my friends. But really, I don't care about myself.

BARDOLPH

Whatever. Stand over there.

MOULDY

And, good Master Corporal Captain, for my old lady's sake, be my friend. She has nobody here to help her do anything once I'm gone. She's old and can't do much by herself. I'll give you forty shillings, sir.

BARDOLPH

Whatever. Stand over there.

FEEBLE

I'll tell you the truth: I don't care one way or the other. You only die once, and we all owe God a death. I won't do anything underhanded. If it's my fate, it's my fate. If not, not. No man is too good to serve his country.

prince, and let it go which way it will, he that dies this year
210   is quit for the next.

BARDOLPH
Well said. Th' art a good fellow.

FEEBLE
Faith, I'll bear no base mind.

Enter FALSTAFF, SHALLOW, *and* SILENCE

FALSTAFF
Come, sir, which men shall I have?

SHALLOW
Four of which you please.

BARDOLPH
215   Sir, a word with you. *(aside to* FALSTAFF*)* I have three pound
to free Mouldy and Bullcalf.

FALSTAFF
Go to, well.

SHALLOW
Come, Sir John, which four will you have?

FALSTAFF
Do you choose for me.

SHALLOW
220   Marry, then, Mouldy, Bullcalf, Feeble, and Shadow.

FALSTAFF
Mouldy and Bullcalf! For you, Mouldy, stay at home till
you are past service.—And for your part, Bullcalf, grow till
you come unto it. I will none of you.

Exeunt MOULDY *and* BULLCALF

SHALLOW
Sir John, Sir John, do not yourself wrong. They are your
225   likeliest men, and I would have you served with the best.

FALSTAFF
Will you tell me, Master Shallow, how to choose a man?
Care I for the limb, the thews, the stature, bulk, and big

Whatever happens, happens. If you die this year, you're paid up for next year.

BARDOLPH

Well said. You're a good man.

FEEBLE

I'm telling you. I won't do anything underhanded.

FALSTAFF, SHALLOW *and* SILENCE *enter.*

FALSTAFF

All right, sir. Which men can I have?

SHALLOW

Any four you choose.

BARDOLPH

Sir, may I have a word with you? *(whispers to* FALSTAFF*)* I've gotten three pounds to free Mouldy and Bullcalf.

FALSTAFF

No kidding. Great.

SHALLOW

Come on, Sir John, which four do you want?

FALSTAFF

You pick.

SHALLOW

All right, then. Mouldy, Bullcalf, Feeble, and Shadow.

FALSTAFF

Mouldy and Bullcalf. Mouldy, you stay home till you're too old to fight. And as for you, Bullcalf, wait till you've reached fighting age. I don't want either of you.

MOULDY *and* BULLCALF *exit.*

SHALLOW

Sir John, Sir John. Don't make a mistake. They're the best men of the bunch, and I want you to have only the best.

FALSTAFF

Master Shallow, are you going to tell me how to choose a soldier? Do you think I care about a man's body,

assemblance of a man? Give me the spirit, Master Shallow.
Here's Wart. You see what a ragged appearance it is. He
230   shall charge you and discharge you with the motion of a
pewterer's hammer, come off and on swifter than he that
gibbets on the brewer's bucket. And this same half-faced
fellow, Shadow, give me this man. He presents no mark to
the enemy. The foeman may with as great aim level at the
235   edge of a penknife. And for a retreat, how swiftly will this
Feeble the woman's tailor, run off! O, give me the spare
men, and spare me the great ones.—Put me a caliver into
Wart's hand, Bardolph.

BARDOLPH
Hold, Wart. Traverse. Thas, thas, thas.

FALSTAFF
240   Come, manage me your caliver: so, very well, go to, very
good, exceeding good. O, give me always a little, lean, old,
chopped, bald shot. Well said, i' faith, Wart. Th' art a good
scab. Hold, there's a tester for thee.

SHALLOW
He is not his craft's master. He doth not do it right. I
245   remember at Mile End Green, when I lay at Clement's
Inn—I was then Sir Dagonet in Arthur's show—there was
a little quiver fellow, and he would manage you his piece
thus. And he would about and about, and come you in, and
come you in. "Rah, tah, tah," would he say. "Bounce,"
250   would he say, and away again would he go, and again would
he come. I shall ne'er see such a fellow.

FALSTAFF
These fellows will do well, Master Shallow.—God keep
you, Master Silence. I will not use many words with you.
Fare you well, gentlemen both. I thank you. I must a dozen
255   mile to-night.—Bardolph, give the soldiers coats.

strength, height, bulk, and overall size? Give me his spirit, Master Shallow! Take a look at Wart. You see how ragged he looks? He can load and fire steadily—as steadily as a tinsmith's hammer. He can advance and regroup fast—faster than a brewer's delivery pail can be refilled. And this skinny guy, Shadow—give me this man. He offers no target to the enemy. The enemy might as well try aiming at a knife's edge. And as for retreating, Feeble, the woman's tailor, will run faster than you can imagine. Oh, give me the spare men and spare me the great ones! Bardolph, give Wart a musket.

BARDOLPH

Here you go, Wart. Present arms! Right shoulder, arms! Left shoulder, arms!

FALSTAFF

Come on, handle your weapon. Yes, good. Very good. Very, very good. Oh, give me a little, skinny, old, dried-out, bald rifleman any day. Good job, Wart. You're a good scab of a guy. Wait, here's a tester for you.

tester = sixpence

SHALLOW

He's no expert. He's not doing it right. I remember up at Mile End Park, when I was at Clement's Inn—I played the fool in the archery pageant. There was a nimble little guy, and he would handle his weapon like this, and he would run all over the place, and he'd charge and charge. "Rat-a-tat tat," he'd say. "Bang!" he'd say. Then he'd run away, then come back. I never saw anybody like him.

FALSTAFF

These guys will be fine, Master Shallow. God bless you, Master Silence—I won't say much to you. Farewell, gentlemen, and thank you. I have to march twelve miles tonight. Bardolph, give the soldiers uniforms.

SHALLOW
Sir John, the Lord bless you. God prosper your affairs. God send us peace. At your return, visit our house. Let our old acquaintance be renewed. Peradventure I will with you to the court.

FALSTAFF
260 Fore God, would you would, Master Shallow.

SHALLOW
Go to. I have spoke at a word. God keep you.

FALSTAFF
Fare you well, gentle gentlemen.
                    Exeunt SHALLOW *and* SILENCE

On, Bardolph. Lead the men away.
                    Exeunt BARDOLPH *and the recruits*

As I return, I will fetch off these justices. I do see the bottom
265 of Justice Shallow. Lord, Lord, how subject we old men are to this vice of lying. This same starved justice hath done nothing but prate to me of the wildness of his youth and the feats he hath done about Turnbull Street, and every third word a lie, duer paid to the hearer than the Turk's tribute.
270 I do remember him at Clement's Inn, like a man made after supper of a cheese paring. When he was naked, he was, for all the world, like a forked radish with a head fantastically carved upon it with a knife. He was so forlorn that his dimensions to any thick sight were invincible. He was the
275 very genius of famine, yet lecherous as a monkey, and the whores called him "mandrake." He came ever in the rearward of the fashion, and sung those tunes to the overscutched huswives that he heard the carmen whistle, and swore they were his fancies or his good-nights.

SHALLOW

God bless you, Sir John. May God bring you good luck, and bring us peace. When you come back, pay us a visit. Let's renew our old friendship. Maybe I'll even come with you to the royal court!

FALSTAFF

I swear, I wish you would, Master Shallow.

SHALLOW

I meant what I said. May God keep you.

FALSTAFF

Farewell, gentle gentlemen.

SHALLOW and SILENCE exit.

March, Bardolph. Lead the men away.

BARDOLPH and the recruits exit.

When I come back, I'll expose these judges for the frauds that they are. I can see through this Judge Shallow. Lord, Lord; we old men sure know how to tell lies! This dried-up old judge has done nothing but go on and on to me about how wild he was when he was as a youth, and how many stunts he pulled in the seedy parts of town. Every third word he speaks is a lie, and he'll tell lies quicker than a Turk will scramble to pay the sultan. I remember him at Clement's Inn: he looked like a man someone carved after dinner out of a scrap of cheese. When he was naked he looked like a mandrake root, with a fanciful head someone had carved in with a knife. He was so skinny that he was invisible to any man with imperfect vision; he truly was the embodiment of starvation. But he was as horny as a monkey: the whores called him "mandrake," because mandrake stimulates the sex drive. He was always a little bit behind the times. He would hear the wagon drivers sing their songs, and then he'd go to his worn-out whores and sing them what he'd

The Turkish Sultan exacted notoriously harsh punishments on those who failed to pay him on time.

280   And now is this Vice's dagger become a squire, and talks as
      familiarly of John o' Gaunt as if he had been sworn brother
      to him, and I'll be sworn he ne'er saw him but once in the
      tilt-yard, and then he burst his head for crowding among
      the Marshal's men. I saw it and told John o' Gaunt he beat
285   his own name, for you might have thrust him and all his
      apparel into an eel-skin; the case of a treble hautboy was a
      mansion for him, a court. And now has he land and beefs.
      Well, I'll be acquainted with him, if I return, and 't shall go
      hard but I'll make him a philosopher's two stones to me. If
290   the young dace be a bait for the old pike, I see no reason in
      the law of nature but I may snap at him. Let time shape, and
      there an end.

                                                                    Exit

heard, pretending he had written them himself. And now this vile stick has become a landowner, and he talks about John of Gaunt like he was his own brother. I swear, he only saw Gaunt once, and that was in the arena at the jousting tournament; John of Gaunt cut Shallow's head with his sword. I saw it all, and I told John of Gaunt that he had beaten his own name, since Shallow was such a gaunt man back then. You could fit him and all his clothes into the skin an eel sheds. An instrument case was as huge as a mansion to him, as big as a courtroom. Now he has land and livestock. Well, I'll be his friend if I come back. He won't like it, but I'll turn him into an unending source of wealth for myself. If small fish can be bait for big fish, I see no reason why I can't snap my jaws at Shallow. Time will tell, and that's all I have to say about that.

He exits.

ACT FOUR
SCENE 1

Enter the ARCHBISHOP *of York,* MOWBRAY, HASTINGS, *and others*

ARCHBISHOP
What is this forest called?

HASTINGS
'Tis Gaultree Forest, an 't shall please your Grace.

ARCHBISHOP
Here stand, my lords, and send discoverers forth
To know the numbers of our enemies.

HASTINGS
5 We have sent forth already.

ARCHBISHOP
'Tis well done.
My friends and brethren in these great affairs,
I must acquaint you that I have received
New-dated letters from Northumberland,
Their cold intent, tenor ,and substance, thus:
10 Here doth he wish his person, with such powers
As might hold sortance with his quality,
The which he could not levy; whereupon
He is retired, to ripe his growing fortunes,
To Scotland, and concludes in hearty prayers
15 That your attempts may overlive the hazard
And fearful melting of their opposite.

MOWBRAY
Thus do the hopes we have in him touch ground
And dash themselves to pieces.

Enter a MESSENGER

ACT FOUR
SCENE 1

ARCHBISHOP *of York,* MOWBRAY, HASTINGS, *and others enter.*

ARCHBISHOP

What's the name of this forest?

HASTINGS

Gaultree Forest, your grace.

ARCHBISHOP

Stop here, sirs. Send out scouts to find out how many soldiers our enemy has.

HASTINGS

We've already done that.

ARCHBISHOP

Well done. My friends and brothers in this great undertaking, I have to share with you that I've received new letters from Northumberland. They have a chilling purpose, tone, and content. He says that he wishes he could be here in person, with an army as strong someone of his rank should have, but he couldn't raise one. So he's going to go to Scotland to increase his power. He prays that your armies will prevail against the terrible power of the enemy.

MOWBRAY

And with that, any hope we had for him is thrown to the ground and dashed to pieces.

A MESSENGER *enters.*

HASTINGS

Now, what news?

MESSENGER

West of this forest, scarcely off a mile,

20   In goodly form comes on the enemy,

And, by the ground they hide, I judge their number

Upon or near the rate of thirty thousand.

MOWBRAY

The just proportion that we gave them out.

Let us sway on and face them in the field.

Enter WESTMORELAND

ARCHBISHOP

25   What well-appointed leader fronts us here?

MOWBRAY

I think it is my Lord of Westmoreland.

WESTMORELAND

Health and fair greeting from our general,

The Prince Lord John and Duke of Lancaster.

ARCHBISHOP

Say on, my Lord of Westmoreland, in peace,

30   What doth concern your coming.

WESTMORELAND

Then, my lord,

Unto your Grace do I in chief address

The substance of my speech. If that rebellion

Came like itself, in base and abject routs,

Led on by bloody youth, guarded with rage,

35   And countenanced by boys and beggary—

I say, if damn'd commotion so appeared

In his true, native, and most proper shape,

You, reverend father, and these noble lords

Had not been here to dress the ugly form

40   Of base and bloody insurrection

HASTINGS

> What's happening?

MESSENGER

> The enemy is west of this forest, and less than a mile away. They look powerful, and, from the amount of space they're taking up, I'd say they have close to thirty thousand soldiers.

MOWBRAY

> That's exactly the number we thought they had. Let's march ahead and engage them in battle.

> WESTMORELAND *enters.*

ARCHBISHOP

> Who's this well-equipped leader coming here to confront us?

MOWBRAY

> I think it's Lord Westmoreland.

WESTMORELAND

> Our general, the Prince Lord John of Lancaster, sends greetings and wishes you good health.

ARCHBISHOP

> Speak in peace, Lord Westmoreland. What's the reason you've come here?

WESTMORELAND

> The most important part of my message is for you, your grace. You, who are a holy man, and these good gentlemen as well—you would not be here, lending dignity to this bloody insurrection, if it appeared as rebellion normally does: like a lowborn mob, led by bloody youths uniformed in rags, and supported by boys and beggars.

With your fair honors. You, Lord Archbishop,
Whose see is by a civil peace maintained,
Whose beard the silver hand of peace hath touched,
Whose learning and good letters peace hath tutored,
45   Whose white investments figure innocence,
The dove and very blessèd spirit of peace,
Wherefore do you so ill translate yourself
Out of the speech of peace, that bears such grace,
Into the harsh and boist'rous tongue of war,
50   Turning your books to graves, your ink to blood,
Your pens to lances, and your tongue divine
To a trumpet and a point of war?

ARCHBISHOP
Wherefore do I this? So the question stands.
Briefly, to this end: we are all diseased,
55   And with our surfeiting and wanton hours
Have brought ourselves into a burning fever,
And we must bleed for it; of which disease
Our late King Richard, being infected, died.
But, my most noble Lord of Westmoreland,
60   I take not on me here as a physician,
Nor do I as an enemy to peace
Troop in the throngs of military men,
But rather show awhile like fearful war
To diet rank minds sick of happiness
65   And purge th' obstructions which begin to stop
Our very veins of life. Hear me more plainly.
I have in equal balance justly weighed
What wrongs our arms may do, what wrongs we suffer,
And find our griefs heavier than our offenses.
70   We see which way the stream of time doth run
And are enforced from our most quiet there
By the rough torrent of occasion,
And have the summary of all our griefs,
When time shall serve, to show in articles;
75   Which long ere this we offered to the King

You, Lord Archbishop—whose diocese is peaceful and law-abiding; whose beard has turned white, signifying a peaceful life; whose education and learning are the products of peaceful times; who is the dove and very blessed embodiment of peace—why are you translating yourself from the graceful language of peace into the harsh, violent language of war? You're turning your books into coffins, your ink into blood, your pens into swords, and your holy words into a trumpet that sounds a call to arms.

ARCHBISHOP

Why am I doing this? That is the question. The short answer is this: we're all sick. We've eaten and drunk too much and stayed up all night, and now we have a burning fever whose only cure is bloodletting. Richard, our late King, was infected with this disease and died from it. But, my good Lord Westmoreland, I'm not here as a physician, nor am I marching with this army as an enemy of peace. What I'm doing is making a frightening show of war, to stop people from indulging all their vices. This will clear the hardening of the arteries which threatens to kill us all. Let me speak more plainly. I've carefully considered the options, weighing the harm our armies are likely to cause against the harm we're already suffering, and I find that our grievances are stronger than our offenses. We can see where things are headed, and the rough times ahead leave us with no choice but to step away from our quiet lives. We have a list of grievances which we can publish at the appropriate time. We offered that list to the King a long time ago, but we could never get an audience with him.

And might by no suit gain our audience.
When we are wronged and would unfold our griefs,
We are denied access unto his person
Even by those men that most have done us wrong.
80   The dangers of the days but newly gone,
Whose memory is written on the earth
With yet appearing blood, and the examples
Of every minute's instance, present now,
Hath put us in these ill-beseeming arms,
85   Not to break peace or any branch of it,
But to establish here a peace indeed,
Concurring both in name and quality.

WESTMORELAND
When ever yet was your appeal denied?
Wherein have you been gallèd by the King?
90   What peer hath been suborned to grate on you,
That you should seal this lawless bloody book
Of forged rebellion with a seal divine
And consecrate commotion's bitter edge?

ARCHBISHOP
My brother general, the commonwealth,
95   To brother born an household cruelty,
I make my quarrel in particular.

WESTMORELAND
There is no need of any such redress,
Or if there were, it not belongs to you.

MOWBRAY
Why not to him in part, and to us all
100   That feel the bruises of the days before
And suffer the condition of these times
To lay a heavy and unequal hand
Upon our honors?

WESTMORELAND
          O, my good Lord Mowbray,
Construe the times to their necessities,

We were wronged, and when we tried to speak to the King about it, we were denied access to him by the very men who had wronged us most. We're in this seemingly unbefitting armor because of the terrible recent violence—the bloodshed from which is still visible on the ground—and because of the terrible things happening now, every minute. We don't want to harm peace in any way. We want instead to establish a peace that's real and meaningful.

WESTMORELAND

When was your request to see the King denied? How has the king harmed you? What lord in the King's court has been sent out to do you wrong? And why would you put your holy stamp of approval on an illegal uprising and give religious blessing to a violent civil war?

ARCHBISHOP

The original text of this difficult passage may be corrupted; its exact meaning is obscure.

The grievances borne by my fellow Englishmen, and the cruel murder of Scroop, my own brother: these are the reasons I've made this fight my own.

WESTMORELAND

There's no need for any repayment like that; and even if there were, you should not be the person to benefit.

MOWBRAY

Why shouldn't he benefit at least a little? Why shouldn't we all benefit, who suffered in these recent battles, and who have allowed our honor to be damaged by the terrible things happening now?

WESTMORELAND

Oh, my good Lord Mowbray, if you think about what is necessary in times of war, you'll see that it is the sit-

105 And you shall say indeed it is the time,
And not the King, that doth you injuries.
Yet for your part, it not appears to me
Either from the King or in the present time
That you should have an inch of any ground
110 To build a grief on. Were you not restored
To all the Duke of Norfolk's seigniories,
Your noble and right well remembered father's?

MOWBRAY
What thing, in honor, had my father lost,
That need to be revived and breathed in me?
115 The King that loved him, as the state stood then,
Was force perforce compelled to banish him,
And then that Harry Bolingbroke and he,
Being mounted and both rousèd in their seats,
Their neighing coursers daring of the spur,
120 Their armèd staves in charge, their beavers down,
Their eyes of fire sparking through sights of steel
And the loud trumpet blowing them together,
Then, then, when there was nothing could have stayed
My father from the breast of Bolingbroke,
125 O, when the King did throw his warder down—
His own life hung upon the staff he threw—
Then threw he down himself and all their lives
That by indictment and by dint of sword
Have since miscarried under Bolingbroke.

WESTMORELAND
130 You speak, Lord Mowbray, now you know not what.
The Earl of Hereford was reputed then
In England the most valiant gentleman.
Who knows on whom fortune would then have smiled?
But if your father had been victor there,
135 He ne'er had borne it out of Coventry;
For all the country in a general voice
Cried hate upon him; and all their prayers and love

uation that harms you, and not the King himself. But as for you in particular, it seems to me that you have no foundation on which to build a quarrel with either the King or your current situation. Wasn't the entire estate of the Duke of Norfolk, your father, just given back to you?

MOWBRAY

What did my father lose that I now need to restore? Richard, the King at the time, loved my father, but given what was happening he had no choice but to banish him. And then, at Coventry, my father and Harry Bolingbroke met in a formal challenge. They were both mounted on their horses and ready to charge. Their horses were neighing, anxiously waiting for their riders' spurs to drive them forward. Their steel-tipped lances were ready for the attack. The visors of their helmets were down. Their eyes were on fire behind the steel slits. The trumpet sounded, and then—when there was nothing that could have stopped my father from killing Bolingbroke—the King prevented the fight by throwing down his royal scepter. That scepter was a symbol of his life; when he threw it down, he threw down his life and the lives of every man that has since died at war under the leadership of Bolingbroke.

The duel between Bolingbroke (now King Henry) and Norfolk (Mowbray's father) occurs in Richard II, 1.3.

WESTMORELAND

You don't know what you're talking about, Lord Mowbray. Bolingbroke at the time was considered the bravest gentleman in England. Who knows who would have won that fight? But even if your father had won, he never would have made it out of Coventry. The whole country hated him, and they loved and prayed for Bolingbroke.

Were set on Hereford, whom they doted on
And blessed and graced, indeed more than the King.
140 But this is mere digression from my purpose.
Here come I from our princely general
To know your griefs, to tell you from his Grace
That he will give you audience; and wherein
It shall appear that your demands are just,
145 You shall enjoy them, everything set off
That might so much as think you enemies.

MOWBRAY
But he hath forced us to compel this offer;
And it proceeds from policy, not love.

WESTMORELAND
Mowbray, you overween to take it so.
150 This offer comes from mercy, not from fear.
For, lo, within a ken our army lies,
Upon mine honor, all too confident
To give admittance to a thought of fear.
Our battle is more full of names than yours,
155 Our men more perfect in the use of arms,
Our armor all as strong, our cause the best.
Then reason will our hearts should be as good.
Say you not then our offer is compelled.

MOWBRAY
Well, by my will, we shall admit no parley.

WESTMORELAND
160 That argues but the shame of your offense.
A rotten case abides no handling.

HASTINGS
Hath the Prince John a full commission,
In very ample virtue of his father,
To hear and absolutely to determine
165 Of what conditions we shall stand upon?

They blessed him and adored him even more than the King. But I digress. I was sent here by our general, the Prince, to hear your grievances, and to tell you that he's prepared to listen to you. If it appears that your demands are legitimate, he'll give you what you want—except for those things which might suggest that you're his enemies.

MOWBRAY

But he's made us force him to listen to us. His offer isn't motivated by love; it's a political move.

WESTMORELAND

Mowbray, you're out of line to think that. His offer is made out of mercy, not fear. Just look, you can see our army from here. I give you my word of honor: that army is so confident, it won't even allow the thought of fear to enter. Our army has more important people than yours, and better soldiers; our armor is every bit as strong as yours, and our cause is better. It's only logical that we should be as courageous as you are. So don't say you've forced the Prince to do anything at all.

MOWBRAY

Well, I say we won't agree to any conference.

WESTMORELAND

That just proves that what you're doing here is shameful. A rotten container falls apart at the touch; likewise, a rotten cause cannot withstand scrutiny and argument.

HASTINGS

Has the King given Prince John his full authorization to listen to our complaint, and address it in any way the Prince sees fit?

WESTMORELAND
> That is intended in the General's name.
> I muse you make so slight a question.

ARCHBISHOP
> Then take, my Lord of Westmoreland, this schedule,
> For this contains our general grievances.
170 Each several article herein redressed,
> All members of our cause, both here and hence,
> That are insinewed to this action,
> Acquitted by a true substantial form
> And present execution of our wills
175 To us and to our purposes confined,
> We come within our awful banks again
> And knit our powers to the arm of peace.

WESTMORELAND
> This will I show the General. Please you, lords,
> In sight of both our battles we may meet,
180 And either end in peace, which God so frame,
> Or to the place of difference call the swords
> Which must decide it.

ARCHBISHOP
>   My lord, we will do so.
>   *Exit* WESTMORELAND

MOWBRAY
> There is a thing within my bosom tells me
> That no conditions of our peace can stand.

HASTINGS
185 Fear you not that. If we can make our peace
> Upon such large terms and so absolute
> As our conditions shall consist upon,
> Our peace shall stand as firm as rocky mountains.

MOWBRAY
> Yea, but our valuation shall be such
190 That every slight and false-derivèd cause,
> Yea, every idle, nice, and wanton reason,
> Shall to the King taste of this action,

WESTMORELAND

That goes without saying. I'm amazed you'd even ask such a foolish question.

ARCHBISHOP

Then, Lord Westmoreland, take this document. It lists our grievances. If each complaint listed here is addressed, and if everyone on our side, both here and elsewhere, is granted a full pardon and immediate satisfaction of our demands, then we'll return to our own boundaries again and work together for the cause of peace.

WESTMORELAND

I'll show this to the general. Please, let's meet at a place where both our armies can see us. Then either let our talks end in peace—God willing!—or let us take the fight to the battlefield where it will be decided.

ARCHBISHOP

My lord, we will do so.

WESTMORELAND exits.

MOWBRAY

Something in my heart tells me that no peace we agree to could possibly last.

HASTINGS

Don't worry about that. If we can come to terms that are as comprehensive as the ones we're insisting upon, then the peace will be as durable as rocky mountains.

MOWBRAY

Yes, but in the future the King will think so poorly of us that every little slight, every false accusation, every tiny, silly, frivolous thing will seem to him to be a revival of this rebellion. Even if we were as devoted to

That, were our royal faiths martyrs in love,
We shall be winnowed with so rough a wind
195   That even our corn shall seem as light as chaff
And good from bad find no partition.

ARCHBISHOP
No, no, my lord. Note this: the King is weary
Of dainty and such picking grievances,
For he hath found to end one doubt by death
200   Revives two greater in the heirs of life;
And therefore will he wipe his tables clean
And keep no telltale to his memory
That may repeat and history his loss
To new remembrance. For full well he knows
205   He cannot so precisely weed this land
As his misdoubts present occasion;
His foes are so enrooted with his friends
That, plucking to unfix an enemy,
He doth unfasten so and shake a friend;
210   So that this land, like an offensive wife
That hath enraged him on to offer strokes,
As he is striking holds his infant up
And hangs resolved correction in the arm
That was upreared to execution.

HASTINGS
215   Besides, the King hath wasted all his rods
On late offenders, that he now doth lack
The very instruments of chastisement,
So that his power, like to a fangless lion,
May offer but not hold.

ARCHBISHOP
                               'Tis very true,
220   And therefore be assured, my good Lord Marshal,
If we do now make our atonement well,
Our peace will, like a broken limb united,
Grow stronger for the breaking.

the King as martyrs are to their causes, he'll regard us so skeptically that even the good things we do for him won't count; he won't be able to distinguish them from the bad.

ARCHBISHOP

No, no, sir. Listen, the king is tired of getting upset over every little thing. He's discovered that ending one problem by killing someone only creates two bigger problems in the people left alive. So from now on, he'll wipe his memory clean, and forget anything that might remind him of the bad things from his past. He knows that he can't just eliminate every single opponent who crops up.

His enemies are rooted in with his friends, to the extent that, if he tries to pull up an enemy, he'll also uproot and discard a friend. This country's like a misbehaving wife, who, just when her husband is about to hit her, holds his baby up, and freezes the intended punishment in the very arm that was poised to apply it.

HASTINGS

Besides, the King has expended all his energy for punishment on the recent rebellion. He has nothing left to punish with. His power is like a lion with no teeth: it can threaten, but it can't do any harm.

ARCHBISHOP

That's true. Rest assured, my good Lord Marshal, if our reconciliation is sincere, then peace will be like a broken bone, which grows stronger for having once been broken.

MOWBRAY
                      Be it so.
Here is returned my Lord of Westmoreland.

Enter **WESTMORELAND**

WESTMORELAND
225   The Prince is here at hand. Pleaseth your lordship
To meet his Grace just distance 'tween our armies.

MOWBRAY
Your Grace of York, in God's name then set forward.

ARCHBISHOP
Before, and greet his Grace.— *(to* **WESTMORELAND***)* My
    lord, we come.

The **ARCHBISHOP**, **MOWBRAY**, **YORK**, **HASTINGS** *and the others
go forward*

Enter Prince John of **LANCASTER** *and officers with him*

LANCASTER
You are well encountered here, my cousin Mowbray.—
230   Good day to you, gentle Lord Archbishop,—
And so to you, Lord Hastings, and to all.—
My Lord of York, it better showed with you
When that your flock, assembled by the bell,
Encircled you to hear with reverence
235   Your exposition on the holy text
Than now to see you here, an iron man talking,
Cheering a rout of rebels with your drum,
Turning the word to sword, and life to death.
That man that sits within a monarch's heart
240   And ripens in the sunshine of his favor,
Would he abuse the countenance of the King,
Alack, what mischiefs might he set abroach
In shadow of such greatness! With you, Lord Bishop,

MOWBRAY

> I hope so. Lord Westmoreland is back.

WESTMORELAND enters.

WESTMORELAND

> The Prince is nearby. If you will, please meet him at a spot halfway between our two armies.

MOWBRAY

> Your grace, Archbishop of York, go forward in God's name.

ARCHBISHOP

> Lead on, and greet his highness. *(to WESTMORELAND)* Sir, we're on our way.

The ARCHBISHOP, MOWBRAY, YORK, HASTINGS, and the others cross the stage.

Prince John of LANCASTER enters, with officers.

LANCASTER

> I'm glad to see you, my cousin Mowbray. Good day to you, gentle Archbishop, and to you, Lord Hastings, and to all. Lord Archbishop, it was better to see you when worshippers—called together by the church bell—surrounded you to hear Biblical sermons than it is to see you here, in armor; cheering a mob of rebels with your war drums, turning your words to weapons, and your life into death.

> When a man is close to the King's heart, and grows strong under the King's protection, only to turn against him—alas! What evils that man will unleash, hidden from view by the King's own reputation! This is exactly how it is with you, Lord Bishop.

It is even so. Who hath not heard it spoken
245   How deep you were within the books of God,
To us the speaker in His parliament,
To us th' imagined voice of God himself,
The very opener and intelligencer
Between the grace, the sanctities, of heaven,
250   And our dull workings? O, who shall believe
But you misuse the reverence of your place,
Employ the countenance and grace of heaven
As a false favorite doth his prince's name,
In deeds dishonorable? You have ta'en up,
255   Under the counterfeited zeal of God,
The subjects of His substitute, my father,
And both against the peace of heaven and him
Have here up-swarmed them.

ARCHBISHOP
Good my Lord of Lancaster,
260   I am not here against your father's peace,
But, as I told my Lord of Westmoreland,
The time misordered doth, in common sense,
Crowd us and crush us to this monstrous form
To hold our safety up. I sent your Grace
265   The parcels and particulars of our grief,
The which hath been with scorn shoved from the court,
Whereon this Hydra son of war is born,
Whose dangerous eyes may well be charmed asleep
With grant of our most just and right desires,
270   And true obedience, of this madness cured,
Stoop tamely to the foot of majesty.

MOWBRAY
If not, we ready are to try our fortunes
To the last man.

HASTINGS
                        And though we here fall down,
We have supplies to second our attempt;
275   If they miscarry, theirs shall second them,

Who hasn't heard how profound your religious knowledge is? To us, you were our representative in God's own parliament. To us, you might as well have been God's own voice: the interpreter and ambassador between God's heavenly ways and our own dull, mortal actions. And now, who would say anything but that you are abusing the holiness of your position, using the outward show of godliness to do terrible things, like a treacherous courtier uses the King's good name? You have pretended to be acting in God's name as you encourage the subjects of God's deputy, my father, to rise up against the peace of both heaven and the King.

ARCHBISHOP

The Hydra was a monster with many heads; each time a head was cut off, a new one would grow in its place.

Good Lord of Lancaster, I am not here as an enemy your father's peace. But, as I told Westmoreland, these tumultuous times have forced us to behave in these monstrous ways, out of common sense and a regard for our own safety. I sent you a detailed list of our grievances, but you angrily shoved it aside. That's why this Hydra of a war has broken out. You can get rid of it by agreeing to the just and right things we demand. If you do that, this disease of war will be cured, and the monster will bow at your feet, tame and obedient.

MOWBRAY

If you don't, we're ready to fight to the last man.

HASTINGS

And if those of us who are here should fail, we have reinforcements standing by. If they fail, they have reinforcements to back them up, and in this way the

And so success of mischief shall be born,
And heir from heir shall hold this quarrel up
Whiles England shall have generation.

LANCASTER
You are too shallow, Hastings, much too shallow
280   To sound the bottom of the after-times.

WESTMORELAND
Pleaseth your Grace to answer them directly
How far forth you do like their articles.

LANCASTER
I like them all, and do allow them well,
And swear here by the honor of my blood,
285   My father's purposes have been mistook,
And some about him have too lavishly
Wrested his meaning and authority.
(to ARCHBISHOP*)* My lord, these griefs shall be with speed
        redressed;
Upon my soul, they shall. If this may please you,
290   Discharge your powers unto their several counties,
As we will ours, and here, between the armies,
Let's drink together friendly and embrace,
That all their eyes may bear those tokens home
Of our restorèd love and amity.

ARCHBISHOP
295   I take your princely word for these redresses.

LANCASTER
I give it you, and will maintain my word,
And thereupon I drink unto your Grace.

HASTINGS
Go, captain, and deliver to the army
This news of peace. Let them have pay, and part.
300   I know it will well please them. Hie thee, captain.
                                        Exit officer

ARCHBISHOP
To you, my noble Lord of Westmoreland.

fight will go on from father to son for all time until
England itself has no more new generations.

LANCASTER

You're not wise enough, Hastings, not wise enough at
all to see into eternity.

WESTMORELAND

Your highness, why not tell them directly what you
think of their list of grievances.

LANCASTER

I agree with all of them, and I admit that they're legitimate. I swear, on my family's honor: my father's
intentions have been misunderstood, and some of his
subordinates have overstepped their authority in exe-
cuting his orders.

(to ARCHBISHOP*)* Sir, we will make good on the wrongs
that have been done to you, I swear on my soul. If this
pleases you, then disperse your armies and send them
back where they came from; we shall do the same.
And here, where both armies can see us, we'll embrace
and drink a friendly toast to one another. The soldiers
will go home with evidence that we're friends once
again.

ARCHBISHOP

I'll take your word as a prince that you'll make good on
these things.

LANCASTER

I give you my word, and I'll keep it. And with that, I
drink a toast to you.

HASTINGS

Go, captain. Tell the army this news of peace. Pay
them, and send them away. I know it will make them
happy. Hurry, captain.

An officer exits.

ARCHBISHOP

Here's to you, good Lord Westmoreland.

WESTMORELAND
I pledge your Grace, and if you knew what pains
I have bestowed to breed this present peace,
You would drink freely. But my love to you
305   Shall show itself more openly hereafter.

ARCHBISHOP
I do not doubt you.

WESTMORELAND
                              I am glad of it.—
Health to my lord and gentle cousin, Mowbray.

MOWBRAY
You wish me health in very happy season,
For I am on the sudden something ill.

ARCHBISHOP
310   Against ill chances men are ever merry,
But heaviness foreruns the good event.

WESTMORELAND
Therefore be merry, coz; since sudden sorrow
Serves to say thus: "Some good thing comes tomorrow."

ARCHBISHOP
Believe me, I am passing light in spirit.

MOWBRAY
315   So much the worse if your own rule be true.

Shouts within

LANCASTER
The word of peace is rendered. Hark how they shout.

MOWBRAY
This had been cheerful after victory.

ARCHBISHOP
A peace is of the nature of a conquest,
For then both parties nobly are subdued,
320   And neither party loser.

WESTMORELAND

I drink to your grace. If you knew how hard I've worked to bring about this peaceful resolution, you'd really drink up. But my love for you will be more apparent from now on.

ARCHBISHOP

I don't doubt it.

WESTMORELAND

I'm glad. And here's to your health, my gentle cousin Lord Mowbray.

MOWBRAY

You wish me good health at a very good moment, because for some reason I'm suddenly feeling ill.

ARCHBISHOP

Men are always merry in the face of bad situations, but a heavy heart predicts a happy event.

WESTMORELAND

So be happy, kinsman. A sudden feeling of melancholy is just a sign that says, "Something good is coming tomorrow."

ARCHBISHOP

Believe me, I'm in really good spirits.

MOWBRAY

Which is not a good thing, if your own rule is correct.

Shouts are heard offstage.

LANCASTER

The news of peace has been announced. Listen to them shout!

MOWBRAY

They sound like they are cheering a victory.

ARCHBISHOP

Peace is a victory of sorts: both sides stop fighting honorably, but neither loses.

LANCASTER
Go, my lord,
And let our army be dischargèd too.

Exit WESTMORELAND

And, good my lord, so please you, let our trains
March by us, that we may peruse the men
We should have coped withal.

ARCHBISHOP
Go, good Lord Hastings,
325   And ere they be dismissed, let them march by.

Exit HASTINGS

LANCASTER
I trust, lords, we shall lie tonight together.

Enter WESTMORELAND

Now, cousin, wherefore stands our army still?

WESTMORELAND
The leaders, having charge from you to stand,
Will not go off until they hear you speak.

LANCASTER
230   They know their duties.

Enter HASTINGS

HASTINGS
My lord, our army is dispersed already.
Like youthful steers unyoked, they take their courses
East, west, north, south, or, like a school broke up,
Each hurries toward his home and sporting-place.

WESTMORELAND
235   Good tidings, my Lord Hastings, for the which
I do arrest thee, traitor, of high treason.—
And you, Lord Archbishop, and you, Lord Mowbray,
Of capital treason I attach you both.

LANCASTER

Go and disperse our army, too, Lord Westmoreland.

WESTMORELAND exits.

Good Archbishop, let's have both our troops march past us here so that we can see the men we would have fought against.

ARCHBISHOP

Go, Lord Hastings, and have them march past before they're dismissed.

HASTINGS exits.

LANCASTER

I hope, sirs, that we'll spend tonight in the same camp.

WESTMORELAND enters.

Cousin, why is our army still standing?

WESTMORELAND

The leaders have orders from you to stand fast, and they won't disperse until they hear you give the order.

LANCASTER

They know how to follow orders.

HASTINGS enters.

HASTINGS

Our army is already dispersed. They've headed off to the east, west, north, and south like young bulls whose yokes have been removed. The men are like children after school, each hurrying toward their homes or the playground.

WESTMORELAND

That's good news, Lord Hastings. And hearing it, I now arrest you, traitor, for high treason. And you, Archbishop, and you, Lord Mowbray. I arrest you both for capital treason.

MOWBRAY
Is this proceeding just and honorable?

WESTMORELAND
240   Is your assembly so?

ARCHBISHOP
Will you thus break your faith?

LANCASTER
                                    I pawned thee none.
I promised you redress of these same grievances
Whereof you did complain, which, by mine honor,
I will perform with a most Christian care.
245   But for you rebels, look to taste the due
Meet for rebellion and such acts as yours.
Most shallowly did you these arms commence,
Fondly brought here, and foolishly sent hence.—
Strike up our drums; pursue the scattered stray.
250   God, and not we, hath safely fought today.—
Some guard these traitors to the block of death,
Treason's true bed and yielder-up of breath.

                                            Exeunt

MOWBRAY

Is this action just and honorable?

WESTMORELAND

Was your rebellion just and honorable?

ARCHBISHOP

Will you break faith with us like this?

LANCASTER

I never promised you my faith. I promised to make good on the grievances you complained of. And, on my honor, I will do that as carefully as possible. But now, you rebels will get exactly what you deserve for the things you've done. You raised armies over nothing, brought them here stupidly, and then foolishly sent them away. Bang on our drums! Capture the soldiers who are scattering away. God, not we, has fought today and won. Guards, escort these traitors to the place of their death. That's where treason belongs, and where they'll draw their last breath.

They exit.

ACT 4, SCENE 2

Alarum. Excursions. Enter FALSTAFF *and* COLEVILE, *meeting*

FALSTAFF
What's your name, sir? Of what condition are you, and of
what place, I pray?

COLEVILE
I am a knight, sir, and my name is Colevile of the Dale.

FALSTAFF
Well, then, Colevile is your name, a knight is your degree,
5   and your place the Dale. Colevile shall be still your name,
a traitor your degree, and the dungeon your place, a place
deep enough so shall you be still Colevile of the Dale.

COLEVILE
Are not you Sir John Falstaff?

FALSTAFF
As good a man as he, sir, whoe'er I am. Do ye yield, sir, or
10   shall I sweat for you? If I do sweat, they are the drops of thy
lovers and they weep for thy death. Therefore rouse up fear
and trembling, and do observance to my mercy.

COLEVILE
I think you are Sir John Falstaff, and in that thought yield
me.

FALSTAFF
15   I have a whole school of tongues in this belly of mine, and
not a tongue of them all speaks any other word but my
name. An I had but a belly of any indifferency, I were
simply the most active fellow in Europe. My womb, my
womb, my womb undoes me. Here comes our general.

ACT 4, SCENE 2

Calls to arms are sounded. Soldiers cross the stage.
FALSTAFF *and* COLEVILE *enter and confront one another.*

FALSTAFF

What's your name, sir? What's your rank, and where are you from?

COLEVILLE

I am a knight, sir. My name is Coleville of the Valley.

FALSTAFF

Well, then, Coleville is your name, your rank is knight, and the valley is where you're from. Coleville will still be your name now that "traitor" is your rank, and the dungeon is where you'll be. It's a place so deep that you'll still be in a kind of valley.

COLEVILLE

Aren't you Sir John Falstaff?

FALSTAFF

I'm as good a man as Falstaff, whoever I am. Will you surrender? Or am I going to have to break a sweat making you surrender? If I sweat, the drops will be the tears of your loved ones, weeping over your death. So you'd better get scared and start to shake, and start praying to me for mercy.

COLEVILLE

I think you are Sir John Falstaff, and so I surrender.

FALSTAFF

My enormous belly can speak in many languages, and each language proclaims my name and my name alone. If I had a moderately sized belly, all I'd be is an anonymous but very successful soldier. But my belly, my belly, my belly blows my cover. Here comes the general.

Enter Prince John of LANCASTER, WESTMORELAND, BLUNT,
and others

LANCASTER
20   The heat is past. Follow no further now.

A retreat is sounded.

Call in the powers, good cousin Westmoreland.
                                        Exit WESTMORELAND
Now, Falstaff, where have you been all this while?
When everything is ended, then you come.
These tardy tricks of yours will, on my life,
25   One time or other break some gallows' back.

FALSTAFF
I would be sorry, my lord, but it should be thus. I never
knew yet but rebuke and check was the reward of valor. Do
you think me a swallow, an arrow, or a bullet? Have I in my
poor and old motion the expedition of thought? I have
30   speeded hither with the very extremest inch of possibility.
I have foundered ninescore and odd posts, and here, travel-
tainted as I am, have in my pure and immaculate valor taken
Sir John Colevile of the Dale, a most furious knight and
valorous enemy. But what of that? He saw me and yielded,
35   that I may justly say, with the hook-nosed fellow of Rome,
"There, cousin, I came, saw, and overcame."

LANCASTER
It was more of his courtesy than your deserving.

FALSTAFF
I know not. Here he is, and here I yield him. And I beseech
your Grace let it be booked with the rest of this day's deeds,
40   or, by the Lord, I will have it in a particular ballad else, with
mine own picture on the top on 't, Colevile kissing my foot;
to the which course if I be enforced, if you do not all show

John of LANCASTER, WESTMORELAND, BLUNT, *and others enter.*

LANCASTER

The danger's over: let's stop here.

The trumpets sound a retreat.

Call off the operation, Westmoreland.

WESTMORELAND *exits.*

Falstaff, where have you been all this time? When everything is over, that's when you start. This habit of laziness of yours will bust a gallows to bits one of these days, mark my words.

FALSTAFF

I'm sorry to hear you say that: I never realized that brave behavior should be rewarded with scolding and admonishing. Do you think I'm a bird, or an arrow, or a bullet? With this old, broken-down body, do you think I can move as fast as thought? I've gotten here as fast as humanly possible. I've burned out more than 180 horses, and—even though I'm spent from all that travel—I've managed, with my extraordinary bravery, to capture Sir John Coleville of the Valley, a brave knight and terrible enemy. But so what? He simply saw me and surrendered. So I can say, just like Julius Caesar, that "I came, I saw, I conquered."

LANCASTER

He was just being polite; it's not as if you did something to deserve it.

FALSTAFF

I don't know about that. Here he is: I turn him over to you. Please, sir, have it added to the record of things accomplished today. If you don't, I'll have a ballad printed about it, with a picture of Coleville kissing my foot on the cover. And if I'm forced to do that, and I

like gilt twopences to me, and I in the clear sky of fame
o'ershine you as much as the full moon doth the cinders of
the element (which show like pins' heads to her), believe
not the word of the noble. Therefore let me have right, and
let desert mount.

45

LANCASTER
Thine's too heavy to mount.

FALSTAFF
Let it shine, then.

LANCASTER
50   Thine's too thick to shine.

FALSTAFF
Let it do something, my good lord, that may do me good,
and call it what you will.

LANCASTER
Is thy name Colevile?

COLEVILE
It is, my lord.

LANCASTER
A famous rebel art thou, Colevile.

FALSTAFF
55   And a famous true subject took him.

COLEVILE
I am, my lord, but as my betters are
That led me hither. Had they been ruled by me,
You should have won them dearer than you have.

FALSTAFF
I know not how they sold themselves, but thou, like a kind
60   fellow, gavest thyself away gratis, and I thank thee for thee.

Enter WESTMORELAND

LANCASTER
Now, have you left pursuit?

don't make you look like counterfeits next to me, and
if my fame doesn't outshine yours like the full moon
outshines the stars (which look like pin pricks in the
sky next to the moon)—well then, you can call me a
liar. Now give me what I deserve, and let my merits
mount on top of each other, in a great pile.

LANCASTER

Your pile would be too heavy for me to bear.

FALSTAFF

Let my merits shine, then.

LANCASTER

You're too dense to shine.

FALSTAFF

Then let it do something that will do me good, whatever you want to call it.

LANCASTER

Is your name Coleville?

COLEVILLE

It is, sir.

LANCASTER

You're a famous rebel, Coleville.

FALSTAFF

And a famous and loyal subject captured him.

COLEVILLE

I'm now in the same situation as my superiors, who
led me here. But if I had been in charge, your victory
would have cost you more than it has.

FALSTAFF

I don't know how much your superiors cost us, but
you, like a generous man, gave yourself away for free,
and I thank you for it.

WESTMORELAND *enters.*

LANCASTER

Have you called off the troops?

WESTMORELAND
Retreat is made and execution stayed.

LANCASTER
Send Colevile with his confederates
To York, to present execution.—
65 Blunt, lead him hence, and see you guard him sure.
Exeunt BLUNT *with* COLEVILE

And now dispatch we toward the court, my lords.
I hear the King my father is sore sick.
Our news shall go before us to his Majesty,
(to WESTMORELAND*)* Which, cousin, you shall bear to
comfort him,
70 And we with sober speed will follow you.

FALSTAFF
My lord, I beseech you give me leave to go through
Gloucestershire, and, when you come to court, stand my
good lord, pray, in your good report.

LANCASTER
Fare you well, Falstaff. I, in my condition,
75 Shall better speak of you than you deserve.
Exeunt all but FALSTAFF

FALSTAFF
I would you had but the wit; 'twere better than your
dukedom. Good faith, this same young sober-blooded boy
doth not love me, nor a man cannot make him laugh. But
that's no marvel; he drinks no wine. There's never none of
80 these demure boys come to any proof, for thin drink doth so
overcool their blood, and making many fish meals, that
they fall into a kind of male green-sickness, and then, when
they marry, they get wenches. They are generally fools and
cowards, which some of us should be too, but for
85 inflammation.

WESTMORELAND

> The order to pull back has been given, and the slaughter has been stopped.

LANCASTER

> Send Coleville and his confederates to York, to be put to death immediately. Blunt, lead him away, and guard him carefully.

> *BLUNT exits with COLEVILLE.*

> And now, let's get going back to the royal court: I understand that the King, my father, is gravely ill. Send news of our victory ahead of us. *(to WESTMORELAND)* You, cousin, will bring him this news and comfort him with it. We'll follow you as quickly as we can.

FALSTAFF

> Sir, please give me permission to go via Gloucestershire. When you get to the court, please vouch for my good work here.

LANCASTER

> Goodbye, Falstaff. By speaking on your behalf as a prince, I'll be speaking better of you than you deserve.

> *Everyone exits except FALSTAFF.*

FALSTAFF

> I wish you had the wit to accomplish that: it would be worth all your land. My goodness, this young, serious-minded boy doesn't like me, and no one can make him laugh. But I guess that's not surprising; after all, he doesn't drink any wine. None of those prim boys ever amount to anything: weak beer and too many fish dinners makes their blood cool. They all turn anemic, like young girls. And then, when they finally get married, they can only father girls because they don't have the stuff to produce sons. Non-drinkers are all generally fools and cowards. The rest of us would probably

A good sherris sack hath a two-fold operation in it. It
ascends me into the brain, dries me there all the foolish and
dull and crury vapors which environ it, makes it
apprehensive, quick, forgetive, full of nimble, fiery, and
delectable shapes, which, delivered o'er to the voice, the
tongue, which is the birth, becomes excellent wit. The
second property of your excellent sherris is the warming of
the blood, which, before cold and settled, left the liver white
and pale, which is the badge of pusillanimity and
cowardice. But the sherris warms it and makes it course
from the inwards to the parts' extremes. It illumineth the
face, which as a beacon gives warning to all the rest of this
little kingdom, man, to arm; and then the vital commoners
and inland petty spirits muster me all to their captain, the
heart, who, great and puffed up with this retinue, doth any
deed of courage, and this valor comes of sherris. So that skill
in the weapon is nothing without sack, for that sets it a-
work; and learning a mere hoard of gold kept by a devil till
sack commences it and sets it in act and use. Hereof comes
it that Prince Harry is valiant, for the cold blood he did
naturally inherit of his father he hath, like lean, sterile, and
bare land, manured, husbanded, and tilled with excellent
endeavor of drinking good and good store of fertile sherris,
that he is become very hot and valiant. If I had a thousand
sons, the first human principle I would teach them should
be to forswear thin potations and to addict themselves to
sack.

Enter BARDOLPH

be the same way, except that we're always drunk. A good sherry wine operates in two ways. First, it rises into the brain and dries out all the foolish, dull, clogged-up fogs that have gathered there. It makes the brain sharp, quick, and inventive; full of nimble, fiery, and beautiful ideas. The voice and tongue give birth to those ideas which, when they grow up, become excellent wit. The second power of good wine is the warming of the blood. Before wine, the blood is cold and sluggish, and this makes the liver—the organ of passion—chilly and pale. A chilly, pale liver is the sign of cowardice and faint-heartedness. But wine warms the blood, making it course from the inner organs to all the extremities. The blood brightens the face, and the rest of the body—which is like a little kingdom in itself—takes that brightening as a signal. Then the spirits of the blood and all the internal organs gather together behind their captain: the heart. The heart draws strength from these followers and, enlarged by them, can accomplish any courageous deed. This is the bravery that comes from wine. Without wine, skill in weaponry doesn't matter. Wine is what sets that skill in motion. Education is nothing more than idle gold in the devil's hands, until wine rouses it and puts it to good use. That's how Prince Harry became valiant. He's taken the cold blood he inherited from his father and—like unproductive farmland—he fertilized it, planted it, and cared for it, through the hard work of drinking vast amounts of good and potent wine. And so now, he's become hot and courageous. If I had a thousand sons, the first rule of behavior I would teach them would be to avoid weak drinks, and get themselves addicted to wine.

BARDOLPH *enters.*

How now, Bardolph?

BARDOLPH
The army is discharged all and gone.

FALSTAFF
115   Let them go. I'll through Gloucestershire, and there will I
visit Master Robert Shallow, Esquire. I have him already
temp'ring between my finger and my thumb, and shortly
will I seal with him. Come away.

Exeunt

What is it, Bardolph?

BARDOLPH

The army is dismissed, and everyone's gone

FALSTAFF

Let them go. I'll head to Gloucestershire. I'll visit Master Robert Shallow, Esquire. I've already got him under my thumb, as soft as wax. Soon I'll seal the deal. Let's go.

They exit.

ACT 4, SCENE 3

Enter KING *Henry, his sons Thomas Duke of* CLARENCE *and Humphrey Duke of* GLOUCESTER, *with* WARWICK *and others*

KING
Now, lords, if God doth give successful end
To this debate that bleedeth at our doors,
We will our youth lead on to higher fields
And draw no swords but what are sanctified.
5   Our navy is addressed, our power collected,
Our substitutes in absence well invested,
And everything lies level to our wish.
Only we want a little personal strength;
And pause us till these rebels now afoot
10   Come underneath the yoke of government.

WARWICK
Both which we doubt not but your Majesty
Shall soon enjoy.

KING
                              Humphrey, my son of Gloucester,
Where is the Prince your brother?

GLOUCESTER
I think he's gone to hunt, my lord, at Windsor.

KING
15   And how accompanied?

GLOUCESTER
                              I do not know, my lord.

KING
Is not his brother Thomas of Clarence with him?

GLOUCESTER
No, my good lord, he is in presence here.

CLARENCE
What would my lord and father?

ACT 4, SCENE 3

KING *Henry, his sons Thomas Duke of* CLARENCE *and Humphrey Duke of* GLOUCESTER, WARWICK, *and others enter.*

KING

Now, my lords: if God grants us a victory in this violent civil war that bleeds at our very doorsteps, I will lead our young people in a greater cause, and fight nothing but holy wars. Our navy is ready, our army is assembled, the leaders who are my subordinates have their orders, and everything is standing by to achieve my main aim. The only drawback is that I'm feeling a little weak. So let's wait a short while, until the rebels, now on the run, are brought back in line and are made obedient again.

WARWICK

We are sure that you'll soon enjoy both good health and the rebels' defeat.

KING

My son Humphrey of Gloucester, where is your brother, Prince Hal?

GLOUCESTER

I think he's gone hunting at Windsor.

KING

Who's with him?

GLOUCESTER

I don't know, father.

KING

Isn't his brother, Thomas of Clarence, with him?

GLOUCESTER

No, father. He's here.

CLARENCE

What is it you'd like, father?

KING
Nothing but well to thee, Thomas of Clarence.
20   How chance thou art not with the Prince thy brother?
He loves thee, and thou dost neglect him, Thomas.
Thou hast a better place in his affection
Than all thy brothers. Cherish it, my boy,
And noble offices thou mayst effect
25   Of mediation, after I am dead,
Between his greatness and thy other brethren.
Therefore omit him not; blunt not his love,
Nor lose the good advantage of his grace
By seeming cold or careless of his will.
30   For he is gracious if he be observed;
He hath a tear for pity and a hand
Open as day for melting charity;
Yet notwithstanding, being incensed he is flint,
As humorous as winter, and as sudden
35   As flaws congealed in the spring of day.
His temper therefore must be well observed.
Chide him for faults, and do it reverently,
When thou perceive his blood inclined to mirth;
But, being moody, give him time and scope
40   Till that his passions, like a whale on ground,
Confound themselves with working. Learn this, Thomas,
And thou shalt prove a shelter to thy friends,
A hoop of gold to bind thy brothers in,
That the united vessel of their blood,
45   Mingled with venom of suggestion
(As, force perforce, the age will pour it in),
Shall never leak, though it do work as strong
As aconitum or rash gunpowder.

CLARENCE
I shall observe him with all care and love.

KING
50   Why art thou not at Windsor with him, Thomas?

KING

Only good things for you, Thomas. Why aren't you with the Prince, your brother? He loves you and you are neglecting him. He cares more about you than any of his other brothers, Thomas; cherish that fact, my boy. After I'm dead, you'll be in a strong position to help maintain good relations between Prince Hal and his brothers.

So don't ignore him. Don't turn away his love, and don't ruin your good relationship with him by seeming cold or distant. He's kind if he gets his way; he has compassion for others, and he's generous with charity. But despite all this, once he gets angry, he becomes like a stone. He can be as tempestuous as winter, and can change himself as suddenly as snowflakes at dawn can turn to hail. So watch his temper.

When he does something wrong, let him know it—gently, and when he's in a happy mood. But when he's ornery, give him room. Wait till his bad mood works itself out, like a beached whale that kills itself by struggling to return to sea. If you can do this, you'll be a shelter for your friends, and a golden chain that links your brothers together. Once they're united, the poison of criticism and rumor—which in this day and age is sure to be aimed at them—can't do them any harm, no matter how explosive and destructive it may be.

CLARENCE

I'll watch over him with as much care and love as possible.

KING

Then why aren't you with him at Windsor?

CLARENCE
He is not there today; he dines in London.

KING
And how accompanied? Canst thou tell that?

CLARENCE
With Poins and other his continual followers.

KING
Most subject is the fattest soil to weeds,
55   And he, the noble image of my youth,
Is overspread with them; therefore my grief
Stretches itself beyond the hour of death.
The blood weeps from my heart when I do shape,
In forms imaginary, th' unguided days
60   And rotten times that you shall look upon
When I am sleeping with my ancestors.
For when his headstrong riot hath no curb,
When rage and hot blood are his counsellors,
When means and lavish manners meet together,
65   O, with what wings shall his affections fly
Towards fronting peril and opposed decay!

WARWICK
My gracious lord, you look beyond him quite.
The Prince but studies his companions
Like a strange tongue, wherein, to gain the language,
70   'Tis needful that the most immodest word
Be looked upon and learned; which, once attained,
Your Highness knows, comes to no further use
But to be known and hated. So, like gross terms,
The Prince will, in the perfectness of time,
75   Cast off his followers, and their memory
Shall as a pattern or a measure live,
By which his Grace must mete the lives of others,
Turning past evils to advantages.

KING
'Tis seldom when the bee doth leave her comb
80   In the dead carrion.

CLARENCE

He's not there today. He's in London.

KING

Who's with him? Do you know?

CLARENCE

Poins, and the usual suspects.

KING

Weeds grow best in the richest soil, and he—like myself at that age—is overrun by them. My sadness, then, cannot end with my death. When I imagine the lawless days and rotten times that you will face when I am dead and sleeping with my ancestors, the blood weeps from my heart.

When Hal's headstrong wildness has free rein; when aggression and passion are his advisors; when he has full opportunity to indulge in his riotous inclinations, then—Oh!—his criminal desires will fly like a bird towards danger and ruin.

WARWICK

Your highness, you've got him all wrong. The Prince is only studying his criminal companions, the way one studies a foreign language. In order to truly learn a language, one must learn even the most immodest curse word—which, as you know, is only learned in order to be identified and, thereafter, avoided. So, like vulgar language, the Prince will get rid of his followers when the time is right. Then they'll live on in his memory as guidelines, by which he'll judge the conduct of others. In this sense, he'll change his past bad deeds to good ends.

KING

It's rare that a bee builds its nest in a dead animal's carcass. The Prince won't leave his current company.

Enter WESTMORELAND

              Who's here? Westmoreland?

WESTMORELAND
    Health to my sovereign, and new happiness
    Added to that that I am to deliver.
    Prince John your son doth kiss your Grace's hand.
    Mowbray, the Bishop Scroop, Hastings, and all
85   Are brought to the correction of your law.
    There is not now a rebel's sword unsheathed
    But peace puts forth her olive everywhere.
    The manner how this action hath been borne
    Here at more leisure may your Highness read
90   With every course in his particular.

KING
    O Westmoreland, thou art a summer bird,
    Which ever in the haunch of winter sings
    The lifting up of day.

Enter HARCOURT

              Look, here's more news.

HARCOURT
    From enemies heaven keep your Majesty,
95   And when they stand against you, may they fall
    As those that I am come to tell you of.
    The Earl Northumberland and the Lord Bardolph,
    With a great power of English and of Scots,
    Are by the shrieve of Yorkshire overthrown.
100   The manner and true order of the fight
    This packet, please it you, contains at large.

KING
    And wherefore should these good news make me sick?
    Will fortune never come with both hands full,
    But write her fair words still in foulest letters?
105   She either gives a stomach and no food—

WESTMORELAND *enters.*

Who's there? Westmoreland?

WESTMORELAND
I wish your highness good health, and happy news
beyond the report I have to deliver! Prince John sends
his respects: Mowbray, the Archbishop, Hastings and
the rest are under arrest. There are no more rebels
anywhere; the olive branch of peace has been
extended everywhere.

Here's a letter explaining what happened. When you
have time, you can read it and learn every detail.

KING

Oh Westmoreland; you're like a summer bird, which
sings the dawn in as winter ends.

HARCOURT *enters.*

Here comes more news.

HARCOURT
May heaven protect your highness from all enemies—
and when they do rise up, may they fall just like the
ones I've come to tell you about. The Earl of
Northumberland and Lord Bardolph, with their
mighty armies of Englishmen and Scotsmen, were
defeated by the Sheriff of Yorkshire. This letter will
tell you the details.

KING

Why am I sick at this good news? Why can't life ever
bring you things with their appropriate comple-
ments? Why is good news so often conveyed in ugly
terms? Life either gives you hunger but no food—

Such are the poor, in health—or else a feast
And takes away the stomach—such are the rich,
That have abundance and enjoy it not.
I should rejoice now at this happy news,
And now my sight fails, and my brain is giddy.
O, me! Come near me, now I am much ill.

GLOUCESTER
Comfort, your Majesty.

CLARENCE
                                   O, my royal father!

WESTMORELAND
My sovereign lord, cheer up yourself, look up.

WARWICK
Be patient, princes. You do know these fits
Are with his Highness very ordinary.
Stand from him, give him air. He'll straight be well.

CLARENCE
No, no, he cannot long hold out these pangs.
Th' incessant care and labor of his mind
Hath wrought the mure that should confine it in
So thin that life looks through and will break out.

GLOUCESTER
The people fear me, for they do observe
Unfathered heirs and loathly births of nature.
The seasons change their manners, as the year
Had found some months asleep and leapt them over.

CLARENCE
The river hath thrice flowed, no ebb between,
And the old folk, time's doting chronicles,
Say it did so a little time before
That our great-grandsire, Edward, sicked and died.

WARWICK
Speak lower, princes, for the King recovers.

which is the experience of poor, healthy people—or it gives you a feast with no appetite—which is how the rich live, who have wealth and abundance but cannot enjoy it. I should be celebrating this good news, and yet my eyesight is failing, and my brain is delirious. Oh God! Come to me, I'm very sick.

GLOUCESTER

Take care, your highness!

CLARENCE

Oh, my royal father!

WESTMORELAND

My lord, feel better; take courage.

WARWICK

Wait a minute, princes. You know his highness has these episodes all the time. Move away from him. Give him air; he'll be all right soon.

CLARENCE

No, no, he can't survive these attacks much longer. His mind's endless worry and concern have so shaken his body that it can barely hold together.

GLOUCESTER

The people are frightening me. They've seen terrible omens: children who seem to have supernatural fathers, and gruesomely deformed infants. The weather is in disarray, as if the calendar discovered some months were fast asleep, and decided to skip over them.

CLARENCE

The river has flooded three times, without receding between floods. The old people—those living history books—say that the last time this happened was when our great-grandfather, King Edward, fell ill and died.

WARWICK

Speak more softly, princes: the King is recovering.

GLOUCESTER

130   This apoplexy will certain be his end.

KING

    I pray you, take me up and bear me hence
    Into some other chamber. Softly, pray.

They carry the KING *to a bed.*

    Let there be no noise made, my gentle friends,
    Unless some dull and favorable hand
135   Will whisper music to my weary spirit.

WARWICK

    Call for the music in the other room.

KING

    Set me the crown upon my pillow here.

CLARENCE

    His eye is hollow, and he changes much.

WARWICK

    Less noise, less noise.

Enter PRINCE HENRY

PRINCE HENRY

                        Who saw the Duke of Clarence?

CLARENCE

140   I am here, brother, full of heaviness.

PRINCE HENRY

    How now! Rain within doors, and none abroad?
    How doth the King?

GLOUCESTER

                    Exceeding ill.

PRINCE HENRY

    Heard he the good news yet? Tell it him.

GLOUCESTER

    He altered much upon the hearing it.

GLOUCESTER

These attacks will be the death of him.

KING

Please, carry me into another room. Quietly. Please.

They carry the KING to a bed.

Please be silent, my friends, unless someone can play some restful, whispering music for my exhausted spirit.

WARWICK

Call the musicians in from the other room.

KING

Put the crown here on my pillow.

CLARENCE

His eyes are sunken, and he seems very pale.

WARWICK

Less noise, less noise!

PRINCE HENRY enters.

PRINCE HENRY

Has anybody seen the Duke of Clarence?

CLARENCE

I'm here, brother, full of sadness.

PRINCE HENRY

What's going on? Raining inside while it's dry outside? How's the King?

GLOUCESTER

Extremely sick.

PRINCE HENRY

Has he heard the good news yet? Tell him.

GLOUCESTER

Yes, he heard it, and it affected him deeply.

PRINCE HENRY
145   If he be sick with joy, he'll recover without physic.

WARWICK
Not so much noise, my lords.—Sweet Prince, speak low.
The King your father is disposed to sleep.

CLARENCE
Let us withdraw into the other room.

WARWICK
Will 't please your Grace to go along with us?

PRINCE HENRY
150   No, I will sit and watch here by the King.

Exeunt all but **PRINCE HENRY**

Why doth the crown lie there upon his pillow,
Being so troublesome a bedfellow?
O polished perturbation, golden care,
That keep'st the ports of slumber open wide
155   To many a watchful night! sleep with it now;
Yet not so sound and half so deeply sweet
As he whose brow with homely biggen bound
Snores out the watch of night. O majesty,
When thou dost pinch thy bearer, thou dost sit
160   Like a rich armor worn in heat of day,
That scald'st with safety. By his gates of breath
There lies a downy feather which stirs not;
Did he suspire, that light and weightless down
Perforce must move. My gracious lord, my father,
165   This sleep is sound indeed. This is a sleep
That from this golden rigol hath divorced
So many English kings. Thy due from me
Is tears and heavy sorrows of the blood,
Which nature, love, and filial tenderness
170   Shall, O dear father, pay thee plenteously.
My due from thee is this imperial crown,
Which, as immediate as thy place and blood,

PRINCE HENRY

If he's sick from joy, then he'll get better without medicine.

WARWICK

Not so loud, sirs. Prince, speak more quietly. Your father the King is trying to sleep.

CLARENCE

Let's go into the other room.

WARWICK

Will you come with us?

PRINCE HENRY

No. I'll stay here with the King.

Everyone exits except **PRINCE HENRY**.

Why does the crown lie there on his pillow, when it's such a troublesome bedfellow? Oh polished aggravation, golden anxiety! You keep the eyelids open wide, to face countless sleepless nights. You sleep with the crown now, father, but you don't sleep as soundly, or half so deeply, as that man whose head is bound with nothing more than a cheap nightcap, who snores through the night. Oh, you crown! When you pinch the person wearing you, you're like a great suit of armor worn on a hot day—you burn the person you're protecting. There's a feather near my father's lips, and it's not moving: if he were breathing, that light, weightless thing would move. My gracious lord! Father! This is a deep sleep indeed—this is a sleep that has removed the golden ring from the heads of many English kings. Father, I owe you tears and a deep grief, and my love, the bonds of family, and a son's tender feelings will make sure that I pay you lavishly. Your debt to me is this kingly crown, which I am owed as your heir-apparent.

Derives itself to me. *(he puts the crown on his head)* Lo,
    where it sits,
Which God shall guard. And put the world's whole
    strength
175   Into one giant arm, it shall not force
This lineal honor from me. This from thee
Will I to mine leave, as 'tis left to me.

                           Exit PRINCE HENRY

KING

    (waking) Warwick! Gloucester! Clarence!

    Enter WARWICK, GLOUCESTER, CLARENCE, *and the rest*

CLARENCE

                           Doth the King call?

WARWICK

    What would your Majesty? How fares your Grace?

KING

180   Why did you leave me here alone, my lords?

CLARENCE

    We left the Prince my brother here, my liege,
Who undertook to sit and watch by you.

KING

    The Prince of Wales? Where is he? Let me see him.
He is not here.

WARWICK

185   This door is open. He is gone this way.

GLOUCESTER

    He came not through the chamber where we stayed.

KING

    Where is the crown? Who took it from my pillow?

WARWICK

    When we withdrew, my liege, we left it here.

(he puts the crown on his head) Look, here it sits, and God will guard it. Even if all the strength in the world were gathered into a single, giant arm, it wouldn't be able to force this inherited honor from me. I will leave this to my son as you've left it to me.

PRINCE HENRY *exits.*

KING

(waking) Warwick! Gloucester! Clarence!

WARWICK, GLOUCESTER, CLARENCE, *and the rest enter.*

CLARENCE

Did you call, sir?

WARWICK

What can we do for you, your highness? How are you feeling?

KING

Why did you leave me alone, sirs?

CLARENCE

We left my brother, Prince Hal, here. He decided to sit with you.

KING

The Prince of Wales? Where is he? I want to see him. He's not here.

WARWICK

This door's open. He went this way.

GLOUCESTER

He didn't come through the room we were in.

KING

Where's the crown? Who took it off my pillow?

WARWICK

When we left, sir, it was here.

KING
The Prince hath ta'en it hence. Go seek him out.
190   Is he so hasty that he doth suppose my sleep my death?
Find him, my Lord of Warwick. Chide him hither.

Exit WARWICK

This part of his conjoins with my disease
And helps to end me. See, sons, what things you are,
How quickly nature falls into revolt
195   When gold becomes her object!
For this the foolish overcareful fathers
Have broke their sleep with thoughts,
Their brains with care, their bones with industry.
For this they have engrossèd and piled up
200   The canker'd heaps of strange-achievèd gold.
For this they have been thoughtful to invest
Their sons with arts and martial exercises—
When, like the bee, tolling from every flower
The virtuous sweets,
205   Our thighs packed with wax, our mouths with honey,
We bring it to the hive and, like the bees,
Are murdered for our pains. This bitter taste
Yield his engrossments to the ending father.

Enter WARWICK

Now, where is he that will not stay so long
210   Till his friend sickness hath determined me?

WARWICK
My lord, I found the Prince in the next room,
Washing with kindly tears his gentle cheeks,
With such a deep demeanor in great sorrow
That tyranny, which never quaffed but blood,
215   Would, by beholding him, have washed his knife
With gentle eyedrops. He is coming hither.

KING

> The Prince has taken it. Go, find him. Is he in such a hurry that he thinks my sleep is my death? Find him, Lord Warwick. Rebuke him, and bring him here.

WARWICK exits.

> Henry's actions join forces with my illness, and together they will kill me. Sons, look at what things you are. See how quickly blood bonds are broken, once money's involved. This is what happens to foolish, overly concerned fathers who ruin their sleep with worry, burden their minds with anxiety, and break their bodies with hard work. This is happens to fathers who amass vast amounts of money, earned in unsavory ways. This is what happens to fathers who have taken care to give their sons good educations, and train them in matters of war. Fathers are like bees, collecting sweet pollen from all the flowers in the world. We pack our thighs full of wax and our mouths full of honey, only to be killed when we return to the hive. This is the bitter fate of the dying father, no matter what he has accumulated in his life.

WARWICK enters.

> Where is that impatient man who can't even wait for his friend, sickness, to put an end to me?

WARWICK

> Sir, I found the Prince in the next room, with tears flowing down his cheeks. He looked so sorrowful that a tyrant—who never drank anything but blood— would, upon seeing him, have washed the blood from his knife with tears. He's on his way.

KING
But wherefore did he take away the crown?

Enter PRINCE HENRY

Lo where he comes.—Come hither to me, Harry.—
Depart the chamber. Leave us here alone.

Exeunt all but the KING *and* PRINCE HENRY

PRINCE HENRY
220　I never thought to hear you speak again.

KING
Thy wish was father, Harry, to that thought.
I stay too long by thee; I weary thee.
Dost thou so hunger for mine empty chair
That thou wilt needs invest thee with my honors
225　Before thy hour be ripe? O foolish youth,
Thou seek'st the greatness that will overwhelm thee.
Stay but a little, for my cloud of dignity
Is held from falling with so weak a wind
That it will quickly drop. My day is dim.
230　Thou hast stol'n that which after some few hours
Were thine without offense, and at my death
Thou hast sealed up my expectation.
Thy life did manifest thou loved'st me not,
And thou wilt have me die assured of it.
235　Thou hid'st a thousand daggers in thy thoughts,
Which thou hast whetted on thy stony heart
To stab at half an hour of my life.
What, canst thou not forbear me half an hour?
Then get thee gone and dig my grave thyself,
240　And bid the merry bells ring to thine ear
That thou art crownèd, not that I am dead.
Let all the tears that should bedew my hearse
Be drops of balm to sanctify thy head;

KING

But why did he take away the crown?

PRINCE HENRY enters.

Look, here he comes. Come here, Harry. *(to the rest)*
Leave the room, and leave us here alone.

Everyone leaves except the KING and PRINCE HENRY.

PRINCE HENRY

I never thought I'd hear you speak again.

KING

You thought that because you wished it to be true. I
live too long for you; you're tired of me. Are you so
desperate for my throne that you would take the honors of kingship before it's your time? Oh you foolish
youth! You long for power that will end up over-
whelming you. Wait a little while. What power I have
left is held together so weakly that the lightest breeze
would blow it away: my life is fading.

You stole something from me that would freely have
been yours in just a few hours. On my deathbed,
you've confirmed all my expectations. All your life
you showed that you didn't love me, and now I will die
certain of it. There are a thousand daggers in your
thoughts, which you've sharpened on your stony
heart with the hopes of stabbing me in the little time
I have left. What? Couldn't you endure me for half an
hour? Then go and dig my grave yourself, and ring the
bells to mark your coronation, not my death. Let all
the tears that should be shed on my hearse be drops of
holy water to bless your head.

Only compound me with forgotten dust.
245 Give that which gave thee life unto the worms.
Pluck down my officers, break my decrees,
For now a time is come to mock at form.
Harry the Fifth is crowned. Up, vanity,
Down, royal state, all you sage counsillors, hence,
250 And to the English court assemble now,
From every region, apes of idleness.
Now, neighbor confines, purge you of your scum.
Have you a ruffian that will swear, drink, dance,
Revel the night, rob, murder, and commit
255 The oldest sins the newest kind of ways?
Be happy, he will trouble you no more.
England shall double gild his treble guilt.
England shall give him office, honor, might,
For the fifth Harry from curbed license plucks
260 The muzzle of restraint, and the wild dog
Shall flesh his tooth on every innocent.
O my poor kingdom, sick with civil blows!
When that my care could not withhold thy riots,
What wilt thou do when riot is thy care?
265 O, thou wilt be a wilderness again,
Peopled with wolves, thy old inhabitants.

PRINCE HENRY
O pardon me, my liege! But for my tears,
The moist impediments unto my speech,
I had forestalled this dear and deep rebuke
270 Ere you with grief had spoke and I had heard
The course of it so far. There is your crown,
And He that wears the crown immortally
Long guard it yours. If I affect it more
Than as your honor and as your renown,
275 Let me no more from this obedience rise,
Which my most inward true and duteous spirit
Teacheth this prostrate and exterior bending.
God witness with me, when I here came in

Just mix me up with the forgotten dust, and give my body—which gave you life—to the worms. Fire my officers, undo my laws; for now the time has come to jeer at authority. Henry the Fifth is crowned: up with foolishness! Down with decorum! Be gone, all you wise advisers! Assemble lazy apes from every region, and make them the royal court of England! Now, you neighboring countries, get rid of your scum. Do you have a criminal who swears, drinks, dances, parties all night, robs, murders, and commits the oldest sins in the newest ways? Then be happy: that man won't trouble you any longer. England will paint over his guilt with gold. England will give him a position, honor, power. Because Henry the Fifth has removed the barriers to anarchy: he's taken the restraining muzzle off the dog of misbehavior, and that wild dog will sink his teeth into the flesh of every decent person. Oh my poor kingdom, sick from this civil war! When all my hard work couldn't keep disorder at bay, what will you do when disorder becomes your caretaker? Oh, you'll be a wilderness again, and all the wolves who lived here once will once again be your only citizens.

PRINCE HENRY

Oh forgive me, your highness. If it weren't for these tears—which are impeding my speech—I would have stopped this harsh scolding before you, in your grief, had spoken and before I had listened so long. There's your crown. May God, who wears the crown eternally, guard it as yours for a long time. If I care for the crown in any way other than as a symbol of your honor and reputation, let me never rise from this kneeling position. It is my deepest and most dutiful feelings which teach my body to bend and bow to you, causing my outer body to reflect my inner feelings. May God be my witness: when I came in here and saw that you

And found no course of breath within your Majesty,
280   How cold it struck my heart! If I do feign,
O, let me in my present wildness die
And never live to show th' incredulous world
The noble change that I have purposèd.
Coming to look on you, thinking you dead,
285   And dead almost, my liege, to think you were,
I spake unto this crown as having sense,
And thus upbraided it: "The care on thee depending
Hath fed upon the body of my father;
Therefore thou best of gold art worst of gold.
290   Other, less fine in carat, is more precious,
Preserving life in med'cine potable;
But thou, most fine, most honored, most renowned,
Hast eat thy bearer up." Thus, my most royal liege,
Accusing it, I put it on my head
295   To try with it, as with an enemy
That had before my face murdered my father,
The quarrel of a true inheritor.
But if it did infect my blood with joy
Or swell my thoughts to any strain of pride,
300   If any rebel or vain spirit of mine
Did with the least affection of a welcome
Give entertainment to the might of it,
Let God forever keep it from my head
And make me as the poorest vassal is
305   That doth with awe and terror kneel to it.

KING
O my son,
God put it in thy mind to take it hence
That thou mightst win the more thy father's love,
Pleading so wisely in excuse of it.
310   Come hither, Harry, sit thou by my bed
And hear, I think, the very latest counsel
That ever I shall breathe. God knows, my son,
By what bypaths and indirect crook'd ways

weren't breathing, my blood ran cold. If I'm lying, may I die as the wild youth I was before, and never live to show the dubious world the transformation I have been planning.

Coming to see you, thinking you were dead—and being nearly dead myself, just thinking that you were—I spoke to this crown as though it were alive. I scolded it like this: "The worry you've caused has eaten my father alive. So you, the best piece of gold, are actually the worst piece of gold. Other gold, perhaps worth less, is more precious, since it at least brings us health when mixed in our drinks. But you— the best, the most honored, the most famous—have consumed the person wearing you." And as I accused it, I put it on my head, to fight against it as an enemy who'd killed my father before my very eyes. It was the fight of a loyal child.

But may God keep it from me forever—making me like the poorest servant bowing down before it in awe and terror—if it in any way made me happy or arrogant, or if any part of me was the least bit pleased to welcome it and the power it brings.

KING

Oh my son, God made you take it from me so that, in pleading your case so beautifully, you would make me love you more! Come here, Harry. Sit by my bed and listen to what I think will be the last advice I ever give. God knows the unusual paths and indirect, crooked ways that led me to this crown.

I met this crown, and I myself know well
315   How troublesome it sat upon my head.
To thee it shall descend with better quiet,
Better opinion, better confirmation,
For all the soil of the achievement goes
With me into the earth. It seemed in me
320   But as an honor snatched with boist'rous hand,
And I had many living to upbraid
My gain of it by their assistances,
Which daily grew to quarrel and to bloodshed,
Wounding supposèd peace. All these bold fears
325   Thou see'st with peril I have answerèd,
For all my reign hath been but as a scene
Acting that argument. And now my death
Changes the mood, for what in me was purchased
Falls upon thee in a more fairer sort.
330   So thou the garland wear'st successively.
Yet though thou stand'st more sure than I could do,
Thou art not firm enough, since griefs are green,
And all my friends, which thou must make thy friends,
Have but their stings and teeth newly ta'en out,
335   By whose fell working I was first advanced
And by whose power I well might lodge a fear
To be again displaced; which to avoid,
I cut them off and had a purpose now
To lead out many to the Holy Land,
340   Lest rest and lying still might make them look
Too near unto my state. Therefore, my Harry,
Be it thy course to busy giddy minds
With foreign quarrels; that action, hence borne out,
May waste the memory of the former days.
345   More would I, but my lungs are wasted so
That strength of speech is utterly denied me.
How I came by the crown, O God forgive,
And grant it may with thee in true peace live.

And I know very well how much anxiety it has caused as I've worn it. It will fall to you in bitter peace, with better support and stronger approval. The stain of its obtainment dies now, with me. On me, the crown seemed like an honor grabbed with a violent hand, and many people lived to remind me that they had helped me take it. Eventually, those daily reminders grew into war and bloodshed, doing damage to the peace. You can see how much pain it's caused me as I've fought my foes. My entire reign has been like a play, in which we rehash that disagreement.

Now my death changes the show. What I bought, you will inherit. You'll wear the crown by right of succession. But even though you have a firmer claim to the crown than I had, it's not firm enough. Anger is still fresh, and my former friends—whom you must make into your friends—have only recently been disarmed. It was their power that first got me the crown, and I feared that same power could take me down. To avoid that, I defeated their rebellion, and planned to lead an army to the Holy Land. I thought that, with nothing to occupy themselves, they'd start eyeing me and my crown.

Therefore, my Harry, make it your policy to focus the distracted minds of the people with foreign wars. Military actions abroad will make people forget about troubling matters in the past. I'd say more, but my lungs are so worn out that I don't have the strength to speak. God forgive me for how I came by the crown, and may he grant that you enjoy it in peace.

PRINCE HENRY
My gracious liege,
350 You won it, wore it, kept it, gave it me.
Then plain and right must my possession be,
Which I with more than with a common pain
'Gainst all the world will rightfully maintain.

Enter Lord John of LANCASTER

KING
Look, look, here comes my John of Lancaster.

LANCASTER
355 Health, peace, and happiness to my royal father.

KING
Thou bring'st me happiness and peace, son John,
But health, alack, with youthful wings is flown
From this bare withered trunk. Upon thy sight
My worldly business makes a period.
360 Where is my Lord of Warwick?

PRINCE HENRY
My Lord of Warwick.

Enter WARWICK *and others*

KING
Doth any name particular belong
Unto the lodging where I first did swoon?

WARWICK
'Tis called Jerusalem, my noble lord.

KING
365 Laud be to God! Even there my life must end.
It hath been prophesied to me many years,
I should not die but in Jerusalem,
Which vainly I supposed the Holy Land.
But bear me to that chamber; there I'll lie.
370 In that Jerusalem shall Harry die.

Exeunt

PRINCE HENRY

My gracious lord, you won it, wore it, kept it, then gave it to me. My possession of it must therefore be honest and lawful. And I will work as hard as I can to defend this crown against any man.

Lord John of LANCASTER *enters.*

KING

Look, look, here comes my son, John of Lancaster.

LANCASTER

Health, peace, and happiness to my royal father!

KING

You bring me happiness and peace, John. But health, unfortunately, has flown from this shrunken body. Now that I've seen you, I have nothing more to do in this world. Where is Lord Warwick?

PRINCE HENRY

Lord Warwick!

WARWICK *and others enter.*

KING

Does the room I first collapsed in have a name?

WARWICK

It's called the Jerusalem Room, your highness.

KING

Praise be to God! That's where I must die. For years it's been predicted that I would die in Jerusalem; I foolishly thought that meant the Holy Land. But carry me to that room, and there I'll lie. In that Jerusalem will Harry die.

They exit.

ACT FIVE
SCENE 1

Enter SHALLOW, FALSTAFF, PAGE, *and* BARDOLPH

SHALLOW
By cock and pie, sir, you shall not away tonight.—What,
Davy, I say!

FALSTAFF
You must excuse me, Master Robert Shallow.

SHALLOW
I will not excuse you. You shall not be excused. Excuses
5 shall not be admitted. There is no excuse shall serve. You
shall not be excused.—Why, Davy!

Enter DAVY

DAVY
Here, sir.

SHALLOW
Davy, Davy, Davy, Davy, let me see, Davy, let me see, Davy,
let me see. Yea, marry, William cook, bid him come
10 hither.—Sir John, you shall not be excused.

DAVY
Marry, sir, thus: those precepts cannot be served. And
again, sir, shall we sow the hade land with wheat?

SHALLOW
With red wheat, Davy. But for William cook, are there no
young pigeons?

DAVY
15 Yes, sir. Here is now the smith's note for shoeing and plow
irons.

ACT FIVE
SCENE 1

SHALLOW, FALSTAFF, BARDOLPH, *and the* PAGE *enter.*

SHALLOW

By gum, sir, you will not leave tonight. Hey, Davy!

FALSTAFF

Please excuse me, Master Robert Shallow.

SHALLOW

I will not excuse you. You will not be excused. Excuses will not be allowed. No excuse will do. You will not be excused. Hey, Davy!

DAVY *enters.*

DAVY

Here, sir.

SHALLOW

Davy, Davy, Davy, Davy, let's see, Davy, let's see, Davy, let's see. Oh yes, right: tell William the cook to come here. Sir John, you will not be excused.

DAVY

Well sir, here's the thing. Those warrants couldn't be served. And once more, sir, should we plant wheat at the field's edges?

SHALLOW

Plant red wheat, Davy. But as for William the cook— aren't there any young pigeons?

DAVY

Yes, sir. Here's the bill from the blacksmith for horse-shoes and plow blades.

SHALLOW
Let it be cast and paid.—Sir John, you shall not be excused.

DAVY
Now, sir, a new link to the bucket must needs be had. And,
sir, do you mean to stop any of William's wages about the
20   sack he lost the other day at Hinckley Fair?

SHALLOW
He shall answer it. Some pigeons, Davy, a couple of short-
legged hens, a joint of mutton, and any pretty little tiny
kickshaws, tell William cook.

DAVY
Doth the man of war stay all night, sir?

SHALLOW
25   Yea, Davy. I will use him well. A friend i' th' court is better
than a penny in purse. Use his men well, Davy, for they are
arrant knaves and will backbite.

DAVY
No worse than they are back-bitten, sir, for they have
marvellous foul linen.

SHALLOW
30   Well-conceited, Davy. About thy business, Davy.

DAVY
I beseech you, sir, to countenance William Visor of Woncot
against Clement Perkes o' th' hill.

SHALLOW
There is many complaints, Davy, against that Visor. That
Visor is an arrant knave, on my knowledge.

DAVY
35   I grant your Worship that he is a knave, sir, but yet, God
forbid, sir, but a knave should have some countenance at his
friend's request. An honest man, sir, is able to speak for
himself when a knave is not. I have served your Worship
truly, sir, this eight years; an if I cannot once or twice in a
40   quarter bear out a knave against an honest man, I have but

SHALLOW

Check the figures and then and pay it. Sir John, you will not be excused.

DAVY

Now, sir, we need some new chain for the bucket. And sir, do you plan to dock William's pay for the wine he lost at the Hinckley fair?

SHALLOW

He'll pay for that. Some pigeons, Davy; a couple of short-legged hens, a leg of lamb, and any fun little fancy dishes. Tell William the cook.

DAVY

Is the soldier staying all night?

SHALLOW

Yes, Davy. I'll take good care of him. A friend at court is better than money in your pocket. Take good care of his men, Davy. They're good-for-nothings, and they'll bite you.

DAVY

No worse than they're bitten, sir. Their clothes are full of lice.

SHALLOW

Good one, Davy. Get on with your work, Davy.

DAVY

Please, sir, rule in favor of William Visor of Woncot in his lawsuit against Clement Perkes of the hill.

SHALLOW

Davy, there are a lot of suits against that Visor. That Visor is a good-for-nothing, as best I can tell.

DAVY

I agree with your honor that he's a good-for-nothing, but God forbid that a good-for-nothing should be denied a favor when his friend asks for one on his behalf. An honest man can speak for himself, but a good-for-nothing can't. I've worked for you for eight years, sir. If I can't get you to rule in favor of a good-

a very little credit with your Worship. The knave is mine
honest friend, sir; therefore I beseech you let him be
countenanced.

SHALLOW
Go to, I say he shall have no wrong. Look about, Davy.

Exit DAVY

45   Where are you, Sir John? Come, come, come, off with your
boots.—Give me your hand, Master Bardolph.

BARDOLPH
I am glad to see your Worship.

SHALLOW
I thank thee with all my heart, kind Master Bardolph, *(to the*
PAGE*)* and welcome, my tall fellow.—Come, Sir John.

FALSTAFF
50   I'll follow you, good Master Robert Shallow.

Exit SHALLOW

Bardolph, look to our horses.

Exeunt BARDOLPH *and* PAGE

If I were sawed into quantities, I should make four dozen of
such bearded hermits' staves as Master Shallow. It is a
wonderful thing to see the semblable coherence of his men's
55   spirits and his. They, by observing of him, do bear
themselves like foolish justices; he, by conversing with
them, is turned into a justice-like servingman. Their spirits
are so married in conjunction with the participation of
society that they flock together in consent like so many wild
60   geese. If I had a suit to Master Shallow, I would humor his
men with the imputation of being near their master; if to his
men, I would curry with Master Shallow that no man could
better command his servants. It is certain that either wise
bearing or ignorant carriage is caught, as men take diseases,
65   one of another. Therefore let men take heed of their
company. I will devise matter enough out of this Shallow to

for-nothing once in a while, then obviously you don't think very much of me. That good-for-nothing is my good friend, sir. So I ask you, please: rule in his favor.

SHALLOW

Stop now; I tell you he won't be wronged. Now get going, Davy.

DAVY *exits.*

Where are you, Sir John? Come, come, come. Take your boots off. Let me shake your hand, Master Bardolph.

BARDOLPH

I'm glad to see you, your honor.

SHALLOW

I thank you with all my heart, Master Bardolph. *(to the PAGE)* Welcome, you tall fellow. Come, Sir John.

FALSTAFF

I'll be right behind you, Master Robert Shallow.

SHALLOW *exits.*

Bardolph, get our horses ready.

BARDOLPH *and the* PAGE *exit.*

If I were cut into pieces, I'd make four dozen bearded broomsticks like this Master Shallow. It's amazing to see the similarity between his men's dispositions and his own. They watch him and behave like foolish judges, and he, by associating with them, turns into a judge-like workman. Their spirits are so closely joined by their intimate involvement, they're like a flock of wild geese that fly in formation. If I needed a favor from Judge Shallow, I would make his men think that I'm a close friend of his. If I needed something from his men, I would flatter Shallow by telling him that no one commands servants better than he does. One thing's for sure: the behavior of a wise man and that of an idiot are contagious, like diseases. They spread from person to person, which is why people

keep Prince Harry in continual laughter the wearing out of
six fashions, which is four terms, or two actions, and a' shall
laugh without intervallums. O, it is much that a lie with a
slight oath and a jest with a sad brow will do with a fellow
that never had the ache in his shoulders. O, you shall see
him laugh till his face be like a wet cloak ill laid up.

SHALLOW
(within) Sir John.

FALSTAFF
I come, Master Shallow; I come, Master Shallow.

Exit

must be careful about the company they keep. I'll come up with enough material about this Shallow to keep Prince Hal laughing nonstop for a year. That's how much time it takes for the current fashion to change six times, or for two lawsuits to be completed. He'll laugh with no intermission. Oh, a lie told with a measure of truth—or a joke told with a serious face—will go far with a young fellow, who has never had his shoulders weighed down by old age or worries. Oh, he'll laugh until his face looks like a wet coat that was hung poorly—it'll be all wrinkled from laughter.

SHALLOW

(offstage) Sir John!

FALSTAFF

Coming, Master Shallow! Coming!

He exits.

ACT 5, SCENE 2

Enter WARWICK *and the Lord* CHIEF JUSTICE

WARWICK
How now, my Lord Chief Justice, whither away?

CHIEF JUSTICE
How doth the King?

WARWICK
Exceeding well. His cares are now all ended.

CHIEF JUSTICE
I hope, not dead.

WARWICK
He's walked the way of nature,
5   And to our purposes he lives no more.

CHIEF JUSTICE
I would his Majesty had called me with him.
The service that I truly did his life
Hath left me open to all injuries.

WARWICK
Indeed, I think the young King loves you not.

CHIEF JUSTICE
10   I know he doth not, and do arm myself
To welcome the condition of the time,
Which cannot look more hideously upon me
Than I have drawn it in my fantasy.

Enter LANCASTER, CLARENCE, GLOUCESTER, *and others*

WARWICK
Here come the heavy issue of dead Harry.
15   O, that the living Harry had the temper
Of he the worst of these three gentlemen!
How many nobles then should hold their places
That must strike sail to spirits of vile sort!

ACT 5, SCENE 2

WARWICK *and the Lord* CHIEF JUSTICE *enter.*

WARWICK

What's happening, my Lord Chief Justice? Where are you going?

CHIEF JUSTICE

How's the King doing?

WARWICK

Very well. All his worries are ended now.

CHIEF JUSTICE

Not dead, I hope.

WARWICK

He's gone down nature's path; for our purposes, he is no longer living.

CHIEF JUSTICE

I wish his majesty had brought me with him. The work I did for him while he was alive makes me very vulnerable, now that he's dead.

WARWICK

Indeed, I think the young King has no love for you.

CHIEF JUSTICE

I know he doesn't. I'm preparing myself to deal with whatever happens, which can't be any worse than what I've imagined.

LANCASTER, CLARENCE, GLOUCESTER, *and others enter.*

WARWICK

Here come the heavy-hearted children of dead Harry. If only the living Harry had the character of the worst of these three young men. Then a lot of noblemen would remain secure, instead of having to step aside to make room for lowlifes.

CHIEF JUSTICE
O God, I fear all will be overturned.

LANCASTER
20 Good morrow, cousin Warwick, good morrow.

GLOUCESTER AND CLARENCE
Good morrow, cousin.

LANCASTER
We meet like men that had forgot to speak.

WARWICK
We do remember, but our argument
Is all too heavy to admit much talk.

LANCASTER
25 Well, peace be with him that hath made us heavy.

CHIEF JUSTICE
Peace be with us, lest we be heavier.

GLOUCESTER
O, good my lord, you have lost a friend indeed,
And I dare swear you borrow not that face
Of seeming sorrow; it is sure your own.

LANCASTER
30 Though no man be assured what grace to find,
You stand in coldest expectation.
I am the sorrier; would 'twere otherwise.

CLARENCE
Well, you must now speak Sir John Falstaff fair,
Which swims against your stream of quality.

CHIEF JUSTICE
35 Sweet princes, what I did I did in honor,
Led by th' impartial conduct of my soul;
And never shall you see that I will beg
A ragged and forestalled remission.
If truth and upright innocency fail me,
40 I'll to the King my master that is dead
And tell him who hath sent me after him.

CHIEF JUSTICE
> Oh God! I'm afraid everything will be turned upside-down.

LANCASTER
> Good morning, cousin Warwick, good morning.

GLOUCESTER AND CLARENCE
> Good morning, cousin.

LANCASTER
> We're all like men who don't remember how to speak.

WARWICK
> We remember how, but what we have to say is so sad that we cannot speak.

LANCASTER
> Well, peace be with the man who has made us sad.

CHIEF JUSTICE
> Peace be with us, or else we'll be even sadder!

GLOUCESTER
> Oh, my good lord, you've lost a friend, indeed. I'm sure you're not borrowing that sorrowful face; it's certainly your own.

LANCASTER
> Even though no man can know what blessings will come his way, he must expect the worst. I am sorry; I wish it were otherwise.

CLARENCE
> Well, now you are only allowed to speak well of Sir John Falstaff, which goes against the nature of a man of your quality.

CHIEF JUSTICE
> Sweet princes, what I did, I did honorably, impartially, and with a clear conscience. You won't see me begging vilely for a pardon, which is sure to be withdrawn as soon as it is given. If truth and honest innocence don't help me, then I'll join my dead King and tell him who sent me.

WARWICK
Here comes the Prince.

Enter PRINCE HENRY *(now King Henry V), attended*

CHIEF JUSTICE
Good morrow, and God save your Majesty.

PRINCE HENRY
This new and gorgeous garment majesty
45   Sits not so easy on me as you think.—
Brothers, you mix your sadness with some fear.
This is the English, not the Turkish court;
Not Amurath an Amurath succeeds,
But Harry Harry. Yet be sad, good brothers,
50   For, by my faith, it very well becomes you.
Sorrow so royally in you appears
That I will deeply put the fashion on
And wear it in my heart. Why then, be sad.
But entertain no more of it, good brothers,
55   Than a joint burden laid upon us all.
For me, by heaven, I bid you be assured,
I'll be your father and your brother too.
Let me but bear your love, I 'll bear your cares.
Yet weep that Harry's dead, and so will I,
60   But Harry lives that shall convert those tears
By number into hours of happiness.

PRINCES
We hope no otherwise from your Majesty.

PRINCE HENRY
You all look strangely on me. *(to the* CHIEF JUSTICE*)* And you
        most.
You are, I think, assured I love you not.

CHIEF JUSTICE
65   I am assured, if I be measured rightly,
Your Majesty hath no just cause to hate me.

WARWICK

Here comes the Prince.

PRINCE HENRY *(now King Henry V) enters, with attendants.*

CHIEF JUSTICE

Good morning, and God save your majesty!

PRINCE HENRY

This new and gorgeous robe of majesty doesn't fit me as comfortably as you think. Brothers, your sadness is mixed with fear. This is the English court, not the Turkish one. I'm not Amurath, who had his brothers killed when he inherited his father King Amurath's crown; I'm a Harry, following another Harry. But be sad, brothers, because truly, it suits you. You look so regal in your sorrow that I will solemnly put it on as well, and wear it in my heart. Be sad, but don't let it be anything more than a burden we all share jointly. I want you to rest assured that as far as I'm concerned, I'll be both your father and your brother now. Just trust me with your love, and you can trust me to care for you. Keep weeping for Harry, who is dead; I will, as well. But one Harry still lives, and he will convert those tears one by one into hours of happiness.

PRINCES

We hope that's exactly what you'll do.

PRINCE HENRY

You're all looking at me strangely. *(to the CHIEF JUSTICE)* You, most of all. I think you're certain that I don't love you.

CHIEF JUSTICE

I'm certain that, if my actions are fairly considered, your majesty will find no just reason to hate me.

PRINCE HENRY
No?
How might a prince of my great hopes forget
So great indignities you laid upon me?
70   What, rate, rebuke, and roughly send to prison
Th' immediate heir of England? Was this easy?
May this be washed in Lethe and forgotten?

CHIEF JUSTICE
I then did use the person of your father;
The image of his power lay then in me.
75   And in th' administration of his law,
Whiles I was busy for the commonwealth,
Your Highness pleasèd to forget my place,
The majesty and power of law and justice,
The image of the King whom I presented,
80   And struck me in my very seat of judgment,
Whereon, as an offender to your father,
I gave bold way to my authority
And did commit you. If the deed were ill,
Be you contented, wearing now the garland,
85   To have a son set your decrees at nought?
To pluck down justice from your awful bench?
To trip the course of law and blunt the sword
That guards the peace and safety of your person?
Nay more, to spurn at your most royal image
90   And mock your workings in a second body?
Question your royal thoughts, make the case yours;
Be now the father and propose a son,
Hear your own dignity so much profaned,
See your most dreadful laws so loosely slighted,
95   Behold yourself so by a son disdained,
And then imagine me taking your part
And in your power soft silencing your son.
After this cold considerance, sentence me,
And, as you are a king, speak in your state

PRINCE HENRY

No? How can a great prince like me forget the terrible wrongs you did me? What were you thinking, to scold, punish, and violently imprison the heir to the English throne? Was this nothing? Should this be dipped in the river of forgetfulness and simply ignored?

CHIEF JUSTICE

I acted with the authority of your father, whose power was vested in me. And when it came to the law—which I was busy enforcing, for the good of the country—you chose to ignore my rank, and the majesty and power of law and justice which I bore as a representative of the King. You struck me in the head, the very location of my judgment. With that action, you committed a crime against your father's own laws. So I did what my power demanded, and imprisoned you. If that was wrong, then—now that you wear the crown—I hope you'll someday be satisfied with a son who mocks your laws, who scorns the judges who rule in your authority, who disrupts the course of law, and blunts the swords that guard your personal peace and safety.

No, even worse than that: a son who disrespects your deputies, and the officers you appoint in your name. Question yourself, and imagine being in your father's position. Be a father, and imagine a son. Listen to your own dignity being profaned. Watch as your most solemn laws are laughed at so lightly. Behold yourself being so disdained by a son. And then imagine that I take your side, and that in your name I gently silence your son. Soberly consider this, and then pronounce my sentence. As king, tell me what I have done that was so unseemly for my station, myself, or my king's authority.

100   What I have done that misbecame my place,
        My person, or my liege's sovereignty.

PRINCE HENRY
        You are right, justice, and you weigh this well.
        Therefore still bear the balance and the sword.
        And I do wish your honors may increase
105   Till you do live to see a son of mine
        Offend you and obey you as I did.
        So shall I live to speak my father's words:
        "Happy am I that have a man so bold
        That dares do justice on my proper son;
110   And not less happy, having such a son
        That would deliver up his greatness so
        Into the hands of justice." You did commit me,
        For which I do commit into your hand
        Th' unstainèd sword that you have used to bear,
115   With this remembrance: that you use the same
        With the like bold, just, and impartial spirit
        As you have done 'gainst me. There is my hand.
        You shall be as a father to my youth,
        My voice shall sound as you do prompt mine ear,
120   And I will stoop and humble my intents
        To your well-practiced wise directions.—
        And, princes all, believe me, I beseech you:
        My father is gone wild into his grave,
        For in his tomb lie my affections,
125   And with his spirit sadly I survive
        To mock the expectation of the world,
        To frustrate prophecies, and to raze out
        Rotten opinion, who hath writ me down
        After my seeming. The tide of blood in me
130   Hath proudly flowed in vanity till now.
        Now doth it turn and ebb back to the sea,
        Where it shall mingle with the state of floods
        And flow henceforth in formal majesty.
        Now call we our high court of parliament,

PRINCE HENRY

> You're right, Chief Justice, and you have considered this well. Therefore, keep your position as judge and enforcer. I hope that your honors increase, and that you live to see a son of mine offend and then obey you, as I have. I will live to speak my father's words: "I am a happy man, to have a man brave enough to punish my own son; and I'm no less happy to have a son that would surrender his greatness, and put himself in the hands of the law."

> You imprisoned me, and for that I charge you to continue in my service, with this reminder: you must always be as courageous, just, and impartial as you were with me. Shake my hand. You'll be like a father to me, and I will say whatever it is you whisper in my ear. I will bow to you, and keep myself humble in the face of your wisdom and experience. And princes, believe me, please: my father lies wild in his grave, for he took my recklessness with him when he died. His sober spirit survives in me, and I will flout the world's expectations. I will prove their prophecies false, and flush out the rotten opinions of those who judged me based on what I once seemed to be.

> My behavior, the tide of my blood, used to flow proudly and vainly. But now, it ebbs and turns back toward the sea, where it will mingle with the ocean's majesty and flow back through my body with formal dignity. Now I will assemble my parliament, and choose such noble officers and advisors that our great

135 And let us choose such limbs of noble counsel
That the great body of our state may go
In equal rank with the best governed nation;
That war, or peace, or both at once, may be
As things acquainted and familiar to us,
140 In which you, father, shall have foremost hand.
Our coronation done, we will accite,
As I before remembered, all our state.
And, God consigning to my good intents,
No prince nor peer shall have just cause to say
145 God shorten Harry's happy life one day.

Exeunt

country will be able to march alongside the best governed nations. We'll become acquainted and familiar with the states of war, peace, or both at once; in this, Chief Justice, my new father, you will be my closest advisor.

Once my coronation has been completed, I will, as I said before, summon all the nobility. And if God endorses my good intentions, no prince or lord will have reason to say that he wishes God would shorten my happy life by even a single day.

They exit.

ACT 5, SCENE 3

Enter FALSTAFF, SHALLOW, SILENCE, DAVY, BARDOLPH, *and the* PAGE

SHALLOW
Nay, you shall see my orchard, where, in an arbor, we will
eat a last year's pippin of my own graffing, with a dish of
caraways, and so forth.—Come, cousin Silence.—And
then to bed.

FALSTAFF
5   Fore God, you have here a goodly dwelling and a rich.

SHALLOW
Barren, barren, barren, beggars all, beggars all, Sir John.
Marry, good air.—Spread, Davy, spread, Davy. Well said,
Davy.

FALSTAFF
This Davy serves you for good uses. He is your servingman
10   and your husband.

SHALLOW
A good varlet, a good varlet, a very good varlet, Sir John. By
the Mass, I have drunk too much sack at supper. A good
varlet. Now sit down, now sit down.—Come, cousin.

SILENCE
Ah, sirrah, quoth he, we shall
15   Do nothing but eat and make good cheer,
(sings) And praise God for the merry year,
When flesh is cheap and females dear,
And lusty lads roam here and there
So merrily,
20   And ever among so merrily.

FALSTAFF
There's a merry heart!—Good Master Silence, I'll give you
a health for that anon.

ACT 5, SCENE 3

FALSTAFF, SHALLOW, SILENCE, DAVY, BARDOLPH, *and the* PAGE *enter.*

SHALLOW

No, you're going to see my orchard. We'll sit in an arbor and eat some of the pippin apples I cross-bred last season, along with some caraway seeds and so on. Come on, Silence. Then we'll go to bed.

FALSTAFF

I swear, you have a good-looking place here, and it's fancy.

SHALLOW

Cheap, cheap, cheap. We're broke, broke, Sir John. But one thing we do have is good air. Set the table, Davy, set the table. Good job, Davy.

FALSTAFF

This Davy does a lot for you. He's your right-hand man as well as your steward.

SHALLOW

A good servant, a very good servant, Sir John. By God, I had too much wine with dinner. A good servant. Now sit down, sit down. Come on, cousin.

SILENCE

Ah, Sirrah, he said. We will:
Do nothing but eat and celebrate,
(sings) And praise God for this happy year,
When flesh is cheap but women are costly,
And lusty men roam here and there,
So merrily,
And always so merrily.

FALSTAFF

That's a merry heart! Master Silence, I'll drink a toast to you in a minute.

SHALLOW
Give Master Bardolph some wine, Davy.

DAVY
Sweet sir, sit. I'll be with you anon. Most sweet sir, sit.
25   Master page, good master page, sit. Proface. What you
want in meat, we'll have in drink, but you must bear. The
heart's all.

Exit DAVY

SHALLOW
Be merry, Master Bardolph. —And, my little soldier there,
be merry.

SILENCE
30   *(sings)* Be merry, be merry, my wife has all,
For women are shrews, both short and tall.
'Tis merry in hall when beards wag all,
And welcome merry Shrovetide.
Be merry, be merry.

FALSTAFF
35   I did not think Master Silence had been a man of this mettle.

SILENCE
Who, I? I have been merry twice and once ere now.

Enter DAVY

DAVY
(to BARDOLPH*)* There's a dish of leather-coats for you.

SHALLOW
Davy!

DAVY
Your Worship, I'll be with you straight.—
40   *(to* BARDOLPH*)* A cup of wine, sir?

SILENCE
(sings) A cup of wine that's brisk and fine,
And drink unto thee, leman mine,
And a merry heart lives long-a.

SHALLOW

Davy, get Master Bardolph some wine.

DAVY

Sit, kind sir; I'll be with you in a second. Very kind sir, please sit. Here's to you! What we lack in food, we make up for in drink. You must endure it; good intentions are what count.

DAVY exits.

SHALLOW

Enjoy yourself, Master Bardolph, and you, my little soldier, enjoy yourself.

SILENCE

Shrovetide = the period of merry-making before the Christian season of Lent (a time of penance and self-denial)

(sings) Enjoy, enjoy! My wife has it all,
Women are shrews, whether they're short or they're tall,
It's a merry party when men laugh and joke,
So let's enjoy ourselves this Shrovetide,
Enjoy, enjoy!

FALSTAFF

I didn't think Master Silence had this in him.

SILENCE

Who, me? I've let loose once or twice in my life.

DAVY enters.

DAVY

(to BARDOLPH) Here's a dish of red apples for you.

SHALLOW

Davy!

DAVY

Yes, sir! I'll be with you in a second. *(to BARDOLPH)* A cup of wine, sir?

SILENCE

(sings) A cup of wine that's fresh and fine,
And drink to you, darling mine,
And a happy heart lives long!

FALSTAFF
 Well said, Master Silence.

SILENCE
45   And we shall be merry; now comes in the sweet o' th' night.

FALSTAFF
 Health and long life to you, Master Silence.

SILENCE
 (sings) Fill the cup, and let it come,
 I'll pledge you a mile to th' bottom.

SHALLOW
 Honest Bardolph, welcome. If thou wantest anything and
      wilt not call, beshrew thy heart.—
50   *(to the* PAGE*)* Welcome, my little tiny thief, and welcome
 indeed too. I'll drink to Master Bardolph, and to all the
 cabileros about London.

DAVY
 I hope to see London once ere I die.

BARDOLPH
 An I might see you there, Davy!

SHALLOW
55   By the Mass, you'll crack a quart together, ha, will you not,
 Master Bardolph?

BARDOLPH
 Yea, sir, in a pottle-pot.

SHALLOW
 By God's liggens, I thank thee. The knave will stick by thee,
 I can assure thee that. He will not out, he. 'Tis true bred!

BARDOLPH
60   And I'll stick by him, sir.

SHALLOW
 Why, there spoke a king. Lack nothing, be merry.
 One knocks at the door within
 Look who's at door there, ho. Who knocks?

                                              Exit DAVY

FALSTAFF

Well said, Master Silence.

SILENCE

And we will enjoy ourselves. Now's the best time of night.

FALSTAFF

Here's to your health and long life, Master Silence.

SILENCE

(sings) Fill the cup, and pass it here,
I'll drink it to the bottom, even if it's a mile down.

SHALLOW

Welcome, honest Master Bardolph. If you want something and don't ask for it, that's your tough luck. *(to the PAGE)* Welcome, my little tiny thief, welcome indeed. I'll drink to Master Bardolph, and to all the good sports around London.

DAVY

I hope to see London once before I die.

BARDOLPH

If I see you there, Davy—

SHALLOW

By God, you'll break open a quart bottle together, ha! Won't you, Master Bardolph?

BARDOLPH

Yessir, in a two-quart glass.

SHALLOW

By God's fingers, I thank you. This rogue will stick with you, I promise you that. He won't fail, he's true blue.

BARDOLPH

And I'll stick with him, sir.

SHALLOW

Spoken like a king. Take whatever you want: enjoy yourselves!

Knocking is heard offstage.

FALSTAFF
> *(to* SILENCE*)* Why, now you have done me right.

SILENCE
65
> *(sings)* Do me right,
> And dub me knight,
> Samingo.
> Is 't not so?

FALSTAFF
> 'Tis so.

SILENCE
70
> Is 't so? Why then, say an old man can do somewhat.

Enter DAVY

DAVY
> An 't please your Worship, there's one Pistol come from the
> court with news.

FALSTAFF
> From the court? Let him come in.

Enter PISTOL

> How now, Pistol?

PISTOL
75
> Sir John, God save you.

FALSTAFF
> What wind blew you hither, Pistol?

PISTOL
> Not the ill wind which blows no man to good. Sweet knight,
> thou art now one of the greatest men in this realm.

NO FEAR SHAKESPEARE

Hey, see who's at the door there! Who's knocking?

DAVY *exits.*

FALSTAFF

(to SILENCE*)* You're really keeping up with me!

SILENCE

(sings) Keep up with me,
Then dub me a knight!
Samingo!
Right?

> Samingo = lyric from "Monsieur Mingo," a drinking song. In Latin, mingo means "I urinate."

FALSTAFF

Right.

SILENCE

Right? Then you've got to admit that an old man can do some things.

DAVY *returns.*

DAVY

Sir, if I may say so, there's someone named Pistol here from the royal court. He's got news.

FALSTAFF

From the royal court? Let him in.

PISTOL *enters.*

What's up, Pistol!

PISTOL

God save you, Sir John.

FALSTAFF

What wind blew you here, Pistol?

PISTOL

Not the evil wind that blows no one toward any good. Sweet knight, you are now one of the hugest men in the country.

SILENCE
By 'r Lady, I think he be, but Goodman Puff of Barson.

PISTOL
80   Puff?
Puff in thy teeth, most recreant coward base!—
Sir John, I am thy Pistol and thy friend,
And helter-skelter have I rode to thee,
And tidings do I bring, and lucky joys,
85   And golden times, and happy news of price.

FALSTAFF
I pray thee now, deliver them like a man of this world.

PISTOL
A foutre for the world and worldlings base!
I speak of Africa and golden joys.

FALSTAFF
O base Assyrian knight, what is thy news?
90   Let King Cophetua know the truth thereof.

SILENCE
(sings) And Robin Hood, Scarlet, and John.

PISTOL
Shall dunghill curs confront the Helicons,
And shall good news be baffled?
Then, Pistol, lay thy head in Furies' lap.

SILENCE
95   Honest gentleman, I know not your breeding.

PISTOL
Why then, lament therefor.

SILENCE

I swear, I think he is—except for the good fellow Puff, from Barson.

PISTOL

Puff? Puff in your face, you degenerate coward! Sir John, I'm your Pistol and your friend, and I rode at full tilt to find you here. I bring you reports, and good luck, and golden times, and happy, valuable news.

FALSTAFF

Then please, deliver this news like a human being who lives in this world.

PISTOL

Damn this world, and the vile little people who live in it! I'm talking about Africa, and its golden joys.

FALSTAFF

Falstaff is aping Pistol's high-flown style. Cophetua was an African king who married a beggar.

Oh, you vulgar Assyrian knight, what is your news? Convey to King Cophetua the story therein.

SILENCE

a lyric from a popular song

(sings) And Robin Hood, Scarlet, and John.

PISTOL

Will junkyard dogs attack the Muses, goddesses of poetry? Will my good news be thwarted this way? Then Pistol, go ahead and plead with the Furies, the goddesses of revenge.

SILENCE

Honest gentleman, I don't know what kind of family you're from.

PISTOL

That's your loss.

SHALLOW
Give me pardon, sir. If, sir, you come with news from the
court, I take it there's but two ways, either to utter them, or
to conceal them. I am, sir, under the King in some
100   authority.

PISTOL
Under which king, besonian? Speak or die.

SHALLOW
Under King Harry.

PISTOL
Harry the Fourth, or Fifth?

SHALLOW
Harry the Fourth.

PISTOL
105   A foutre for thine office!—
Sir John, thy tender lambkin now is king.
Harry the Fifth's the man. I speak the truth.
When Pistol lies, do this (*he makes an obscene gesture*) and
         fig me, like
The bragging Spaniard.

FALSTAFF
110   What, is the old king dead?

PISTOL
As nail in door. The things I speak are just.

FALSTAFF
Away, Bardolph.—Saddle my horse.—Master Robert
Shallow, choose what office thou wilt in the land,
'tis thine. Pistol, I will double-charge thee with dignities.

BARDOLPH
115   O joyful day! I would not take a knighthood for my fortune.

PISTOL
What, I do bring good news!

FALSTAFF
Carry Master Silence to bed.—Master Shallow, my Lord
Shallow, be what thou wilt. I am Fortune's steward. Get on

SHALLOW

Forgive me saying so, sir, but if you've got news from the court, then you have only two choices: you can either tell it or not tell it. I have some authority from the King, you know.

PISTOL

From which king, you beggar? Speak, or die.

SHALLOW

For King Henry.

PISTOL

Henry the Fourth, or Fifth?

SHALLOW

Henry the Fourth.

PISTOL

Then screw your position! Sir John, your tender little lamb is now the king. Henry the Fifth's the man, and I speak the truth. When Pistol tells a lie, do this *(he makes an obscene gesture)* and tell me to go screw myself, like some crazy Spaniard.

FALSTAFF

What? Is the old King dead?

PISTOL

As a doornail: these things I say are true.

FALSTAFF

Get going, Bardolph! Saddle up my horse. Master Robert Shallow, pick whatever job you want in the whole country: it's yours. Pistol, I'll pile honors on you.

BARDOLPH

Oh happy day! I wouldn't even trade a knighthood for my new, good fortune.

PISTOL

There you go! I brought good news!

FALSTAFF

Carry Master Silence to bed. Master Shallow—Lord Shallow—call yourself whatever you want. I'm in

120   thy boots. We'll ride all night.—O sweet Pistol!—Away,
    Bardolph!

Exit BARDOLPH

    Come, Pistol, utter more to me, and withal devise
    something to do thyself good. Boot, boot, Master Shallow.
    I know the young King is sick for me. Let us take any man's
    horses. The laws of England are at my commandment.
125   Blessed are they that have been my friends, and woe to my
    Lord Chief Justice!

PISTOL
    Let vultures vile seize on his lungs also!
    "Where is the life that late I led?" say they.
    Why, here it is. Welcome these pleasant days.

Exeunt

charge of all the luck in the world! Get your boots on. We'll ride through the night. Oh sweet Pistol! Get going, Bardolph!

BARDOLPH *exits.*

Pistol, tell me more, and help me think of something good we can do for you. Boots, boots, Master Shallow! I know the young King is dying to see me. Let's just take anybody's horses; I rule the laws of England now! Blessed are those who have been my friends, and watch out, Lord Chief Justice!

PISTOL

May vultures eat out his lungs, too! You know the old saying, "What happened to the life I used to lead?" Well, they're here; welcome to these pleasant days.

They exit.

ACT 5, SCENE 4

Enter BEADLES, *dragging in* MISTRESS QUICKLY *and* DOLL
TEARSHEET

MISTRESS QUICKLY
No, thou arrant knave. I would to God that I might die, that
I might have thee hanged. Thou hast drawn my shoulder
out of joint.

FIRST BEADLE
The Constables have delivered her over to me, and she shall
5   have whipping cheer enough, I warrant her. There hath
been a man or two lately killed about her.

DOLL TEARSHEET
Nut-hook, nut-hook, you lie! Come on, I 'll tell thee what,
thou damned tripe-visaged rascal: an the child I now go
with do miscarry, thou wert better thou hadst struck thy
10   mother, thou paper-faced villain.

MISTRESS QUICKLY
O the Lord, that Sir John were come! I would make this a
bloody day to somebody. But I pray God the fruit of her
womb might miscarry.

FIRST BEADLE
If it do, you shall have a dozen of cushions again; you have
15   but eleven now. Come, I charge you both go with me, for the
man is dead that you and Pistol beat amongst you.

DOLL TEARSHEET
I'll tell you what, you thin man in a censer, I will have you
as soundly swinged for this, you bluebottle rogue, you
filthy famished correctioner. If you be not swinged, I'll
20   forswear half-kirtles.

FIRST BEADLE
Come, come, you she knight-errant, come.

ACT 5, SCENE 4

BEADLES *enter,* dragging DOLL TEARSHEET *and*
MISTRESS QUICKLY.

beadles =
parish officers

MISTRESS QUICKLY
No, you horrible rogue! I wish to God I were dead, so
I could have you hanged. You dislocated my shoulder!

FIRST BEADLE
The street cops handed her over to me, and she'll be
whipped through and through, I promise. She's been
involved in a couple of murders.

DOLL TEARSHEET
Pig, Pig! You lie! Come on! I'll tell you what, you
damned flabby-faced moron: if I have a miscarriage
now, you'll wish you'd hit your own mother, you
pasty-faced villain!

MISTRESS QUICKLY
Oh God, I wish Sir John would come! He'd make
somebody bleed for this. I pray to God that she has a
miscarriage!

FIRST BEADLE
Well, if she does, you'll have twelve cushions on your
couch again. You have only eleven now, since she's
wearing one of them under her dress. I order both of
you to come with me: the man that you two and Pistol
beat up is dead.

DOLL TEARSHEET
I'll tell you what, you stick-figure; I'll have you beaten
soundly for this. You blue-coated rogue, you filthy,
starving correctioner! If you aren't walloped for this,
I'll swear off skirts.

FIRST BEADLE
Come on, come on, you little night sinner, come on.

MISTRESS QUICKLY
O God, that right should thus overcome might! Well, of
sufferance comes ease.

DOLL TEARSHEET
Come, you rogue, come, bring me to a justice.

MISTRESS QUICKLY
25   Ay, come, you starved bloodhound.

DOLL TEARSHEET
Goodman Death, Goodman Bones!

MISTRESS QUICKLY
Thou atomy, thou!

DOLL TEARSHEET
Come, you thin thing, come, you rascal.

FIRST BEADLE
Very well.

Exeunt

MISTRESS QUICKLY

Oh God! I can't believe that right is overcoming might! Well, challenges build character.

DOLL TEARSHEET

Come on, you bastard, come on. Bring me to a judge.

MISTRESS QUICKLY

Yeah, come on, you starved dog.

DOLL TEARSHEET

Master Death! Master Bones!

MISTRESS QUICKLY

You skeleton, you!

DOLL TEARSHEET

Come on, you thin thing; come on, you lean deer!

FIRST BEADLE

Very well.

They exit.

ACT 5, SCENE 5

Enter two GROOMS, *strewing rushes*

FIRST GROOM
More rushes, more rushes.

SECOND GROOM
The trumpets have sounded twice.

FIRST GROOM
'Twill be two o'clock ere they come from the coronation.
Dispatch, dispatch.

Exeunt

Enter FALSTAFF, SHALLOW, PISTOL, BARDOLPH, *and* PAGE

FALSTAFF
5   Stand here by me, Master Robert Shallow. I will make the
King do you grace. I will leer upon him as he comes by, and
do but mark the countenance that he will give me.

PISTOL
God bless thy lungs, good knight!

FALSTAFF
Come here, Pistol, stand behind me.— *(to* SHALLOW*)* O, if
10   I had had time to have made new liveries, I would have
bestowed the thousand pound I borrowed of you. But 'tis
no matter. This poor show doth better. This doth infer the
zeal I had to see him.

SHALLOW
It doth so.

FALSTAFF
15   It shows my earnestness of affection—

SHALLOW
It doth so.

FALSTAFF
My devotion—

ACT 5, SCENE 5

groom = an officer in the royal household

Two GROOMS enter, strewing rushes to cover the floors.

FIRST GROOM
More rushes; more rushes.

SECOND GROOM
The trumpets have blown twice.

FIRST GROOM
It'll be two o'clock before they arrive from the coronation. Hurry, hurry.

They exit.

FALSTAFF, SHALLOW, PISTOL, BARDOLPH, *and the* PAGE *enter.*

FALSTAFF
Stand here near me, Master Robert Shallow. I'll make the King do good things for you: I'll throw him a look as he passes by. Just watch the face he'll make at me.

PISTOL
God bless your lungs, good knight.

FALSTAFF
Come here, Pistol. Stand behind me. *(to SHALLOW)* Oh, if I'd had time to make new clothes I would have spent the thousand pounds I borrowed from you. But it doesn't matter. These poor clothes are better; it shows how desperate I was to see him.

SHALLOW
It does indeed.

FALSTAFF
It shows how sincerely I love him—

SHALLOW
It does indeed.

FALSTAFF
My devotion—

SHALLOW
It doth, it doth, it doth.

FALSTAFF
As it were, to ride day and night, and not to deliberate, not
20   to remember, not to have patience to shift me—

SHALLOW
It is best, certain.

FALSTAFF
But to stand stained with travel and sweating with desire to
see him, thinking of nothing else, putting all affairs else in
oblivion, as if there were nothing else to be done but to see
25   him.

PISTOL
'Tis *semper idem*, for *obsque hoc nihil est*;
'tis all in every part.

SHALLOW
'Tis so indeed.

PISTOL
My knight, I will inflame thy noble liver, and make thee
30   rage. Thy Doll and Helen of thy noble thoughts is in base
durance and contagious prison, Haled thither by most
mechanical and dirty hand. Rouse up revenge from ebon
den with fell Alecto's snake, for Doll is in. Pistol speaks
nought but truth.

FALSTAFF
35   I will deliver her.

Shouts within, and the trumpets sound

PISTOL
There roared the sea, and trumpet-clangor sounds.

SHALLOW

It does, it does, it does.

FALSTAFF

In a word, to ride all night; not to stop and think, not to dawdle, not to take the time to change my clothes—

SHALLOW

It is best, no doubt about it.

FALSTAFF

Standing here filthy from traveling, and sweating with my desire to see him; thinking of nothing else, disregarding everything, as if the only thing in the world that mattered was seeing him.

PISTOL

These Latin phrases translate as "Ever the same" and "Apart from this, there is nothing."

That's how it is. Nothing else matters. *Semper idem. Obsque hoc nihil est.*

SHALLOW

That's exactly right.

PISTOL

Knight, I'll fire up your noble liver and make you enraged. Doll, the goddess of your thoughts, is imprisoned in a horrible jail, tossed there by a heartless and filthy hand. Stoke up dark revenge from your deepest belly and set loose the serpents of hell. Doll is in. Pistol speaks nothing but the truth.

FALSTAFF

I'll set her free.

Shouts are heard offstage. Trumpets play.

PISTOL

That was the roar of the sea. The clanging trumpet sounds!

> *Enter* PRINCE HENRY *and his train, the Lord* CHIEF JUSTICE
> *among them*

FALSTAFF
God save thy Grace, King Hal, my royal Hal.

PISTOL
The heavens thee guard and keep, most royal imp of fame!

FALSTAFF
God save thee, my sweet boy!

KING
40   My Lord Chief Justice, speak to that vain man.

CHIEF JUSTICE
(to FALSTAFF*)* Have you your wits? Know you what 'tis to
    speak?

FALSTAFF
My King, my Jove, I speak to thee, my heart!

KING
I know thee not, old man. Fall to thy prayers.
How ill white hairs become a fool and jester.
45 I have long dreamt of such a kind of man,
So surfeit-swelled, so old, and so profane;
But being awaked, I do despise my dream.
Make less thy body hence, and more thy grace;
Leave gormandizing. Know the grave doth gape
50 For thee thrice wider than for other men.
Reply not to me with a fool-born jest.
Presume not that I am the thing I was,
For God doth know—so shall the world perceive—
That I have turned away my former self.
55 So will I those that kept me company.
When thou dost hear I am as I have been,
Approach me, and thou shalt be as thou wast,
The tutor and the feeder of my riots.
Till then I banish thee, on pain of death,
55 As I have done the rest of my misleaders,

PRINCE HENRY *enters with a procession of attendants, including the* CHIEF JUSTICE.

FALSTAFF

God save your grace, King Hal! My royal Hal!

PISTOL

The heavens guard and protect you, you royal child of fame!

FALSTAFF

God save you, my sweet boy!

PRINCE HENRY

My Lord Chief Justice, go speak to that arrogant man.

CHIEF JUSTICE

(to FALSTAFF*)* Have you lost your mind? Do you know what you're doing, talking like that?

FALSTAFF

My King! My God! I'm talking to you, my heart!

KING

I know you not, old man. Get down on your knees and pray, for white hair doesn't sit well on a fool and a clown. I have dreamed about such a man for a long time: a man so swollen with excess, so old and so obscene. But now that I have awakened, I despise that dream. Let your body lessen, and your manners increase; leave behind your overindulgence, and know that the grave gapes three times as wide for you than any other man. Don't answer me with a foolish joke. Do not assume that I am what I was; for God knows, I have turned my back on my former self, and I will do the same to those who were my companions. When you hear that I am as I was, then come to me, and you will once again be what you were: the teacher and nurse to my wild, riotous ways.

Until then, I banish you, on pain of death, as I have done to the other men who once misled me. Do not

Not to come near our person by ten mile.
For competence of life I will allow you,
That lack of means enforce you not to evils.
And, as we hear you do reform yourselves,
60   We will, according to your strengths and qualities,
Give you advancement. *(to* CHIEF JUSTICE*)* Be it your
       charge, my lord,
To see performed the tenor of my word.—
Set on.

> *Exeunt* PRINCE HENRY, *the* CHIEF JUSTICE,
> *and the attendants.*

FALSTAFF
Master Shallow, I owe you a thousand pound.

SHALLOW
65   Yea, marry, Sir John, which I beseech you to let me have
home with me.

FALSTAFF
That can hardly be, Master Shallow. Do not you grieve at
this. I shall be sent for in private to him. Look you, he must
seem thus to the world. Fear not your advancements. I will
70   be the man yet that shall make you great.

SHALLOW
I cannot well perceive how, unless you should give me your
doublet and stuff me out with straw. I beseech you, good Sir
John, let me have five hundred of my thousand.

FALSTAFF
Sir, I will be as good as my word. This that you heard was
75   but a color.

SHALLOW
A color that I fear you will die in, Sir John.

FALSTAFF
Fear no colors. Go with me to dinner.—Come, Lieutenant
Pistol.—Come, Bardolph.—I shall be sent for soon at
night.

come within ten miles of me. I'll grant you a modest allowance to live on, so that poverty will not lead you into evil. When I hear that you have reformed your ways, I will promote you as you deserve. *(to* CHIEF JUSTICE*)* It's your job to see this order carried out. Let's go.

PRINCE HENRY, *the* CHIEF JUSTICE, *and the attendants exit.*

FALSTAFF

Master Shallow, I owe you a thousand pounds.

SHALLOW

Yes, indeed, Sir John. And I'd like to take it home with me.

FALSTAFF

That can't happen, Master Shallow. Don't let this upset you; I'll get a private invitation to see him. Look, he has to appear this way to the world. Don't worry about your good fortunes: I'm still the man who will make you great.

SHALLOW

I don't know how you're going to do that, unless you give me your jacket and fill me out with stuffing. Please, Sir John, let me have five hundred of my thousand.

FALSTAFF

Sir, I'm as good as my word. What you heard here a minute ago was just a color; it was a pretense.

SHALLOW

A color that I fear you'll be buried in, Sir John.

FALSTAFF

Stop worrying about colors: come to lunch with me. Come, Lieutenant Pistol. Come, Bardolph. He'll call for me tonight.

Enter the Lord CHIEF JUSTICE *and Prince John of* LANCASTER; *officers with them*

CHIEF JUSTICE
80   Go, carry Sir John Falstaff to the Fleet.
    Take all his company along with him.

FALSTAFF
    My lord, my lord—

CHIEF JUSTICE
    I cannot now speak. I will hear you soon.—
    Take them away.

PISTOL
85   *Si fortune me tormenta, spero me contenta.*

> *Exeunt all but Prince John of* LANCASTER *and*
> *the* CHIEF JUSTICE

LANCASTER
    I like this fair proceeding of the King's.
    He hath intent his wonted followers
    Shall all be very well provided for,
    But all are banished till their conversations
90   Appear more wise and modest to the world.

CHIEF JUSTICE
    And so they are.

LANCASTER
    The King hath called his parliament, my lord.

CHIEF JUSTICE
    He hath.

LANCASTER
    I will lay odds that, ere this year expire,
95   We bear our civil swords and native fire
    As far as France: I beard a bird so sing,
    Whose music, to my thinking, pleased the King.
    Come, will you hence?

> *Exeunt*

The Lord CHIEF JUSTICE, *Prince John of* LANCASTER, *and officers enter.*

CHIEF JUSTICE

Go, take Sir John Falstaff away to jail, and take all his companions with him.

FALSTAFF

My lord, my lord—

CHIEF JUSTICE

I can't talk now. I'll listen to you later. Take them away.

PISTOL

Si fortuna me tormenta, spero me contenta.

"If fortune torments me, hope contents me." Pistol's motto is a garbled mix of French, Spanish, and Italian.

Everyone exits except John of LANCASTER *and the* CHIEF JUSTICE.

LANCASTER

The King's fair dealings please me. He wants to ensure that his old companions are provided for, but he banishes them until they can behave more properly and presentably.

CHIEF JUSTICE

That they are.

LANCASTER

The King's assembled his parliament, sir.

CHIEF JUSTICE

He has.

LANCASTER

I'll bet that, before the year ends, we'll launch an invasion of France. I heard a little bird singing about it, and I think the music pleased the King. Come, will you leave with me?

They exit.

EPILOGUE

Enter the EPILOGUE.

First my fear; then my curtsy, last my speech. My fear is
your displeasure my curtsy my duty; and my speech, to beg
your pardons. If you look for a good speech now, you undo
me, for what I have to say is of mine own making, and what
indeed I should say will, I doubt, prove mine own marring.
But to the purpose, and so to the venture. Be it known to
you, as it is very well, I was lately here in the end of a
displeasing play to pray your patience for it and to promise
you a better. I meant indeed to pay you with this, which, if
like an ill venture it come unluckily home, I break, and you,
my gentle creditors, lose. Here I promised you I would be,
and here I commit my body to your mercies. Bate me some,
and I will pay you some, and, as most debtors do, promise
you infinitely. And so I kneel down before you, but, indeed,
to pray for the Queen.

If my tongue cannot entreat you to acquit me, will you
command me to use my legs? And yet that were but light
payment, to dance out of your debt. But a good conscience
will make any possible satisfaction, and so would I. All the
gentlewomen here have forgiven me; if the gentlemen will
not, then the gentlemen do not agree with the
gentlewomen, which was never seen before in such an
assembly.
One word more, I beseech you: if you be not too much
cloyed with fat meat, our humble author will continue the

EPILOGUE

The Epilogue is the actor who delivers the epilogue.

The EPILOGUE *enters.*

EPILOGUE

First, I'll tell you what I'm afraid of. Then, I'll bow, and finally, I'll make a speech. I fear that this play displeased you; I bow to you out of duty; and finally, I make this speech to ask you for forgiveness. If you're expecting a good speech now, then I'm in trouble. For I wrote the words I'm about to say, and I'm sure that what I'm about to say will end up getting me in trouble. But I'll get to the point, and thus I'll get to the danger. You should know—as you seem to—that I recently came on this stage at the end of some other lousy play, to ask you to be patient and to promise you a better play the next time. I had intended to pay you back for that play with this one. If you didn't like this play, then—like a businessman who has gambled on a risky venture—I am bankrupt; and you, my sweet creditors, are out of luck. I promised you I would be here, and here I stand to submit myself to your mercy. Give me some mercy and I'll promise to pay you back again another time. That's how debtors do it: they always promise to repay.

If my talking can't convince you to let me off the hook, then would you like me to dance? And yet, that would be a cheap payment, to dance myself out of debt. But a person with a good conscience will always seek to pay his debts, and I would do the same. All the women here have forgiven me: if the men won't, then the men don't agree with the women, which has never happened in a theater audience before.

Just one more thing, if you don't mind. If fatty meat hasn't clogged you up yet, our playwright will con-

story, with Sir John in it, and make you merry with fair Katherine of France, where, for anything I know, Falstaff shall die of a sweat, unless already he be killed with your hard opinions; for Oldcastle died a martyr, and this is not the man. My tongue is weary; when my legs are too, I will bid you good night.

30

tinue the story with Sir John in it, and entertain you with the beautiful Princess Katharine of France. And speaking of France, as far as I know, Falstaff will die there of the sweating disease—unless, that is, he's already been killed by your low opinions of him. Oldcastle died a martyr, and this is not him. My mouth is tired; when my legs are, too, I'll say goodnight and take a bow.

In an early version of 1 Henry IV, the character of Falstaff was called Sir John Oldcastle. The name was changed upon the insistence of the historical Sir John Oldcastle's descendants, who were highly influential in England at the time.

SPARKNOTES LITERATURE GUIDES

1984

The Adventures of Huckleberry Finn

The Adventures of Tom Sawyer

The Aeneid

All Quiet on the Western Front

And Then There Were None

Angela's Ashes

Animal Farm

Anna Karenina

Anne of Green Gables

Anthem

Antony and Cleopatra

Aristotle's Ethics

As I Lay Dying

As You Like It

Atlas Shrugged

The Autobiography of Malcolm X

The Awakening

The Bean Trees

The Bell Jar

Beloved

Beowulf

Billy Budd

Black Boy

Bless Me, Ultima

The Bluest Eye

Brave New World

The Brothers Karamazov

The Call of the Wild

Candide

The Canterbury Tales

Catch-22

The Catcher in the Rye

The Chocolate War

The Chosen

Cold Mountain

Cold Sassy Tree

The Color Purple

The Count of Monte Cristo

Crime and Punishment

The Crucible

Cry, the Beloved Country

Cyrano de Bergerac

David Copperfield

Death of a Salesman

The Death of Socrates

The Diary of a Young Girl

A Doll's House

Don Quixote

Dr. Faustus

Dr. Jekyll and Mr. Hyde

Dracula

Dune

Edith Hamilton's Mythology

Emma

Ethan Frome

Fahrenheit 451

Fallen Angels

A Farewell to Arms

Farewell to Manzanar

Flowers for Algernon

For Whom the Bell Tolls

The Fountainhead

Frankenstein

The Giver

The Glass Menagerie

Gone With the Wind

The Good Earth

The Grapes of Wrath

Great Expectations

The Great Gatsby

Grendel

Gulliver's Travels

Hamlet

The Handmaid's Tale

Hard Times

Harry Potter and the Sorcerer's Stone

Heart of Darkness

Henry IV, Part I

Henry V

Hiroshima

The Hobbit

The House of Seven Gables

I Know Why the Caged Bird Sings

The Iliad

Inferno

Inherit the Wind

Invisible Man

Jane Eyre

Johnny Tremain

The Joy Luck Club

Julius Caesar

The Jungle

The Killer Angels

King Lear

The Last of the Mohicans

Les Miserables

A Lesson Before Dying

The Little Prince

Little Women

Lord of the Flies

The Lord of the Rings

Macbeth

Madame Bovary

A Man for All Seasons

The Mayor of Casterbridge

The Merchant of Venice

A Midsummer Night's Dream

Moby Dick

Much Ado About Nothing

My Antonia

Narrative of the Life of Frederick Douglass

Native Son

The New Testament

Night

Notes from Underground

The Odyssey

The Oedipus Plays

Of Mice and Men

The Old Man and the Sea

The Old Testament

Oliver Twist

The Once and Future King

One Day in the Life of Ivan Denisovich

One Flew Over the Cuckoo's Nest

One Hundred Years of Solitude

Othello

Our Town

The Outsiders

Paradise Lost

A Passage to India

The Pearl

The Picture of Dorian Gray

Poe's Short Stories

A Portrait of the Artist as a Young Man

Pride and Prejudice

The Prince

A Raisin in the Sun

The Red Badge of Courage

The Republic

Richard III

Robinson Crusoe

Romeo and Juliet

The Scarlet Letter

A Separate Peace

Silas Marner

Sir Gawain and the Green Knight

Slaughterhouse-Five

Snow Falling on Cedars

Song of Solomon

The Sound and the Fury

Steppenwolf

The Stranger

Streetcar Named Desire

The Sun Also Rises

A Tale of Two Cities

The Taming of the Shrew

The Tempest

Tess of the d'Urbervilles

The Things They Carried

Their Eyes Were Watching God

Things Fall Apart

To Kill a Mockingbird

To the Lighthouse

Treasure Island

Twelfth Night

Ulysses

Uncle Tom's Cabin

Walden

War and Peace

Wuthering Heights

A Yellow Raft in Blue Water